Windows 95® and NT Programming

with the Microsoft® Foundation Class Library

LIMITED WARRANTY AND DISCLAIMER OF LIABILITY

ACADEMIC PRESS, INC. ("AP") AND ANYONE ELSE WHO HAS BEEN INVOLVED IN THE CREATION OR PRODUCTION OF THE ACCOMPANYING CODE ("THE PRODUCT") CANNOT AND DO NOT WARRANT THE PERFORMANCE OR RESULTS THAT MAY BE OBTAINED BY USING THE PRODUCT. THE PRODUCT IS SOLD "AS IS" WITHOUT WARRANTY OF ANY KIND (EXCEPT AS HEREAFTER DESCRIBED), EITHER EXPRESSED OR IMPLIED, INCLUDING, BUT NOT LIMITED TO, ANY WARRANTY OF PERFORMANCE OR ANY IMPLIED WARRANTY OF MERCHANTABILITY OR FITNESS FOR ANY PARTICULAR PURPOSE. AP WARRANTS ONLY THAT THE MAGNETIC DISKETTE(S) ON WHICH THE CODE IS RECORDED IS FREE FROM DEFECTS IN MATERIAL AND FAULTY WORKMANSHIP UNDER THE NORMAL USE AND SERVICE FOR A PERIOD OF NINETY (90) DAYS FROM THE DATE THE PRODUCT IS DELIVERED. THE PURCHASER'S SOLE AND EXCLUSIVE REMEDY IN THE EVENT OF A DEFECT IS EXPRESSLY LIMITED TO EITHER REPLACEMENT OF THE DISKETTE(S) OR REFUND OF THE PURCHASE PRICE, AT AP'S SOLE DISCRETION.

IN NO EVENT, WHETHER AS A RESULT OF BREACH OF CONTRACT, WARRANTY OR TORT (INCLUDING NEGLIGENCE) WILL AP OR ANYONE WHO HAS BEEN INVOLVED IN THE CREATION OR PRODUCTION OF THE PRODUCT BE LIABLE TO PURCHASER FOR ANY DAMAGES, INCLUDING ANY LOST PROFITS, LOST SAVINGS OR OTHER INCIDENTAL OR CONSEQUENTIAL DAMAGES ARISING OUT OF THE USE OR INABILITY TO USE THE PRODUCT OR ANY MODIFICATIONS THEREOF, OR DUE TO THE CONTENTS OF THE CODE, EVEN IF AP HAS BEEN ADVISED OF THE POSSIBILITY OF SUCH DAMAGES, OR FOR ANY CLAIM BY ANY OTHER PARTY.

Any request for replacement of a defective diskette must be postage prepaid and must be accompanied by the original defective diskette, your mailing address and telephone number, and proof of date of purchase and purchase price. Send such requests, stating the nature of the problem, to Academic Press Customer Service, 6277 Sea Harbor Drive, Orlando, FL 32887, 1-800-321-5068. APP shall have no obligation to refund the purchase price or to replace a diskette based on the claims of defects in the nature or operation of the product.

THE RE-EXPORT OF UNITED STATES ORIGIN SOFTWARE IS SUBJECT TO THE UNITED STATES LAWS UNDER THE EXPORT ADMINISTRATION ACT OF 1969 AS AMENDED. ANY FURTHER SALE OF THE PRODUCT SHALL BE IN COMPLIANCE WITH THE UNITED STATES DEPARTMENT OF COMMERCE ADMINISTRATION REGULATIONS. COMPLIANCE WITH SUCH REGULATIONS IS YOUR RESPONSIBILITY AND NOT THE RESPONSIBILITY OF AP.

Windows 95® and NT Programming

with the Microsoft® Foundation Class Library

William H. Murray
Montrose, PA

Chris H. Pappas
Vestal, NY

AP PROFESSIONAL

Boston San Diego New York
London Sydney Tokyo Toronto

This book is printed on acid-free paper 

AP PROFESSIONAL
1300 Boylston Street, Chestnut Hill, MA 02167
World Wide Web Site at http://www.apnet.com

An imprint of ACADEMIC PRESS, INC.
A Division of HARCOURT BRACE & COMPANY

United Kingdom Edition published by
ACADEMIC PRESS LIMITED
24-28 Oval Road, London NW1 7DX

Library of Congress Cataloging-in-Publication Data
Murray, William, 1943-
Windows 95 and NT programming with the Microsoft foundation class library / William H. Murray, Chris H. Pappas
p. cm.
Includes bibliographical references and index.
ISBN 0-12-511890-2 (alk. paper). -- ISBN 0-12-511891-0
1. Microsoft Windows (Computer file) 2. Microsoft Windows NT
3. Operating systems (Computers) 1. Pappas, Chris H., 1953-
II. Title.
QA76.76.063M868 1996
005.26'2--dc20
96-1380
CIP

Printed in the United States of America
96 97 98 99 IP 9 8 7 6 5 4 3 2 1

Contents

Introduction **xi**

Chapter 1 An Introduction to 32-Bit Windows 95 and NT **1**

Reasons for Developing Windows 95 and Windows NT Applications 3
Key Elements of Windows 95 and Windows NT 5
Getting Started 20
In the Next Chapter... 22

Chapter 2 Windows 95 and NT Concepts and Terminology **23**

Windows versus Windows 24
Creating the "Look" 25
Object Classes to the Rescue 29
Using Object-Oriented Technology 30
Communication via Messages 36
Standard Windows Resources 41
Standard Windows Functions 42
A First Look At WINDOWS.H 43
Understanding the Style of Windows Code 44
The Seven Fundamental Steps For Developing Windows Programs 46
In The Next Chapter... 47

Chapter 3 Important Programming Elements 49

Understanding the Windows Screen Coordinate System 50
Using ShowWindow() 69
Updating Window Features with SetClassLong() 70
Standard Windows Controls and Dialog Boxes 70
Giving Virtual Keys Meaning 74
An Introduction to System Timers 76
Understanding 32-Bit Memory Management 78
In The Next Chapter... 83

Chapter 4 A Procedure-Oriented Approach 85

Which Language and Which Approach? 85
Key Programming Elements 87
Handles 88
WinMain() and the Callback Function 89
A Procedure-Oriented Windows Application 89
Visual C/C++ Compiler Project Workspaces 107
Compiler Options 112

Chapter 5 Foundations for Object-Oriented Programming 115

Procedure-Oriented Programming 116
Object-Oriented Programming 116
C++ and Object-Oriented Programming 118
Object-Oriented Definitions and Terminology 118
The C++ Class 122
The Derived C++ Class 131
An Object-Oriented Stack 132

Chapter 6 The Microsoft Foundation Class (MFC) Library 135

Class Hierarchy 136
CObject 136
Classes Not Based on CObject 146
More on MFC Classes 148

Chapter 7 An Object-Oriented Approach 149

Why Switch? 150
Design Techniques 151
Key MFC Features 152
A Parent Class, CObject 152

Parent Class Hierarchy 156
An MFC Application, WinVerMFC.cpp 159
File Sizes 168

Chapter 8 The AppWizard, a Code Generator 169

Code Generators 170
The NoWiz Application 172
Why and How Did They Do That? 185
Working with the AppWizard and ClassWizard 188
Understanding the AppWizard's Code 198
It Looks the Same to Me 210

Chapter 9 Adding Icon, Cursor, Bitmap, Font, and Sound Resources 211

Microsoft Developer Studio's Bitmap Editors 212
Microsoft's Sound Recorder 225
Font Resources 226
Adding Resources to the AddRes Project 232
Adding an Icon 236
Adding Sound 237
Adding a Bitmap 238
Adding a Font 240
Using the ClassWizard 240

Chapter 10 Adding Menu and Keyboard Accelerators 245

Menus and Keyboard Accelerators 246
Base Code 247
Changing Drawing Colors from a Menu 248
Working with MenuColor Project Files 256
More Menus? 270

Chapter 11 Adding Dialog Boxes 271

Dialog Boxes Are Resources 272
Important Dialog Controls 275
Base Code 277
A New About Dialog Box for the DataEntry Project 278
A Data Entry Dialog Box for the DataEntry Project 280
Using a Common Dialog Box 294
More Dialog Boxes? 302

Chapter 12 Understanding Graphics Primitives **303**

The Graphics Device Interface 304
Important Drawing Primitives 310
Graphics Tools 315
Simple Applications Using GDI Tools and Techniques 320
More Graphics Shapes? 326

Chapter 13 Common Controls **327**

Base Code 327
A ToolBar Control with ToolTips 329
A Slider Control 338
A Spin Button Control 348
More Controls? 357

Chapter 14 Complete MFC Applications **359**

Base Code 359
A Word Processor Project 360
A Bar Chart Application 365

Chapter 15 OLE Concepts **389**

Understanding OLE 390
Objects, Files, and Data 391
OLE Containers and Object Embedding 392
OLE and Linked Applications 395

Chapter 16 Developing OLE Applications **405**

Containers 406
Servers 424
A Word on OLE Automation 442

Chapter 17 Custom Controls **443**

OLE Custom Controls 445
Custom Control Events 455
Custom Control Methods and Properties 455
Custom Control Persistence 456
Custom Control Containers 456

Chapter 18 Developing Custom Controls 457

Creating a Default Custom Control 458
Understanding the ControlWizard's Code 462
Creating a Real Clock Control 472
Responding to Mouse Events 477
More Custom Controls? 483

Chapter 19 A Screen Saver Application 487

Saucer Files 488
A Special Build Operation 500
Running the Screen Saver 500
More Screen Savers 503

Index 505

Introduction

We attended a Microsoft Developers Conference on Windows NT in San Francisco in 1992. During the conference, Microsoft evangelists began hinting at the importance of programming with the Microsoft Foundation Class library (MFC). We noted that not many participants were taking advantage of the object-oriented features of the MFC library. The evangelists also suggested that programmers should master the concepts of object linking and embedding and custom controls. During the time that followed, OLE has grown to OLE 2 and the use of the MFC library has grown tremendously. OLE and customs controls will be major features in 32-bit Windows 95 and NT applications.

You may have already discovered that object-oriented programming techniques are not mere extensions of procedure-oriented concepts. There is a price to be paid when moving into this new development arena. You will find, however, that once you are over this learning curve, a whole new world of programming will be open to you. In terms of Windows 95 and

Windows NT programming, the MFC library provides a whole collection of objects to make programming easier.

This book is built around the Visual C++ compiler and associated tools provided in the Microsoft Developer Studio. The Developer Studio provides an integrated approach when working with all of the components and tools involved with Windows 95 and Windows NT code development.

Chapters 1 through 3 will teach you the basic Windows programming concepts and terminology as they relate to the Windows 95 and Windows NT operating systems. Chapter 4 discusses the procedure-oriented approach to developing Windows applications. You'll learn the weaknesses of this approach and why programmers are switching to object-oriented programming. Chapter 5 serves as a base for object-oriented concepts and definitions, as they will relate to development work in future chapters. Chapters 6 and 7 will get you well on your way to writing simple applications with the MFC library. By the time you reach Chapter 8, you'll be ready to learn the techniques involved with Microsoft's AppWizard. The AppWizard is an automatic code generator. Chapters 9 through 14 focus on including various Windows resources in an application. These include menus, toolbars, dialog boxes, common controls, and so on. Chapters 15 and 16 will teach you the fundamentals of OLE containers and servers. With the help of the AppWizard and ClassWizard, you'll be developing complex OLE applications in no time at all. Chapters 17 and 18 are devoted to the development and understanding of custom controls. Custom controls give an application a unique look and flair. Using the ControlWizard makes the development of custom much easier.

This book makes certain assumptions about you as a programmer and about the software and hardware platforms that you will be developing your applications on. As a C or C++ programmer, you should be familiar with procedure-oriented Windows programming such as that found in Cross-Platform Programming for Windows by Murray and Pappas and published by Osborne/McGraw-Hill. For software, you should be running Windows 95 or Windows NT and have the latest version of Microsoft Developer Studio (Visual C++ compiler) installed. When installing the compiler, we selected all available development options. For hardware, we strongly recommend a 100 Mhz Pentium computer with CD-ROM, 16 MB RAM, and a 540 MB hard drive. At this speed, full compiles will typically be under a minute.

Welcome to the world of object-oriented Windows development!

The Authors

Chapter 1

An Introduction to 32-Bit Windows 95 and NT

Unless you have been on some other planet for the last year, you undoubtedly recognize this Start button! Everywhere you turn—television, cable, satellite, newspaper, magazines, billboards, hundreds of other promotional campaigns or the stock market—you see this famous Windows 95 icon. As such, you already know, *the* reason for learning how to develop an application for Windows 95. And if you are a Windows NT user, hang on—a matching icon is on its way imminently.

You might be asking yourself the question, "Why has this new operating system garnered so much attention?" First, you cannot ignore Microsoft's purported $40 million—dollar advertising campaign. More importantly, Windows 95 and Windows NT provide the programmer and end user with so many advantages over their ancestral Windows 3.*x*/MS-DOS roots that most, if not all, Windows 3.*x* and earlier users will naturally want to upgrade. The following list highlights just a few of the features Microsoft is including in Windows 95:

- Networking
- InfoCenter universal in-box (electronic mail, fax)
- Explorer (a vastly improved shell)
- WordPad (a full-featured word processor)
- Microsoft Paint (a full-featured paint program)
- Hypterterminal (a full-featured telecommunications package)

Finally comes the statement made by Rick Sherlund, a Wall Street analyst for Goldman Sachs: Microsoft "should dominate the market for desktop software for the next 10 years." Whether you like it or not, accept these facts:

- Microsoft runs the show.
- Evolutionary changes are much easier for the market to accept.
- When choosing platforms for which to develop software, remember that what ultimately matters is not technical excellence but market penetration.
- Market penetration leads to standardization.
- Windows 95 will be the standard desktop computing platform for the next five years.

Windows 95 and Windows NT unleash the full potential of 32-bit microprocessors without ignoring older, 16-bit Windows applications. End users can still run their current Windows 3.*x* applications, while simultaneously taking advantage of full 32-Bit Windows 95 and Windows NT programs.

Windows 95 and Windows NT are full 32-bit operating systems; thus, your programs will not require any of the confusing memory management schemes required under DOS. Windows 95, however, still has a few links (for compatibility purposes) to its 16-bit past, so it can still take advantage of memory managers, such as Microsoft's MemMaker.

Note: *Many developers view Windows 95 as a scaled-down version of Windows NT. This is simply not the case. Windows 95 could be more accurately viewed as a (very) scaled-up version of Windows 3.11 for WorkGroups.*

This book is designed to teach you how to quickly and efficiently write applications for Windows 95 and Windows NT using the Microsoft Foundation Class Library, known as MFC. In addition, the book teaches you how to use the latest techniques for program development, including the use of Microsoft's AppWizard and ClassWizard tools. Along the way you learn why an object-oriented approach to Windows development is best, why Microsoft is emphasizing its use, and why you should abandon the procedure-oriented approach.

To use this book effectively, you should be a C/C++ programmer with a little experience in writing traditional procedure-oriented programs. You will need the Microsoft Visual C++ compiler (version 4.0). Microsoft has been gaining tremendous ground with new developments in the Visual C++ compiler. This compiler is designed to efficiently generate 32-bit Win32 code for its new generation of operating systems—Windows 95 and Windows NT. Experts in the field agree that the Visual C++ compiler, and the MFC programming approach, may soon be the *only* approach to this environment—so much so that companies such as Borland International may soon drop their proprietary object-window-packaging, known as OWL (Object Windows Library), and license the MFC Library.

Reasons for Developing Windows 95 and Windows NT Applications

Imagine a future of information interchange that was language independent, hardware and software indifferent, and file format transparent. Imagine a future where universal knowledge was virtually at your fingertips; a future free of cryptic protocols, translation algorithms, and inaccessible domains. Imagine "information at your fingertips." The operating system of the future will be able to do all of these things:

- Access information from any source
- Communicate with others
- Easily store, retrieve, and browse information
- Integrate various kinds of information
- Take everyday business procedures and automate them

This almost unbelievable scenario is the goal of the visionary software engineers at Microsoft. Windows 95 already includes many of these features in its document-centric approach, and the next release of Windows NT will include even more. We are on the evolutionary migration path towards tapping vast storehouses of universal knowledge.

Objects Are Everything

The goals for "information at your fingertips" include creating, using, organizing, and finding information regardless of what or where it is. This requires a consistent object model representation for application or system information. This scalable, easy-to-use object model gives the user a personal work space that can be customized and controlled and that is extremely flexible.

Objects provide a consistent look to all of the controls for the visual interface, regardless of the data source: CD, camcorder, VCR, or laser disk. The object-model representation of information will take into consideration what kind or class of data is being represented. It will also consider where the information is found (the context), independent of the implementation (or provider). For example, a faxed message has certain common characteristics, regardless of whether the fax was just received over the phone or transferred from an internal message center. However, the object-model would differentiate unique features, or the quality of the service. Design emphasis will shift totally to that of an object-based philosophy, where there will be one model for all interactions, regardless of type (users, processes, documents, or devices).

To fully understand and appreciate Windows 95 and Windows NT, you must start with each product's goals and target audiences. From the user's viewpoint, Windows 95, with its new user interface, is the most updated version of Windows yet. Windows 95 was designed to be a document-centric environment. A document-centric environment means that documents open the applications (type the name of a word processor document and that document will start the word processor automatically), not the more common method of opening Microsoft Word and searching for the file to edit.

Under Windows 95 and Windows NT, the emphasis is on creating, editing, manipulating, storing and retrieving data.

The Windows NT operating system was designed as a 32-bit, high-end, secure computing platform. Windows NT is targeted for the developer, power end-user, corporate MIS-manager, multihardware-platform, and network-server implementors. The next version of Windows NT will appear more like Windows 95 and less like Windows 3.1, while retaining all of its present power. If rumors are to be believed, the next Windows NT beta should appear in February or March of 1996.

Windows 95 and Windows NT are 32-bit preemptive multitasking operating systems that combine the ease of use and proven productivity of the older 16-bit nonpreemptive version of Windows (3.1) with the power and advanced capabilities of a new high-end operating system. Windows NT also unlocks the potential of a wide range of advanced PC hardware because it runs on Intel-based 80x86 microprocessors and RISC architectures, and it supports symmetric multiprocessing, or MIPS. Thus, Windows NT extends your investment in hardware, but it does not do so at the expense of previous investments in software. Both Windows 95 and Windows NT run all carefully developed 16-bit applications written for MS-DOS and Windows 3.1. Carefully developed programs are those that follow Microsoft's rules for program development.

Upward compatibility makes Windows 95 and Windows NT a safe platform for future application development. Windows 95 offers the advantages of plug-and-play, which frees the user from having to configure applicable hardware items such as modems, printers, and mice. The Windows NT hardware interface enables it to take advantage of all current I/O technologies, from CD audio to real-time video, and to evolve with future developments. The real success for all of the generations of Microsoft Windows can be summed up in one sentence: "It makes people more productive than ever before."

Key Elements of Windows 95 and Windows NT

Many users are so profoundly happy with their Windows 3.*x* version that they can't understand the hoopla about Windows 95 or Windows NT. As good as Windows 3.*x* is, there is still a lot of room for improvement. The following discussion explains the features that make Windows 95 and Windows NT the platform for development well into the next century.

Beginnings: Windows 95 and Windows NT

The Windows NT development group began laying their foundations back in the late 1980s, and the Windows 95 development group in the early 1990s. The Windows NT development team was headed by Dave Cutler and included expert software engineers with experience in designing Windows, UNIX, VMS, and OS/2. The first successful boot of Windows NT took place in late 1989 on an Intel i860. In early 1990, Microsoft made the decision to base the Windows 95 and Windows NT operating systems on a Windows-based 32-bit API (application program interface). Microsoft then focused its design around the Intel and RISC architectures.

Windows 95 and Windows NT As Operating Systems

Compared to the conventional 16-bit MS-DOS operating system with Windows 3.1, the Windows 95 and Windows NT operating systems offer considerable advantages to both users and programmers. Individually, the three primary capabilities (graphics-oriented user interface, multitasking, and hardware independence) are not new. What is innovative is attempting to combine all three of them into a single microcomputer operating system! Windows NT still retains the "look" of Windows 3.x; Windows 95, however, presents a whole new user interface.

Common User Interface The most obvious capability provided by Windows is the standardized graphics-oriented user interface. This consistent user interface uses pictures, or *icons*, to represent drives, files, subdirectories, and many of the operating system commands and actions. Most Windows applications make use of both the keyboard and mouse interfaces. Although most functions of Windows applications can be controlled through the keyboard, using the mouse is often easier for many tasks. With a common interface, the user will no longer have to spend long hours learning to use a new application program, because all Windows applications have an intuitive feel. This consistent user interface is achieved by using subroutines built directly into Windows to construct menus and dialog boxes. For example, all menus have the same keyboard and mouse interface because Windows, not the application itself, handles the job.

Preemptive Multitasking A multitasking operating system allows the user to have several applications, or several instances of the same application, running concurrently. At any time, the user can move the windows on the screen, change their size, switch between different applications, and exchange information among windows. One of the main differences between Windows 3.1 (WIN32s), and Windows 95 and Windows NT (Win32) is true preemptive multitasking. While the visual interface between all Windows versions may appear similar, what is going on in the background is completely different.

With the 16-bit version of Windows 3.1, you could have several applications loaded, but only one of them could actually use the processor at any given time. The distinction between a task that was processing and one that was merely running was important. Under Windows 95 and Windows NT, the processor automatically switches between applications and does not have to wait for the currently executing program to release control of the processor. This is true preemptive multitasking.

Windows also provides a third state called "active." An active application is the one receiving the user's attention or focus. Just as only one application can be processing at any given instant, so there can be only one active application at a time. However, there can be any number of concurrently running tasks. Partitioning up the microprocessor's time is the responsibility of Windows 95 and Windows NT. They control the sharing of the microprocessor by using queued input and messages.

Before the advent of true multitasking operating systems, application programs had exclusive control of all the computer's resources, including the input and output devices, memory, the video display, and even the CPU itself. Under Windows, however, all of these valuable resources must be shared. For example, a standard C/C++ program no longer has access to all the memory not used by the system or the program itself.

Greatly Improved Memory Management Next to the microprocessor itself, memory is the second most important shared resource under Windows 95 and Windows NT. With more than one application running at the same time, the applications must cooperate to share memory in order not to exhaust the resource. Additionally, as new programs are started up and old ones are terminated, memory can become fragmented. Windows 95 and Windows NT are capable of consolidating free memory space by moving blocks of code and data in memory. Windows 95 and Windows NT permit applications to "overcommit" memory. That is, an application can contain more code than will actually fit into memory at one time. Windows 95 and Windows NT can discard code from memory and later reload the code from the program's executable (.exe) file.

In addition, Windows 95 and Windows NT allow the user to have several instances, or copies, of the same program running concurrently. To conserve space, Windows 95 and Windows NT share the same code. Programs running under Windows 95 and Windows NT can even share routines with other programs. The files that contain these shared routines are called *dynamic link libraries* or DLLs. Windows 95 and Windows NT include the mechanism to link the program with the routines in the DLLs at run time.

Queue-based Input Under Windows, an application does not make explicit calls to read from the keyboard or mouse input devices. Instead, keyboard and mouse input are treated as a shared resource under Windows. No longer can a C/C++ program read directly from the keyboard by means of a **getchar()** function call. Windows itself receives all input from the keyboard, mouse, and timer in the *system queue.* It is the queue's responsibility to redirect the input to the appropriate application by copying it from the system queue into the application queue. When the application is ready to process any input, it reads from its queue and dispatches a message to the appropriate window. This input is provided in a uniform format called an *input message.* All input messages specify the system time, state of the keyboard, scan code of any depressed key, position of the mouse, and which mouse button has been pressed (if any), as well as information specifying which device generated the message.

The good news is that all keyboard, mouse, and timer messages have the identical format and are all processed in the same manner. Additionally, with each message, Windows provides a device-independent virtual key code that identifies the key (it doesn't matter which type of keyboard it is on), the device-dependent scan code generated by the keyboard, and the status of other keys on the keyboard, such as NUM LOCK, ALT, SHIFT, and CTRL. With the keyboard and mouse being a shared resource, one keyboard and one mouse must supply all the input for each program running under Windows. With the keyboard, all input messages go directly to the currently active window. However, mouse messages are handled differently; they are sent to the window that is immediately beneath the mouse cursor.

Windows allows a program to set a timer so that one of its windows receives a message at periodic intervals. Timer messages are very similar to keyboard and mouse messages in that they go directly into the program's message queue. There are also other messages that get into a program's message queue as a result of the program calling certain Windows functions. These functions will be discussed individually as they occur in example programs in future chapters.

Message-based Communication Windows uses what is called a *message system* to disseminate information in a multitasking environment. From the application's viewpoint, a message can be seen as a notification that some event of interest has occurred, which may or may not require a specific action. These events may be initiated by the user, such as clicking or moving the mouse, changing the size of a window, or making a menu selection. The signaled event, however, could also be generated by the application. For example, Microsoft Excel could have finished a recalculation, resulting in a need to update a displayed bar chart. In this case, Excel would send itself an "update window" message. It is also possible for Windows to generate messages, as in the case of a "close session" message. In this example, Windows must inform each application of the intent to shut down. One last major message source could be an instrument monitoring program, indicating that a critical nuclear process had reached the specified pressure. Regardless of the source of the message, your program must take the appropriate action.

There are two major points to keep in mind when thinking about the role of messages in Windows.

First, it is through the message system that Windows achieves its multitasking capabilities. The message system makes it possible for Windows to share the processor among different applications. Each time Windows sends a message to the application program, it also grants processor time.

Secondly, the role of messages under Windows is to enable an application to respond to events in the environment, whether these events are generated by the application itself, by other concurrently running applications, by the user, or by Windows. Each time an event occurs, Windows makes a note of it and distributes an appropriate message to the interested applications. Thus, at the simplest level, the most important task for all versions of Windows is to process messages!

Hardware Independence Historically, hardware devices change at a much faster rate than operating systems. Consider, for example, the number of new printers introduced each year. Another advantage provided by Windows is hardware device independence. This section will concentrate on a discussion on how device independence is accomplished.

Windows frees the programmer from having to account for every possible variety of monitor, printer, input device, and CPU available! Currently, a non-Windows application must be written to include drivers for every possible device that it uses. This has always been one of the major inefficiencies in software development. For example, to make an application capable of printing on any printer, the developer must furnish a different driver for each printer type that may be encountered. This requires many software companies to write essentially the same device driver over and over. For instance, essentially the same Hewlett Packard LaserJet 5 driver would be needed for WordPerfect, Microsoft Word, AutoCad, and so on. Under DOS, each software company would have to develop their own driver.

All Windows versions allow each device driver—for a video display, printer, keyboard, or mouse—to be written only once. Instead of each software company writing its own complete set, the hardware company writes one driver for the Windows environment. Microsoft includes many drivers with Windows, and others are available from the hardware or software manufacturer. One of the enhancements available with Windows is external support for font cartridges. This capability has been incorporated into the Hewlett-Packard LaserJet driver, for example. When Windows is installed, it includes one driver for each device in the current system. Whenever a command to print or draw is sent from an application, Windows feeds the output through the appropriate driver. Incorporating the necessary drivers directly into the system eliminates a great deal of redundant programming effort.

Since applications interact directly with windows rather than with any specific device driver, from the programmer's perspective, application development has become easier. When a command is sent from the application to draw a filled rectangle, Windows will automatically carry out the task. By the same token, each device driver works with every Windows application. Developers save time, and users no longer have to worry whether each new application will support their favorite generic-brand digitizer pad. Windows achieves this device independence by specifying the capabilities the hardware must have in conjunction with the Software Development and/or Device-Driver kits.

Every routine, regardless of its complexity, can be broken down into a minimal set of operations required for a device. For example, not every plotter is capable of drawing an ellipse. As an application developer, however, you can still use the kit routines to draw an ellipse, even if the plotter has no specific ellipse capabilities. Since every plotter connected to Windows must be minimally capable of drawing a line, Windows can break the ellipse routine down into a series of small lines.

In terms of input, Windows is also able to specify a set of minimum capabilities to ensure your application will receive only valid, predefined input. Windows has predefined a set of legal keystrokes. In other words, Windows predefines all the keystrokes that a Windows application can possibly receive. The valid keystroke set is very similar to that produced by the keyboard. Should a manufacturer produce a keyboard containing keys that do not exist in the Windows list of acceptable keys, the manufacturer would also have to supply additional software that would translate these "illegal" keystrokes into Windows legal keystrokes. This predefined input covers all input devices, including the mouse. Therefore, even if someone should develop a six-button mouse, you won't have to worry about compatibility issues. The manufacturer would again have to supply the software necessary to convert all mouse input to Windows' predefined possibilities for mouse-button clicks.

Plug-and-Play Windows 95 supports a feature called Plug-and-Play. Plug-and-Play will allow hardware devices designed for Windows 95 to be inserted into computers with no additional hardware or software adjustments. Imagine plugging in a serial port, parallel port, sound card, or modem, and doing nothing else!

Reusable Dynamic Link Libraries Just about all of Microsoft Windows' capabilities come from a set of dynamic link libraries, called DLLs, which enhance the base operating system and provide a powerful and flexible graphics user interface. Dynamic link libraries contain predefined functions that are linked with an application program when it is loaded (dynamically), instead of when the executable (.exe) file is generated (statically). Windows did not originate the idea of linking libraries to application code, however. The C/C++ language depends heavily on libraries to implement standard functions for different systems. For example, the linker copies C/C++ run-time library functions, such as **getchar()** and **printf()**, into a program's executable file.

This collection of routines save a programmer from having to re-create a new procedure for a common operation such as reading in a character or formatting output. Programmers can build their own libraries to include additional capabilities such as changing a font and justifying text. The new function can then be made available as a general tool, eliminating redundant design. As mentioned earlier, Windows libraries are dynamically linked. With dynamically linked libraries the linker does not copy the library functions into the program's executable file. Instead, while the program is executing, it makes calls to the functions in the library. An immediate advantage of this technique is memory conservation. No matter how many applications are running, there is only one copy of the library in the computer's RAM memory at a time.

Microsoft's new library format for Windows DLLs is more versatile. While they have retained the same format as any other DOS executable file (although they cannot themselves be executed), they can hold anything programs hold. In addition to functions, DLLs can also encode data and even incorporate graphics resources such as cursor shapes and bitmaps. Windows DLLs expand the range of shared resources and save programmers even more time. Technically, when an application makes a call to a Windows function, the compiler must generate machine code for a call to the function that is located in one of the Windows DLLs. This presents a problem, since until the program is actually running under Windows, the address of the Windows function is unknown.

The solution to this problem is called *delayed binding* or *dynamic linking*. New linkers allow a program to have calls to functions that cannot be fully resolved at link time. Only when the program is loaded into memory to be run are the far function calls resolved. Windows allows your compiler to take advantage of "import libraries" that are used to properly prepare a Windows program for dynamic linking. These import libraries contain a record for each Windows function that your application can call. This record defines the Windows module that contains this function and, in many cases, an ordinal value (a numeric value) that corresponds to the function in the module.

For example, a Windows application could make a call to the Windows **PostMessage()** function. When you link the program, the linker finds the **PostMessage()** function listed in the library. The linker obtains the ordinal number for the function and embeds this information in the program's executable (.exe) file. When the program is run, Windows then links the call the program makes with the actual **PostMessage()** function.

Win16 versus Win32

Technically speaking, Windows 3.x is a sophisticated application that requires MS-DOS. It is not, although it may appear to be, a full-fledged operating system. Windows 3.*x* is optimized for x86 machines and uses only a small amount of system resources. For example, Windows 3.*x* operates very well with just 4 MB of RAM. By its very nature, Windows 3.*x* is a nonpreemptive operating environment that is very DOS dependent. Windows 95 and Windows NT are *not* based on 16-bit MS-DOS, although several DOS components have been "discovered" in Windows 95.

Both Windows 95 and Windows NT are 32-bit operating systems. Windows 95 works well with 6 to 8 MB of RAM while Windows NT works best with 16 MB of RAM. Windows NT also operates on multiple hardware platforms with multiple processors. For example, you may have a server running Windows NT that uses four RISC microprocessors! Both Windows 95 and Windows NT run 16-bit and 32-bit applications. This feature allows upward compatibility with older MS-DOS and Windows 3.*x* applications. The following discussion highlights several new components of the Windows 95 and Windows NT operating systems.

Platform Independence One of Microsoft's major goals for Windows NT was system portability. They have succeeded. Windows NT applications are portable across several of the most popular architectures. *Hardware portability* enables code to be moved from one microprocessor to another with as little rewriting as possible. This portability allows developers and end users alike to benefit from being able to have the same operating system run on different systems. As a result, with Windows NT you can now have salespeople in the field use a Windows interface on their pen-based systems that matches the one on their portable computers, which matches the networked microcomputer at the office and the minicomputer in the development lab.

For the enduser, there is only one set of commands to learn. For the developer, there is only one product to design. Both are happy. Financially, there is also only one initial outlay for a cross-system interface. Portability is a matter of degree. The real question is not whether software will port, but how difficult it is to port. Windows NT excels in portability. First, Windows NT is written not in a hardware-restrictive assembly language, but in portable C. C is a programming language available on all development or host architectures.

Second, Windows NT minimizes the amount of code that interacts directly with the hardware. Third, since it is impossible to avoid hardware-dependent code, these routines have been localized. By not spreading hardware-dependent algorithms throughout the entire operating system, Windows NT makes porting easy. Each target environment need only replace those code sections specific to their architecture. Specifically,

Windows NT encapsulates hardware-dependent code inside a dynamic-link library known as the *hardware abstraction layer*, or HAL. The HAL intercepts hardware interaction, such as I/O interrupts and memory access, with a layer of software. The HAL layer takes care of the communication between the standard Windows NT operation and the hardware-dependent implementation. This allows the core of Windows NT to remain unchanged from architecture to architecture.

All-Platform Compatibility with Win32s With the tremendous cost of software development, designing one application that runs on multiple software platforms offers money and time savings advantages. It is extremely easy to write one Windows application that can be compiled to run under Windows 3.*x*, Windows 95, or Windows NT. This software portability does not exist between DOS, Windows, OS/2, and the UNIX operating systems. The success of this software portability between Windows 3.*x*, Windows 95, and Windows NT lies in the Win32s and Win32 APIs (application program interfaces). Table 1.1 lists the Win32s enhancements to Windows 3.1.

Table 1.1: Improvements of Win32s over Win16

Feature	*Description*
32-bit addressing	Win32 processes access a flat, 32-bit address space instead of the segmented address space of Win16
32-bit heap	Win32 heap allocation routines such as **HeapAlloc()** and **HeapFree()** are supported
Exception handling	The Win32s API also provides this Win32 capability.
Shared memory	Win32s provides some of the interprocess memory sharing support of Win32
Virtual memory	Allows control over a program's address space; for example, some Win32 virtual memory functions and features are provided in Win32s
File I/O	Win32s provides its own file I/O functions, replacing the MS-DOS functions used by Win16 programs, but incompatible with Win32 applications
Universal thunks	Win32s allows a Win32 application to call Win16 Dynamic Link Libraries (DLLs).

Specifically, Windows NT takes full advantage of all Win32 API features and offers access to multiple processors, distributed processing, networking, and security. Windows NT has full access to all Win32 functions and features, including **AngleLine()** and 32-bit world coordinate features. Windows 95 also uses the 32-bit Win32 API, but is currently restricted in its access to multiple processors and security features. Additionally, Windows 95 does not have access to all Win32 functions and features.

For example, Windows 95 uses a 16-bit world coordinate system and does not allow access to certain functions, such as **AngleLine()**. The official word from Microsoft is that Windows 95 will support all functions that are supported in both Win32 and Win32s—in 32-bit mode! Table 1.2 list those features exclusive to Win32 and *not* supported by Win32s.

Windows 3.*x* can use a limited set of Win32 functions. However, these functions must be accessed through the 16-bit Win32s API.

Multiprocessing Very soon you are going to see a proliferation of microcomputers containing more than one microprocessor. It

Table 1.2: Win32 features not supported by Win32s

Feature	*Description*
GDI improvements	The 32-bit GDI is capable of drawing paths, bezier curves, and rotating bitmaps
Multithread support	Unlike Windows 3.1, which is a single-threaded environment, Win32 supports multithreads and processes
Network API	Win32 provides mail slots and named pipes
Security	Win32 provides user security to Windows NT, which is not available under Win16 or Win32s and is not currently supported by Windows 95.
Tape backup	Win32 provides tape backup support
Remote procedure call (RPC)	Win32 allows the control of an application from a different computer via network communication
Console API	Character-based application development is not supported under Win32s

seems that one high-speed Pentium just isn't enough! For those high-end users, Windows NT can take advantage of multiprocessor architectures. Each additional processor added to the system delivers a linear increase in performance. A Windows NT application can allocate each thread (subtask or procedure) of the program to its own processor. Windows NT can even dedicate individual processors to system-level tasks. With this design, both the application and the operating system receive the benefits of multiprocessing. All of this is accomplished without any modifications to the application. Windows NT automatically takes full advantage of symmetric multiprocessing whenever available. Therefore, the user immediately benefits from improved performance through this transparent conversion.

Scalability *Scalability* is a term that refers to an operating system's ability to run on different platforms. Windows NT runs on computers ranging from notebooks to super-servers, Intel-based, MIPS-based, and Alpha systems, and symmetric multiprocessing machines.

Distributed Computing One of the design goals behind Windows 95 and Windows NT involved information sharing. The workplace has evolved from a company having one large mainframe computer to the proliferation of smaller and cheaper microcomputers. As a result of this hardware metamorphosis, there has come a need for these isolated microcomputer systems to communicate with one another. Windows 95 and Windows NT solve this software and hardware handshaking by directly incorporating networking capabilities into the operating systems.

Security Today, more than ever, data security is an issue of which more and more individuals and corporations are becoming aware. Once data storage and retrieval moved from one large mainframe to networked microcomputers, MIS managers began worrying seriously about data security. Naturally, this was not just a concern of the individual corporation, but was also an even more serious matter for the U.S. government. The government saw the need to secure one user's resources from another and to prevent any one user from garnering all of the systems resources at any moment in time. Although such security is not currently a part of Windows 95, Windows NT targets the United States Department of Defenses Class C2 security level.

This standard defines what is known as a discretionary, or need-to-know, level of protection. It also defines a set of standards that allows privilege level audit capabilities. Basically, a C2-compliant operating system allows the owner of a system resource to decide who can access it. A system monitor keeps track of who is accessing the data and at what time. The U.S. government standard encompasses security levels from D (lowest security level) through A (highest security level). The fundamental structure of Windows NT will allow its security rating to migrate to the higher security levels.

Windows Open Systems Architecture Through the use of their Windows Open Systems Architecture (WOSA), Microsoft has defined an open set of network interface standards for file-sharing, print-sharing, database access, electronic mail, and system configuration and administration. WOSA allows end-users of Windows 95 and Windows NT to access multivendor information services.

Crash Management Under Windows 95 or Windows NT, the system crashes experienced under Windows 3.*x* are a thing of the past. Windows 95 and Windows NT are robust platforms with proven stability and integrity. Through advanced memory protection schemes, Windows 95 and Windows NT prevent business-critical applications from experiencing any data corruption. Neither the operating system, nor any single process can bring a program down, because each is given its own unique memory space. Windows 95 and Windows NT also protect from system crashes by isolating each application from direct hardware access. Windows 95 and Windows NT check each request for validity and correct privilege level. Finally, new file systems for Windows 95 and Windows NT provide many file fixes, such as a full recovery system, to quickly restore file integrity. The new file systems maintain a transaction log that insures the integrity of the disk structure even if there is a system shutdown.

Virtual Memory Windows 95 and Windows NT both take advantage of a flat or linear programming platform, as opposed to the segmented platforms of the past. Both users and developers can benefit from applications that demand large amounts of RAM for peak performance. These full 32-bit operating systems, combined with a 64-bit address capability, essentially eliminate all architectural limits for your applications. One of the major goals for Windows 95 and Windows NT was the operating system's ability to run an MS-DOS or 16-bit Windows application as-is. This is quite an undertaking, because each environment views physical memory in a unique manner.

Microsoft's solution was to allow each of the Windows 95 and Windows NT environment subsystems to view memory in a manner corresponding to what each 16-bit application expects. With a 32-bit flat address virtual memory system, an application's *virtual address space* represents a set of addresses available to a process and any of its threads. At run time, the virtual memory manager translates or maps each virtual address into an actual physical address. Since the operating system is doing a validation between virtual address and physical addresses, it prevents individual processes from bumping into each other.

Many systems running Windows 95 and Windows NT do not have access to large quantities of physical memory. Instead, when the virtual memory manager detects a shortage of physical memory, it automatically transfers (or pages) some of the physical memory's contents to disk. Paged data frees up the store of available physical memory. This allows needed code or data to be moved into memory. Whenever a virtual address maps to paged information, these operating systems automatically load or reload the needed data. Windows 95 and Windows NT are sophisticated enough to customize themselves to whatever physical RAM is available. They do this by dynamically balancing physical RAM between paged memory and a file cache.

Comparison of Windows 95 and Windows NT

The list of features that each version of Windows provides is indeed confusing. Table 1.3 provides a summary of features for each version of Windows.

If we are to believe the rumors that abound concerning these operating systems, then the next version of Windows NT will incorporate the Windows 95 interface. This version of Windows NT went to beta in February of 1996. Eventually, however, Windows 95 will merge into Windows NT as Microsoft's single operating system! Do you believe it?

Table 1.3: Features of Windows 95 and Windows NT.

Feature	*Windows Version*		
	3.1	*95*	*NT*
32-bit preemptive multitasking		*	*
Auto hardware detection		*	*
Automatic recovery from a system failure			*
C-2 security level			*
Crash protection between Win16 apps			*
Data protection			*
Desktop user profiles		*	*
Fully exploits 386 to Pentium platforms		*	*
LAN connectivity and peer-to-peer networking		*	*
New interface		*	
Open networking architecture		*	*
Open system management architecture		*	*
Plug-and-play technology		*	
Remote access services		*	*
Runs IBM Presentation Manager			*
Runs MS-DOS device drivers	*	*	
Runs on PowerPC, MIPS, Alpha RISC systems			*
Runs Win16 device drivers	*	*	
Secure user profiles			*
Supports disk compression	*	*	
Supports MS-DOS	*	*	many
Supports multiple file systems + FAT			*
Supports multiple processors			*
Supports OpenGL		soon	*
Supports SNMP and DMI standards		*	*
Supports Win16 applications	*	*	*
Supports Win32 applications		*	*
Win32 APIs		*	*
Win32s APIs	*	*	*

Getting Started

The intent of this book is to help moderately experienced C/C++ programmers make the transition to writing applications that use the Microsoft Windows APIs. The text covers how to use all popular Windows 95 and Windows NT functions, messages, and data structures to carry out useful tasks common to Windows applications. Thus, you will learn how to write common code that can be compiled and run under Windows 95 and Windows NT. However, you'll also learn how to write code targeted for specific environments, such as Windows 95 or Windows NT.

The C/C++ programming language is the preferred development language for Windows applications. Many of the programming features of Windows were designed with the C/C++ programmer in mind. Windows applications can also be developed in Microsoft's Visual Basic, Borland's Delphi, and assembly language, but these languages present additional challenges and/or limitations that are typically avoided when writing applications in C/C++.

Required Software

To build all of the Windows applications in this book, you will need to have a variety of tools. For Windows 95 and Windows NT application development, you will need the following:

- A 32-bit C/C++ compiler. Again, we recommend either the Microsoft or Borland compilers.
- Either Windows 95 or Windows NT running on your system.
- Access to the Win32 API (usually provided by the compiler manufacturer).

System Requirements

All versions of Windows will work with 80386 or higher processors and at least 100 MB hard drives. Windows 3.*x* will work well with 4 MB of RAM. We feel that 6-8 MB of RAM is required for good performance under Windows 95, and 12-16 MB of RAM when using Windows NT.

For optimal performance for developers, we recommend the following system configuration for the best overall performance and ease-of-use:

- Audio board—Microsoft or Sound Blaster
- CD-ROM—4*x* or 6*x* speed CD-ROM Drive
- Floppy disk type—1.44 MB 3.5"
- Hard disk—1 GB (minimum)
- Main system—Pentium running at 100 MHZ (or greater).

- Mouse—Microsoft Mouse
- RAM—16 MB
- Video—32-bit local video bus graphics adapter

In the Next Chapter...

You have now been introduced to Windows, from its distinguished genealogy through Microsoft's visionary plans for the future. The next chapter will begin by explaining fundamental Windows concepts and vocabulary necessary to begin developing Windows 95 and Windows NT applications.

Chapter 2

Windows 95 and NT Concepts and Terminology

Before you can begin programming a Windows application, you need to understand those concepts and terms specific to multitasking, object-oriented GUI (graphical user interface) applications. These new concepts and terms can be broken down into two distinct areas, visual and behind-the-scenes. Visual features include standard Windows items such as title bars, icons, radio buttons, push buttons, menus, and scroll bars. Behind-the-scenes features include invoking functions and recognizing and responding to messages.

Just as in any technical area of study—for example, digital logic—knowing the correct terminology is important for correctly communicating with others. For this reason, all of the Windows features have been given a name and an associated usage. This chapter will introduce you to the basic vocabulary that will enable you to confidently discuss and develop Windows applications.

Windows versus Windows

To begin, Windows, in this book, refers to the two Microsoft operating systems, Windows 95 and Windows NT. The term window refers specifically to a rectangular portion of the screen representing a program, with an application-independent format. To endusers, this window is the visual interface between the user and the application generating the window. To the application, this window is the rectangular area of the screen under the control of the application. How the application was written determines the window's shape, size, and screen location. In Windows, whenever the user launches an application, a new window is created. Whenever the user selects a window control or option, the program responds. One of the ways to terminate an application is to simply close its window.

A window represents much more than a simple rectangle painted on the screen. This visual interface also relates directly to specific application features, such as terminating the program. In this sense, a window represents the fundamental substructure of the Windows system and is just as important as this visual user-application information exchange. For example, while the window itself represents the graphics-oriented user interface, it is also the visible manifestation of a multitasking and hardware-independent environment. The visible overlap of applications conveys to the user the true multitasking capabilities of Windows. Because the screen is partitioned into different windows, the user can direct input to a specific application within the multitasking environment by using the keyboard or mouse to select one of the concurrently running applications. Windows then intercepts the user's input and allocates any necessary resources (such as the processor or memory) as needed.

With each window representing an individually executing application, you can easily see how this window metaphor highlights the hardware-independent substructure of Windows. From each application's viewpoint, its window is the screen. However, since Windows does not permit applications to access the physical screen directly, all interaction must be performed through the window. Because of the intervention by

Windows, it doesn't matter to the application that the window may only be a portion of the entire display; to the application, the window is the entire display. It is Windows itself that sits between each application and any interaction between specific devices, such as the keyboard, monitor or printer, making all necessary translations.

CREATING THE "LOOK"

One of the main objectives of Windows was making every new application you purchase as easy as possible to learn. One way Windows accomplishes this is by requiring every Windows application to behave in a certain manner and contain common, recognizable features. A brief list of shared characteristics would include the Help menu and related capabilities, control boxes, About boxes, and so on. These commonalities give Windows a comforting predictability from application to application (see Figure 2.1). The discussion that follows describes each of these components in detail.

Figure 2.1: Common Windows components.

The Window Border

Working from the outside in, all windows are bounded by a border. The border consists of the lines that frame a window. To the newcomer, the border may appear only to delineate one application window from another. However, by moving the mouse pointer over a border and holding down the left mouse button, the user can usually alter a window's size and shape.

The Window Title Bar

In a multitasking environment, knowing which concurrently executing application you are using is important. For this reason, all application windows have a title bar at the top, displaying the application's name. The title bar itself is centered in Windows NT and placed just to the right of the applications icon under Windows 95. The title is printed left-justified in this area. Writing the code necessary to title your application is as simple as passing its title string—for example, "My Program"—to the **CreateWindow()** function. **CreateWindow()** assigns this string to the main window object's title data member (data members are functionally the same as an older high-level language's record fields).

The Control Box

The upper-left corner of all title bars contains a control box. Under Windows NT, the control box is drawn as a small square box with a flat, shadowed rectangle. Under Windows 95, the control box is usually an application-supplied and visually related icon.

The System Menu

When the user clicks on an application's control box, a drop-down system menu is displayed. The system menu lists several standard options, such as Restore, Move, Size, Minimize, Maximize, and Close (Windows NT includes a Switch To option).

The Minimize Box

The window's minimize box appears on the upper right-hand corner of the window. Under Windows NT, this is a small downward-pointing arrow that causes the window to shrink to a small picture, or icon. Windows 95 uses an underscore symbol to represent a collapsed window.

The Maximize Box

The upper right-hand corner of a window also houses the maximize box. Under Windows NT, this is a small upward-pointing arrow that causes the window to expand to full size. Windows 95 uses a small rectangle with a heavy bar at the top to represent an expanded window and title bar area. When the window is maximized, this image changes to either a downward-pointing arrow or two overlapped rectangles, representing the option to unzoom the application back to original proportions.

The Terminate Box

Windows 95 also includes one additional icon in the upper right-hand corner of the window, representing the terminate box. This is a small rectangle with a heavy "X" drawn in it, used to terminate an application whenever the user clicks the mouse over the icon.

The Vertical Scroll Bar

Scroll bars in general are not required window features. However, so many programs use them that they almost appear to be a standard window control. Windows demands that vertical scroll bars be drawn on the right-hand side of the client area. Vertical scroll bars have arrows at either end, pointing in opposite directions; a colored band; and a transparent window block, sometimes called the thumb. The thumb shows the position of the currently displayed contents in relation to the document as a whole, which is represented visually by the colored band. Also, the size of the thumb gives you an indication of the size of image in the window.

A program uses the vertical scroll bar to select which page of a multiple-page file will be displayed to the window. Clicking either arrow shifts the display one line at a time. Clicking the thumb below the upward arrow and then dragging it causes screen output to rapidly move to any portion of the application's screen output. One of the best uses for the vertical scroll bar is for moving through a multiple-page word processing document.

The Horizontal Scroll Bar

Just like vertical scroll bars, horizontal scroll bars are optional window controls. If an application uses a horizontal scroll bar, it appears at the bottom of the window and runs the extent of the client area. It has arrows at its extremes that point in opposite directions, a colored band, and a transparent window block, or thumb. The thumb shows the position of the currently displayed contents in relation to the document as a whole, which is represented by the colored band.

Typically, horizontal scroll bars are used to shift the display left or right, choosing which set of multiple columns of information you would like displayed. Clicking either arrow causes the screen image to shift one column at a time. Clicking the thumb to the right of the left-pointing arrow and then dragging the thumb causes the screen output to rapidly shift horizontally to any portion of the application's screen output. One of the best uses for the horizontal scroll bar is to move through multiple columns of a spreadsheet application in which all the columns of information cannot fit into one window's width.

The Menu Bar

All Windows applications have a menu bar, which sits immediately below the title bar. The menu bar is used for making menu and submenu selections (menu items are always left-justified within the menu bar). These selections can be made by pointing and clicking the menu command, or alternatively by using a "hot-key" combination. Hot-key combinations often use the ALT key in conjunction with a letter shown in bold and underlined, as the "F" is in the command File shown earlier in Figure 2.1.

The Client or Work Area

The largest portion of a window, occupying the most screen real estate, is the client area. The client area is the application's primary location for output. It is the application's responsibility, not Windows', to manage the client area of the window, and only the application can output to the client area.

OBJECT CLASSES TO THE RESCUE

At this point you are familiar with the most common components and features of a standard Windows window. From a programming perspective, the good news is that you do not have to write the bare-bones code to create each one of them. Instead you use off-the-shelf, reusable windows objects. There may even be an occasion where you will want to create two windows with a similar appearance and behavior. An excellent example of this involves the Windows Paint program. Paint allows users to clip or copy a portion of a graphics image by running two instances (or copies) of Paint. The information is copied from one instance of Paint to the other. It is therefore logical that each instance of Paint look and behave like its counterpart. Therefore, each instance of Paint must have its own window with an identical "look and feel."

Windows accomplishes this commonality by creating new applications based on existing window classes. Windows allows a programmer to create windows with a wide variety of characteristics. They may be of different sizes, be placed on different areas of the display, have different text in the caption bars, have different display colors, or use different mouse cursors. Every window that you create in a Windows application must be based on a window class. Five of these window classes have already been registered by Windows during its initialization phase. You can also have your application register its own classes.

Windows specifies some of a window's characteristics as parameters to the **CreateWindow()** function. Other parameters are specified in a separate window class structure. In order to allow several windows to be created and based on the same window class, a window class needs to be registered. Once registered, the class becomes available to all programs running under Windows. Windows of similar appearance and behavior can be grouped into classes to reduce the amount of information that needs to be maintained.

Each window class has its own shareable window class structure, so there is no needless replication of the window class parameters. Also, since two windows of the same class use the same functions and any associated subroutines, you get maximum code reuse. The most important characteristic of shared classes, however, is that they all share the same "look and feel."

Using Object-Oriented Technology

One of the most important goals of any GUI interface is a common look and familiar mode of operation between different applications. If the coding for this look and user interaction were left up to the individual programmer, two things would happen. First, there would be no common look. Every programmer would have a different idea of how to draw and place an object, and how it should interface with the user. Second, hardly any programs would ever get written. This later problem deals with the coding complexity involved in doing ground-up graphical-user-interface design. Fortunately, we are in the age of object-oriented programming. When you are programming for Windows, you are actually using object-oriented programming. Instead of writing the GUI code yourself, you merely use a previously written object. These objects provide the "look and feel" end users anticipate.

By definition, in object-oriented programming, an object is an abstract data type that consists of a data structure and various functions that act on the data structure. Additionally, objects receive messages that can cause them to change. For example, a graphics object, such as a vertical scroll bar, is a collection of data that can be manipulated as a single entity and is presented to the user as part of the visual interface. In particular, a graphics object represents both the data and the functions dealing with the presentation of the data. Some examples of graphics objects include menus, title bars, control boxes, and scroll bars. The next section describes several new graphics objects that affect the user's view of an application.

Icon Objects

A familiar proverb says that one picture is worth a thousand words; accordingly, icons can be very powerful. They attract the user's attention. Icons relate to program actions in the same way assembly language mnemonics are translated into machine-code instructions. Icons and mnemonics are visual symbols associated with some sort of action. In the case of a mnemonic, this is a readable abbreviation for some action. In the case of an icon, you have a small symbol used to remind the user of a particular operation, idea, or product. For example, when a spreadsheet application is minimized, it could display a very small histogram icon to remind the user the application is still running. Clicking the histogram would cause Windows to bring the application to active status. Windows provides several stock icons, including a question mark, exclamation point, asterisk, and an upturned palm. Using various Windows tools, users can create their own device-independent color icon designs. The function **DrawIcon()** allows an application to easily place an icon within the client area.

Cursor Objects

A Windows cursor is a graphic symbol, unlike the blinking underscore of DOS. The graphic symbol changes according to the placement of the pointing device; this helps to show the operations currently available. The best example of this would be the change from the standard Windows arrow cursor to the small hourglass cursor that indicates a pause while a selected command is being executed. Incorporated into Windows are several stock cursors: the original diagonal arrow, a vertical arrow, an hourglass, cross hairs, an I-beam, and several others. Using the Windows tools, your application can also create its own unique cursors.

Caret Objects

Unlike a cursor object, a caret is a graphic symbol showing the user where input will be received. While a typical Windows window contains many graphic markers, only the caret blinks. Most of the time mouse input is associated with a cursor and keyboard input with a caret. However, the mouse can move or change the input emphasis of a caret. To help clarify the difference between a cursor and a caret, remember that Windows carets behave most like the standard DOS cursor. An example is the I-beam caret provided for you automatically in dialog boxes. Unlike icons and cursors, an application must create its own carets by using the **CreateCaret()** and **ShowCaret()** functions. Except for the automatic I-beam dialog-box caret, there are no stock carets.

Message Box Objects

There will be many occasions when a program will want to inform the user of a particular action. For these purposes there are message box objects. A message box is a pop-up window that contains a title, an icon, and a message. Figure 2.2 shows a standard message box.

Programs easily generate message boxes with a simple call to the function **MessageBox()**. **MessageBox()** creates, displays, and receives the user's response from the message box. In a syntax similar to assigning data items to a structure member, your program need only supply the message title; the message itself; instructions on which stock icon to use (if any); and, if applicable, the stock response to use (such as OK). Other stock user responses include Yes/No, Yes/No/Cancel, OK/Cancel, Retry/Cancel. Your program can also access standard icons such as IconExclamation, IconAsterisk, IconQuestion, and IconHand.

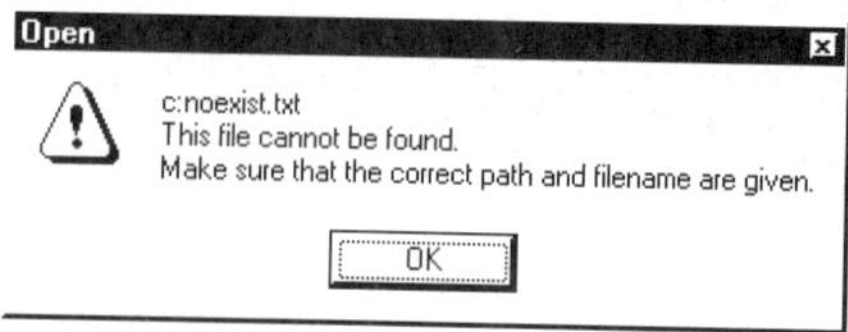

Figure 2.2: A Windows 95 message box.

Dialog Box Objects

Dialog boxes are very similar to message boxes, except that they receive more complex types of user responses other than simple selections of fixed options. Dialog boxes are also pop-up windows; however, dialog boxes are primarily used to receive input from the user. Figure 2.3 shows a Windows 95 Plus! Desktop Themes dialog box.

A dialog box allows an application to receive information one field or box of information at a time, rather than one character at a time. The look and feel of a dialog box is determined automatically by Windows. Dialog boxes are considered program resources because their contents are specific to a particular application. You use your C/C++ compiler's resource editor to define dialog box objects.

Font Objects

If you understand the simple definition of an object, meaning the syntactic combination of data members (remember, a member is no different from a record field), bundled with all

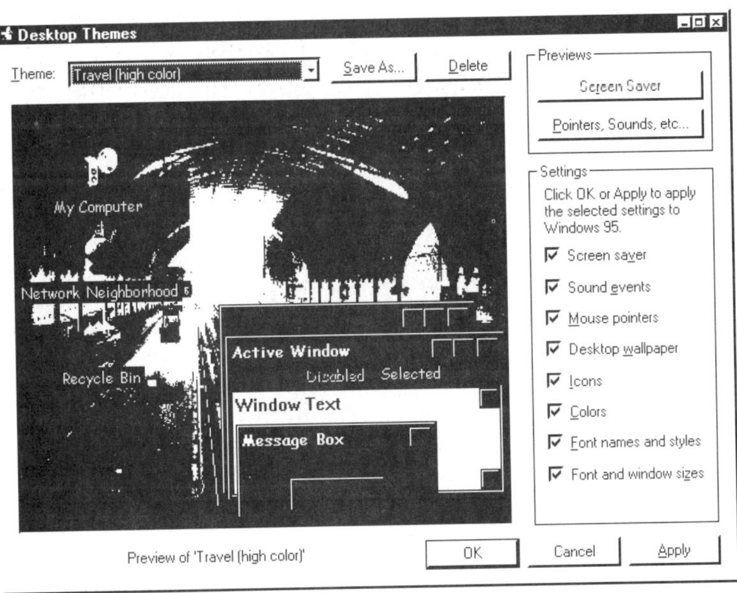

Figure 2.3: A Windows 95 Plus! Desktop Themes dialog box.

of the function members that make the object do something, you'll understand why even fonts are considered objects. Long gone are the days when the characters displayed on your monitor came from a single character ROM built into your system. On the contrary, today's applications seem to have unlimited font capabilities, from typefaces, to point sizes, to the standard bold, italics, and underline styles.

Your programs use font objects, to define a complete set of characters from one typeface, all with a certain size and style. Fonts can be manipulated to give text a variety of appearances. By using built-in routines, Windows allows for the dynamic modification of a typeface, including boldface or italic, underlining, or changing the font size. Windows provides all of the necessary functions for displaying text anywhere within the client area. Even better, because of Windows' device independence, an application's output will have a consistent appearance from one output device to the next.

Bitmap Objects

You can think of a bitmap object as a small picture. There are two basic uses for bitmaps. First, bitmaps are used to draw pictures on the display. For example, Windows uses many small bitmaps to draw arrows in scroll bars; display check marks when the user selects pull-down menu options; and draw the system menu box, the size box, and many others. Bitmaps are also used for creating brushes, which will be covered shortly. These pixel pictures are stored in memory. Bitmaps are used whenever an application wants to quickly display a graphics image. Because the object is being transferred directly from memory, it can be displayed faster than the code necessary to re-create the image can be executed.

For all of their display-speed characteristics, bitmaps do have their disadvantages. First, depending on their size, bitmaps can occupy an unpredictably large portion of memory. For each pixel being displayed, there has to be an equivalent representation in memory. Displaying the same bitmap in color versus a monochrome rendering requires much more memory. In a monochrome bitmap, one bit can define a pixel as on or off. However, a color bitmap using 16 colors requires that each pixel be represented by 4 bits. In computer work, a nibble is 4 bits. Thus, as the resolution of the graphics image increases, so does the memory requirements. And what about today's 64-bit graphics devices!

A less serious disadvantage, as there are ways of coding around this, is that a bitmap is a composite picture, meaning that you cannot break apart its individual components. Take, for example, a bitmap of a personal computer. The user cannot go into this bitmap and click only on the image of the monitor to select it separately from the entire system. However, if the bitmap had been constructed from a series of routines, an application would be able to change the data supplied to these routines and modify the picture. For example, an application could modify the personal computer drawing routine to include a monitor, system unit, keyboard, and so on.

Pen Objects

You might not realize that all Windows applications use pen objects to draw lines and outline shapes. Pen objects have three basic characteristics: line width, style (dotted, dashed, solid, and so on), and color. Under Windows, a pen for drawing black lines and one for drawing white lines are always available to each application. The black pen is the default pen. Of course, you can always create your own pens. One good example of an alternative pen style is the dashed line many spreadsheet applications use to highlight user-selected groups of cells.

Brush Objects

Many graphics applications use a small picture of a tipped paint can dribbling paint to represent a flood-fill type operation. In Windows, brushes are used to paint colors and flood-fill areas with predefined patterns. A Windows brush has a minimum size of 8 x 8 pixels and, like a pen, has three basic characteristics: size, pattern, and color. With their 8 x 8 pixel minimum, brushes are said to have a pattern, not a style, as pens do. A brush's appearance may come from a compiler-supplied definition such as solid color to hatched to diagonal, or from an application-supplied bit pattern.

COMMUNICATION VIA MESSAGES

Because the term multitasking does not mean multihardware, something has to take control of directing I/O from each concurrently running application down to the one system all applications are sharing. Windows takes charge of the single system's keyboard, video display, mouse, parallel and serial ports, memory, and program execution. It is important to realize that Windows accomplishes all that it does because of its hardware dominance. For example, it is only by taking control of the hardware that Windows can partition the display screen into separate windows.

By managing the hardware, Windows can intercept all user input and distribute that input, as messages, to the appropriate applications. Finally, it is only through the total control of the hardware that Windows can ensure that an application can interface with a variety of output devices, thereby creating a "virtual machine." Under Windows, an application does not write directly to the screen, process any hardware interrupts, or output directly to the printer. Instead, the application uses the appropriate Windows functions, or it waits for an appropriate message to be delivered. Applications development under Windows must now incorporate the processing of the application and the user's view of the application through Windows. In Chapter 1 you learned that the Windows message system is the underlying structure used to disseminate information in a multitasking environment.

From an application's viewpoint, a message is a notification that some event of interest has occurred—an event that may or may not require a specific action. These events may have been initiated by the user by clicking, moving the mouse, changing the size of a window, or making a menu selection. However, the signaled event could have been generated by the application.The net effect of all of this is that applications must now be totally oriented toward processing of messages. Applications must be capable of awakening, determining the appropriate action based on the type of message received, taking that action to completion, and returning to sleep. As a result of this new communication, Windows applications are significantly different from their older DOS counterparts. Under Windows

3.1, more than 2300 function calls were available. Windows 95 and Windows NT have access to even more.

Windows divides message processing into three general layers, called EXECUTIVE, GDI (graphics device interface), and USER. The EXECUTIVE module is responsible for memory management, loading and running an application, and scheduling. The GDI contains all of the routines to create and display graphics. The USER module takes care of all other application requirements.

Standard Message Formats

In this next section you will take a closer look at the message system, examining the format and sources of messages, several common message types, and the ways in which both Windows and your application go about processing messages. The purpose of a message is to notify your program that an event of interest has occurred. Technically, a message is of interest not just to the application, but to a specific window within that application. Therefore, every message is addressed to a window.

There are actually two categories of message queues: the Windows system message queue, and each concurrently running program's message queue. Each message in the system message queue must eventually be transferred to a program's message queue. The program's message queue stores all messages for all the windows in that program. The following four parameters are associated with all messages: a window handle (identifying which window is receiving the message), a message type, a lParam, value and a wParam value. Under Windows 3.*x*, handles are 16 bits, message types are 16 bits, LPARAM is 32 bits, and WPARAM is 16 bits. Under Windows 95 and NT, handles are 32 bits, messages are 32 bits, LPARAM is 32 bits and WPARAM is now 32 bits. (Because the parameter types are defined as symbolic constants [LPARAM and WPARAM] instead of standard data types, their specific meaning can be easily redefined for each target platform.)

The window handle in an object-oriented programming environment is simply an identifier of an object, which corresponds to the particular window to which the message is addressed. Frequently, this handle will reference an object (defined in the form of a data structure) that is located in a moveable portion of memory. It is important to realize that, even though the portion of memory can be moved, the handle remains the same. This allows Windows to manage memory efficiently while leaving the relocation invisible to the application. Because multiple windows can be created based on the same window class, a single window function could process messages for more than one window within a single program. Under these circumstances, the application would use the handle to determine which window was receiving the message.

The message type obtains its meaning from one of several symbolic constants defined in the standard windows.h header file discussed later in this chapter. Under Windows, each message type is represented by a two-character mnemonic followed by the underscore character and, finally, a descriptor to complete the message. The most common message types include WM_CREATE, WM_PAINT, WM_CLOSE, WM_COPY, and WM_PASTE. Other message types include control window messages BM_xxxxxxxxxx, edit control messages EM_xxxxxxxxxx, and list box messages LB_xxxxxxxxxx (where xxxxxxxxxx represents different message types within the same category). If this list is not sufficient, your application can create and register its own types. Application-specific message types are not shared by other applications and are one way of generating private message types.

The contents of these last two parameters, LPARAM and WPARAM, provide any additional information necessary to interpret the message, and therefore vary depending on the message type. Examples of the types of information that would be passed include which key was just struck, the position of the vertical or horizontal scroll bar elevators, the selected pop-up menu item, the position of the mouse, and even the status of the mouse buttons.

Who Sends Messages?

Basically, there are four sources for a message. An application can receive a message from the user, from Windows itself, from the application program itself, or from another application. It is through the underlying structure of messages that

Windows is capable of multitasking. Therefore, all messages must be processed by Windows.

Typical, user input messages include keystroke information, mouse movements, point-and-click coordinates, menu selections, the location of scroll bar elevators, and so on. Your application program will devote a great deal of time to processing user messages.

When Windows itself is posting an application-specific message, Windows is usually signaling a state change—for example, when the user clicks an application's icon to make that application active. In this case, Windows tells the application that its main window is being opened, that its size and location are being modified, and so forth. Windows-originated messages can be either responded to or ignored, depending on the current state of an application,.

To facilitate application-to-application message posting, Microsoft has developed the DDE (dynamic data exchange) protocol. Currently, most applications written for Windows do not take full advantage of the fourth type of message source, intertask communication. However, this category will become increasingly important as more and more applications use this integration capability.

Processing Messages

Application-specific processing of recognized message types is usually performed by functions. A Windows application will have a procedure for processing each type of message that is of interest to any of its windows. However, different windows may respond differently to messages of the same type. For example, one application may have two windows that respond in different ways to the press of the mouse button.

The first window may respond by changing the background color; the second window may respond by placing cross-hatching on a spreadsheet. Since the same message can be interpreted differently by different windows, you can understand why Windows addresses each message to a specific window within an application. Not only will the application have a different procedure to handle each message type, it will need a procedure to handle each message type for each window. The window procedure is used to group together all the message-type procedures for a Windows application.

The Standard Message Loop

All of the standalone functions your program uses to process messages are triggered by what is called the Windows application message processing loop. Each application will contain procedures to create and initialize windows, which are followed by the message processing loop, and finally by some required closing code. The message loop is responsible for processing a message delivered by Windows to the main body of the program. Here the program acknowledges the message and requests Windows to send it to the appropriate window procedure for processing. Then the window procedure executes the desired action.

As you have already seen, messages can be sent from one of two queues, either the system queue or the application's message queue. The message queue and dispatching priority are two factors that can influence the sequence in which a message is processed. Messages are first placed in the system queue. When a message reaches the front of the queue, it is sent over to the appropriate application's message queue. This dual mode allows Windows to keep track of all messages while allowing each application to track only those messages that pertain to it. Most messages go into these queues as you would expect, in first-in first-out order (FIFO). These are called synchronous messages. Most Windows applications use this type of dispatching method.

However, there are occasions when Windows will push a message to the end of the queue, thereby preventing it from being dispatched. Messages of this type are called asynchronous messages. Care must be taken when sending an asynchronous message that overrides the application's normal sequence of processing. There are three types of asynchronous messages: paint, timer, and quit. A timer message, for example, causes a certain action to take effect at a specified time, regardless of the messages to be processed at that moment. Therefore, a timer message will cause all other messages in the queue to be pushed farther from the queue front.

Windows also has asynchronous messages that can be sent to other applications. This scenario is unique in that the receiving application doesn't put the message into its queue. Instead, the message immediately calls the receiving application's appropriate window procedure, where the message then executes.

How does Windows dispatch messages that are pending for several applications at once? Windows settles this issue in one of two ways. One method of message processing is called dispatching priority. Each time Windows loads an application, it sets the application's priority to one of the following four levels:

```
HIGH_PRIORITY_CLASS
IDLE_PRIORITY_CLASS
NORMAL_PRIORITY_CLASS
REALTIME_PRIORITY_CLASS
```

However, an application can change its priority. All things being equal, Windows would then settle any dispatching contention by sending messages to the highest-priority application. A data communications application is an example of a program that might need to raise its priority level. If your system were connected to a distant host computer, you would want to process the information being sent long-distance as soon as possible.

Normally, an application with a properly chosen priority level won't need to change a message's priority. Since tampering with an application's priority level is very uncommon, Windows must have another method for dispatching messages to concurrent applications with the same priority level. Beside processing the messages in the queue, whenever Windows sees that a particular application has a backlog of unprocessed messages, it hangs on to any new messages for that application while continuing to dispatch other messages to other applications.

Standard Windows Resources

In general, a resource represents data that is included in a program's executable (.exe) file, although, technically speaking, it does not reside in a program's normal data segment. The graphics objects described earlier included icons, cursors, carets, message boxes, dialog boxes, fonts, bitmaps, pens, and brushes. These are all examples of Windows resources. When Windows loads a program into memory for execution, very often it will leave all of the resources on the disk. One example of this is when the user first requests to see an application's About dialog box. Before Windows can display the About box, it must first access the disk to copy this information from the program's executable file into memory.

To make the most efficient reuse of memory possible, an application typically defines its resources as read-only and discardable. The latter allows Windows to discard the resource whenever more memory is required. Under Windows 3.*x*, resources are essentially unowned, and should the resource be requested again, Windows simply reads the disk and reloads the data into memory. Thus, multiple instances of the same application running concurrently (for instance, a word processor) will not only share the application's program code, but its resource definitions as well. Under Win32 resources are owned by the application and not shareable.

Standard Windows Functions

The following list contains some of the most frequently used message processing functions: **RegisterWindowMessage()**, **PostMessage()**, and **DispatchMessage()**. Officially called the API (application program interface), parameters are passed via the stack to the various modules that make up Windows. Under Windows 3.*x*, Windows functions returned 16-bit integer addresses. However, under Windows 95 and Windows NT, these addresses are now 32 bits because they are no longer the shorter 2-byte integer-offset addresses, but instead a full 4-byte integer-linear address.

Calling Convention

As just discussed, parameters to all Windows functions are passed via the stack. In a C/C++ program, for example, first function parameters are pushed onto the stack, and then the function is called. Normally, the parameters are pushed starting from the rightmost parameter and going to the leftmost parameter. Upon return from the function, the calling procedure must adjust the stack pointer to a value equal to the number of bytes originally pushed onto the stack. In Windows, however, things look slightly different.

One of the most frequently observed function modifiers seen in Windows applications is the WINAPI modifier. The WINAPI modifier instructs the C/C++ compiler to push parameters from left to right, with the called function having the responsibility to adjust the stack before the return. It is no longer the job of the calling procedure to adjust the stack.

Windows uses this calling convention because it turns out to be more space efficient. Therefore, the Microsoft C/C++ compiler understands that any function declared with the symbolic constant WINAPI is to use the more efficient calling convention. However, the efficiency of using the WINAPI calling convention comes with its own set of problems. This calling sequence makes coding functions with a variable number of parameters more difficult. For this reason Windows C/C++ compiler still uses __cdecl when prototyping variable argument functions.

A First Look At WINDOWS.H

Many Windows functions work with their own specified data types and variables, which your program can access. These variables and types are defined in previously mentioned header files. To use certain functions, you must include the header file in which they are defined. This is accomplished by placing an #include statement in your source program. Technically, the #define statements found in these header files associate a numeric constant with a text identifier—for example:

```
#define WM_CREATE 0x0001
```

The C/C++ compiler will use the hexadecimal constant 0x0001 as a replacement for WM_CREATE during preprocessing. Other typedef statements may appear a bit unusual—for example:

```
typedef int   INT
typedef float FLOAT
```

In Microsoft C/C++, both int and float are reserved words. Your applications should use the uppercase INT and FLOAT for one very good reason: should you decide to port your application over to another C/C++ compiler, it would certainly be much easier to change the typedef statements within the header file than to change all the occurrences of a particular identifier.

You may be interested to know that the original version of windows.h contained Windows specific constants, type, and function prototypes, and occupied a mere 110 kilobytes. However, with the advent of Win32 and the introduction of Windows 95 and Windows NT, this file became too unwieldy. The information contained in this header file increased from 110 kilobytes to over 567 kilobytes. Currently, windows.h simply points to more than 28 separate #include files containing this information. These files now contain more than 350 constant declarations, the typedef declarations, and more than 2000 Windows function declarations. This explains just one of the reasons it takes so long to compile a Windows application.

Understanding the Style of Windows Code

Even if you already know how to code in C or C++, you may initially find Windows source code a little confusing. Not only does this new code contain never-before-seen functions, but how things are defined appears to be unique. The name for this style of coding is known as "Hungarian" style. Officially, this "Hungarian" style of notation can be credited to the Microsoft programmer Charles Simonyi. In Hungarian notation, variable names begin with a lowercase letter or letters that describe the data type of the variable. This variable name prefix is then followed by the name of the variable, which is represented by a meaningful use of upper- and lowercase letters. This approach allows each variable to have attached a mnemonic representing the variable's data type. For example:

```
LONG LPARAM
unsigned int UINT
```

By prefacing each identifier with a reminder of its data type (L for LongPARAM and U for UnsignedINT), you can actually avoid some very common mistakes before compiling your program. The following statement looks harmless but is incorrect and may go unchecked.

```
Variable1 = Variable2;
```

However, using Hungarian notation, you would undoubtedly catch the following mistake:

```
ivariable1 = uvariable2;
```

Hopefully, the following list will bring you "on board" as quickly as possible to the more frequently used Windows type prefixes:

Prefix	*Data Type Represented*
a	atom
b	BOOL (integer)
by	BYTE (unsigned character)
c	character (ANSI ASCII 8-bit)
dw	DWORD (unsigned long)
fn	function
h	HANDLE (unsigned integer)
hDC	HANDLE to a device context
i	integer (16-bits in Windows 3.x, 32-bits under Windows 95 and NT)
id	integral id value
l	LONG (long)
lp	long (far) pointer
lpsz	long pointer to null-terminated string
n	short integer
np	near (short) pointer
p	pointer
pfn	function pointer
pst	pointer to a structure
psz	pointer to null-terminated string
pv	pointer to void
s	string
sz	NULL (/0) terminated string
u	unsigned
v	void
w	WORD (unsigned 16-bit value)
w	character (UNICODE 16-bit)
x	short (when used as the X coordinate)
y	short (when used as the Y coordinate)

The Seven Fundamental Steps For Developing Windows Programs

All programming languages have a systematized set of steps required to build the majority of applications. Under Windows these common steps involve the following:

1. A call to **WinMain()**, where program execution begins, along with any additional Windows/C/C++ functions.
2. Application-specific menu creation, and menu descriptions stored in a resource script file.
3. Optional creation of the application's dialog boxes.
4. Optional creation of icons, cursors, and bitmaps.
5. Defining the project.
6. Compiling and linking all related files.
7. Debugging.

As you can quickly see, creating an actual Windows application will require the use of several project development tools. Following is a brief look at these tools.

The Visual C/C++ Compiler

When developing a Windows application the project file, and its associated options, controls how the application will be built. In Chapter 4 you will learn more about project options for building Windows applications.

The Resource Editor

You use your C/C++ compiler's resource editors to create application-specific menus, dialog boxes, icons, cursors, and bitmaps. The use of these editors is almost intuitive, but on-line help is provided should you run into a problem.

The Resource Compiler

Frequently, a Windows application will use its own resources, such as menus, icons, and dialog boxes. Each of these resources must be predefined in a file called a resource script file. The resource compiler does pretty much what its name suggests: it compiles the resource, and the additional information is added to the application's final executable (.exe) file by the project utility. This approach allows Windows to load and use the resources from the executable file.

Using the Linker

All Windows applications can be linked with the C/C++ linker under the management of the project utility, which resolves all external references.

In The Next Chapter...

Because a Windows application presents the user with an incredibly rich array of features, mastering Windows application development takes some time. The first two chapters of this book have introduced you to all that Windows is capable of performing, along with a foundational foreword to Windows terminology. In the next few chapters, you will be taught the fundamentals of creating good Windows applications. Later chapters will illustrate the programming techniques necessary to use advanced Windows capabilities.

Chapter 3

Important Programming Elements

Over the last couple of years, more and more individuals have gravitated towards Microsoft Windows as their home, and now office, operating system. Therefore, it is quite possible that your only experience with Windows has been that of an end user. As such, you would easily agree that Microsoft Windows is an easy-to-use, intuitive graphical environment that maximizes your efficiency and use of hardware resources.

However, as easy as Microsoft windows is to use, if you have never written Windows code before now, you are in for quite a surprise. The difference in the learning curve for a Windows user versus a Windows programmer is quite dramatic. Don't worry—this book does not assume that you have already programmed in Windows. The good news is that learning to master Windows application development is no more difficult than mastering any new programming concept.

For example, can you remember how confused you were when your professor introduced the topic of subroutines, and tried to explain the differences between procedures and functions? How long did it take you to really understand the difference? Or, do you remember when your instructor told you never to use the same name of function within the body of the function itself? If your instructor did not go into any detail explaining why this could create a problem, you likely accepted this as some sort of compiler restriction. However, sooner or later you learned about recursion a function that calls itself. Probably the first time you encountered the concept of one-dimensional arrays, you were awestruck—then came multidimensional arrays. Then there was dynamic memory allocation, and pointer types!

Most professional programming courses present programming concepts using an incremental scale of complexity. This pedagogical approach worked to your advantage—as you mastered simpler programming fundamentals, you logically moved on to more complex material. Unfortunately, the ease of use provided by all Windows applications comes at the cost of programming complexity. The software engineers that developed Windows have presented you with a large array of programming features that will require patience to master completely. This chapter begins by explaining the more common Windows programming elements, which are then used by many of the example programs throughout the following chapters.

Understanding the Windows Screen Coordinate System

Windows, by design, uses what is called a *GUI* (graphical user interface). Basically, this means the most frequently used types of program operations are represented by pictures (visual objects) and replace their older-style command line equivalents. These pictures (operations) have specific names, such as client areas, scroll bars, visual controls, fonts, menus, and much more to which you were introduced in the last chapter.

From a programming perspective, then, all of these visual objects need positioning on the display device. Windows makes visual object placement very simple with an all-encompassing array of functions that allow you to display text and graphics in whichever coordinate system most logically or physically maps your application's needs to the display context. However, before you can begin placing visual objects, you need to understand the various concepts involved in using the Windows coordinate systems. While there are eight official coordinate system modes, the good news is that the majority of application's can use the default coordinate system, MM_TEXT.

The Eight Fundamental Mapping Modes

Just about all of Windows' visual object placement functions accept coordinate values or size arguments, in the form of X and Y. The X parameter indicates the position on the horizontal axis, and the Y parameter, the position on the vertical axis. For example, one of the more popular text placement functions is called **TextOut()**. **TextOut()** uses its X and Y arguments to specify the output text's row and column position.

Learning to use the Windows coordinate systems is a bit confusing at first until you understand its goal. Windows' goal is to allow the programmer to develop one application that will correctly display its visual objects, regardless of the particular end user's hardware configuration. In order to accomplish this, Windows separates actual physical device coordinates from those used by the application. However, based on the mapping mode, whenever Windows actually processes an output request, it then needs to map these virtual coordinates to the end user's physical device coordinates.

Windows allows an application to specify these virtual X and Y coordinates in what it calls *logical units*. Under Windows 3.*x* and Windows 95, the range of useful values for X and Y extends from -32,768 to +32,767. Under Windows NT, these values extend from -2,147,483,648 to +2,147,483,647.

Note: *Under Windows 3.x, the X and Y values are 16 bits. Under Windows 95, the values are 32 bits, but currently only the lower 16 bits are used. Under Windows NT, all 32 bits are used.*

Remember, however, that you cannot use these virtual coordinates to do any actual physical output. Instead, the GDI output functions map these logical coordinates into correct physical screen coordinates for output. This mapping between virtual logical coordinates and actual physical screen coordinates makes your life as a programmer much simpler. The Windows GUI design goal is achieved. You write one application, targeted for any display device, and Windows takes care of translating all logical coordinates to realistic hardware coordinates! This translation of logical units to device units (actual screen coordinates) is determined by the application when it selects a mapping mode and related viewport.

All eight mapping modes require the application to specify coordinates using a signed integer data type. All mapping modes define two categories: the mapping mode's origin and the X and Y axes orientation. Table 3.1 lists the eight mapping modes defined in the Windows 95 or Windows NT, wingdi.h header file.

In addition to the eight fundamental mapping modes, there are three additions: MM_MIN, MM_MAX, and MM_MAX_FIXEDSCALE, which are just different ways (aliases) to refer to one of the eight standard modes.

Your application sets its mapping mode with a simple call to the function **SetMapMode(hdc,iMapMode)**. The *iMapMode* argument contains one of the eight mapping modes listed in the table. MM_TEXT is the default Windows mapping mode. Should an application need to retrieve its current mapping mode, the program calls the Windows function **GetMapMode(hdc)** as seen in this short coded example:

```
iMapMode = GetMapMode ( hdc );
```

In this next section you will explore how the different mapping modes affect the output of a string using the Windows

Table 3.1: The eight fundamental Mapping Modes and Aliases

Mapping Mode		*Orientation*		*Unit Measures*
MM_TEXT	1	right	down	pixels
MM_LOMETRIC	2	right	up	0.1 mm
MM_HIMETRIC	3	right	up	0.01 mm
MM_LOENGLISH	4	right	up	0.01 inch
MM_HIENGLISH	5	right	up	0.001 inch
MM_TWIPS	6	right	up	1/1440 inch
MM_ISOTROPIC	7	either	either	user-defined, X =Y
MM_ANISOTROPIC	8	either	either	user-defined, X!=Y
MM_MIN	1	alias for		MM_TEXT
MM_MAX	8	alias for		MM_ANISOTROPIC
MM_MAX_FIXEDSCALE	6	alias for		MM_TWIPS

TextOut(hdc,x,y,lpszString,iCount) function. When the mapping mode is MM_TEXT (the default), logical units are mapped directly to physical units, or pixels. If the **TextOut()** function had been passed an X value of 5 and a Y value of 15, the text output would begin five pixels from the left of the client area and 15 pixels from the top.

When the MM_LOENGLISH mapping mode is used with the **TextOut()** function, an X value of 200 and a Y value of -300 outputs the text two inches from the left of the client area and three inches from the top. Did you notice the -300? When the mapping modes MM_LOENGLISH, MM_HIENGLISH, MM_LOMETRIC, MM_HIMETRIC, or MM_TWIPS are used, all logical coordinates are expressed in physical measurements, with the origin at the upper-left corner of the selected area. Moving down the display requires a negative value.

Since the mapping mode is an attribute of a device context, the only time the mapping mode will come into play is when the application is using a GDI function that requires a handle to the device context. In order for you not to become confused, you must remember that all non-GDI functions use the device coordinate system, which returns values in device units, which are pixels.

The Three Coordinate Systems

Windows expresses all device coordinate systems in terms of pixels. The X axis increases in value going from left to right. The Y axis increases in value from the top of the display to the bottom. For example, many Windows functions, such as **CreateWindow()**, **MoveWindow()**, **GetWindowRect()** (which obtains, in terms of screen coordinates, the position and size of the whole window), **WindowFromPoint()**, **GetMessagePos()**, **GetCursorPos()**, and **SetCursorPos()**, use the *screen coordinate system* described in the preceding section. Windows uses the *whole-window coordinate system* to define the application's entire window.

Whole-window coordinates provide access to an application's caption bar, main menu, any scroll bars, and the window frame itself. The **GetWindowDC()** function will map logical coordinates in GDI functions into whole-window coordinates. Of the three device coordinate systems, *client area coordinates* are the most frequently used. In this system the upper-left corner of the client area is (0,0). When the **GetDC()** or **BeginPaint()** function is used, logical coordinates are translated into client area coordinates. When necessary, converting from screen coordinates to client area coordinates is as easy as making the appropriate function call to either **ScreenToClient()** or **Client-ToScreen()**.

Mapping Logical Units to Viewports

You now know that Windows maps logical coordinates to device coordinates based on two criteria: the mapping mode selected and the particular function used to obtain the device context. Actually, there's more to the story. The mapping mode is used to define the mapping of the window's coordinates or logical units to the viewport or device coordinates. A *viewport* is defined in device coordinates, or pixels, and usually refers to the client area. However, if the application has made a call to **GetWindowDC()** or **CreateDC()**, the coordinates returned will refer to the whole-window or to screen coordinates, respectively. Regardless, the point (0,0) is at the upper-left corner of the specified area, with X values increasing from left to right, and Y values increasing from top to bottom. A *window,* in this context, refers to logical coordinates. These logical coordinates may be pixels, inches, millimeters, or user-defined units. Logical window coordinates are passed to GDI functions.

Using MM_SOTROPIC to Change Viewport and Window Extents

Your application can use either the MM_ISOTROPIC or MM_ANISOTROPIC mapping modes to change the viewport or window extent. This allows an application-defined scaling factor for translating logical and device coordinates. The MM_ISOTROPIC mapping mode provides a metric mapping mode where logical units on the X axis are identical to those of the Y axis. This mapping mode allows an application to display images with the correct aspect ratio, regardless of the aspect ratio of the display device itself. Choosing the MM_ANISOTROPIC mapping mode allows an application to use arbitrary axes while providing equal logical units for both axes.

Application-Specific Coordinates

Your application should always use the MM_ISOTROPIC mapping mode whenever it needs to use identical X and Y physical distances. The following code segment does this with a function call to **SetMapMode()**. In addition, with this mapping mode your application must also make a call to the function **SetWindowExtEx()**, which sets the X and Y extents of the window associated with the device context. For this example, the logical size of the logical window will be fixed to the constants (350,350). The third function call, to **SetViewportExtEx()**, passes the parameters that define the actual height and width of the client area. When Windows adjusts these extents, it has to fit the logical window within the physical viewport. Therefore, Windows makes the best use of space whenever **SetWindowExtEx()** is called before **SetViewportExtEx()**. The last function call, to **SetViewportOrgEx()**, sets the logical point (0,0) to the device point (0,0).

```
SetMapMode       (                  hdc,MM_ISOTROPIC  );
SetWindowExtEx   (                  hdc,350,350,NULL  );
SetViewportExtEx ( hdc,xClientView,yClientView,NULL  );
SetViewportOrgEx (                      hdc,0,0,NULL  );
```

As you already know, if the mapping mode is defined as MM_HIENGLISH and, for example, the **TextOut()** function is passed an X value of 200 and a Y value of -300, the text output would begin two inches from the left of the client area and three inches from the top. The -300 was necessary because the default window and viewport origins were (0,0). This meant that the only way to display anything in the client area was to use negative values for Y. Since this can become quite disconcerting, why not just reset the logical origin? Assuming that *yClientView* is the height of the client area in pixels, you can accomplish this with the following statement:

```
SetViewportOrgEx ( hdc,0,yClientView,NULL );
```

This relocates the logical origin to the lower-left corner of the client area. As a result, you now use positive values to move text up the display. This approach can be used for all five of the "measurable" mapping modes.

Determining a Window's Initial Location, Dimensions, Styles, Icons, and Cursors

Whenever your application wants to create and define the characteristics of an overlapped, popup, or child window, it calls the function **CreateWindow()** or **CreateWindowEx()**. This section is designed to explain the syntax and meaning behind the various parameters. The following coded statement illustrates a sample function call to **CreateWindow()**:

```
HWND CreateWindow ( lpszClassName,lpszWindowName,dwStyle,
                    x,y,nWidth,nHeight,hwndParent,hmenu,
                    hinst,lpParam );
```

A function call to **CreateWindowEx()** looks very similar:

```
HWND CreateWindowEx ( lpszClassName,lpszWindowName,
                      dwStyle,x,y,nWidth,nHeight,
                      hwndParent,hmenu,hinst, lpvCreateParams );
```

Your application must call one function or the other. **CreateWindowEx()** has a few more capabilities. However, either function can be used to create an overlapped, popup, or child window, and to specify the window's class, title, and style. Also, either function can set the window's initial position and size. Both functions send all the necessary messages—for example, WM_CREATE, WM_GETMINMAXINFO, and WM_NCCREATE—to the window. For example, selecting the WS_VISIBLE style option causes the function to send the window messages to activate and display the window. Listing 3.1 lists each formal argument.

Listing 3.1: Description of CreateWindow()'s Formal Arguments

lpszClassName(LPCSTR) points to a null-terminated character string naming the window's class.

lpszWindowName(LPCSTR) points to a null-terminated character string that identifies the window.

dwStyle (DWORD) specifies the window style(see Tables 2 through 9).

x(int) defines the initial X-coordinate position of the window.

y(int) defines the initial Y coordinate position of the window.

nWidth(int), defines window width using device units.

nHeight(int), defines window height using device units.

hWndParent(HWND) identifies the parent window for the window that is about to be created. Overlapped windows must not have a parent (hWndParent must be NULL). A valid parent handle must be passed when creating a child window.

hMenu(HMENU) depends on the window's style and specifies a menu or a child-window identifier.

hInstance(HANDLE) identifies the instance of the module to be identified with the window.

lpParam contains the address of window-creation information. The window being created may access this data when the CREATESTRUCT structure is passed to the window by either WM_NCCREATE or WM_CREATE.

---

dwStyle can be created from the various parameters in Tables 3.2 through 3.9. Table 3.2 lists several of the control classes available to *dwStyle*.

Table 3.2: Available Control Classes

Class	*Meaning*
BUTTON	BUTTON controls look like small rectangular child windows that displays a button the user can turn on or off with a press of the mouse button. Buttons usually change display appearance when selected and deselected. **BUTTON Control Styles** BS_AUTOCHECKBOX BS_AUTORADIOBUTTON BS_AUTO3STATE BS_CHECKBOX BS_DEFPUSHBUTTON BS_GROUPBOX BS_LEFTTEXT BS_OWNERDRAW BS_PUSHBUTTON BS_RADIOBUTTON BS_3STATE
EDIT	EDIT controls look like small, rectangular child windows in which the user can enter text from the keyboard. Input focus can be changed by pressing the mouse button or using TAB. Edit control classes allow the user to repeatedly select the input focus, make entries, backspace over mistakes, and reenter information. The user inserts text whenever the control display exhibits a flashing caret. **EDIT Control Styles** ES_LEFT

continued on the next page

Table 3.2: Continued

Class	*Meaning*
	ES_CENTER ES_RIGHT ES_MULTILINE ES_UPPERCASE ES_LOWERCASE ES_PASSWORD ES_AUTOVSCROLL ES_AUTOHSCROLL ES_NOHIDESEL ES_OEMCONVERT ES_READONLY ES_WANTRETURN
LISTBOX	LISTBOX controls enumerate a list of character strings. They are used when an application needs to present a list of name, such as available file names, from which the user can select. Options are selected by moving the mouse and clicking the selected item. This causes the item to be highlighted and a notification of the choice to be passed to the parent window. Whenever the list is long, LISTBOX controls can be used in conjunction with SCROLLBAR controls. **LISTBOX Control Styles** LBS_NOTIFY LBS_SORT LBS_NOREDRAW LBS_MULTIPLESEL LBS_OWNERDRAWFIXED LBS_OWNERDRAWVARIABLE LBS_HASSTRINGS LBS_USETABSTOPS LBS_NOINTEGRALHEIGHT LBS_MULTICOLUMN LBS_WANTKEYBOARDINPUT LBS_EXTENDEDSEL LBS_DISABLENOSCROLL
COMBOBOX	A COMBOBOX control consists of a selection field similar to an EDIT control plus a list box. The list box may be displayed at all times or may be dropped down when the user selects a "pop box" next to the selection field.
SCROLLBAR	SCROLLBAR controls display a stretched rectangular box containing a page position reference, sometimes called a thumb, along with direction arrows at both ends. The user selects a position within the list by sliding the thumb up or down the bar. SCROLLBAR controls are identical in appearance to scroll bars used in ordinary windows; however, they may appear anywhere within a window.

Table 3.2: Continued

Class	*Meaning*
	Automatically associated with the SCROLLBAR control is a SIZEBOX control. This small rectangle allows the user to change the size of the window. **SCROLLBAR Control Styles** SBS_BOTTOMALIGN SBS_HORZ SBS_LEFTALIGN SBS_RIGHTALIGN SBS_SIZEBOX SBS_SIZEBOXBOTTOMRIGHTALIGN SBS_SIZEBOXTOPLEFTALIGN SBS_TOPALIGN SBS_VERT
STATIC	STATIC controls are used whenever an application wants to identify, box, or separate other controls, or to define a simple text field, box, or rectangle. STATIC controls, therefore, only output information. **STATIC Control Styles** SS_BLACKFRAME SS_BLACKRECT SS_CENTER SS_GRAYFRAME SS_GRAYRECT SS_ICON SS_LEFT SS_LEFTNOWORDWRAP SS_NOPREFIX SS_RIGHT SS_SIMPLE SS_USERITEM SS_WHITEFRAME SS_WHITERECT

Table 3.3 shows available window styles.

Table 3.3: Available Window Styles

Style	*Meaning*
WS_BORDER	Places a border around a window.
WS_CAPTION	Places a title bar in the window.

continued on the next page

Table 3.3: Continued

Style	*Meaning*
WS_CHILD	Creates a child window. Not used with WS_POPUP style windows.
WS_CLIPCHILDREN	When creating a parent window, the WS_CLIPCHILDREN window style prohibits drawing of the parent window within the area occupied by any child window.
WS_CLIPSIBLINGS	For WS_CHILD styles only. This style clips all other child windows whenever a particular child window receives a paint message. Without this, it would be possible to draw within the client area of another child window.
WS_DISABLED	Builds an initially disabled window.
WS_DLGFRAME	Builds a double-bordered window without a title.
WS_EX_ACCEPTFILES	Indicates that a window created with this style accepts drag-drop files.
WS_EX_DLGMODALFRAME	Builds a window with a double border that can contain an optional title bar. This style can be used only in the dwEx-Style.
WS_EX_NOPARENTNOTIFY	Indicates that a child window created in this style will not send the WM_PARENTNOTIFY message to its parent window when the child window is created or destroyed.
WS_EX_TOPMOST	Specified that a window created with this style should be placed above all non-topmost windows and stay above them even when the window is deactivated.
WS_EX_TRANSPARENT	Indicates that a window created with this style is transparent. Any windows that are beneath the window are not obscured by the window.
WS_GROUP	Used only by dialog boxes. This window style defines the first control of a group of controls. The user can move from one control to another by using the direction keys.
WS_HSCROLL	Builds a window with a horizontal scroll bar.
WS_MAXIMIZE	Builds a window of maximum size.
WS_MAXIMIZEBOX	Builds a window that includes a maximize box.
WS_MINIMIZE	Builds a window of minimum size.

Table 3.3: Continued

Style	*Meaning*
WS_MINIMIZEBOX	Builds a window that includes a minimize box.
WS_OVERLAPPED	Builds an overlapped window.
WS_OVERLAPPEDWINDOW	Uses the WS_CAPTION, WS_OVERLAPPED, WS_THICKFRAME, and WS_SYSMENU styles to create an overlapped window.
WS_POPUP	Builds a pop-up window. Not to be used with the WS_CHILD style.
WS_POPUPWINDOW	Uses the WS_BORDER, WS_POPUP, and WS_SYSMENU styles to create a pop-up window.
WS_SYSMENU	Builds a window with a system-menu box displayed in its title bar. When used with a child window, this style builds a close box instead of the standard system-menu box. WS_SYSMENU is used only with windows that include title bars.
WS_VISIBLE	Builds a window that is automatically displayed. Can be used with overlapped and pop-up windows.

Table 3.4 lists several of the BUTTON class control styles available to *dwStyle*.

Table 3.4: Available BUTTON Class Control Styles

Style	*Meaning*
BS_AUTOCHECKBOX	Analogous to BS_CHECKBOX, except that the button automatically toggles its state when the user selects it by pressing the mouse button.
BS_AUTORADIOBUTTON	Analogous to BS_RADIOBUTTON, except that when the button is selected, a BN_CLICKED message is sent to the application, removing check marks from any other radio buttons in the group.
BS_AUTO3STATE	Analogous to BX_3STATE, except that the button automatically toggles its state when the user selects it by pressing the mouse button.

continued on the next page

Table 3.4: Continued

Style	*Meaning*
BS_CHECKBOX	Specifies a small rectangular button that can be checked. The check box is shown in bold when it is selected.Any associated text is printed to the right of the button.
BS_DEFPUSHBUTTON	Specifies a small elliptical bold-bordered button. Usually used to identify a user's default response. Any associated text is displayed within the button.
BS_GROUPBOX	Specifies a rectangular region bounding a button group. Text is displayed within the rectangle's upper-left corner.
BS_LEFTTEXT	Forces text to be displayed on the left side of the radio button or check box button. Can be used with the control styles, BX_3STATE.
BS_OWNERDRAW	Identifies an "owner-draw" button. The parent window is notified whenever a button is clicked. This notification includes a request to paint, invert, and then disable the button.
BS_PUSHBUTTON	Specifies a small elliptical button containing the specified text. This control sends a message to the parent window whenever the user clicks the button.
BS_RADIOBUTTON	Specifies a small circular button with a border that is shown in bold when it has been selected with a click. The parent window is also notified via a message. A subsequent click produces a normal border, and another message is sent to the parent window to indicate the change.
BS_3STATE	Analogous to BS_CHECKBOX, but the button can be grayed as well as checked. The grayed state is a visual reminder that the current check box has been disabled.

Table 3.5 lists several of the EDIT class control styles available to *dwStyle*.

Table 3.5: Available EDIT Class Control Styles

Style	*Description*
ES_AUTOHSCROLL	Scrolls text automatically to the right 10 characters whenever the user enters data at the end of a line. When the user presses ENTER< the text scrolls back to the left-edge border.
ES_AUTOVSCROLL	Scrolls text up automatically one page when the user presses ENTER at the last line.

Table 3.5: Continued

Style	*Description*
ES_CENTER	Centers text.
ES_LEFT	Uses flush-left text alignment.
ES_LOWERCASE	Translates all characters to lowercase as they are typed.
ES_MULTILINE	Generates a multiple-line editing control. When used in conjunction with the ES_AUTOVSCROLL style, scrolls text vertically when the user presses ENTER. If ES_AUTOVSCROLL style is not specified, the system beeps when the user presses ENTER; no more lines can be displayed. A similar condition exists when used with the ES_AUTOHSCROLL style. If selected, the style will allow the user to remain on the same line, shifting text to the left. When deactivated, text not fitting on the same line within the window causes a new line to be created. ES_MULTILINE styles can include scroll bars.
ES_NOHIDESEL	Supersedes the default action, preventing the EDIT control from hiding the selection whenever the control loses the input focus. ES_NOHIDESEL does not invert the selection when the control receives the input focus.
ES_OEMCONVERT	Translates text entered in the EDIT control from the Windows character set to the OEM character set and then back again.
ES_PASSWORD	Outputs each character as an asterisk (*) as the character is typed.
ES_READONLY	Disables the user's ability to type or edit text.
ES_UPPERCASE	Translates all characters to uppercase as they are typed.
ES_RIGHT	Forces flush-right text alignment.
ES_WANTRETURN	Appends a carriage return when the user presses the ENTER key.

Table 3.6 lists several of the LISTBOX class control styles available to *dwStyle*.

Table 3.6: Available LISTBOX Class Control Styles

Style	*Meaning*
LBS_DISABLENOSCROLL	Prevents vertical scroll bar display for a list box when the box does not contain enough items to scroll.
LBS_EXTENDEDSEL	Facilitates multiple item selection by using the SHIFT key and the mouse or by using special keys.

continued on the next page

Table 3.6: Continued

Style	*Meaning*
LBS_HASSTRINGS	Keeps the memory and pointers for strings that appear in "owner-draw" list boxes. LBS_HASSTRINGS allows the application to use the LB_GETTEXT message to retrieve the text for a particular string.
LBS_MULTICOLUMN	Specifies a multicolumn list box that is scrolled horizontally.
LBS_MULTIPLESEL	Permits selection of any number of strings, with the string selection toggling each time the user clicks or double-clicks the string.
LBS_NOINTEGRALHEIGHT	Identifies the size of the list box as being exactly the size specified by the application when the list box was created.
LBS_NOREDRAW	Guarantees that the LISTBOX display is not updated when changes are made.
LBS_NOTIFY	Guarantees that, whenever the user clicks or double-clicks a string, the parent window receives an input message.
LBS_OWNERDRAWFIXED	Specifies that the owner of the list box is responsible for drawing its contents; the items in the list box are the same height.
LBS_OWNERDRAWVARIABLE	Specifies that the owner of the list box is responsible for drawing its contents; however, unlike LBS_OWNERDRAWFIXED, the strings are of variable height.
LBS_SORT	Outputs alphabetically sorted LISTBOX strings.
LBS_STANDARD	Outputs alphabetically sorted LISTBOX strings, sending a message to the parent window whenever the user clicks or double-clicks a string. The LISTBOX contains a vertical scroll bar and borders on all sides.
LBS_USETABSTOPS	Designates a list box that recognizes and expands all tab characters when drawing strings. The default tab positions into 32 dialog units. Using the **GetDialogBaseUnits()** function, an application can obtain the current dialog base units in pixels. One horizontal dialog unit is equal to one fourth of the current dialog base width unit. Dialog base units are calculated on the height and width of the current system font.

Table 3.6: Continued

Style	*Meaning*
LBS_WANTKEYBOARDINPUT	Guarantees that, whenever the user presses a key and the list box has the input focus, the owner of the list box receives WM_VKEYTOITEM or WM_CHARTOITEM messages.

Table 3.7 shows several of the COMBOBOX class control styles available to *dwStyle*.

Table 3.7: Available COMBOBOX Class Control Styles

Style	*Meaning*
CBS_AUTOHSCROLL	Scrolls text automatically in the EDIT control to the right whenever the user types a character at the end of the line.
CBS_DISABLENOSCROLL	Inhibits vertical scroll bar display for a list box when the box does not contain enough items to scroll.
CBS_DROPDOWN	Inhibits list box display unless the user selects an icon next to the selection field.
CBS_DROPDOWNLIST	Substitutes the EDIT control with a static text item that displays the current selection in the list box.
CBS_HASSTRINGS	Permits GETTEXT to return the text for a particular item.
CBS_NOINTEGRALHEIGHT	Specifies text as having no integral height.
CBS_OEMCONVERT	Specifies an OEM convert.
CBS_OWNERDRAWFIXED	Specifies that the owner of the list box is responsible for drawing its contents; the items in the list box are the same height.
CBS_OWNERDRAWVARIABLE	Specifies that the owner of the list box is responsible for drawing its contents; however, unlike LBS_OWNERDRAWFIXED, the strings are of variable height.
CBS_SIMPLE	Shows the list box at all times. The current selection in the list box is displayed in the EDIT control.
CBS_SHORT	Sorts strings automatically, that are entered into the list box. This style does not apply to "owner-draw" combo boxes.

Table 3.8 lists several of the SCROLLBAR class control styles available to *dwStyle*.

Table 3.8: Available SCROLLBAR Class Control Styles

Style	*Meaning*
SBS_BOTTOMALIGN	Frequently used with SBS_HORZ style. Using the system-default scroll bar height, SBS_BOTTOMALIGN aligns the scroll bar with the bottom edge of the rectangle defined by x, y, nWidth, and nHeight.
SBS_HORZ	Identifies a horizontal scroll bar. The height, width, and position of the scroll bar are determined by the **CreateWindow()** function if neither SBS_BOTTOMALIGN nor SBS_TOPALIGN style is requested.
SBS_LEFTALIGN	Frequently used with SBS_VERT style. Using the system-default scroll bar height, SBS_LEFTALIGN aligns the left edge of the scroll bar with the left edge of a rectangle defined by x, y, nWidth, and nHeight.
SBS_RIGHTALIGN	Frequently used with SBS_VERT style. Using the system-default scroll bar height, SBS_RIGHTALIGN aligns the lower-right corner of the scroll bar with the right edge of the rectangle defined by x, y, nWidth, and nHeight.
SBS_SIZEBOX	Identifies a size box. The height, width, and position of the size box are determined by the **CreateWindow()** function if neither the SBS_SIZEBOXBOTTOMRIGHTALIGN nor the SBS_SIZEBOXTOPLEFTALIGN style is selected.
SBS_SIZEBOXBOTTOMRIGHT-ALIGN	Frequently used with the SBS_SIZEBOX style. Using the system-default scroll bar height, SBS_SIZEBOXBOTTOMRIGHTALIGN aligns the scroll bar with the lower-right corner of the rectangle defined by x, y, nWidth, and nHeight.
SBS_SIZEBOXTOPLEFTALIGN	Frequently used with the SBS_SIZEBOX style. Using the system-default scroll bar height, SBS_SIZEBOXTOPLEFTALIGN aligns the upper-left corner of the scroll bar with the upper-left corner of the rectangle defined by x, y, nWidth, and nHeight.
SBS_TOPALIGN	Applies the system-default scroll bar height, SBS_TOPALIGN aligns the scroll bar along the top edge of the rectangle defined by x, y, nWidth, and nHeight.

Table 3.8: Continued

Style	*Meaning*
SBS_VERT	Identifies a vertical scroll bar. The height, width, and position of the scroll bar are determined by the **CreateWindow()** function if neither the SBS_RIGHTALIGN nor the SBS_LEFTALIGN style is requested.

Table 3.9 lists several of the STATIC class control styles available to *dwStyle*.

Table 3.9: Available STATIC Class Control Styles

Style	*Meaning*
SS_BLACKFRAME	Identifies a box with a black frame.
SS_BLACKRECT	Identifies a black-filled rectangle.
SS_CENTER	Takes the given text and centers it within a simple rectangle. All text is formatted. Any text not fitting on one line is automatically wrapped to the next line and centered.
SS_GRAYFRAME	Identifies a gray-framed box.
SS_GRAYRECT	Identifies a gray-filled rectangle.
SS_ICON	Sizes and displays an icon, automatically, within the dialog box.
SS_LEFT	Similar to SS_CENTER, except the text displayed within the rectangle is aligned flush left. This includes automatic word wrap and flush-left alignment of the next line.
SS_LEFTNOWORDWRAP	Switches word wrapping off.
SS_NOPREFIX	Substitutes the usual interpretation of the ampersand (&). Normally, Windows interprets an ampersand in the control's text as an accelerator prefix character; this causes the next character to be underlined. If a static control is to contain no underlined text, SS_NOPREFIX (when used with the bitwise logical operator OR) can be used with other styles.
SS_RIGHT	Similar to SS_CENTER, except the text displayed within the rectangle is aligned flush right. This includes automatic word wrap and flush-right alignment of the next line.

continued on the next page

Table 3.9: Continued

Style	*Meaning*
SS_SIMPLE	Identifies a rectangle that will display a single line of flush-left text.
SS_USERITEM	Identifies a user-defined item.
SS_WHITEFRAME	Identifies a white-framed box.
SS_WHITERECT	Identifies a white-filled rectangle.

Table 3.10 lists several of the extended styles that available to *dwExStyle*.

As you can readily see from Tables 3.2 through 3.10, a call to either function, **CreateWindow()** or **CreateWindowEx()**, gives your application the ability to create just about any type of window your application could possibly need.

Table 3.10: Available Extended Styles

Style	*Meaning*
WS_EX_ACCEPTFILES	Windows created with this style will accept drag-drop files.
WS_EX_DLGMODALFRAME	Creates a window with a double border. It may also be created with a title bar if the WS_CAPTION style flag is used in the dwStyle parameter.
WS_EX_NOPARENTNOTIFY	A child window is created, and no WM_PARENTNOTIFY message is sent to its parent window when the child window is created or destroyed.
WS_EX_TOPMOST	Creates a window with this style and placed above all non-topmost windows. It will stay above them even when deactivated. **SetWindowPos()** can add or remove this attribute.
WS_EX_TRANSPARENT	A window with this style is transparent. Any windows that are beneath the window are not obscured by the window. WM_PAINT messages are received after all sibling windows have been updated.

Using ShowWindow()

Just creating a window with a call to **CreateWindow()** or **CreateWindowEx()** doesn't automatically display the window. After a window is created, Windows needs to be instructed to show it with a call to the function **ShowWindow()**. However, each application must make a call to the **ShowWindow()** function using the *nCmdShow* parameter obtained from the **WinMain()** function.

```
ShowWindow ( hWnd,nCmdShow );
```

Subsequent calls to **ShowWindow()** must come from the window states defined in Table 3.11.

Table 3.11: Available Window States

State	*Meaning*
SW_HIDE	Hides the window and passes activation to another window.
SW_MINIMIZE	Minimizes the window and activates the top-level window in the window manager's list.
SW_RESTORE	Does the same work as SW_SHOWNORMAL.
SW_SHOW	Activates the window and displays it in its current position and at its current size.
SW_SHOWMAXIMIZED	Activates the window and displays it fully maximized.
SW_SHOWMINIMIZED	Activates the window and displays it as an icon.
SW_SHOWMINNOACTIVATE	Displays the window as an icon; the window that is currently active remains active.
SW_SHOWNA	Displays the window in its current state; whichever window is currently active remains active.
SW_SHOWNOACTIVATE	Displays the window in its most recent position and at its most recent size; whichever window is currently active remains active.
SW_SHOWNORMAL	Activates and displays the window. If the window had been an icon or was zoomed, Windows will restore the window to its original position and size.

If you are curious about the somewhat similar constants, W_MINNOACTIVATE and SW_SHOWMINIMIZED, SW_MINNOACTIVATE does not make the window the active window, but SW_SHOWMINIMIZED does.

Updating Window Features with SetClassLong()

If, while your program is executing, you need to change a particular window's characteristics, your program makes a call to the function **SetClassLong()**:

```
SetClassLong ( hWnd,nIndex,dwNewLong );
```

The first argument (*hWnd*) identifies the handle of the target window. The second argument (*nIndex*) designates the index of the value to change in the **WNDCLASSA** data structure. The *dwNewLong* parameter specifies the replacement value (LONG). The following code sequence calls **SetClassLong()** to change the background color of a window by using the BLACK_BRUSH value:

```
switch( message )
 case WM_CREATE:
            GetClassLong   (            hWnd,GCL_HBRBACKGROUND );
            DeleteObject   (                              hWnd );
            SetClassLong   ( hWnd,GCL_HBRBACKGROUND,BLACK_BRUSH );
            InvalidateRect (                     hWnd,NULL,TRUE );
            UpdateWindow   (                              hWnd );
            break;
```

Standard Windows Controls and Dialog Boxes

Windows employs several types of visual objects, such as controls and dialog boxes, which allow the user to easily interact with the application. These predefined child windows have features and capabilities other window styles do not. There are several ready-made control classes. Controls have their characteristics and functions defined by their window class, just as any other window would. The window function determines how the window will appear to the user. It also determines what actions are to be taken based on the user's responses.

An Introduction to Static Controls

The simplest control to understand and use is the *static control*. You can think of a static control as a small window containing text or a graphics image such as an icon. Static controls are usually used in combination with other controls to enhance their visual interface. Unlike the other control types, static controls do not accept any user responses.

An Introduction to Push-Button Controls

One step above the static control in complexity is the *push-button control*. The push-button control looks like a small rectangle with rounded corners, which contains text—for example, the frequently seen OK and CANCEL push-buttons. Clicking the push button causes the application to take some form of immediate action.

An Introduction to Radio-Button Controls

Your application uses a *radio-button control* to create an open circle with text to its right. With a single mouse click, the user can select the circle, turning the associated control on or off. Selected radio-button controls have the circle filled in. Radio buttons work like the buttons on your car radio. You can select only one at a time. (Ever tried to play two stations at once?) Radio buttons list mutually exclusive application options.

A typical Windows application will logically group radio buttons, allowing the user to select only one of the mutually exclusive choices. When the user selects a second radio-button control, the previously selected item is deselected. For example, you could use radio-button controls to give the user a list of disk drives to select from. Naturally, you can read from only one drive at a time. Selecting both Drive C and Drive A has no meaning. Properly designed radio buttons, or logically related groups of radio buttons, automatically prevent the user from incorrectly interacting with the application.

An Introduction to Check-Box Controls

Check-box controls are similar to, yet different from, radio-button controls. You can visually distinguish a *check-box control* from a radio button by the small square, instead of the round circle, with text to its right. Unlike radio buttons, check-box controls allow the application to logically relate application-specific options that are not mutually exclusive. In other words, the check-box control permits concurrent selections. For example, a desktop publishing application could present the user with several text-format options—bold, underlining, italic, subscripts, and so on—that could be combined in numerous ways.

An Introduction to List Boxes

Moving up in control complexity and capabilities, there is the *list-box control*. A list-box control not only responds to mouse input (as do radio buttons and check boxes), but it also accepts keyboard input. Applications typically use list-box controls to list character strings—for example, file names. The user can select one or sometimes several items.

List-box control styles options include list boxes that have their contents automatically sorted (LBS_SORT), that automatically notify the parent window of a selection (LBS_NOTIFY), and that can include scroll bar styles (WS_VSCROLL). When an LBS_STANDARD style is chosen, all three of these styles are selected.

The user interacts with list-box options by simply pressing the space bar to accept the selected option, or by double-clicking with the mouse. Either response will cause Windows to highlight the text in the selected character string. List-box messages returned include LBN_SELCHANGE and LBN_DBLCLK (if the mouse button was pressed). Retrieving the index of the selected character string is as easy as making a call to **SendDlgItemMessage()**, using LB_GETCURSEL (the selected item's index) and LB_GETTEXT (which contains a copy of the selected text).

An Introduction to Edit Boxes

The most complex type of control is the Windows *edit-box control*, which in effect operates very much like a mini-word processor, allowing the user to enter and edit text. The application can define an EDIT control with multiple-line editing and scrolling by selecting the appropriate control style (ES_MULTILINE,

ES_AUTOHSCROLL, or ES_AUTOVSCROLL). The last two options shift the window horizontally or vertically whenever the user enters text extending beyond the box's borders.

An Introduction to Scroll Bar Controls

Scroll bars are very common feature of Windows applications. *Scroll-bar controls* permit the user to move through lists, text, columns of information, or graphics displays that do not fit on a single screen (see Chapter 2, "The Vertical Scroll Bar" and "The Horizontal Scroll Bar" sections).

The vertical and horizontal scroll bars allow the user to see the part of the surface that, because of the size constraints of the active window or screen, is temporarily out of view. With the two scroll bars, the user can shift the displayed image up and down, left or right.

Actually, there are two types of scroll bars used by Windows: window scroll bars and scroll bar controls. As you've already seen, the **CreateWindow()** function wears many hats. As it turns out, the function is also responsible for adding horizontal window scroll bars (WS_HSCROLL) or vertical window scroll bars (WS_VSCROLL).

Vertical scroll bars are always displayed along the right side of the window and extend the full height of the client area. Horizontal scroll bars are always positioned at the bottom of the window and extend the full width of the client area. The following highlights how to add scroll bars to a window:

```
CreateWindow ( lpszClassName,        // a registered ClassName
               "Adding Scroll Bars", // window title
               WS_VSCROLL |
               WS_HSCROLL,           // adds scroll bars
               CW_USEDEFAULT,        // default x position
               0,                    // default y position
               CW_USEDEFAULT,        // default width
               0,                    // default height
               NULL,                 // no parent window
               NULL,                 // Use class' menu
               hInstance,            // owning window
               NULL                  // no window creation data
               );
```

Technically speaking, scroll bar controls are considered child windows. Your application can define their size and dimension, and they can be placed anywhere within the client area of the window. They are created by making a call to (you guessed it) **CreateWindow()**. This call requests the creation of a child window that contains a scroll bar.

Giving Virtual Keys Meaning

These days, not only cross-platform development is a big topic—so, too, is developing single application that will handle multiple-language keyboard input. This means that the key marked J may be used to enter a kanji glyph. To help developers with this situation, Windows has defined a set of virtual key codes. This set of virtual keys defines the set of all possible keystrokes that can occur in the Windows environment. This set of keystrokes is defined in winuser.h and constitutes the only keystrokes a Windows application can receive.

Your application uses this virtual key code to recognize if that particular key was either pressed or released. Because the developers of Windows defined virtual keys for many different hardware configurations, some virtual key codes cannot be generated on an IBM system. Table 3.12 lists these identifiers along with the numeric key codes and the keyboard key that corresponds to the virtual key.

Table 3.12: Windows Standard Virtual Key Codes

Required Windows Virtual Key	*winuser.h Constants*	*Keyboard Symbol*	*Hex Number*
No	VK_LBUTTON		01
No	VK_RBUTTON		02
Yes	VK_CANCEL	Ctrl-Break	03
No	VK_MBUTTON		04
Yes	VK_BACK	Backspace	08
Yes	VK_TAB	Tab	09
No	VK_CLEAR	Keypad #5	0C
Yes	VK_RETURN	Enter	0D
Yes	VK_SHIFT	Shift	10
Yes	VK_CONTROL	Ctrl	11
Yes	VK_MENU	Alt	12
No	VK_PAUSE		13
Yes	VK_CAPITAL	Caps Lock	14
Yes	VK_ESCAPE	Esc	1B

Table 3.12: Windows Standard Virtual Key Codes

Required Windows Virtual Key	*winuser.h Constants*	*Keyboard Symbol*	*Hex Number*
Yes	VK_SPACE	Spacebar	20
Yes	VK_PRIOR	PgUp	21
Yes	VK_NEXT	PgDn	22
No	VK_END	End	23
Yes	VK_HOME	Home	24
Yes	VK_LEFT	Left arrow	25
Yes	VK_UP	Up arrow	26
Yes	VK_RIGHT	Right arrow	27
Yes	VK_DOWN	Down arrow	28
No	VK_SELECT		29
No	VK_PRINT		2A
No	VK_EXECUTE		2B
No	VK_SNAPSHOT		2C
Yes	VK_INSERT	Ins	2D
Yes	VK_DELETE	Del	2E
No	VK_HELP		2F
Yes		Keyboard 0-9	30-39
Yes		A-Z	41-5A
No	VK_NUMPAD0	Keypad 0	60
No	VK_NUMPAD1	Keypad 1	61
No	VK_NUMPAD2	Keypad 2	62
No	VK_NUMPAD3	Keypad 3	63
No	VK_NUMPAD4	Keypad 4	64
No	VK_NUMPAD5	Keypad 5	65
No	VK_NUMPAD6	Keypad 6	66
No	VK_NUMPAD7	Keypad 7	67
No	VK_NUMPAD8	Keypad 8	68
No	VK_NUMPAD9	Keypad 9	69
No	VK_MULTIPLY	Keypad *	6A
No	VK_ADD	Keypad +	6B
No	VK_SEPARATOR		6C
No	VK_SUBTRACT	Keypad -	6D
No	VK_DECIMAL	Keypad .	6E
No	VK_DIVIDE	Keypad /	6F
Yes	VK_F1	F1	70
Yes	VK_F2	F2	71
Yes	VK_F3	F3	72
Yes	VK_F4	F4	73
Yes	VK_F5	F5	74
Yes	VK_F6	F6	75
Yes	VK_F7	F7	76
Yes	VK_F8	F8	77
Yes	VK_F9	F9	78
Yes	VK_F10	F10	79

Table 3.12: Windows Standard Virtual Key Codes

Required Windows Virtual Key	*winuser.h Constants*	*Keyboard Symbol*	*Hex Number*
No	VK_F11	F11	7A
No	VK_F12	F12	7B
No	VK_F13		7C
No	VK_F14		7D
No	VK_F15		7E
No	VK_F16		7F
No	VK_F17		80
No	VK_F18		81
No	VK_F19		82
No	VK_F20		83
No	VK_F21		84
No	VK_F22		85
No	VK_F23		86
No	VK_F24		87
No	VK_NUMLOCK	Num Lock	90
No	VK_SCROLL	Scroll Lock	91
No	VK_LSHIFT		
No	VK_RSHIFT		
No	VK_LCONTROL		
No	VK_RCONTROL		
No	VK_LMENU		
No	VK_RMENU		
No	VK_ATTN		
No	VK_CRSEL		
No	VK_EXCEL		
No	VK_EREOF		
No	VK_PLAY		
No	VK_ZOOM		
No	VK_NONAME		
No	VK_PA1		
No	VK_OEM_CLEAR		

An Introduction to System Timers

A *timer* is an internal routine, given to all Windows applications, that repeatedly measures a specified interval in milliseconds. Each time the interval (or *time-out value*) elapses, the system notifies the window associated with the timer. Because the accuracy of a timer depends on the system clock rate and how often the application retrieves messages from the message queue, the time-out value is only approximate. Windows 3.*x* is a nonpreemptive multitasking environment. The main purpose of a timer is to provide a method whereby a large, time-consuming process can be subdivided into smaller, interruptible tasks. In Windows 3.*x*, each subtask is activated whenever it receives a WM_TIMER message. This prevents any one application from monopolizing the CPU.

Timers are still needed under Windows 95's and Windows NT's preemptive multitasking environments, so that (with the correct priority), Windows can take control of the processor as needed. Additionally, Windows timers can be used to activate a preset alarm used in a scheduling program, generate an auto save for a word processor at predefined intervals, control the speed of a graphics display, control the update for a clock display, and many other meaningful uses.

What Makes the Timer Tick?

The **SetTimer()** function uses the *uElapseMs* parameter to define the elapsed time (in milliseconds) between timer events. The interval can range from 1 to 65,535 milliseconds, or up to 65.5 seconds. For example, if *uElapseMs* were 4000 milliseconds, Windows would send the application program a WM_TIMER message about every four seconds. The *pfnTimerFunc* parameter to **SetTimer()** points to the procedure-instance address of the callback function. The Windows WM_TIMER message is accomplished through a virtualized MS_DOS call implemented in Win32. The message instructs it to decrement each of the system timer counters set by Windows. Whenever the count reaches 0, a WM_TIMER message is sent to the application's message queue. After this, the counter is set back to its original starting value. Since all Windows applications receive the WM_TIMER messages from the normal message queue, the application won't suddenly be interrupted in the middle of an important process.

When writing an application that uses system timers, however, the developer must be careful to enable the application to continue proper execution if there are no timers available. There are approximately 16 timers available at any one time. Therefore, applications should stop any timer messages no longer needed by making a call to the **KillTimer()** function.

Effective Use of Timers

There are two basic approaches Windows uses to process timers. The first, and the easiest approach to use includes error checking. This method involves a call to the **SetTimer()** function from the **WinMain()** function or during the processing of a WM_CREATE message. This approach gives the application the earliest means of dealing with an unavailable timer. It is ended by terminating the timer with a call to **KillTimer()** in response to a WM_DESTROY message. With this method, all WM_TIMER messages are sent directly to the normal window function. The second approach to using the timer causes Windows to send the WM_TIMER message to a function within the application program (a callback function) instead of to the **WinMain()** function.

Understanding 32-Bit Memory Management

The dramatic evolution of Windows has greatly affected the way memory is allocated and accessed. For example, under Windows NT an application can access up to two gigabytes of virtual address space. This virtually unlimited domain, however, has the typical size-versus-speed trade off associated with all virtual storage. For this reason, it is still imperative that all Windows applications manage this resource. Windows 95 uses a page-based memory management scheme. With paging, Windows 95 and the CPU fool applications into believing there is more system memory than is actually available. When memory requirements exceed actual memory, Windows 95 will swap information to the hard drive.

Next to the particular microprocessor you are using to run Windows, the next most significant factor influencing the speed of your Windows applications is the amount of available memory. When you want to execute multiple programs, Windows will attempt to place as many of these programs into system memory as possible. However, it seems no matter how much memory you purchase, you never have enough just when you want it! If you attempt to load several large programs under Windows, the majority of your system memory may be allocated. At this point, any additional programs you invoke will cause Windows to make space for the program in memory by temporarily taking a current application out of memory and placing it on the fixed disk. One can quickly see that, as the number of programs executing becomes very large, the amount of memory and disk swapping that Windows must perform increases proportionately.

Because of this slow disk access-time limitation, disk input and output operations are one of the major causes of computer processing delays. Performance is also degraded by the additional overhead required by all disk I/O operations generated by the frequent swapping.

All Windows applications work on information when it is in RAM memory. This means that everything must eventually get into memory. For example, before Windows can draw a menu or icon, the description of the menu and the contents of the icon must be loaded into memory. The picture becomes even more complex, since Windows also requires the display context, code segments, data segments, the window itself, and on and on, to reside in memory before they can be executed. Considering the tremendous amount of memory required by the Windows graphics-oriented environment, as well as the fact that Windows accomplishes its multitasking in a finite amount of memory, you begin to appreciate why memory management is such an important issue in Windows application development.

Operating System Control

The following example demonstrates just how quickly a typical Windows application can use up memory. As soon as the user selects a program by double-clicking the application's name in the Program Manager (or through the Start Menu), the first instance of the application begins to execute. For a minimal application, this would require Windows to load at least one code segment and data segment, for a total of two objects loaded into memory. On top of this, each Windows application must register a window class and create a window of that class. Most Windows applications use at least one menu and an icon. Total objects in memory: six. Now consider what Windows must do to manage this finite memory resource.

Suppose the user chooses to start a second instance of the application. The second instance shares the same code segment as its predecessor, along with the application's icon. However, the second instance has its own data segment. While the second instance has a window of the same class as the first instance, it is still a new window object. Because of the modifications (selection, activation, and deactivation of options) each instance can make, the menu of the first instance cannot be shared with the second instance. This brings the memory-object total to nine.

Finally, most Windows applications create their own font, pen, and brush. Total objects: 12. A poorly written Windows application (one not sharing objects) would cause the second instance to create its own font, pen, and brush, bringing the memory object tally to 15, and the application hasn't even done anything yet! As you can see, memory gets consumed at a startling rate in the Windows environment, since graphics objects are an integral part of an application's basic functioning and multiple instances can be invoked at any moment. You can, however, minimize the amount of space an application requires by using special memory management techniques.

User Control

Naturally, there is no way Windows could guess how much memory an application will need at any particular moment. For this reason, it is up to each application to manage this limited resource. Though Windows does provide several memory management routines for your application to use, memory itself is a different type of resource, since Windows is unable to abstract or separate it from the application. While Windows is quite capable of mediating the use of a display or printer, it cannot arbitrate an application's need for memory.

Each Windows application controls how much memory it requires, while at the same time specifying how much memory is unavailable for other applications to use. This last point highlights the need for each Windows application to manage memory efficiently. You can enhancing the overall performance of Windows applications by remembering four basic memory management principles:

1. When possible, share objects.
2. Keep object size as small as possible.

3. Make objects relocatable.
4. Minimize the number of objects created.

Reducing the Number of Objects The first approach to reducing the number of objects is to share objects as much as possible, rather than forcing each task to create its own copy of the object. The second is to make certain that unused objects are not accidentally left in memory. All objects can be considered shareable whenever the object is not likely to be modified during program execution. Under these conditions the object can be shared not only by multiple instances of an application, but also between different applications. Icons, standard cursors, and user-created brushes, pens, and objects are all examples of shareable objects.

Reducing Object Size The first method involved in reducing an object's size is making sure you segment your code. Follow Microsoft's recommendation of limiting the size of your code segments to 4 kilobytes; this will also minimize the amount of code you have lying around in memory at one time. You can also reduce the final size of an object by allocating the minimum amount of memory required to represent the object.

One example of this approach would involve a disk file containing both graphics and text information. At one point in the application, only the text information is required. Rather than dynamically allocating a portion of memory large enough to contain the entire text, a better approach would be to allocate enough memory for a small number of records, read more records, reallocate memory, and so on. With this last approach the amount of memory used most closely represents the actual size of the object.

Ever hear someone say, "One picture is worth a thousand words"? When it comes to the use of memory, however, it might be better to use the thousand words. The last method in reducing the size of memory objects involves the conservative use of bitmaps. The problem with bitmaps is the tremendous amounts of memory they can require. Additionally, because of varying display resolutions, the size of a bitmap is somewhat unpredictable. On a monochrome monitor, a bitmap may occupy 100 × 100 / 8 (1 bit per pixel) bytes; on another device, 200 × 200 / 2 (4 bits per pixel for 16 colors) bytes. A high-resolution graphics full-screen bitmap would require 1024 × 1024 × 3 (24-bit color resolution), or a whopping 3072 kilobytes of memory!

Using Relocatable Objects New memory objects are created each time an application is started. Each time Windows loads an object into memory, it uses tangential pieces of memory. When the application terminates, the memory objects are removed. This dynamic memory allocation-deallocation process is most efficient whenever Windows is told that it can move or relocate an object. A poorly written Windows application will create and then subsequently destroy fixed memory objects, thereby fragmenting memory.

Since Windows will allocate only contiguous memory for each subsequent object, it is quite possible that a memory fragment will not be large enough for the new object. If the fragmentation is severe enough, an out-of-memory error can be generated—even though sufficient total memory is actually available. The solution is to allow Windows to move objects within memory dynamically.

If you are unfamiliar with the object-oriented programming you are probably flinching at the thought of moveable memory objects. Frequently, memory objects are kept track of with pointers. Moving memory objects would then require acquiring new pointers—a dynamic variable nightmare! In an object-oriented programming environment, handles keep track of objects. Technically, a handle is a pointer—but not to the memory object. Instead, handles are pointers to pointers. A program needs only to know where to look (the handle) for the object; Windows supplies the address of the object (the pointer pointed to by the handle).

Windows can create two types of objects, nonrelocatable and relocatable. By choosing the latter type, relocatable, you allow Windows to move memory objects to maximize memory "real estate." About the only time an application will need to lock or mark a memory object as nonrelocatable is when it needs to write or read data in an object or when it is subscript-indexing through the object. Any Windows application that creates a relocatable object can subsequently lock the object and eventually return it to the original relocatable state as needed. It is best to keep locked objects to an absolute minimum between messages. Leaving a memory object locked while waiting for new messages can create additional problems if the new message is not addressed to the nonrelocatable memory object.

In The Next Chapter...

With these last two chapters, you now understand the fundamentals and components of a Windows application. In the next chapter you will begin building your first cross-platform Windows applications. Chapter 4 also demonstrates how to manage the various project options available with your compiler.

Chapter 4

A Procedure-Oriented Approach

In the previous chapters you have learned about the evolution of Win32, as well as many Windows 95 and Windows NT terms and concepts. Those concepts include developing applications that have a common graphical interface and an ability to share system resources with other applications, and that operate in a device-independent manner.

In this chapter you will learn how to combine these terms and concepts into a simple, but functional, procedural-oriented Windows application.

Which Language and Which Approach?

All computer programming languages have their advantages and disadvantages. Assembly language, for example, is ideal for time-sensitive programming applications. The problem with assembly language is that it is an unstructured language that takes a great deal of time to master. Pascal is a great language to use when introducing new programmers to a structured programming environment. The problem with Pascal is its rigid structure, its lack of support when dealing with Windows functions, and the fact that it was not designed as an object-oriented language.

If you examine Windows programming books at your local bookstore, you might find books that teach Windows programming in assembly language, BASIC, Fortran, Pascal, and so on. You will also notice that the vast majority of programming books revolve around one language, C or C++. Why? There are many reasons why the C/C++ language has evolved as the de facto standard.

First, from the initial version of Windows, Microsoft has used C as its language of choice. Early programmers were provided with C source code in software development tool kits (SDKs) provided by Microsoft. Charles Petzold's *Programming Windows* or Murray and Pappas's *Windows Programming—An Introduction* were the earliest Windows programming books available to the public. They used the C programming language.

Secondly, Borland and Microsoft developed powerful optimizing C compilers that were easy to use, produced tight code, and easily integrated the vast function libraries required by Windows.

As the programming advantages in C become more apparent, the interest in Pascal continued to decrease. Microsoft all but abandoned Pascal, choosing Visual Basic as its alternative language to C for Windows development. Borland maintained their interest in Pascal and eventually designed the Delphi environment as an alternative to C for developing Windows applications.

During this time, there was a gentle but steady movement among C programmers, from a procedure-oriented programming approach to an object-oriented programming approach. While other languages can make claims to object-oriented components, only C++ with its STRUCT and CLASS capabilities does it in a natural manner.

Note: *You'll learn about the advantages of object-oriented programming starting in Chapter 5.*

During a Microsoft Developer's Conference held in San Francisco in 1993, Microsoft "strongly" encouraged developers who had not designed object-oriented Windows applications using the Microsoft Foundation Class library to do so immediately. It was a warning about things to come.

So, what was coming? Well, of course, Windows 95 and Windows NT, OLE (Object Linking and Embedding), and a whole host of tools, called Wizards, for developing applications. Here is the catch—all of this works best with object-oriented programming. As a matter of fact, Microsoft's Wizards only build object-oriented code which is closely tied to the Microsoft Foundation Class Library. No programmer who has gone around the track once or twice would want to design OLE applications without the help from these Wizards.

Now, if object-oriented coding is so good, why does this chapter teach and explain a simple procedure-oriented application? Roots! To best understand the object-oriented approach requires an understanding of what Windows programming is all about. Also remember, that we are in a transition period. There will be plenty of books and magazine articles that contain the traditional procedure-oriented approach. So, while the trend is toward object-oriented coding, it is still wise to understand the procedure-oriented approach.

Key Programming Elements

The first things you will notice about any Windows application are a large number of new data types and structures. These data types and structures are defined in header files, such as windows.h. Tables 4.1 and 4.2 offer a list of the most frequently encountered Win32 data types and structures.

Table 4.2 shows the most frequently encountered Win32 structures.

Procedure-oriented Windows programming relies on making calls to Windows functions. The information in the two tables will help you understand the types of parameters being passed to and from these Windows functions.

Table 4.1: Most Frequently Encountered windows Data Types

Data Type	*Description*
BOOL	A value
BSTR	A 32-bit character pointer
BYTE	An unsigned 8-bit integer
COLORREF	A 32-bit color value
DWORD	A 32-bit unsigned integer
LONG	A 32-bit signed integer
LPARAM	A 32-bit parameter passed to a window procedure or callback function
LPCRECT	A 32-bit pointer to a constant
LPCSTR	A 32-bit pointer to a constant character string
LPSTR	A 32-bit pointer to a character string
LPCTSTR	A 32-bit pointer to a constant character string
LPTSTR	A 32-bit pointer to a character string
LPVOID	A 32-bit pointer to an unspecified type
LRESULT	A 32-bit value return value from a window procedure or callback function
POSITION	Denotes the position of an element in a MFC collection class
UINT	A 32-bit unsigned for Win32
WNDPROC	A 32-bit pointer to a window procedure
WORD	A 16-bit unsigned integer
WPARAM	A 32-bit value passed as a parameter to a window procedure or callback function for Win32.

Handles

Procedure-oriented Windows applications make extensive use of handles. A *handle* is a unique number used to identify many

Table 4.2: Most Frequently Encountered Win32 Structures

Structure	*Description*
MSG	Defines the fields of a message structure
PAINTSTRUCT	A structure used when painting within the client area of a window
RECT	A structure defining the bounds of a rectangle
WNDCLASSEX	An extended window class structure, which includes hIconSm and CbSize

different types of elements. These objects can include brushes, controls, icons, memory allocation, menus, output devices, pens, and windows.

WinMain() and the Callback Function

All procedure-oriented Windows applications contain two required elements: the **WinMain()** function and a *window* function. The Visual C/C++ compiler requires that you name the main body of your program **WinMain()**. **WinMain()** is the entry point for a Windows application, just as **main**() serves as the entry point for a standard C/C++ program.

The required *window* function (not **WinMain()**) has a unique role in a Windows application. It has a unique role because a Windows application never directly accesses any Windows functions. Instead, a request is made to Windows to carry out the specified task. Thus, all Windows applications must have a window function. This windows function is called a callback function. The *callback* function is registered with Windows and is called back whenever Windows executes an operation on a window.

These two functions will be examined more closely in our example application.

A Procedure-Oriented Windows Application

This procedure-oriented application will be named WinVer.cpp. This application will demonstrate the use of many of the components necessary to create and display a Window. Many of these components were discussed in Chapter 2. The application will also demonstrate how to draw several simple graphics figures and determine which operating system, Windows 95 or Windows NT, the application is running under. The code in this application is basic Windows code that appears in almost all Win32 procedure-oriented applications. As such, it can be considered boilerplate code or a static template.

Here is the complete WinVer.cpp application.

```
//
// WinVer.cpp
// A 32-bit application for Windows 95 or Windows NT.
// This simple application illustrates the older
// procedure-oriented approach for designing
// Windows 95 and/or Windows NT applications.
// The program determines if your operating system is
// Windows 95 or Windows NT?
// Copyright (c) 1996 William H. Murray and Chris H. Pappas

#include <windows.h>
#include <stdio.h>
#include <string.h>

LRESULT CALLBACK WndProc(HWND,UINT,WPARAM,LPARAM);

char szProgName[]="ProgName";

int WINAPI WinMain(HINSTANCE hInst,HINSTANCE hPreInst,
                   LPSTR lpszCmdLine,int nCmdShow)
{
  HWND hWnd;
  MSG lpMsg;
  WNDCLASSEX wcApp;

  wcApp.lpszClassName=szProgName;
  wcApp.hInstance =hInst;
  wcApp.lpfnWndProc =WndProc;
  wcApp.hCursor =LoadCursor(NULL,IDC_ARROW);
  wcApp.hIcon =NULL;
  wcApp.hIconSm =NULL;
  wcApp.cbSize =sizeof(WNDCLASSEX);
  wcApp.lpszMenuName =0;
  wcApp.hbrBackground=GetStockObject(WHITE_BRUSH);
  wcApp.style =CS_HREDRAW|CS_VREDRAW;
  wcApp.cbClsExtra =0;
  wcApp.cbWndExtra =0;
```

```
  if (!RegisterClassEx (&wcApp))
    return 0;
  hWnd=CreateWindow(szProgName,"Windows 95 or Windows NT?",
                    WS_OVERLAPPEDWINDOW,CW_USEDEFAULT,
                    CW_USEDEFAULT,CW_USEDEFAULT,
                    CW_USEDEFAULT,(HWND)NULL,(HMENU)NULL,
                    (HANDLE)hInst,(LPSTR)NULL);
  ShowWindow(hWnd,nCmdShow);
  UpdateWindow(hWnd);
  while (GetMessage(&lpMsg,NULL,0,0)) {
    TranslateMessage(&lpMsg);
    DispatchMessage(&lpMsg);
  }
  return(lpMsg.wParam);
}
LRESULT CALLBACK WndProc(HWND hWnd,UINT messg,
                         WPARAM wParam,LPARAM lParam)
{
  HDC hdc;
  PAINTSTRUCT ps;
  DWORD dwVersion;
  char szVersion[25];
  int i;

  dwVersion=GetVersion();

  switch (messg)
  {
    case WM_PAINT:
      hdc=BeginPaint(hWnd,&ps);

      Ellipse(hdc,10,10,210,210);
      Ellipse(hdc,220,10,540,210);

      for (i=60;i>10;i-=10)
        Rectangle(hdc,320-i,380-i,320+i,380+i);

        if (dwVersion < 0x80000000) {
          wsprintf(szVersion,
                   "This is Windows NT, Version %u.%u",
                   (LOBYTE(LOWORD(dwVersion))),
                   (HIBYTE(LOWORD(dwVersion))));
          TextOut(hdc,210,240,szVersion,strlen(szVersion));
        } else {
          wsprintf(szVersion,
                   "This is Windows 95, Version %u.%u",
                   (LOBYTE(LOWORD(dwVersion))),
                   (HIBYTE(LOWORD(dwVersion))));
```

```
        TextOut(hdc,210,240,szVersion,strlen(szVersion));
        }
      ValidateRect(hWnd,NULL);
      EndPaint(hWnd,&ps);
      break;

    case WM_DESTROY:
       PostQuitMessage(0);
       break;

    default:
       return(DefWindowProc(hWnd,messg,wParam,lParam));
  }
  return(0);
}
```

In the following sections we'll take a look at each part of this program and discuss its function.

The WinMain() Function

Remember that the Visual C/C++ compiler requires procedure-oriented Windows applications to have a **WinMain()** function. The job of the **WinMain()** function is to do the following:

- Register the application's window class type
- Perform any required initializations
- Create and initiate the application's message processing loop
- Terminate the program after receiving a WM_QUIT message

You'll notice that the **WinMain()** function is passed four parameters. The following code segment illustrates these parameters as they are used in the WinVer.cpp application:

```
int WINAPI WinMain(HINSTANCE hInst,HINSTANCE hPreInst,
                   LPSTR lpszCmdLine,int nCmdShow)
```

Here **WinMain()** uses the WINAPI return calling convention discussed in Chapters 2 and 3. WINAPI is actually defined as FAR PASCAL. The FAR PASCAL return type is a remnant of the early days when the Pascal parameter passing convention was preferred to that of C. If you examine early Windows programming books, they probably use FAR PASCAL return type. The first formal parameter to **WinMain()** is *hInst,* which contains the current instance handle of the application. This number uniquely identifies the program when it is running under Windows.

The second formal parameter, *hPreInst*, will always contain a NULL value under Win32.

Note: *Under Windows 3.x, hPreInst was used to indicate if there were any previous copies of the program running.*

Under Win32, each application runs in its own separate address space. Thus, *hPreInst* will always return a NULL.

The third parameter, *lpszCmdLine*, is a pointer to a null-terminated string. This string is used by the application's command-line arguments if they exist. This parameter will contain a NULL value if it was started using the Run command.

The fourth and last formal parameter is *nCmdShow*. The **int** value stored in *nCmdShow* represents one of many predefined constants defining the possible ways a window can be displayed. These can be values such as SW_SHOWNORMAL, SW_SHOWMAXIMIZED, and SW_MINIMIZED. These values were discussed in Chapter 3.

Registering the Windows Class

The windows created for a Windows application are based upon a predefined window class. The **WinMain()** function registers the application's main window class. Window classes are based on a combination of fonts, caption bars, icons, size, placement, user-selected styles, and so on. Thus, the window class serves as a template that allows these items to be specified.

Standard C/C++ structure types are used for all window class definitions. The following portion of code is taken directly from the winuser.h header file.

```
typedef struct tagWNDCLASSEXW {
    UINT        cbSize;
    UINT        style;
    WNDPROC     lpfnWndProc;
    int         cbClsExtra;
    int         cbWndExtra;
    HINSTANCE   hInstance;
    HICON       hIcon;
    HCURSOR     hCursor;
    HBRUSH hbrBackground;
```

```
    LPCWSTR lpszMenuName;
    LPCWSTR lpszClassName;
    HICON hIconSm;
} WNDCLASSEXW, *PWNDCLASSEXW, NEAR *NPWNDCLASSEXW, FAR *LPWNDCLASSEXW;
```

The header file contains a *typedef* statement defining the structure type **WNDCLASSEXW** (a UNICODE-compatible definition) from which **WNDCLASSEX** is derived under Win32. Currently, only Windows 95 makes use of the hIconSm structure member.

Your application can define a custom window class by using this structure and filling the structure member's fields with the information about your window class.

Table 4.3 explains the various fields within the **WNDCLASSEX** structure. A zero or NULL in any structure member field usually means that the information is not provided or a default value is to be used.

Table 4.3: WNDCLASSEX Structure Field Definitions

Field Name	*Description*	
size	Defines the size of the structure.	
style	The class style. Styles can be combined by using the bitwise logical OR operator. Values for the style field can include:	
	Value	*Meaning*
	CS_BYTEALIGNCLIENT	Uses byte boundaries in the X direction. Aligns a window's client area.
	CS_BYTEALIGNWINDOW	Uses byte boundaries in the X direction. Aligns the window.
	CS_CLASSDC	Assigns a window class its own display context that can be shared by instances.
	CS_DBCLKS	Sends a double-click message to a window.
	CS_GLOBALCLASS	Defines a global window class.
	CS_HREDRAW	A horizontal size change will trigger a redraw of the window.
	CS_KEYCVTWINDOW	Performs a virtual key conversion.

Table 4.3: WNDCLASSEX Structure Field Definitions

Field Name	*Description*	
	CS_NOCLOSE	Deactivates the close option on the system menu.
	CS_NOKEYCVT	Deactives virtual key conversion.
	CS_OWNDC	Assigns each window instance its own display context.
	CS_PARENTDC	Provides the parent window's display context (DC) to the window class.
	CS_SAVEBITS	Saves the portion of the screen image that is obscured by a window.
	CS_VREDRAW	A vertical size change will trigger a redraw of the window.
lpfnWndProc	Is a pointer to the window function that will carry out the tasks for the window.	
cbClsExtra	Defines the number of extra bytes to allocate for the WNDCLASSEX structure (usually is NULL).	
cbWndExtra	Defines the number of extra bytes to allocate for all additional structures created using this window class (usually is NULL).	
hInstance	Defines the instance of the application registering the window class	
hIcon	Specifies the icon to be used whenever the window is minimized. A standard cursor size.	
hCursor	Defines the cursor to be used for the window. Typically it is set to NULL.	
hbrBackground	Defines a brush to be used for painting the window's background. This can be the handle to a physical brush or it can be a color value. If a color value is used it must be one of the following standard system colors listed. (a 1 is added to the chosen color.) COLOR_ACTIVEBORDER COLOR_ACTIVECAPTION COLOR_APPWORKSPACE COLOR_BACKGROUND COLOR_BTNFACE COLOR_BTNHIGHLIGHT COLOR_BTNSHADOW COLOR_BTNTEXT	

Continued on the next page

Table 4.3: Continued

Field Name	*Description*
	COLOR_CAPTIONTEXT COLOR_GRAYTEXT COLOR_HIGHLIGHT COLOR_HIGHLIGHTTEXT COLOR_INACTIVEBORDER COLOR_INACTIVECAPTION COLOR_INACTIVECAPTIONTEXT COLOR_MENU COLOR_MENUTEXT COLOR_SCROLLBAR COLOR_WINDOW COLOR_WINDOWFRAME COLOR_WINDOWTEXT
lpszMenuName	A pointer to a null-terminated string, indicating the resource name of a menu. Value can be NULL.
lpszClassName	A pointer to a null-terminated string. Gives the name of the window class. This name must be unique in order to avoid confusion when sharing a window class among applications
hIconSm	Specifies the small icon used by Windows 95.

The following listing shows how the WNDCLASSEX structure is implemented in our sample program.

```
WNDCLASSEX wcApp;
  wcApp.lpszClassName=szProgName;
  wcApp.hInstance=hInst;
  wcApp.lpfnWndProc=WndProc;
  wcApp.hCursor=LoadCursor(NULL,IDC_ARROW);
  wcApp.hIcon=NULL;
  wcApp.hIconSm=NULL;
  wcApp.cbSize=sizeof(WNDCLASSEX);
  wcApp.lpszMenuName=0;
  wcApp.hbrBackground=GetStockObject(WHITE_BRUSH);
  wcApp.style=CS_HREDRAW|CS_VREDRAW;
  wcApp.cbClsExtra=0;
  wcApp.cbWndExtra=0;
  if (!RegisterClassEx (&wcApp))
    return 0;
```

In this example, the application is assigned a generic name, "szProgName," for the window's *wcApp.lpszClassName*. You should assign a unique class name for each new window class you define.

The second **WNDCLASSEX** field, *hInstance*, is assigned the value returned in *hInst*, after the **WinMain()** function is invoked, indicating the current instance of the application. *lpfnWndProc* points to the address of the window function that will carry out all of the window's tasks. For the template application, the function is called **WndProc()**.

Note: *The named assigned to the WndProc() function is a user-defined name. Thus, the function must be prototyped before encountering the assignment statement.*

The *wcApp.hCursor* field uses the **LoadCursor()** function to load a predefined IDC_ARROW cursor. A NULL value is assigned for the function's handle. The *wcApp.hIcon* field is assigned a NULL value, since no icon will be used. Likewise, *wcApp.hIconSm* is NULL, since no specific Windows 95 icon is specified.

The value for *wcApp.cbSize* is determined with the use of the **sizeof()** function. In this case, the function will determine the size of the WNDCLASSEX structure.

The *wcapp.lpszMenuName* member is assigned a 0 value. In this instance, Windows understands that the class has no menu. If it did, the menu would have a name and it could appear between quotation marks. The *wcApp.hbrBackground* member uses the **GetStockObject()** function to return a handle to a brush used to paint the background color of the client area. In this case, the function returns a handle to one of Windows predefined brushes; WHITE_BRUSH.

The *wcApp.style* window class style has been set to CS_HREDRAW logically ORed with CS_VREDRAW. All window class styles have identifiers defined in a header file, such as windows.h or winuser.h. These class styles start with CS_. Each identifier represents a bit value. The bitwise OR operation | is used to combine these bit flags. The two parameters that are used (CS_HREDRAW or CS_VREDRAW) instruct Windows to redraw the entire client area whenever the horizontal or vertical size of the window is changed.

The *wcApp.cbClsExtra* and *wcApp.cbWndExtra* fields are assigned a 0 value. These optional fields are used to indicate the count of extra bytes that may have been reserved at the end of the window class structure and the window data structure used for each window class.

You have probably noticed that a couple of lines of code from the previous listing that have not been explained:

```
    .
    .
    .
if (!RegisterClassEx (&wcApp))
  return 0;
```

This **if** statement is responsible for registering the window class. It does this by sending the **RegisterClassEx()** function a pointer to the window class structure. If Windows cannot register the window class, **RegisterClassEx()** will return a 0, terminating the program.

Creating Your First Window

A window is created with a call to the Windows **CreateWindow()** function. While the window class defines the general characteristics of a window, which allows the same window class to be used for many different windows, the parameters to **CreateWindow()** specify more detailed information about the window.

Defining and then registering a window class has nothing to do with actually displaying a window in a Windows application.

The **CreateWindow()** function uses the information passed to it to describe the window's class, instance handle, menu handle, parent handle, screen position, style and title. The call to **CreateWindow()** for the WinVer.cpp application uses the following parameter values:

```
hWnd=CreateWindow(szProgName,"Windows 95 or Windows NT?",
                  WS_OVERLAPPEDWINDOW,CW_USEDEFAULT,
                  CW_USEDEFAULT,CW_USEDEFAULT,
                  CW_USEDEFAULT,(HWND)NULL,(HMENU)NULL,
                  (HANDLE)hInst,(LPSTR)NULL);
```

The first field, *szProgName*, defines the window's class, followed by the title to be used for the window. The style of the window is the third parameter; WS_OVERLAPPEDWINDOW. This is a standard Windows style that represents a normal overlapped window with a caption bar, a system menu box, minimize and maximize icons, and a window frame.

The next six parameters use either CW_USEDEFAULT or NULL. CW_USEDEFAULT values are used to represent the initial X and Y positions and X and Y size of the window. NULL values are used for the the parent window handle and window menu handle. Each of these fields has been assigned a default value. The *hInst* field contains the instance handle of the program, followed by a NULL indicating that no additional parameters are used.

CreateWindow() returns the handle of the newly created window when it is successful. If the function fails, a NULL is returned.

Showing and Updating a Window

In order to actually display a window, it is necessary to make a call to the **ShowWindow()** function. The following portion of code is from the WinVer.cpp application:

```
ShowWindow(hWnd,nCmdShow);
```

The *hWnd* parameter holds the handle of the window created by the call to the **CreateWindow()** function. The second parameter, *nCmdShow*, determines how the window is initially displayed. This initial display is described as the window's *visibility state*.

Values for the *nCmdShow* parameter can specify that the window is to be displayed as a normal window (SW_SHOWNNORMAL), or several other possibilities found in the winuser.h header file. For example, SW_SHOWMINNOACTIVE would cause the window to be drawn as an icon. If SW_SHOWMAXIMIZED was used, the active window would fill the entire display.

The final step for displaying a window involves a call to the Windows **UpdateWindow()** function:

```
UpdateWindow(hWnd);
```

Calling the **ShowWindow()** function with a SW_SHOWNORMAL parameter causes the function to erase the window's client area with the background brush specified in the window's class. It is the call to the **UpdateWindow()**

function that allows the client area to be painted. This is achieved by generating a WM_PAINT message. The WM_PAINT message is discussed in more detail later in this chapter.

The Message Loop

All procedure-oriented Windows applications require a message loop. Windows does not send input from the mouse or keyboard directly to an application. Instead, it places all input into the application's message queue. This queue contains messages generated by Windows or the application or even messages posted by other applications.

Messages are nothing more than a number sent to a function or object, triggering that code segment to perform a specified action. Messages are defined in header files.

Once the **WinMain()** function has created and displayed the window, it is the application's responsibility to create a message processing loop. While several different programming approaches are possible, the most common technique is to use a **while** loop. For example:

```
while (GetMessage(&lpMsg,NULL,0,0)) {
  TranslateMessage(&lpMsg);
  DispatchMessage(&lpMsg);
}
```

GetMessage() The **GetMessage()** function is used to retrieve the next message to be processed from the application's message queue. The function copies the message into the message structure pointed to by the pointer *lpMsg* and sends it to the window function when appropriate.

If the second parameter is NULL, the function will retrieve any of the messages for any window that belongs to the application. In this example, the last two parameters are set to zero. This instructs the function not to apply any *message filters*. A message filter is used to restrict retrieved messages. These filters are *wMsgFilterMin* and *wMsgFilterMax*. The filter values give the numeric filter extremes to apply.

Typically, an application can return control to Windows any time before starting the message loop. For example, an application will normally make certain that all steps leading up to the message loop have executed properly. Once the message loop has been entered, however, only WM_QUIT message can terminate the loop. This causes the processing to proceed to the main loop's closing routine.

TranslateMessage() The **TranslateMessage()** function converts virtual-key messages into character messages. This function is only necessary for applications that need to process character input from the keyboard. The **TranslateMessage()** function creates an ASCII character message, WM_CHAR, from a WM_KEYDOWN and WM_KEYUP message. The keyboard interface will remain in effect as long as this function is included in the message loop.

DispatchMessage() The **DispatchMessage()** function is responsible for sending the current message to the correct window procedure. This function makes it easy to add additional windows and dialog boxes to your application. **DispatchMessage()** will automatically route each message to the appropriate window procedure.

The Window Function

Recall that all Windows applications must include a call to the **WinMain()** function and a separate Windows callback function. A callback function is necessary because a Windows application never directly accesses any Windows function. Instead, each application must make a request to Windows to carry out a specified operation.

A callback function is registered with Windows and is called back whenever Windows executes an operation on a window. The size of the callback function varies from application to application. The callback function may be very small, only processing one or two messages, or it may be large and complex.

The following code segment illustrates the WinVer.cpp callback function. In this portion of code, the application-specific statements have been removed.

```
LRESULT CALLBACK WndProc(HWND hWnd,UINT messg,
                         WPARAM wParam,LPARAM lParam)
{
  HDC hdc;
```

```
  PAINTSTRUCT ps;
  switch (messg)
  {
    case WM_PAINT:
      hdc=BeginPaint(hWnd,&ps);

      .
      .
      .

      ValidateRect(hWnd,NULL);
      EndPaint(hWnd,&ps);
      break;

    case WM_DESTROY:
      PostQuitMessage(0);
      break;

    default:
      return(DefWindowProc(hWnd,messg,wParam,lParam));
  }
  return(0);
}
```

Notice that this callback function only processes two messages: WM_PAINT and WM_DESTROY.

Windows has several hundred different messages it can send to the window function. Window messages start with the WM_ identifier. These identifiers are *symbolic constants* found in various Windows header files. The use of symbolic constants makes program code easier to read than the use of their numeric equivalents. Table 4.6 shows a partial list of these messages.

Table 4.4: WM_ Window Messages Defined in winuser.h

Message	*Value*
WM_ACTIVATE	0x0006
WM_ACTIVATEAPP	0x001C
WM_ASKCBFORMATNAME	0x030C
WM_CANCELMODE	0x001F
WM_CHAR	0x0102
WM_CHARTOITEM	0x002F
WM_CHILDACTIVATE	0x0022
WM_CLEAR	0x0303
WM_CLOSE	0x0010
WM_COMMAND	0x0111

Table 4.4: Continued

Message	*Value*
WM_COMMNOTIFY	0x0044
WM_COMPACTING	0x0041
WM_COMPAREITEM	0x0039
WM_COPY	0x0301
WM_CREATE	0x0001
WM_CTLCOLORBTN	0x0135
WM_CTLCOLORDLG	0x0136
WM_CTLCOLOREDIT	0x0133
WM_CTLCOLORLISTBOX	0x0134
WM_CTLCOLORMSGBOX	0x0132
WM_CTLCOLORSCROLLBAR	0x0137
WM_CTLCOLORSTATIC	0x0138
WM_CUT	0x0300
WM_DELETEITEM	0x002D
WM_DESTROY	0x0002
WM_DESTROYCLIPBOARD	0x0307
WM_DRAWCLIPBOARD	0x0308
WM_DRAWITEM	0x002B
WM_ENABLE	0x000A
WM_ENDSESSION	0x0016
WM_ERASEBKGND	0x0014
WM_FONTCHANGE	0x001D
WM_FULLSCREEN	0x003A
WM_GETDLGCODE	0x0087
WM_GETFONT	0x0031
WM_GETHOTKEY	0x0033
WM_GETTEXT	0x000D
WM_GETTEXTLENGTH	0x000E
WM_HOTKEY	0x0312
WM_HOTKEYEVENT	0x0045
WM_HSCROLL	0x0114
WM_HSCROLLCLIPBOARD	0x030E
WM_ICONERASEBKGND	0x0027
WM_INITDIALOG	0x0110
WM_INITMENU	0x0116
WM_INITMENUPOPUP	0x0117
WM_KEYDOWN	0x0100
WM_KEYFIRST	0x0100
WM_KEYLAST	0x0108
WM_KEYUP	0x0101
WM_KILLFOCUS	0x0008
WM_LBUTTONDBLCLK	0x0203
WM_LBUTTONDOWN	0x0201
WM_LBUTTONUP	0x0202

Continued on the next page

Table 4.4: Continued

Message	*Value*
WM_MDIACTIVATE	0x0222
WM_MDICASCADE	0x0227
WM_MDICREATE	0x0220
WM_MDIDESTROY	0x0221
WM_MDIGETACTIVE	0x0229
WM_MDIMAXIMIZE	0x0225
WM_MDINEXT	0x0224
WM_MDIRESTORE	0x0223
WM_MDISETMENU	0x0230
WM_MDITILE	0x0226
WM_MENUCHAR	0x0120
WM_MENUSELECT	0x011F
WM_MOUSEACTIVATE	0x0021
WM_MOUSEFIRST	0x0200
WM_MOUSELAST	0x0209
WM_MOUSEMOVE	0x0200
WM_MOVE	0x0003
WM_NEXTDLGCTL	0x0028
WM_NULL	0x0000
WM_OTHERWINDOWCREATED	0x0042
WM_OTHERWINDOWDESTROYED	0x0043
WM_PAINT	0x000F
WM_PAINTCLIPBOARD	0x0309
WM_PAINTICON	0x0026
WM_PALETTECHANGED	0x0311
WM_PALETTEISCHANGING	0x0310
WM_PARENTNOTIFY	0x0210
WM_PASTE	0x0302
WM_POWER	0x0048
WM_QUERYDRAGICON	0x0037
WM_QUERYNEWPALETTE	0x030F
WM_QUERYOPEN	0x0013
WM_QUEUESYNC	0x0023
WM_QUIT	0x0012
WM_RBUTTONDBLCLK	0x0206
WM_RBUTTONDOWN	0x0204
WM_RBUTTONUP	0x0205
WM_SETCURSOR	0x0020
WM_SETFOCUS	0x0007
WM_SETFONT	0x0030
WM_SETHOTKEY	0x0032
WM_SETREDRAW	0x000B
WM_SETTEXT	0x000C
WM_SHOWWINDOW	0x0018

Table 4.4: Continued

Message	*Value*
WM_SIZE	0x0005
WM_SIZECLIPBOARD	0x030B
WM_TIMECHANGE	0x001E
WM_TIMER	0x0113
WM_VSCROLL	0x0115
WM_VSCROLLCLIPBOARD	0x030A
WM_WINDOWPOSCHANGED	0x0047
WM_WINDOWPOSCHANGING	0x0046

These identifiers can be divided into different categories: client area repainting, window creation, destroying a window, iconization of a window, moving a window, menu item selection, mouse manipulation of scroll bars, resizing a window, and so on.

Like most Windows functions, the first parameter to the **WndProc()** function is *hWnd*. Recall that this value represents the handle to the window that Windows will send the message to. Note that it is possible for one function to process messages for several windows created from the same window class. This handle is used by the window function to determine which window is to receive the message.

The second parameter to the function, *messg*, specifies the actual message being processed. Recall that this message is defined in winuser.h or a related header file. The parameters *wParam* and *lParam* are used to pass any additional information needed to process the given message.

This function continues by defining several variables; *hdc* is the handle for the display context, and *ps* is associated with a PAINTSTRUCT structure. This structure stores information about the client area. When messages are to be processed in a procedure-oriented window function, they are usually processed with the use of a simple C/C++ switch statement. As you will learn in Chapter 7, this switch statement is often an area where errors occur when programming.

The WM PAINT Message In The WinVer.cpp application, the first message to be processed is WM_PAINT. The Windows paint message is responsible for calling the **BeginPaint()** function. The **BeginPaint()** function prepares the window, identified by the *hWnd handle,* for painting. The structure, PAINTSTRUCT (*&ps*), is filled with information about the area to be painted. **BeginPaint()** returns a handle to the device context (DC) for the window.

This device context is supplied with several default items, including a default pen, brush, and font. The default pen draws in black. It is one pixel wide and draws a solid line. The default brush is white with a solid brush pattern. The default font is the system font. All of the display functions used by Windows require a handle to the device context.

In Windows it is possible for one application to display a window or dialog box over another application's window. This creates a problem whenever one application is closed or moved—namely, a hole on the screen where the first applications window once appeared. Windows solves this problem by sending the application a WM_PAINT message.

Windows sends WM_PAINT messages under the following conditions:

- When the application's area needs repainting because of a recently closed application, menu, or dialog box that has hidden a portion of a client area
- When a window needs resizing
- When using scroll bar functions
- When calling the functions InvalidateRect() or InvalidateRgn()

Windows will mark as corrupted any portion of an application's window that has been overlaid by another window, dialog box, or menu. This corrupted portion is marked as invalid. Windows keeps track of the diagonal coordinates of this invalidated rectangle. The presence of an invalid rectangle prompts Windows to send a WM_PAINT message.

If multiple invalidated regions exist, Windows will adjust the invalid rectangle coordinates to encapsulate all invalid regions. Thus, only one WM_PAINT is sent, rather than one for each invalid region.

WM_PAINT messages can be forced by making a call to the **InvalidateRect()** function. This is the function that marks the application's client area as being invalid. By calling the **GetUp-**

dateRect() function, an application then obtains the coordinates of the invalid rectangle. Finally, a call to the **ValidateRect()** function validates any rectangular region in the client area and removes any pending WM_PAINT messages.

WndProc() ends by calling the **EndPaint()** function. **EndPaint()** is used whenever an application is finished outputting information to the client area and when it is all right to remove the display context.

Drawing in the Client Area The trick in this simple application, in addition to drawing several graphics shapes, is obtaining the Windows version information. This information is available by calling the **GetVersion()** function. This function returns a DWORD value. If the MSB (most significant bit) is a zero, the operating system is Windows NT. Thus, a check is made to see if that bit is not set with the hexadecimal number 0x80000000. If the operating system is not Windows NT, it must be Windows 95. After all, this is a 32-bit application!

The WM DESTROY Message WM_DESTROY messages help terminate an application. These messages can be generated by the system menu or from within the application itself.

The DefWindowProc() Function The **DefWindowProc()** function is used to empty the application's message queue of any unrecognized and unprocessed messages. This function ensures that all of the messages posted to the application are processed.

Visual C/C++ Compiler Project Workspaces

Your Microsoft Visual C++ compiler is fully integrated with the Windows GDI environment. From within your compiler, Windows applications can be written, compiled, debugged, linked, and executed.

The *project workspace* is your key to success when working within the compiler's integrated environment. Microsoft's project workspaces use .mdp file extensions, while Microsoft make files use the .mak file extension. Here are some tips for creating project workspaces for your Windows applications.

Tips for Getting It Together

Use the Visual C++ compilers editor to write your Windows application. When the application is completed, select the File menu and chose the New menu item. This process will envoke the New dialog box window, shown in Figure 4.1. From the list of items, choose Project Workspace and click on OK. This selection will display yet another dialog box. This is the New Project Workspace dialog box, shown in Figure 4.2. Here the project is named and its type is selected (application), along with the platform (WIN32) and the drive and directory for the files. A subdirectory option is also available. Click on the Create button when you are satisfied with your choices. Next, use the Insert menu to select the Files into Project... menu item, as shown in Figure 4.3. From this dialog box you can locate and group all of the files necessary for your project. In this example, only the source code, WinVer.cpp, is required. Select Close when all files have been added.

It is also possible to set the build target for the application. From the Build menu select the Settings... menu item, as shown in Figure 4.4. Two versions are provided. The debug version is

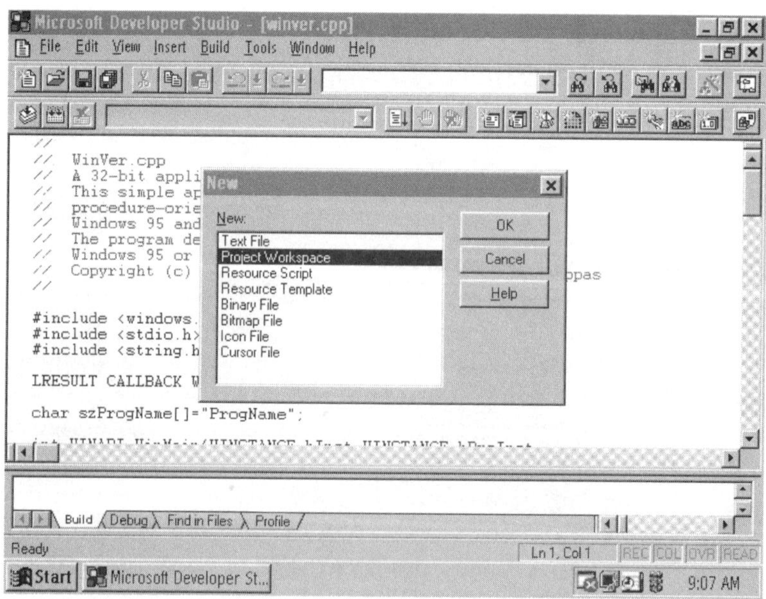

Figure 4.1: Select the Project Workspace option in Microsoft's New File dialog box.

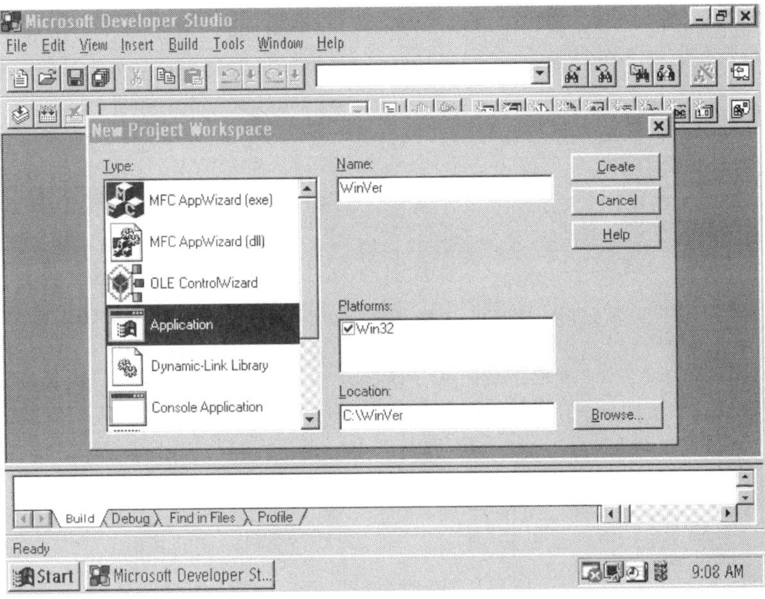

Figure 4.2: Microsoft's New Project Workspace dialog box allows you to name and configure the project.

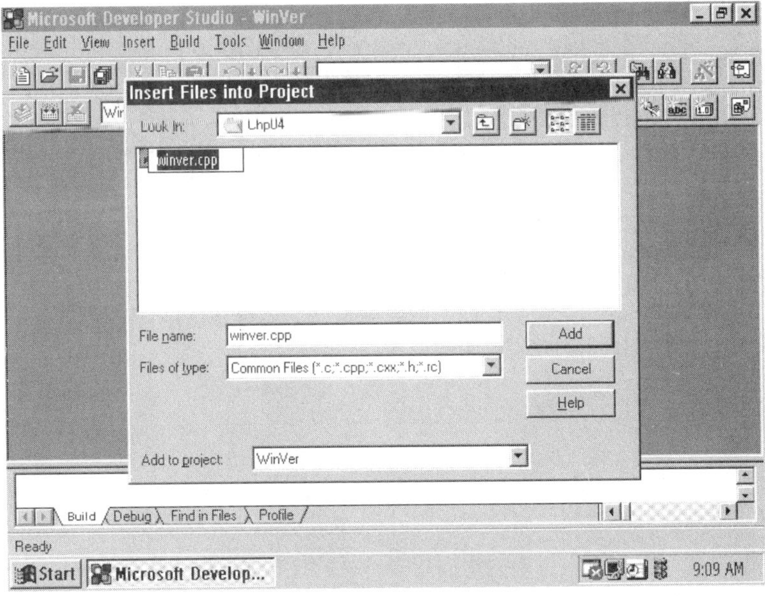

Figure 4.3: Microsoft's Project Files dialog box allows you to select the files required for building your application.

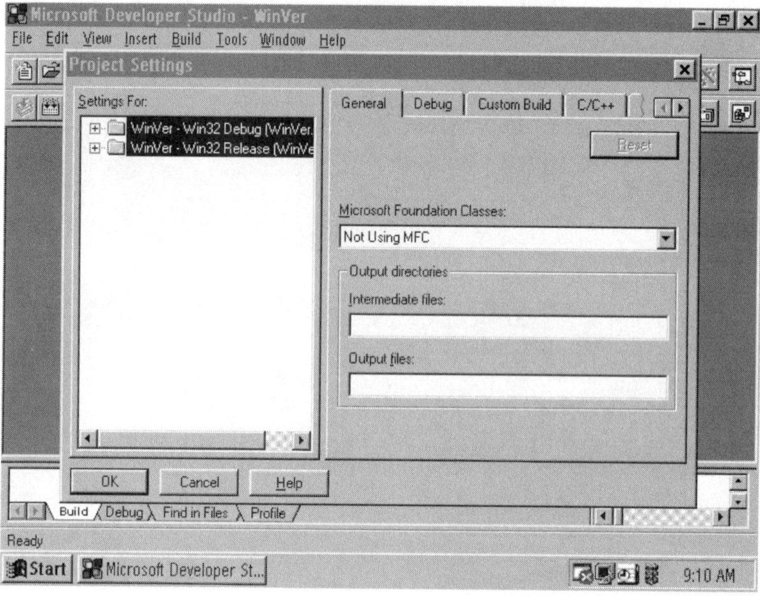

Figure 4.4: Microsoft's Settings... Menu item allows the operating platform to be identified and configured.

useful when developing new applications, but increases the application's executable file size. You'll want to choose the release version when your project is fully functional, for the smallest executable file size.

Once this process is completed, the application can be built from the Build menu by selecting the Rebuild All menu item, as shown in Figure 4.5. Once this is completed you will have an executable file (.exe), ready to run, on your hard disk.

Execute the application. If you are running under Windows NT, you will see a screen similar to the one shown in Figure 4.6.

On the other hand, you are probably running under Windows 95 (isn't everybody?), so expect to see a screen similar to Figure 4.7.

Remember, every application in this book, whether procedure-oriented or object-oriented, will need a project workspace. All project workspaces are created in essentially the same manner. As applications become more involved, you'll add additional items to the project file list (see Figure 4.3). These additional items can and will include multiple source files (.cpp), header files (.h), and various resource files.

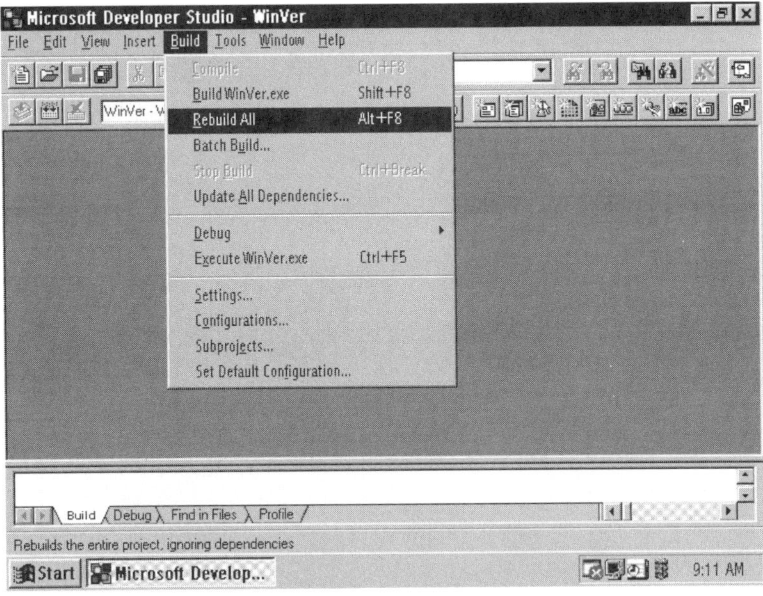

Figure 4.5: From Microsoft's Build menu, select the Rebuild All menu item to produce an executable file for this project.

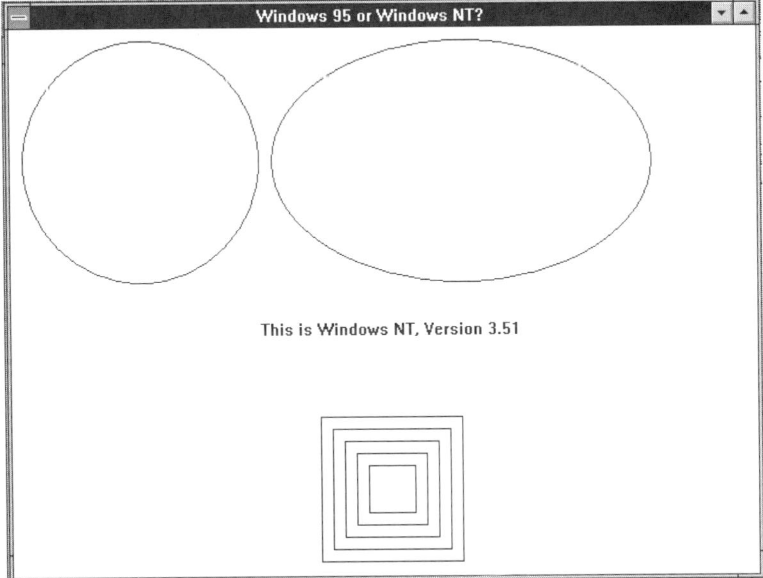

Figure 4.6: The WinVer.cpp application running under Windows NT.

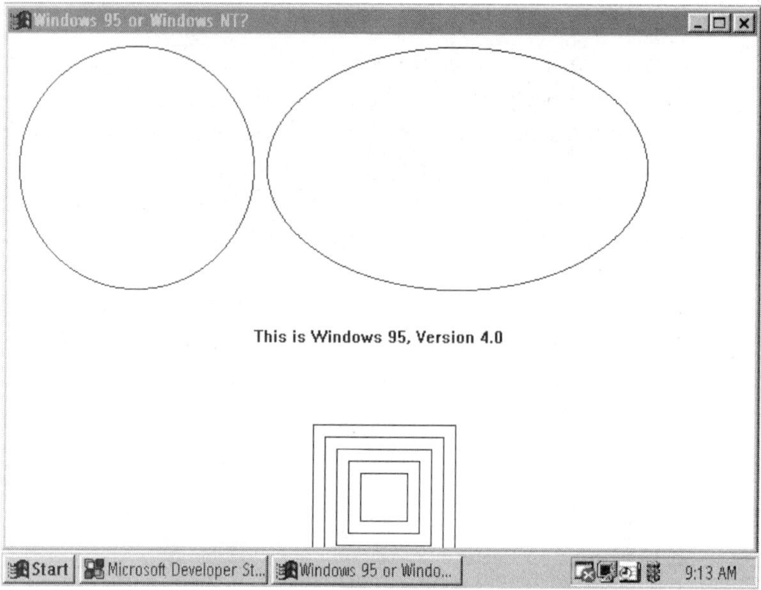

Figure 4.7: The WinVer.cpp application running under Windows 95.

Compiler Options

The Microsoft Visual C++ compiler is an optimizing compiler. In the previous section, you built a procedure-oriented application using the compiler's defaults. There are certain options that you might want to consider: file size and executable speed. For example, there is often a 2:1 ratio in file sizes between the debug and release versions of the same application.

File Sizes

Various optimizations can be selected from the Build menu by selecting the Settings... menu item. The Project Settings dialog box, shown earlier in Figure 4.4, will appear. Select the C/C++ folder to view the Optimizations list box. If you want the compiler to optimize for minimum executable file size, select Minimize Size from the list.

The resulting application will be the smallest possible executable file, but not necessarily the fastest!

Executable Speed

If you want the compiler to optimize for the fastest executable file, select Maximize Speed from the list.

The resulting application will be the fastest possible executable, but not necessarily the smallest file!

For small applications, such as WinVer.cpp, the resulting file sizes are often the same, regardless of the option selected. For example, for either option, the debug version resulted in a file approximately 72 KB in size. The release version was approximately 39 KB in size. Remember these numbers. We'll compare them to an object-oriented application in Chapter 7.

Chapter 5

Foundations for Object-Oriented Programming

Most programmers are faced with a steep learning curve as they move from the procedure-oriented Windows environment illustrated in Chapter 4 to the object-oriented environment using the MFC library. This chapter is designed to help you quickly grasp object-oriented concepts, terminology, and definitions.

This chapter first discusses the general differences between a procedure-oriented approach and an object-oriented approach. You'll then learn the terms associated with object-oriented programming, such as encapsulation, hierarchy, inheritance, objects, and polymorphism.

Next, you will learn of a new C++ type, called a class, which serves as the foundation for developing object libraries. The details of how the C++ **class** type forms this foundation are then discussed. The chapter concludes with a non-Windows application using classes.

Procedure-Oriented Programming

Chapter 4 illustrated the traditional procedure-oriented approach to developing Windows applications. A procedural approach is common among all structured languages including C, C++, and Pascal. You also know that in a non-Windows application, a procedure-oriented C or C++ program is structured in such a way that there is typically a main function and possibly one or more functions (subroutines) that are called from the main function. This is a top-down approach. Here, the main function is usually short, assigning the work to the remaining functions in the program. Program execution flows from the top of the main function and terminates at the bottom of the same function.

In this type of program, code and data are separate. Procedures define what is to happen to data, but the two never become one. All of this changes in object-oriented programming. The procedural approach suffers from several disadvantages, the chief of which is program maintenance. When additions or deletions are to be made to the program code, as in a word processor or database program, often the entire program must be rewritten to include the new routines. This approach takes enormous amounts of time in initial development and finally debugging. Program maintenance demands a better approach.

Object-Oriented Programming

Object-oriented programs (oops) offer solutions to the problems of procedure-oriented programming. However, object-oriented solutions function differently from the traditional procedural approach. Object-oriented solutions require a new programming strategy that is often difficult for procedure-oriented programmers to grasp. This chapter will introduce you to the concepts that make up object-oriented programming in C++. If you studied the application in Chapter 4, you have already had a taste of object-oriented programming. Yes, even while you were in a procedure-oriented environment, you were working with various message handlers and functions that are proto-objects. Now, by using C++ you can form real objects by using the new **class** data type. A class provides a set of values (data) and the operations (methods or member functions) that act on those values. Once the C++ class is formed, the resulting objects can be manipulated by using messages.

It is the message component of object-oriented languages that is most useful to Windows applications. In an object-oriented environment, objects hold the data (member data) and the methods (member functions) for working on that data. This is the first time these two items have been combined into one working concept. Now, objects contain the data and the methods for working on that data.

The object-oriented approach offers several advantages to the programmer. First, object-oriented programming offers a solution to program maintenance. Initially, object-oriented programs are easier to read and understand. The overall complexity of a program is controlled by allowing only the necessary details to be viewed by the programmer. Another advantage is program modification (adding or deleting features). Features can often be added or deleted—for example, such as in a word processor or database program—by simply adding or deleting objects. Since new objects can inherit everything from a parent object, it is only necessary to add or delete items that differ. Another advantage is that you can use the same object many times. Well-designed objects can be saved in a toolkit of useful routines that you can easily insert into new code, with few or no changes to that code. This, of course, is the basis for the MFC library, which will be introduced in the next chapter.

In your programming experience, you may have discovered a technique for converting a C program to a C++ program and vice versa. If this is the case, it is because you learned that substitutions, such as switching **printf** with **cout** for I/O streams, are relatively easy. This is an easy switch because the conversion is from and to a procedural programming structure, it doesn't matter whether you are writing C or C++ code. However, object-oriented programming is exclusively in the C++ realm, since C does not provide the **class** type. There is no simple substitution that can be made to convert a procedure-oriented application to an object-oriented application. Whole applications have to be reworked, with traditional functions being replaced with objects. You may agree that it is often easier to discard the old program and create an object-oriented program from scratch. The need to completely rewrite an application is a distinct disadvantage to converting from a procedure-oriented program to an object-oriented program.

C++ AND OBJECT-ORIENTED PROGRAMMING

What does C++ have that makes it a suitable language for developing object-oriented programs? You already know the answer—the **class** data type. It is the **class** type that gives the language the ability to build objects. C++ offers several additional advantages to the object-oriented environment. These advantages include operator overloading, less emphasis on the preprocess, and strong typing. C++ is a language that was designed, not retrofitted, for object-oriented programming.

Object-oriented programming has its own unique definitions and terminology, which we'll examine in the next section. Understanding these terms and definitions will help you form a better understanding of object-oriented programming.

OBJECT-ORIENTED DEFINITIONS AND TERMINOLOGY

Object-oriented programming is a programming technique that allows you to view concepts as a variety of objects. Objects allow you can represent the tasks that are to be performed, their interaction, and any given conditions that must be observed. A data structure often forms the basis of an object. The **struct** type can form an elementary class or object. Messages can be used to communicate with objects. Using messages for communication is similar to calling a function in a procedure-oriented program. When an object receives a message, methods contained within the object respond. *Methods* are similar to the functions of procedure-oriented programming. However, unlike functions, methods are part of an object's definition.

The C++ **class** type is an extension of the **struct** type. It forms the required abstract data type for object-oriented programming. Classes usually contain related items that share attributes. Object can be considered an instance of a class. As an example, Figure 5.1 illustrates a simple Microprocessor class.

Assume that the Microprocessor class is described in the program's code. This class might include a description of items that are common to all Intel microprocessors and data concerning heat buildup. At run time, three additional objects of the Microprocessor class can be created. They could include the Pentium Pro, the Pentium, and the 80486. The additional objects might include details of features and data common to each individual model. For example, a Pentium Pro is an object that describes a particular type of microprocessor. It is an instance of the Microprocessor class.

If a message is sent to the instance of the Microprocessor class (similar to a call to a function) with instructions to select a 150 MHz microprocessor, that message could be utilized only by the Pentium Pro (at least at the time of this writing) object of the class. Only the Pentium Pro currently has a clock rate of 150 MHz.

Class libraries, such as the MFC library, have emerged containing many object types. The remaining chapters of this book are devoted to a detailed investigation of the MFC library.

Before examining the MFC library, it is a good idea to become familiar with several concepts that relate to C++ and object-oriented programming. The next few sections describe these concepts.

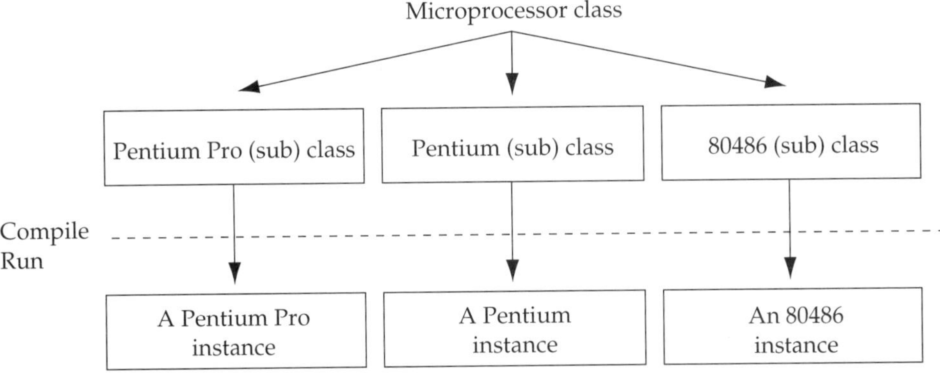

Figure 5.1: A simple class

Encapsulation

Encapsulation refers to the manner in which an object combines its member data and member functions (methods) into a single structure. Figure 5.2 shows how data fields and methods can be combined to build an object.

An object's description is usually part of a C++ class and includes the object's internal structure, how the object interacts with other objects, and what form of protection is used to isolate the functional details of the object outside of the class. The C++ **class** type does all of this.

In a class, the functional details of an object are controlled by using private, public, and/or protected descriptors. The *public* section is used for the interface information (methods) that makes the class reusable across applications. If data or methods are contained in the public section, they are available outside the class. The *private* section of a class limits the availability of data or methods to the class itself. Most typically, data is placed in the private section. A *protected* section containing data or methods is available to the class and any derived subclasses.

Class Hierarchy

The objects formed from the a class description are *instances* of the class. In this manner, the C++ class serves as a *boilerplate* for creating objects. It is thus possible to create a *class hierarchy* where there is a parent class and several child classes. The basis

OBJECT

Data Field	METHOD: Member Function
Data Field	METHOD: Member Function
	METHOD: Member Function
Data Field	METHOD: Member Function

Figure 5.2: Data fields and methods build an object.

for doing this revolves around *derived* classes. In object-oriented programming, parent classes are used for more generalized tasks while derived child classes are used for specific actions. For example, the Microprocessor class discussed earlier could contain data and methods common to the entire microprocessor line, such as pin-outs, temperature ratings, and case sizes. Child classes derived from the parent, such as the Pentium Pro, Pentium, and 80486, could contain items specific to the class. For example, the Pentium Pro was introduced with a clock speed of 150 MHz.

Inheritance

Inheritance refers to the ability of a class to inherit properties from a class of objects. Here, the parent class serves as a boilerplate for the derived class and can be modified in several ways, including overloading and altering access privileges. When an object inherits attributes from a single parent, it is referred to as *single inheritance.* When multiple parents are involved, it is called *multiple inheritance.* Inheritance allows reuse of a class definition without requiring major code changes. Inheritance also supports reusable code, since child classes are extensions of parent classes.

Polymorphism

In object-oriented programming, common messages can be sent to the parent class object and all derived subclass objects. This is called *polymorphism.*

Polymorphism allows each subclass object to respond to the message format in a manner appropriate to its definition. Consider a class hierarchy used for gathering data. The parent class could be responsible for gathering the name, address, telephone number, and Social Security number of an individual. The child class could then gather additional information based on, for example, the zip code provided in the address. In this manner the parent class gathers general information common to all child classes, while the child class gathers detailed information relating to a specific item. Here a common data-gathering message is sent to the parent and child class, with both the parent and child classes responds, and if necessary, passes the message to the parent class.

Virtual Functions

Polymorphism gives an object the ability to respond to messages when the object's exact type is not known. You send the message as if it is going to the most general class, but the appropriate child responds based on the type of the actual instance. This is possible because of *late binding*. Here, the addresses are determined dynamically at run time, as opposed to statically at compile time. Late binding is achieved with the use of *virtual functions*. Virtual functions are defined in the parent class whenever subsequent derived classes will overload the member function by redefining the function's implementation. When virtual functions are used, messages are passed to a pointer that points to the object instead of directly to the object.

Virtual functions use a table for address information. The table is initialized at run time by using a constructor. A constructor is called whenever an object of the class is created. The purpose of the constructor, at the point, is to link the virtual function with the table of address information. The address of the virtual function is not known at compile time. It is simply given the position in the table (determined at run time) of addresses that will contain the address for the function.

THE C++ CLASS

In this section we'll examine the formal syntax for defining a class and see several simple examples of its implementation. The definition of a C++ class begins with the use of the **class** keyword. The class *name* (tag type) follows the keyword. You'll notice that the data part of the class is similar to the C and C++ **struct** type. Examine this listing:

```
class type {
  type var1
  type var2
  type var3
  type var4
      .
      .
      .
```

```
public:
  member function 1
  member function 2
  member function 3
        .
        .
        .
} name associated with class type;
```

Class member variables follow the class declaration. These variables are private to the class by default and can be accessed only by class member functions. Class member functions usually follow a public declaration. This form allows access to class member functions from external calling routines. All class member functions have access to public, private, and protected parts of a class.

Here is an example of a class:

```
class trig
  { double data_value;
public:
  void set_value(double);
  double get_sine(void);
  double get_cosine(void);
  double get_tangent(void);
} deg;
```

This class has a type (tag name) **trig**. A private variable, *data_value*, will share degree values among the various member functions. Four functions make up the member functions of the class. They are **set_value(), get_sine(), get_cosine(),** and **get_tangent().** The name that is associated with this class type is *deg*. This example is an exception, since the association of a variable name with the class name is most frequently done in the **main()** function.

A Simple C++ Class

The visibility of class member variables is by default private. Member variables are accessible only to member functions of the class. Member functions must be declared public if they are to have visibility beyond the class. Here is a complete programming example:

```
//
// TRIGCLASS.CPP
// This program uses a simple class and introduces
```

```
// the concept of private and public parts.
// This program uses a class to obtain the trigonometric
// value for given angle.
// Copyright (c) Chris H. Pappas and William H. Murray, 1996

#include <iostream.h>
#include <math.h>

const double DEG_TO_RAD=0.01745329;

class trig {
  double data_value;
public:
  void set_value(double);
  double get_sine(void);
  double get_cosine(void);
  double get_tangent(void);
} deg;

void trig::set_value(double ang)
{
  data_value=ang;
}

double trig::get_sine(void)
{
  double answer;

  answer=sin(DEG_TO_RAD*data_value);
  return (answer);
}
double trig::get_cosine(void)
{
  double answer;

  answer=cos(DEG_TO_RAD*data_value);
  return (answer);
}

double trig::get_tangent(void)
{
  double answer;

  answer=tan(DEG_TO_RAD*data_value);
  return (answer);
}
main()
{
  // set angle to 35.0 degrees
  deg.set_value(35.0);

  cout << "The sine of the angle is: "
       << deg.get_sine() << endl;
```

```
cout << "The cosine of the angle is: "
     << deg.get_cosine() << endl;
cout << "The tangent of the angle is: "
     << deg.get_tangent() << endl;
return (0); }
```

The *data_value* variable is private to the class, by default, and is thus accessible only by the member functions of the class. Notice that the member functions themselves have been declared public in visibility and are accessible from outside the class. Each class member, however, has access to all other class members.

In most cases, class member functions are defined outside of the class. When this is the case, class member functions are usually defined immediately after the class has been defined and before the **main()** function. Nonmember functions are still defined after the function **main()** and are prototyped in the normal fashion.

Constructors and Destructors

A *constructor* is a class member function. Constructors are used to initialize class variables or allocate memory storage. A constructor *always* has the same name as the class it is defined within. Constructors can also accept arguments and be overloaded. A constructor is executed automatically when an object of the **class** type is created. *Free store objects* are objects created with the **new** operator and serve to allocate memory for the created objects. Constructors are generated by Microsoft's Visual C/C++ compiler if they are not explicitly defined.

A *destructor* is also a special class member function. Destructors are used to return memory allocated by free store memory. The destructor also uses the same name as the class it is defined in; however, that name is preceded by the tilde character. Destructors are automatically called when the **delete** operator is applied to a class pointer or when a program passes beyond the scope of a class object. Destructors cannot accept an argument and may not be overloaded. Destructors are generated by Microsoft's Visual C/C++ compiler if they are not explicitly defined.

Constructors have another practical use. Constructors can be used to initialize private class variables. In the following example, the private data member is initialized with the use of a constructor—in this case, 578 pennies.

```
class coin {
  int value;

public:
  coin() {value=578;}                        // constructor
  ~coin() {cout << "Conversion complete";}   // destructor
  int quarter_conversion(void);
  int dime_conversion(int);
  int nickel_conversion(int);
};
```

In this small portion of code, the member functions are defined outside of the class itself and are not shown here. Access to class variables is always through class member functions. Again, recall that the constructor is considered a member function.

A more significant reason for using a constructor is in using free store memory. In the next portion of code, a constructor is used to allocate memory for the *mystring* pointer with the **new** operator. A destructor is also used to release the allocated memory back to the system when the object is destroyed. This is accomplished with the use of the **delete** operator.

```
class use_string {
  char *mystring
  int string_length;

public:
  use_string(char *) {mystring=new char[string_length];}
  ~use_string() {delete mystring;}
  void input_data(char *);
  void output_data(char *); };
```

The memory which **new** allocates to the pointer *mystring* can only be deallocated with a call to **delete**. Thus, memory is allocated to pointers in constructors and deallocated in destructors. This process ensures that if the variable assigned to the class passes out of its scope, the allocated memory will be returned. Memory allocation can be considered dynamic and is most useful in programs that use linked lists. The memory used by the **int** and **float** data types is automatically restored to the system without the need for **new** and **delete**.

Overloading Class Member Functions

Class member functions can be overloaded just like ordinary C++ functions. *Overloading* a class member function means that more than one function can have the same function name in the current scope. It is the responsibility of the compiler to select the correct function based upon the number and types of arguments used when the function call is made. A classic example of overloading is illustrated below. This class is used to determine the absolute value of a number, whether it is an integer or double. The task is accomplished with the use of the **abs()** and **fabs()** functions, which return integer and double results.

```
//
// ABSOLUTE.CPP
// Program illustrates class member function overloading.
// Program finds the absolute value of an integer
// and a double.
// Copyright (c) Chris H. Pappas and William H. Murray, 1996
//

#include <iostream.h>
#include <math.h>
#include <stdlib.h>

class absolute {
public:
  int value(int);
  double value(double);
};

int absolute::value(int test_data)
{
  int answer;

  answer=abs(test_data);
  return (answer);
}

double absolute::value(double test_data)
{
  double answer;

  answer=fabs(test_data);
  return (answer); }

main()
{
  absolute neg_value;
```

```
  cout << "The absolute value is: "
       << neg_value.value(-437)
       << endl;
  cout << "The absolute value is: "
       << neg_value.value(-437.1234)
       << endl;
  return (0);
}
```

Here the dot operator is used, along with the member function name, to pass a negative integer and negative double value. The program selects the proper member function based upon the type (integer or double) of argument passed with the function name. The positive value returned by each function is printed to the screen.

Friend Functions

Friend functions can be used to access the private data members of a class. Remember that member data is private by default. Member data is usually shareable only with member functions of the class. Friend functions allow the sharing of private class information with nonmember functions. Friend functions can share the same class resources as member functions.

This special group of functions also offer the advantage that they are external to the class definition itself. This is illustrated in the following listing:

```
//
// FRIEND.CPP
// Program illustrates the concept of friend functions.
// Program will collect a string of date and time
// information from system. Time information will
// be determined and converted into seconds.
// Copyright (c) Chris H. Pappas and William H. Murray, 1996
//

#include <iostream.h>
#include <stdlib.h>
#include <string.h>
#include <time.h>

class time_value {
  long secs;
  friend char * current_time(time_value);  //friend function
```

```
public:
  time_value(char *);
};

// constructor
time_value::time_value(char *tm)
{
  char *hours,*minutes,*seconds;

  // data is returned as a string:
  // (day month date hours:minutes:seconds year)
  // skip three tokens, (day, month and date)
  hours=strtok(tm," ");
  hours=strtok(0," ");
  hours=strtok(0," ");

  // collect time information from string
  hours=strtok(0,":");
  minutes=strtok(0,":");
  seconds=strtok(0," ");

  // convert data to long type and accumulate seconds.
  secs=atol(hours)*3600;
  secs+=atol(minutes)*60;
  secs+=atol(seconds);
}

char * current_time(time_value);  // prototype

main()
{
  // get the time and date string
  struct tm *ptr;
  time_t ltime;
  ltime=time(NULL);
  ptr=localtime(&ltime);

  time_value tz(asctime(ptr));

  cout  <<  "The date and time information: "
        <<  asctime(ptr)
        <<  endl;
  cout  <<  "The total number of seconds: "
        <<  current_time(tz) << endl;
  return (0);
}

char * current_time(time_value tz)
{
  char *ctbuf; ctbuf=new char[40]; long int
  total_seconds;
```

```
    total_seconds=tz.secs;
    ltoa(total_seconds,ctbuf,10);
    return (ctbuf);
}
```

Notice in the class definition the use of the keyword **friend** along with the description of the **current_time()** function. When you examine the previous listing you will also notice that this function is external to the class and appears after the **main()** function description. In other words, it appears as a traditional C/C++ function.

In the function **main()**, the computer's time is obtained with the use of *time_t* and its associated structure *tm*. In this program, *ltime* is the name of the variable associated with *time_t*. Local time is initialized and retrieved into the pointer *ptr* with the next two lines of code. By using **asctime(ptr)**, the pointer will point to an ASCII string of date and time information.

```
struct tm *ptr;
time_t ltime;
ltime=time(NULL);
ptr=localtime(&ltime);

time_value tz(asctime(ptr));
```

The date and time string is formatted in the following manner: day month date hours:minutes:seconds year 0

For example:

```
Tue Nov 21 14:22:32 1995
```

The string information that is retrieved is sent to the class by associating *tz* with the class **time_value**:

```
time_value tz(asctime(ptr));
```

The constructor **time_value(char** *) is used to define the code used to convert the string information into integer data. The conversion process uses the **strtok()** function.

The date/time information is returned in a unique format. To process this string information in order to determine the number of seconds, the **strtok()** function must use a space as the delimiter. This is necessary in order to skip over the day, month, and date information in the string. Initially, the variable *hours* initially collects unwanted tokens. The space delimiters are followed by a colon (:) delimiter. This is used in collecting the hour and minute tokens from the string. The number of seconds can be obtained by reading the string until another space is encountered. The time information is then converted to a **long** type for storing the total number of seconds. The variable *secs* is private to the class but accessible to the friend function.

The friend function uses the number of accumulated seconds in *tz.seconds* and converts it back to a character string. The memory for string storage is allocated with the **new** operator. The newly created string is a result of using the friend function.

While friend functions offer some interesting programming possibilities when programming with C++ classes, they should be used with caution.

The Derived C++ Class

A *derived class* is an extension or inheritance of an existing class. The existing class is called the *base* or *parent class,* and the derived class is called a *subclass* or *child class.* A derived class provides a means for expanding or customizing the capabilities of a parent class, without the need to re-create the parent class itself. A common interface is possible between derived classes sharing a common parent.

Any class can serve as a parent class. Classes derived from the parent will reflect the parent's description. The derived class can add additional features to those of the parent class. For example, the derived class can modify access privileges, add new members, or overload existing members. When derived classes overload parent member functions, they are said to be *virtual member functions.*

A derived class is described by using the following syntax:

```
class derived-class-type :(public/private/protected) . . .
      parent-class-type { . . . .};
```

For example, here is a simple derived class description:

```
class working:public consumer { . . . .};
```

In this case, the derived class tag is **working**. The parent class has public visibility, and its tag is **consumer**.

A third visibility specifier is often used with derived classes. This is the protected specifier. A protected specifier is the same as a private specifier, with the added feature that class member functions and friends of derived classes are given access to the class. Thus, classes use three visibility specifiers: public, private, and protected.

An Object-Oriented Stack

As a final object-oriented example, the following program illustrates how an object-oriented stack can be implemented.

The **stack** class provides six member functions: **clear()**, **top()**, **empty()**, **full()**, **push()**, and **pop()**. Stack operations occur in the normal FILO (first-in, last-out) manner.

```
//
// STACK.CPP
// Program shows object-oriented programming
// with a classical stack operation.
// Copyright (c) Chris H. Pappas and William H. Murray, 1996
//

#include <iostream.h>
#include <string.h>

#define maxlen 80

class stack {
  char init_string[maxlen];
  int value;

public:
  void clear(void);
  int empty(void);
  int full(void);
  char pop(void);
  void push(char chr);
  char top(void);
};

void stack::clear(void)
{
  value=0;
}

int stack::empty(void)
{
  return (value==0);
}

int stack::full(void)
{
```

```
return (value==maxlen-1);
}

char stack::pop(void)
{
  return (init_string[value--]);
}

void stack::push(char character)
{
  init_string[++value]=character;
}

char stack::top(void)
{
  return (init_string[value]);
}

main()
{
  stack thestack;
  char str[11]="abcdefghij";

  // clear the stack
  thestack.clear();

  // load the string, char-by-char, on the stack
  cout  <<  "Load character on stack"
        <<  endl;
  for(int i=0;i<strlen(str);i++) {
    if (!thestack.full())
      thestack.push(str);
      cout <<  str
           << endl;
   }

   // unload the stack, char-by-char
   cout  << "Unload character from stack"
         << endl;
   while (!thestack.empty())
      cout  << thestack.pop()
            << endl;

   return (0);
}
```

Characters from the string are pushed one character at a time onto the stack. The stack is then unloaded one character at a time. Loading and unloading are done from the stack top, so the first character loaded on the stack is pushed the lowest in the stack.

Observe in the following listing that the "a" character was pushed onto the stack first. It should be no surprise that it is also the last character popped off the stack.

```
Load character on stack
a
b
c
d
e
f
g
h
i
j

Unload character from stack
j
i
h
g
f
e
d
c
b
a
```

This is a simple example. It lacks many object-oriented concepts such as inheritance, memory management, and polymorphism. It is, nevertheless, a simple object-oriented program.

Examine the program code and find to object-oriented and class features discussed earlier in this chapter. In the next chapter, you'll learn how many of these components are incorporated into the MFC library.

Chapter 6

The Microsoft Foundation Class (MFC) Library

In the previous chapter, you learned the reasons for developing parent classes and the techniques for deriving child classes from those parents. In this chapter, you will learn how Microsoft developed a family of classes that can be called upon when developing object-oriented Windows applications. This family of classes is called the Microsoft Foundation Class (MFC) library.

The use of a class library is a radical departure from the use of functions in traditional procedure-oriented programming. Class libraries are the exclusive property of the developer. The MFC is owned and licensed by Microsoft Corporation. It should be no surprise you that in the early days of object-oriented programming for Windows, Borland and Microsoft went their separate ways. Borland first released the Object Windows Library (OWL) and made a tremendous effort to move away from procedure-oriented programming. Microsoft introduced the Microsoft Foundation Class (MFC) library and warned developers that object-oriented programming with the MFC (of course) was the development path to take. At this writing, it seems apparent that the MFC is or will become the standard for class libraries. Borland has announced that it plans to provide the OWL and license the MFC starting with the release of version 5 of the Borland C++ compiler. The common denominator among all C/C++ compiler manufacturers will be the MFC library. This fact will certainly limit the usefulness of the OWL for those that continue to use that library. The use of the OWL will decrease because developers will look toward the MFC library as the common library that will be the basis of their object-oriented programming needs.

The strategies for developing a good library as well as simple program development will be discussed in Chapter 7. In this chapter, we will take a careful look at how the MFC library has evolved to version 4.0 in terms of class hierarchy.

Class Hierarchy

The MFC library is a collection of related classes. The relationship of one class to another depends upon where it falls in the class hierarchy for the MFC. For example, CTabCtrl and CSliderCtrl are two closely related classes. CSemaphore and CPropertySheet are not as closely related. However, in the larger scheme, they are all descendents of the CObject class. CObject is the base class for all derived MFC classes. CObject is discussed in more detail in Chapter 7 as it relates to the development of a simple programming example. In the following sections, we'll examine the class hierarchy of the MFC as it has evolved over the past several years. You'll gain a better understanding of how the various classes interact in the MFC, and perhaps understand how your applications can further derive child classes from this important library. There are a few classes that are not derived from CObject; they will be examined, also.

CObject

CObject is the base class for almost all derived MFC classes. In the hierarchy scheme, groups of related classes are derived immediately from CObject, as shown in the following list:

```
CObject -
  Arrays
  CCmdTarget (architecture)
  Control
  Database
  Drawing Objects
  Exceptions
  File
  Graphics
  Lists
  Maps
  Menus
  Sockets
  Synchronization
```

The contents of each of these categories along with a short description of their use will be examined in the sections which follow.

Arrays

The CArray class allows arrays the use of arrays that shrink and grow as needed. They are most closely associated with normal C/C++ arrays. Memory is allocated to the upper bound. CArray is part of the template-based collection classes. As such, it provides a type-safe collection for containing objects of any type.

All remaining classes are not of the template-based collection type. These classes are used to efficiently manipulate and store the array data types mentioned.

```
CObject -
  CArray
  CByteArray
  CDWordArray
  CObArray
  CPtrArray
  CStringArray
  CUIntArray
  CWordArray
```

CCmdTarget (Architecture)

CCmdTarget is the base class for all classes of objects that receive and respond to messages. Messages are sent by menus, dialog boxes, controls, and so on. These commands are sent from interface objects to target objects.

```
CObject -
  CCmdTarget
    CWinThread
    CWinApp
      COleControlModule
    CDocTemplate
      CSingleDocTemplate
      CMultiDocTemplate
    COleObjectFactory
    COleTemplateServer
    COleDataSource
    COleDropTarget
    COleMessageFilter
    CConnectionPoint
    CDocument
      COleDocument
        COleLinkingDoc
          COleServerDoc
            CRichEditDoc
  CDocItem
    COleClientItem
      CRichEditCntrlItem
  COleServerItem
  CWnd
```

For example, CDocTemplate serves as the base class for all document templates. This class is not used directly. Instead, either CSingleDocTemplate or CMultiDocTemplate would be selected. CSingleDocTemplate is a template for documents using the single document interface (SDI). CMultiDocTemplate is a template for documents using the multiple document interface (MDI).

CWnd This class is the base class for all window classes in the MFC library. The CWnd class lets you create a main window or child window for the application. A class is derived from CWnd, then member variables and functions are added. Other classes are derived from CWnd, including CDialog, CFrameWnd, CMDIChildWnd, CMDIFrameWnd, CView, and so on.

```
CObject -
  CCmdTarget
    CWnd
      Control Bars
      Controls
      Dialog Boxes
```

```
Frame
Property Sheets
Views
```

Control Bars These control bars are most closely associated with a frame window. They include buttons, dialog template, status panes, and so on. They are easy to use because they are integrated with the frame window. CControlBar is the base class for CDialogBar, COleResizeBar, CStatusBar and CToolBar.

```
CObject -
  CCmdTarget
    CWnd
      CControlBar
        CDialogBar
        COleResizeBar
        CStatusBar
        CToolBar
```

Controls Control classes provide an interface between Windows controls, such as buttons, combo boxes, list boxes, sliders, tabs, and toolbars, and your application. Classes ending with "Ctrl" are part of the common control being used extensively by programmers today.

```
CObject -
  CCmdTarget
    CWnd
      CAnimateCtrl
      CButton
        CBitmapButton
      CComboBox
      CEdit
      CHeaderCtrl
      CHotKeyCtrl
      CListBox
        CCheckListBox
        CDragListBox
      CListCtrl
      COleControl
      CProgressCtrl
      CRichEditCtrl
      CScrollBar
      CSliderCtrl
      CSpinButtonCtrl
      CStatic
      CStatusBarCtrl
      CTabCtrl
```

```
CToolBarCtrl
CToolTipCtrl
CTreeCtrl
```

For example, common controls are used in dialog boxes, form views, record views, and so on. Common controls function as child windows that send notification messages to the parent window when events occur in the control. These messages can include WM_NOTIFY and WM_COMMAND Windows messages.

Dialog Boxes The CDialog class is the base class used for all dialog boxes. An object based on this class is made up of a dialog template and a class derived from CDialog.

```
CObject -
  CCmdTarget
    CWnd
      CDialog
        CCommonDialog
          CColorDialog
          CFileDialog
          CFindReplaceDialog
          CFontDialog
          COleDialog
            COleBusyDialog
            COleChangeIconDialog
            COleChangeSourceDialog
            COleConvertDialog
            COleInsertDialog
            COleLinksDialog
              ColeUpdateDialog
            COlePasteSpecialDialog
            COlePropertiesDialog
          CPageSetupDialog
          CPrintDialog
        COlePropertyPage
        CPropertyPage
```

Member variables can be added to the derived dialog class for storing data received by controls contained in the dialog box.

Frame The CFrameWnd is the base class for frame windows. It supports a single document interface (SDI), overlapped, or popup frame window. In a user application, a class is derived from CFrameWnd, then member variables are added to store specific data for the particular application. Frame windows can be created by using **Create()** or **LoadFrame(),** or via document template.

```
CObject -
  CCmdTarget
    CWnd
      CFrameWnd
        CMDICChildWnd
        CMDIFrameWnd
        CMiniFrameWnd
        COleIPFrameWnd
      CSplitterWnd
```

Property Sheets The CPropertySheet class is used to create property sheets or tab dialog objects. Property sheets contain a CPropertySheet object and at least one CPropertyPage object. Property sheets are displayed via the framework as a window with tab indices. Property Sheets can relieve the congestion found on single-sheet dialog boxes.

```
CObject -
  CCmdTarget
    CWnd
      CPropertySheet
```

Views The CView class is the base class for all view classes. A view becomes part of a document and serves as an interface between the document and the user.

```
CObject -
  CCmdTarget
    CWnd
      CView
        CCtrlView
          CEditView
          CListView
          CRichEditView
          CTreeView
      CScrollView
        CFormView
          CDaoRecordView
          CRecordView
```

A view is simply the child of a frame window. New views are constructed by the framework and attached to a document as requested. Views receive commands from the frame window.

Control

An image list is a group of images of the same size. Image lists are used to manage large groups of icons and bitmapped images.

```
CObject -
  CImageList
```

Database

The CDatabase class, allows an object to represent a connection to a data source. A data source might be provided by a database application such as Microsoft Access.

A CDaoDatabase class, also allows an object to represent a connection to a data source. The basic difference between this class and CDatabase is that CDaoDatabase gains access to data via the Data Access Object (DAO). This object is based on the Microsoft Jet database engine. The CDatabase object, on the other hand, gains access through the Open Database Connectivity (ODBC).

```
CObject -
  CDatabase
  CRecordset
  CLongBinary
  CDaoDatabase
  CDaoQueryDef
  CDaoRecordset
  CDaoTableDef
  CDaoWorkspace
```

Drawing Objects

The CGdiObject class is the base class for Windows GDI objects. These objects include bitmaps, brushes, palettes, pens, and so on. User classes are based on classes derived from CGdiObject.

```
CObject -
  CGdiObject
    CBitmap
    CBrush
    CFont
    CPalette
    CPen
    CRgn
```

For example, the CBrush class encapsulates a Windows brush. A CBrush object can be used by any CDC member function.

Exceptions

In this group, CException serves as the base class for all exceptions in the MFC library. The derived exception classes include CArchiveException, CDaoException, CDBException, CFileException, CMemoryException, CNotSupportedException, COleDispatchException, COleException, CResourceException, and CUserException.

```
CObject -
  Cexception
    CArchiveException
    DDaoException
    CDBException
    CFileException
    CMemoryException
    CNotSupportedException
    COleException
    COleDispatchException
    CResourceException
    CUserException
```

Specific exceptions are captured using one of the previously mentioned classes. All exceptions can be captured with the CException class.

File

The CFile class serves as the base class for all MFC file classes using unbuffered disk input/output. Text files and memory files can also be supported via a derived child class.

```
CObject -
  CFile
    CMemFile
    COleStreamFile
    CSocketFile
    CStdioFile
```

For example, a CStdioFile class object can be used for a C run-time stream file. These files are buffered and can be used in text or binary mode.

Graphics

The CDC class provides device-context objects for use in a device context. The device context can be the normal client area or a window, or, for example, a printer.

Member functions are provided for all GDI graphics work, including coordinate system manipulation, clipping, device extents, and graphics figures.

```
CObject -
  CDC
    CCleintDC
    CMetaFileDC
    CPaintDC
    CWindowDC
```

CPaintDC, for example, encapsulates calls to **BeginPaint()** and **EndPaint()**. CPaintDC objects are used to respond to a WM_PAINT message. They are typically located in the OnPaint message-handler member function.

Lists

The CList class acts, for example, as a double-linked list for ordered lists. Sequential searches are used to find list element by value or index. Element insertion can be fast at the beginning or end of the list.

The CStringList class, for example, supports lists of CString objects. In this case, comparisons are done by value (characters instead of addresses).

```
CObject -
  CList
  CPtrList
  CObList
  CStringList
```

Maps

The CMap class serves, for example, as a dictionary collection class. This class links specific keys to values, making retrieves or deletes very efficient.

Some classes serve very specific purposes. For example, the CMapWordToPtr class is used to support maps of void pointers keyed by 16-bit words (pointers).

```
CObject -
  CMap
  CMapWordToPtr
  CMapPtrToWord
  CMapPtrToPtr
  CMapWordToOb
  CMapStringToPtr
  CMapStringToOb
  CMapStringToString
```

Menus

The CMenu class encapsulates HMENU. Cmenu provides the functionality for all menu implementation, including creating, updating, and destroying.

```
CObject -
  CMenu
```

Sockets

The CAsyncSocket class provides support for a Windows socket. Applications must handle blocking, order differences, and various string conversions. Sockets are used in Windows communications.

```
CObject -
  CAsyncSocket
    CSocket
```

Synchronization

The CSyncObject class allows the synchronization of objects. For example, CSemaphore is derived from CSyncObject. CSemaphore supports semaphores, which are used to limited the number of threads in a processes. CSemaphore object are used to hold the count on the number of threads accessing a resource.

```
CObject -
  CSyncObject
    CCriticalSection
    CEvent
    CMutex
    CSemaphore
```

Classes Not Based on CObject

There are several small groups of classes not based on CObject. These groups are briefly discussed in the following sections.

Automation

These classes are typically used to encapsulate a particular type of OLE automation. For example, the COleCurrency class is used to create objects that encapsulate the CURRENCY data type of OLE automation. The CURRENCY data type is used for financial calculations or for any fixed-point calculation requiring accuracy.

```
COleCurrency
COleDateTime
COleDateTimeSpan
COleVariant
```

Object Model

These classes provide run-time object support. For example, CArchive is a class that permits a complex network of objects to be saved in a permanent binary form. This form exists even after the objects are deleted. The process of making data persistent is called *serialization*.

```
CArchive
CDumpContext
CRuntimeClass
```

Structures

These classes provide structures for other MFC classes. For example, the framework uses the CCreateContext structure when implementing a frame windows and views. The structure provides the required information for connecting the components of a document and the view of the document's data.

```
CCommandLineInfo
CCreateContext
CFileStatus
CMemoryState
CPrintInfo
```

Support

This group of classes offers support for the indicated item. For example, the CDataExchange class provides support for the dialog data exchange (DDX) and dialog data validation (DDV) routines. The object provides context information needed for DDX and DDV to take place.

```
CCmdUI
CDaoFieldExchange
CDataExchange
CFieldExchange
COleDataObject
COleDispatchDriver
CPropExchange
CRectTracker
CWaitCursor
```

Synchronization

The CSingleLock class allows objects to represent the access-control mechanism used in controlling access to a resource in a multithreaded program. In the same way, the CMultiLock class is used when multiple objects are needed.

```
CMultiLock
CSingleLock
```

Typed Templates

These classes are often used as type-safe wrappers. For example, the CTypedPtrArray class supplies a wrapper for objects of class CPtrArray or CObArray. The type-checking facility of C++ helps eliminate mismatched pointer errors.

```
CTypedPtrArray
CTypedPtrList
CTypedPtrMap
```

Types

These classes are similar to needed Windows structures. For example, the CRect class is similar to RECT structure. CRect includes member functions required to manipulate CRect objects and Windows RECT structures.

```
CPoint
CRect
CSize
CString
CTime
CTimeSpan
```

Wrappers

These classes are used to encapsulates the functionality of a font or picture object and the appropriate interface. These classes are used when it is desirable to customize font or picture properties for an application.

```
CFontHolder
CPictureHolder
```

More on MFC Classes

This chapter was designed to be a very brief overview of the MFC class hierarchy. In Chapter 7, you'll learn more detail about CObject and the related classes necessary to build complete Windows applications with the MFC library.

Chapter 7

An Object-Oriented Approach

In this chapter, we'll examine Microsoft's solution to making object-oriented programming easier. The Microsoft Visual C++ compiler provides a class library containing a new set of tools for the development of C++ and C++ Windows applications. While the Microsoft Foundation Class (MFC) library is available in 16- and 32-bit versions, only the 32-bit version will be discussed in this book. The 32-bit version is used exclusively for Windows 95 and Windows NT applications. The 32-bit version offers an expanded library providing additional class support for control bars, property sheets, OLE, etc.

This chapter examines the advantages of using the Microsoft Foundation Class library for Windows code development. It discusses terms, definitions, and techniques that are common across all Microsoft Foundation Class versions. The material you learn in this chapter is important for all MFC code developed in later chapters.

You'll also contrast the object-oriented programming application with the procedure-oriented application from Chapter 4, in terms of code size for both the source and executable files.

WHY SWITCH?

The Foundation Class library provides easy-to-use objects for the programmer. Windows, from its very inception, has followed many principles of object-oriented programming design, within the framework of a non–object-oriented language such as C. Many of these features were discussed in Chapters 1 through 4 of this book. The use of the C++ language for developing 32-bit Windows applications is a natural. That combination can take full advantage of object-oriented programming features. The Microsoft development team designed a library that includes a comprehensive implementation of the Windows Application Program Interface (API). This library encapsulates the most important data structures and API function calls within a group of reusable classes.

Class libraries, in general, offer many advantages over the traditional function libraries used by procedure-oriented programmers. These advantages include the following:

- Encapsulation of code and data within the class
- Final classes that appear to be natural extensions of the language
- Inheritance capabilities
- Reduced code size as a result of well-designed class libraries
- Reduction of function and variable name collisions

By using the Microsoft Foundation Class (MFC) library, the code required to establish a window has been reduced to approximately one-third the length of a conventional application. This translates into more time for application development. It allows you, the developer, to spend less time communicating with Windows and more time developing your application's code.

Design Techniques

To make the library easy to use, the design team set design principles and guidelines that had to be followed. These principles and guidelines include the following:

- Capture the power of C++ without overwhelming the programmer
- Power and efficiency must strike a balance in the design of class libraries
- The class library must be portable from one platform to another—for example, Windows 95 or Windows NT
- The transition from the use of API function calls to the use of class libraries is to be as simple as possible
- Traditional functions calls can be mixed with the class libraries

From the onset, the design team felt that a well-designed application had to start with a well-designed class library. The MFC classes are designed to be small in size and fast in execution speed. The current implementation of the MFC is easy to use with speeds approaching those of the older function libraries of C.

The MFC classes were developed so that new classes were named in a fashion similar to the function names known by experienced procedure-oriented Windows programmers. Microsoft achieved these results by carefully naming and designing class features. The "mixed-mode" concept was also implemented. With this approach, classes and traditional function calls can be intermixed in the same source code.

The original version of the MFC was designed to be portable. Windows NT was already on the market, and these programmers knew that Windows 95 was on the horizon. This dynamic architecture allowed the classes to be easily scaled to the growing Windows environment. Thus, the Microsoft Foundation Class library is fully integrated across both platforms, Windows NT and Windows 95.

KEY MFC FEATURES

Class libraries for Windows are available from other C++ compiler manufacturers, but Microsoft claims several real advantages for its Foundation Class library:

- Data object type determination at run time. T his permits a dynamic manipulation of a field when classes are instantiated.
- Diagnostic support that includes the ability to send information about objects to a file and also to validate member variables.
- Extensive exception-handling design that makes application code less subject to failure.
- Reduction of switch/case statements that are prone to error. Messages are mapped to member functions within a class. Direct message-to-method mapping is available for all messages.
- Same class-naming convention as the conventional function-based Windows API. Thus, the action of a method is immediately recognizable from its name.
- Small code means fast implementation. With minimal object code overhead, MFC applications execute almost as quickly as conventional C Windows applications.
- Support for all Windows controls, dialog boxes, functions, GDI graphics, messages, menus, and dialog boxes.
- Support for the Component Object Model.

Traditional procedure-oriented Windows programmers will appreciate two of these features. First, the familiar class-naming convention and the message-to-method mapping. Secondly, the elimination of error-prone switch/case statements, such as the one shown in the WinVer.cpp application of Chapter 4.

As a developer you will appreciate Microsoft's commitment to better diagnostics and the small code overhead imposed by the MFC library.

A PARENT CLASS, COBJECT

A class library, such as the MFC, develops a hierarchy of classes by deriving characteristics from a base or parent class.

Microsoft uses a few classes as base or parent classes. Additional classes, in the library, are then derived from the parent classes. **CObject** is the one parent class used extensively in developing Windows applications. The MFC library header files, located in the MFC/INCLUDE subdirectory, provide a wealth of information on defined classes.

CObject is defined in the afx.h header file. This code has been edited slightly for clarity.

```
class CObject
{
public:
  virtual CRuntimeClass* GetRuntimeClass() const;

virtual ~CObject();
  void* operator new(size_t, void* p);
  void* operator new(size_t nSize);
  void operator delete(void* p);
  void* operator new(size_t nSize,
                    LPCSTR lpszFileName, int nLine);

protected:
  CObject();

private:
  CObject(const CObject& objectSrc);
  void operator=(const CObject& objectSrc);

public:
  BOOL IsSerializable() const;
  BOOL IsKindOf(const CRuntimeClass* pClass) const;
  virtual void Serialize(CArchive& ar);
  virtual void AssertValid() const;
  virtual void Dump(CDumpContext& dc) const;

public:
  static CRuntimeClass AFXAPI_DATA classCObject;
};
```

If you view the previous listing, notice which components make up this class definition. First, like most class definitions, **CObject** is divided into public, protected, and private parts. **CObject** also provides normal and dynamic type checking and serialization. Dynamic type checking allows the type of object to be determined at run time. The state of the object can be saved to a storage medium, such as a disk, through a concept called *persistence.* This object persistence permits class member functions to also be persistent, permitting retrieval of object data.

Child classes are derived from parent classes. **CGdiObject** and **CDC** are examples of classes derived from **CObject**. Here is a portion of the **CDC** definition found in the afxwin.h header file. Again, this partial listing has been edited for clarity.

```
class CDC : public CObject
{
  DECLARE_DYNCREATE(CDC)
public:

// Attributes
  HDC m_hDC;
  HDC m_hAttribDC;
  operator HDC() const;
  HDC GetSafeHdc() const;
      .
      .
      .
  static CDC* PASCAL FromHandle(HDC hDC);
  static void PASCAL DeleteTempMap();
  BOOL Attach(HDC hDC);
  HDC Detach();

  virtual void SetAttribDC(HDC hDC);
  virtual void SetOutputDC(HDC hDC);
  virtual void ReleaseAttribDC();
  virtual void ReleaseOutputDC();

  BOOL IsPrinting() const;

  CPen* GetCurrentPen() const;
  CBrush* GetCurrentBrush() const;
  CPalette* GetCurrentPalette() const;
  CFont* GetCurrentFont() const;
  CBitmap* GetCurrentBitmap() const;

// Constructors
  CDC();
  BOOL CreateDC(LPCTSTR lpszDriverName,
                LPCTSTR lpszDeviceName,
    LPCTSTR lpszOutput, const void* lpInitData);
  BOOL CreateIC(LPCTSTR lpszDriverName,
                LPCTSTR lpszDeviceName,
    LPCTSTR lpszOutput, const void* lpInitData);
  BOOL CreateCompatibleDC(CDC* pDC);

  BOOL DeleteDC();
      .
      .
      .
```

```
// Drawing-Attribute Functions
  COLORREF GetBkColor() const;
  int GetBkMode() const;
  int GetPolyFillMode() const;
  int GetROP2() const;
  int GetStretchBltMode() const;
  COLORREF GetTextColor() const;
     .
     .
     .
  CPoint GetCurrentPosition() const;
  CPoint MoveTo(int x, int y);
  CPoint MoveTo(POINT point);
  BOOL LineTo(int x, int y);
  BOOL LineTo(POINT point);
  BOOL Arc(int x1, int y1, int x2, int y2,
          int x3, int y3, int x4, int y4);
  BOOL Arc(LPCRECT lpRect, POINT ptStart, POINT ptEnd);
  BOOL Polyline(LPPOINT lpPoints, int nCount);
     .
     .
     .
  BOOL Rectangle(int x1, int y1, int x2, int y2);
  BOOL Rectangle(LPCRECT lpRect);
  BOOL RoundRect(int x1, int y1, int x2,
                int y2, int x3, int y3);
  BOOL RoundRect(LPCRECT lpRect, POINT point);
```

CDC and its member functions allow drawing all of the basic graphics primitives for Windows. These graphics primitives include lines, circles, arcs, polylines, rectangles, rounded rectangles, and so on.

While Microsoft has provided detailed information about the MFC library, it is not really necessary to completely understand the class definitions to use them efficiently.

For example, in traditional C Windows applications, the **DeleteObject()** function can be called with the following syntax:

```
DeleteObject(hPen); /*hPen is the pen handle*/
```

In C++, when using the MFC library, the same results will be achieved by accessing the member function with the following syntax:

```
newpen.DeleteObject(); //newpen is current pen
```

While this is a simple example, you should see that switching between C Windows function calls and class library objects can be intuitive. Microsoft has used this same approach in developing all Windows classes. This makes for a very easy transition from the traditional function calls used in procedure-oriented applications to Microsoft Foundation Class library objects.

Parent Class Hierarchy

Table 7.1 lists important 32-bit MFC library classes. All classes in this table are derived from **Cobject**.

Table 7.1: MFC Parent Class Hierarchy

```
Cobject
  CException
    CMemoryException
    CFileException
    CArchiveException
    CNotSupportedException
    CUserException
    COleException
      COleDispatchException
    CDBException
  CFile
    CStdioFile
    CMemFile
    COleStreamFile
  CDC
    CClientDC
    CWindowDC
    CPaintDC
    CMetaFileDC
  CGdiObject
    CPen
    CBrush
    CFont
    CBitmap
    CPalette
    CRgn
  CMenu
  CArray
  CByteArray
  CWordArray
  CDWordArray
```

Table 7.1: Continued

- CPtrArray
- CObArray
- CStringArray
- CUIntArray
- CList
- CPtrList
- CObList
- CStringList
- CMap
- CMapWordToPtr
- CMapPtrToWord
- CMapPtrToPtr
- CMapWordToOb
- CMapStringToPtr
- CMapStringToOb
- CMapStringToString
- CDatabase
- CRecordSet
- CLongBinary
- **CCmdTarget**
    - CWinThread
        - CWinApp
    - CDocTemplate
        - CSingleDocTemplate
        - CMultiDocTemplate
    - COleObjectFactory
        - COleTemplateServer
    - COlcDataSource
    - COleDropSource
    - COleDropTarget
    - COleMessageFilter
    - CDocument
        - COleDocument
            - COleLinkingDoc
                - COleServerDoc
    - CDocItem
    - COleClientItem
    - COleServerItem
- **CWnd**
    - CFrameWnd
        - CMDIChildWnd
        - CMDIFrameWnd
        - CMiniFrameWnd
        - COleIPFrameWnd
    - CControlBar
        - CToolBar

Continued on the next page.

Table 7.1: Continued

```
        CStatusBar
        CDialogBar
        COleResizeBar
    CSplitterWnd
    CPropertySheet
    CDialog
        COleDialog
            COleInsertDialog
            COleChangeIconDialog
            COlePasteSpecialDialog
            COleConvertDialog
            COleBusyDialog
            COleLinksDialog
                COleUpdateDialog
    CFileDialog
    CColorDialog
    CFontDialog
    CPrintDialog
    CFindReplaceDialog
    CPropertyPage
    CView
        CScrollView
            CFormView
                CRecordView
    CEditView
    CStatic
    CButton
        CBitmapButton
    CListBox
    CComboBox
    CScrollBar
    CEdit
```

Table 2 is a list of 32-bit Run-time Object Model Support.

Table 7.2: Run-Time Object Model Support

```
CArchive
CCmdUI
CCreateContext
CDataExchange
CDumpContext
CFieldExchange
CFileStatus
CMemoryState
```

Table 7.2: Continued

```
COleDataObject
COleDispatchDriver
CPoint
CPrintInfo
CRect
CRectTracker
CRuntimeClass
CSize
CString
CTime
CTimeSpan
CTypedPtrArray
CTypedPtrList
CTypedPtrMap
```

Tables 7.1 and 7.2 will help you maintain an understanding of where classes fit into the overall hierarchy as you continue your study of the MFC in future chapters. Mark this spot!

An MFC Application, WinVerMFC.cpp

In Chapter 4, we developed a simple procedure-oriented application named WinVer.cpp. The purpose of that application was to do the following:

- Draw simple GDI graphics in the client area
- Establish a window on the screen
- Illustrate the older procedure-oriented approach to Windows programming
- Make a calculation to determine whether the operating system was Windows NT or Windows 95

In this section, we'll tackle the same goals, except this time we'll write object-oriented code and take advantage of the MFC library.

The WinVerMFC.h Header File

The WinVerMFC.h header file is used to indicate class definitions that are unique to the application. The definitions for two classes are contained in this file. First, **CMainWnd** is derived from Microsoft's **CWinApp**. Next, **CWinVerMFCApp** is derived from Microsoft's **CFrameWnd**.

Here is the WinVerMFC.h header file listing:

```
class CMainWnd : public CFrameWnd
{
public:
  CMainWnd();
  afx_msg void OnPaint();
  DECLARE_MESSAGE_MAP();
};

class CWinVerMFCApp : public CWinApp
{
public:
  BOOL InitInstance();
};
```

Note: *Putting these class definitions in a separate header file is a matter of style—a style of programming encouraged by Microsoft.*

The class **CWinVerMFC** overrides the member function, **InitInstance()**, of **CWinApp**. You will find that overriding member functions occurs frequently. By overriding **InitInstance()**, you can customize the initialization and execution of the application. In **CWinApp**, it is also possible to override **InitApplication()**, **ExitInstance()**, and **OnIdle()**, but for most applications this will not be necessary.

Here is an edited portion of the **CWinApp** class description, as found in the afxwin.h header file:

```
class CWinApp : public CObject
{
  DECLARE_DYNAMIC(CWinApp)
public:
  CWinApp(const char* pszAppName=NULL);
  void SetCurrentHandles();

  const char* m_pszAppName;
  HANDLE m_hInstance;
  HANDLE m_hPrevInstance;
  LPSTR m_lpCmdLine;
  int m_nCmdShow;

CWnd* m_pMainWnd;

  HCURSOR LoadCursor(LPSTR lpCursorName);
  HCURSOR LoadCursor(WORD nIDCursor);
```

```
    HCURSOR LoadStandardCursor(LPSTR lpCursorName);
    HCURSOR LoadOEMCursor(WORD nIDCursor);

    HICON LoadIcon(LPSTR lpIconName);
    HICON LoadIcon(WORD nIDIcon);
    HICON LoadStandardIcon(LPSTR lpIconName);
    HICON LoadOEMIcon(WORD nIDIcon);

    BOOL PumpMessage();

    virtual BOOL InitApplication();
    virtual BOOL InitInstance();

    virtual int Run();

    virtual BOOL PreTranslateMessage(MSG* pMsg);
    virtual BOOL OnIdle(LONG lCount);
    virtual int ExitInstance();

protected:
  MSG m_msgCur;
};
```

The **CWinApp** class is responsible for establishing and implementing the Windows message loop. Message loops were discussed in Chapters 2 to 4. This action alone eliminates many lines of repetitive code.

As you continue examining the WinVerMFC.h header file, notice that **CMainWnd** contains a function declaration, **OnPaint()**, and the addition of a message map. For member functions such as **OnPaint()**, the **afx_msg** keyword is used instead of **virtual**. **OnPaint()** is a member function of the **CFrameWnd** class that the **CMainWnd** class overrides. This allows the client area of the window to be altered. The **OnPaint()** function is automatically called when a WM_PAINT message is sent to a **CMainWnd** object.

DECLARE_MESSAGE_MAP is used in virtually all object-oriented MFC Windows applications. This permits class overrides when handling certain messages. (See the body of the source code.) The MFC makes use of message maps, instead of virtual functions, because it is more space efficient.

The WinVerMFC.CPP Application File

The C++ source code file is straightforward. Examine the complete WinVerMFC.cpp file, which follows, and notice the length of the code listing.

```
//
// WinVerMFC.cpp
// A 32-bit application for Windows 95 or Windows NT.
// This application illustrates the newer
// object-oriented approach for designing
// Windows 95 and/or Windows NT applications.
// The program determines if your operating system is
// Windows 95 or Windows NT.
// Copyright (c) 1996 William H. Murray and Chris H. Pappas
//

#include <afxwin.h>
#include "WinVerMFC.h"

CWinVerMFCApp theApp;

CMainWnd::CMainWnd()
{
  Create(NULL,"Windows 95 or Windows NT?",
         WS_OVERLAPPEDWINDOW,rectDefault,NULL,NULL);
}

void CMainWnd::OnPaint()
{
  CPaintDC dc(this);

  DWORD dwVersion;
  char szVersion[25];
  int i;

  dwVersion=GetVersion();

  dc.Ellipse(10,10,210,210);
  dc.Ellipse(220,10,540,210);

  for (i=60;i>10;i-=10)
    dc.Rectangle(320-i,380-i,320+i,380+i);

if (dwVersion < 0x80000000) {
  wsprintf(szVersion,
          "This is Windows NT, Version %u.%u",
          (LOBYTE(LOWORD(dwVersion))),
          (HIBYTE(LOWORD(dwVersion))));
    dc.TextOut(210,240,szVersion,strlen(szVersion));
  } else {
    wsprintf(szVersion,
            "This is Windows 95, Version %u.%u",
            (LOBYTE(LOWORD(dwVersion))),
            (HIBYTE(LOWORD(dwVersion))));
    dc.TextOut(210,240,szVersion,strlen(szVersion));
    }
}
```

```
BEGIN_MESSAGE_MAP(CMainWnd,CFrameWnd)
  ON_WM_PAINT()
END_MESSAGE_MAP()

BOOL CWinVerMFCApp::InitInstance()
{
  m_pMainWnd=new CMainWnd();
  m_pMainWnd->ShowWindow(m_nCmdShow);
  m_pMainWnd->UpdateWindow();

  return TRUE;
}
```

The previous object-oriented code listing produces a program with equivalent results to the WinVer.cpp application from Chapter 4. In the next sections we'll examine the details concerning the various parts of this source code file.

The afxwin.h Header File The first header file to be included in the source code listing is afxwin.h. The afxwin.h header file provides the entrance to the world of MFC programming. This header file is equivalent to the windows.h header file used by procedure-oriented applications. Like its windows.h counterpart, this header file calls all subsequent header files, including windows.h, as they are needed. Using one header file also aids in creating precompiled header files. Precompiled header files save time when repeated compilation is being done during application development.

Note: *You'll see extremely large precompiled header files, files with .pch extensions, after you build an application. They are only useful where subsequent rebuilds will take place.*

We recommend that you print a copy of afxwin.h for future reference as you develop applications using the MFC library.

Note: *The 32-bit version of afxwin.h is approximately 100 pages in length.*

The CFrameWnd Class The application window, established by the **CMainWnd** class, is defined from the base class, **CFrameWnd.** Here, the CMainWnd constructor defines the window style:

```
CMainWnd::CMainWnd()
{
  Create(NULL,"Windows 95 or Windows NT?",
         WS_OVERLAPPEDWINDOW,rectDefault,NULL,NULL); }
```

The constructor for the class, **CMainWnd()**, calls the **Create()** member function to establish initial window parameters. In this application, the window's style and caption are provided as parameters. It is also possible to specify a menu name and an accelerator table with the **Create()** member function.

Here is a small edited portion of **CFrameWnd**, also found in the afxwin.h header file:

```
class CFrameWnd : public CWnd
{
  DECLARE_DYNAMIC(CFrameWnd)

protected:
  HANDLE m_hAccelTable;

public:
  static const CRect rectDefault;

  CFrameWnd();

  BOOL LoadAccelTable(const char FAR* lpAccelTableName);
  BOOL Create(const char FAR* lpClassName,
              const char FAR* lpWindowName,
              DWORD dwStyle = WS_OVERLAPPEDWINDOW,
              const RECT& rect = rectDefault,
              const CWnd* pParentWnd = NULL,
              const char FAR* lpMenuName = NULL);

public:
  virtual ~CFrameWnd();
  virtual CFrameWnd* GetParentFrame();
  virtual CFrameWnd* GetChildFrame();

protected:
virtual BOOL PreTranslateMessage(MSG* pMsg); };
```

Notice that the first parameter in the **Create()** member function allows a class name to be specified in compliance with the traditional Windows API **RegisterClass()** function. Normally, this will be set to NULL in the applications you develop, and a class name will not be required.

Using Member Functions Recall that the derived **CWinVerMFCApp** class object overrode the **InitInstance()** member function. Here is how this application implements **InitInstance()**:

```
BOOL CWinVerMFCApp::InitInstance()
{
  m_pMainWnd=new CMainWnd();
```

```
  m_pMainWnd->ShowWindow(m_nCmdShow);
  m_pMainWnd->UpdateWindow();

  return TRUE;
}
```

The **new** operator invokes the constructor, **CMainWnd**, discussed in the previous section. The *m_pMainWnd* member variable (*m_* indicates a member variable) holds the location for the application's main window. The member function, **ShowWindow()**, is required to display the window on the screen. The parameter *m_nCmdShow* is initialized by the application's constructor. The **UpdateWindow()** member function displays and paints the window being sent to the screen.

The Constructor The application's constructor is invoked at startup with this piece of code:

```
CWinVerApp theApp;
```

The application code for this example is very simple and straightforward. The application merely establishes a window; it does not permit you to draw anything in the window.

The OnPaint() Message Handler The function part of this application results from the inclusion of the **OnPaint()** message handler function. Examine the following portion of source code:

```
void CMainWnd::OnPaint()
{
  CPaintDC dc(this);

  DWORD dwVersion;
  char szVersion[25];
  int i;

  dwVersion=GetVersion();

  dc.Ellipse(10,10,210,210);
  dc.Ellipse(220,10,540,210);

  for (i=60;i>10;i-=10)
    dc.Rectangle(320-i,380-i,320+i,380+i);

  if (dwVersion < 0x80000000) {
      wsprintf(szVersion,
              "This is Windows NT, Version %u.%u",
              (LOBYTE(LOWORD(dwVersion))),
              (HIBYTE(LOWORD(dwVersion))));
```

```
    dc.TextOut(210,240,szVersion,strlen(szVersion));
  } else {
    wsprintf(szVersion,
            "This is Windows 95, Version %u.%u",
            (LOBYTE(LOWORD(dwVersion))),
            (HIBYTE(LOWORD(dwVersion))));
    dc.TextOut(210,240,szVersion,strlen(szVersion));
    }
}
```

A device context is created for handling WM_PAINT messages. Any Windows GDI functions are encapsulated in the device context in this section. When the **OnPaint()** function has ended, the destructor for **CPaintDC** is called automatically.

The actual code used in this portion of the program is identical to the code used in the procedure-oriented application, WinVer.cpp, in Chapter 4. Return to Chapter 4 for a discussion of how the correct version of the operating system is being determined.

This application uses a fairly short message map, as the following code indicates:

```
BEGIN_MESSAGE_MAP(CMainWnd,CFrameWnd)
  ON_WM_PAINT()
END_MESSAGE_MAP()
```

Two classes are specified by BEGIN_MESSAGE_MAP: **CMainWnd** and **CFrameWnd**. **CMainWnd** is the target class, and **CFrameWnd** is a class based on **CWnd**. The **ON_WM_PAINT()** function handles all WM_PAINT messages and directs them to the **OnPaint()** member function just discussed. In later chapters you'll see many additional functions added to the message map.

Remember that one of the biggest advantages of using message maps is the elimination of error-prone switch/case statements. Switch/case statements are a hallmark of procedure-oriented Windows applications.

Building the WinVerMFC Application

In Chapter 4 you learned how to enter your program code in the compiler's editor, and also how to create a project workspace and set various compiler options. Developing MFC applications is done in the same manner. Enter the source code, WinVerMFC.cpp, and the header file code, WinVerMFC.h, for this application. Next, create a project workspace named WinVerMFC. When you create the project workspace, make sure that you mark it as an MFC application. This can be done from the compiler's Build menu by selecting the Settings... menu item. When the selection is made, the Project Settings dialog box will appear, as shown in Figure 7.1. From the list box, select the option Use MFC in a Static Library. Otherwise, you will get a series of strange errors when building the executable.

Once you have entered the source and header code and created a project workspace with the proper compiler options set, the time has arrived to build the application. From the compiler's Build menu, select the Rebuild All menu item. If no errors occur, run the application. Of course, the screen will look just like its procedure-oriented counterpart from Chapter 4, as shown in Figure 7.2.

This 32-bit application can also be run under Windows NT.

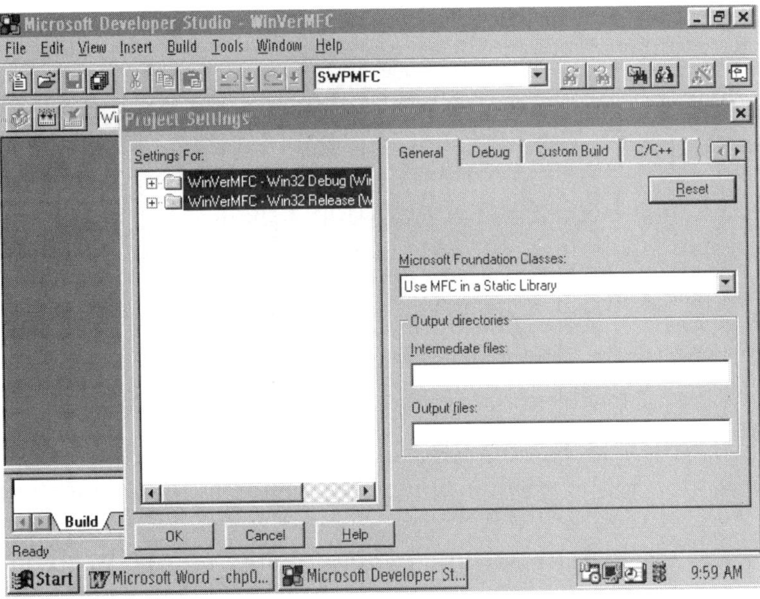

Figure 7.1: Selecting a static MFC library for the build operation.

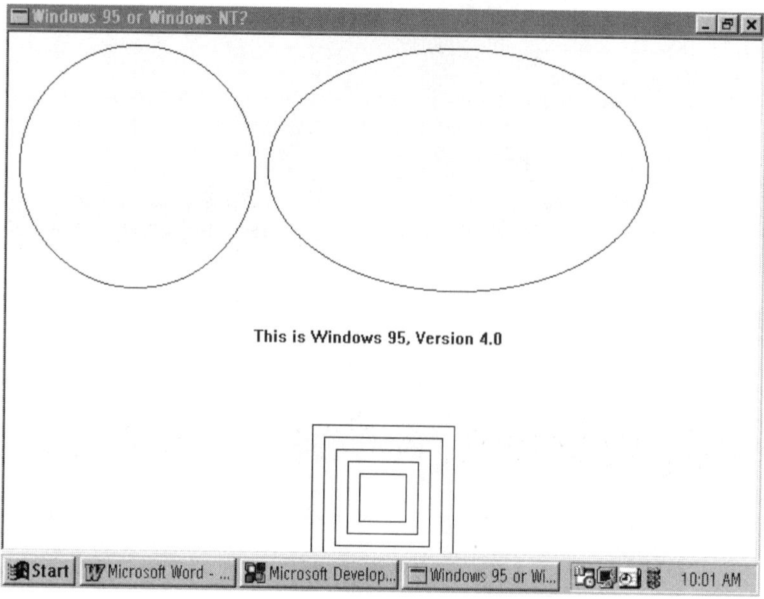

Figure 7.2: The window created by WinVerMFC.cpp when running under Windows 95.

FILE SIZES

Remember that the Microsoft Visual C++ compiler is an optimizing compiler. In Chapter 4 we built a similar procedure-oriented example using the compiler's defaults. Let's compare file sizes between the procedure-oriented version and the object-oriented version developed in this chapter.

In Chapter 4, the debug version of the procedure-oriented WinVer.cpp application was approximately 72 KB in size. The release version was approximately 39 KB in size.

If you check your file sizes in this chapter, you'll find that the object-oriented WinVerMFC.cpp version has a debug file size of 932 KB and a release version size of 99 KB.

So, while the source code file lengths are much shorter for equivalent MFC applications, there is a penalty in executable file sizes to be paid when using the MFC library. The questions you must answer are: Does it matter? Is it worth it?

In the following chapters, we'll try to give you sound reasons for adopting the MFC library and the object-oriented approach.

Chapter 8

The AppWizard, a Code Generator

This chapter will introduce you to the use of Microsoft's Wizards for application development. The Microsoft AppWizard is an automatic MFC code generator that allows the programmer to specify features for an application. At this point you may be unsure why a code generator is necessary. This chapter will examine the history of Windows program development, before the use of code generators, and then make a strong case for their use. The two programming examples in this chapter will parallel the example program, WinVerMFC.cpp, developed in Chapter 7.

The first programming example will develop a single source code application whose project workspace is named NoWiz. The second programming example will develop a similar application with the use of the AppWizard. Its project workspace is named WithWiz.

As you work with the AppWizard, you might be surprised that the code generator generates several source code files for each application. Do not be alarmed. You'll discover, for example, that the source code in WithWiz is essentially the same code you will see in NoWiz. Microsoft AppWizard breaks application code into functioning units. For example, if an application is named WithWiz, you might find these five files: StdAfx.cpp, WithWiz.cpp, MainFrm.cpp, WithWizDoc.cpp, and WithWizView.cpp. The WithWiz.cpp is the main source code file for the application. The MainFrm.cpp file is used to describe the document interface for the application. The WithWizDoc.cpp file is used to describe the document data. The WithWizView.cpp file is used for viewing objects. These separate source code files are combined by the linker into a single executable application. In this case, the file would be named WithWiz.exe.

Code Generators

In Chapters 4 and 7 you learned how to develop simple procedure-oriented and object-oriented Windows applications. Since almost every Windows application establishes a basic window in the same manner, this code could be used again and again. As such, it could be copied or "boilerplated" from one application to another. Actually, the unique part of both programs found in Chapters 4 and 7 was only about 15 code lines in length. This, of course, begs the question: Why do you need a code generator when writing this code is so easy? The question is simple; the answer is multifaceted.

The Good Old Days

In 1985, Microsoft released the first version of Windows. Almost as quickly, authors such as Charles Petzold, William Murray, and Chris Pappas published C programming books for Windows. These were the good old days! Programming books concentrated on getting programmers started in the new Windows environment. People needed to know what cursors, icons, scroll bars, menus, dialog boxes, and bitmaps were and how to use them. Programs were short and to the point—

teaching a few new concepts in each chapter. These books seldom contained program code that exceeded five or six book pages in length. In the good old days, there was no need for a code generator.

For example, if a program developer saw that one application would be similar to a previous application, the developer simply cut and pasted the code from one application to the next. This redundant code could be considered a static template, with basically no changes from one application to another. The use of static code templates worked well for short procedure-oriented applications.

Life was not to remain so easy, however. Since 1985, users and programmers have learned the language of Windows. Even if you have never implemented the code for a menu or dialog box, you certainly know what they are and how they function within the Windows environment. As Windows, hardware, and compilers evolved, users and programmers alike wanted more. Life and programming was moving toward the fast lane.

Life in the Fast Lane

As hardware and software evolved, Windows evolved with it. From a sleepy 16-bit DOS overlay, we now work in a true powerful 32-bit multitasking environment under Windows 95 or Windows NT. Multitasking capabilities in Windows increased the demand for the ability to connect multiple applications. OLE was introduced as Microsoft's solution for object linking and embedding. The seamless connection was made—but not without a price.

During its evolutionary trip, Windows had continued to add new functions. Functions for multimedia sound and video, task bars, tool tips, and security more than doubled the original number of function calls. However, no evolutionary step made as many changes as the inclusion of OLE. Almost overnight, the slope of the Windows learning curve tripled. If you wanted to be a Windows programmer and be able to write applications across the broad capabilities for this environment, then you were faced with a huge task: understanding hundreds of new function calls and how to implement them.

There were a few daring pioneers who actually tackled this task and wrote procedure-oriented OLE applications. But hundreds of hours of work were involved with these projects.

Microsoft quickly saw the problem and quickly went to work on a solution. That solution is the AppWizard and ClassWizard, contained in the Visual C++ compiler. The AppWizard is a dynamic code generator that creates MFC object-oriented code templates with a set of customizable features. These features include editing, file and printing capabilities, OLE container and server support, database support, and so on.

The AppWizard instantly puts you on the Windows interstate highway, doing 65 mph., in the fast lane. Buckle up—it's the law!

The NoWiz Application

You will see shortly that Microsoft's AppWizard typically generates five separate object-oriented source code files and five separate header files. The linker then combines these files to produce the executable application.

In this section, you will see an application written with a single source code file and single header file. After all, this is the style that most C/C++ programming books use when developing simple applications. We'll then show you how Microsoft divides a single source code application into five separate source code files. Once you have seen how this is done, future AppWizard files should be less of a mystery to you.

Remember, the purpose of this section is not to build an application or explain application code. This section will illustrate how a single source code file can be broken into five source code components, similar to the technique by which Microsoft's AppWizard generates project code.

A NoWiz.rc Resource File

The AppWizard generates resource files which describe a variety of Windows resources. These resources typically include menu, dialog box, keyboard accelerator, and string table descriptions. All of these resources are described in detail in Chapters 9 through 11. We have to give you this file, without a lot of description, because it is generated by the AppWizard for even the simplest applications. This file will be named NoWiz.rc:

```
//Microsoft Visual C++ generated resource script.

#include "resource.h"

#define APSTUDIO_READONLY_SYMBOLS
//
// Generated from the TEXTINCLUDE 2 resource.
//

#include "afxres.h"

#undef APSTUDIO_READONLY_SYMBOLS

#ifdef APSTUDIO_INVOKED

//
// TEXTINCLUDE
//

1 TEXTINCLUDE DISCARDABLE
BEGIN
  "resource.h0"
END

2 TEXTINCLUDE DISCARDABLE
BEGIN
  "#include ""afxres.h"""
  "0"
END

3 TEXTINCLUDE DISCARDABLE
BEGIN
     "#define _AFX_NO_SPLITTER_RESOURCES\r\n"
     "#define _AFX_NO_OLE_RESOURCES\r\n"
     "#define _AFX_NO_TRACKER_RESOURCES\r\n"
     "#define _AFX_NO_PROPERTY_RESOURCES\r\n"
   "\r\n"
   "#if !defined(AFX_RESOURCE_DLL)||defined(AFX_TARG_ENU)\r\n"
   "#ifdef _WIN32\r\n"
   "LANGUAGE 9, 1\r\n"
   "#pragma code_page(1252)\r\n"
   "#endif\r\n"
   "#endif"
   "0"
END

#endif
```

```
//
// Icon
//

IDR_MAINFRAME           ICON        DISCARDABLE       "NoWiz.ico"

#if !defined(AFX_RESOURCE_DLL)   || defined(AFX_TARG_ENU)
#ifdef _WIN32
LANGUAGE 9, 1
#pragma code_page(1252)
#endif
IDR_NOWIZTYPE           ICON        DISCARDABLE       "NoWizDoc.ico"
#endif

#if !defined(AFX_RESOURCE_DLL) || defined(AFX_TARG_ENU)
#ifdef _WIN32
LANGUAGE 9, 1
#pragma code_page(1252)
#endif
//
// Menu
//

IDR_MAINFRAME MENU PRELOAD DISCARDABLE
BEGIN
  POPUP "&File"
  BEGIN
    MENUITEM "&New\tCtrl+N",          ID_FILE_NEW
    MENUITEM "&Open...\tCtrl+O",      ID_FILE_OPEN
    MENUITEM "&Save\tCtrl+S",         ID_FILE_SAVE
    MENUITEM "Save &As...",           ID_FILE_SAVE_AS
    MENUITEM SEPARATOR
    MENUITEM "Recent File",           ID_FILE_MRU_FILE1,GRAYED
    MENUITEM SEPARATOR
    MENUITEM "E&xit",                 ID_APP_EXIT
  END
  POPUP "&Edit"
  BEGIN
    MENUITEM "&Undo\tCtrl+Z",         ID_EDIT_UNDO
    MENUITEM SEPARATOR
    MENUITEM "Cu&t\tCtrl+X",          ID_EDIT_CUT
    MENUITEM "&Copy\tCtrl+C",         ID_EDIT_COPY
    MENUITEM "&Paste\tCtrl+V",        ID_EDIT_PASTE
  END
  POPUP "&Help"
  BEGIN
    MENUITEM "&About NoWiz...",       ID_APP_ABOUT
  END
END
```

```
//
// Accelerator
//

IDR_MAINFRAME ACCELERATORS PRELOAD MOVEABLE PURE
BEGIN
  "N",              ID_FILE_NEW,          VIRTKEY,CONTROL
  "O",              ID_FILE_OPEN,         VIRTKEY,CONTROL
  "S",              ID_FILE_SAVE,         VIRTKEY,CONTROL
  "Z",              ID_EDIT_UNDO,         VIRTKEY,CONTROL
  "X",              ID_EDIT_CUT,          VIRTKEY,CONTROL
  "C",              ID_EDIT_COPY,         VIRTKEY,CONTROL
  "V",              ID_EDIT_PASTE,        VIRTKEY,CONTROL
  VK_BACK,          ID_EDIT_UNDO,         VIRTKEY,ALT
  VK_DELETE,        ID_EDIT_CUT,          VIRTKEY,SHIFT
  VK_INSERT,        ID_EDIT_COPY,         VIRTKEY,CONTROL
  VK_INSERT,        ID_EDIT_PASTE,        VIRTKEY,SHIFT
  VK_F6,            ID_NEXT_PANE,         VIRTKEY
  VK_F6,            ID_PREV_PANE,         VIRTKEY,SHIFT END

//
// Dialog
//

IDD_ABOUTBOX DIALOG DISCARDABLE 0, 0, 217, 55
CAPTION "About NoWiz"
STYLE DS_MODALFRAME | WS_POPUP | WS_CAPTION | WS_SYSMENU
FONT 8, "MS Sans Serif"
BEGIN
  ICON              IDR_MAINFRAME,IDC_STATIC,11,17,20,20
  LTEXT             "NoWiz Version 1.0",IDC_STATIC,40,10,119,8,
                     SS_NOPREFIX
  LTEXT             "Copyright \251 1996",IDC_STATIC,40,25,119,8
  DEFPUSHBUTTON     "OK",IDOK,178,7,32,14,WS_GROUP
END

//
// Version
//

VS_VERSION_INFO     VERSIONINFO
    FILEVERSION1,0,0,1
    PRODUCTVERSION 1,0,0,1
  FILEFLAGSMASK 0x3fL
#ifdef _DEBUG
  FILEFLAGS 0x1L
#else
  FILEFLAGS 0x0L
#endif
```

```
   FILEOS 0x4L
   FILETYPE 0x1L
   FILESUBTYPE 0x0L
 BEGIN
   BLOCK "StringFileInfo"
   BEGIN
          BLOCK "040904B0"
     BEGIN
       VALUE "CompanyName", "\0"
       VALUE "FileDescription", "NOWIZ MFC Application\0"
       VALUE "FileVersion", "1, 0, 0, 1\0"
       VALUE "InternalName", "NOWIZ\0"
       VALUE "LegalCopyright", "Copyright \251 1995\0"
       VALUE "LegalTrademarks", "\0"
       VALUE "OriginalFilename","NOWIZ.EXE\0"
       VALUE "ProductName", "NOWIZ Application\0"
       VALUE "ProductVersion", "1, 0, 0, 1\0"
     END
   END
   BLOCK "VarFileInfo"
   BEGIN
     VALUE "Translation", 0x409, 1200
     END
END

//
// DESIGNINFO
//

#ifdef APSTUDIO_INVOKED
GUIDELINES DESIGNINFO DISCARDABLE
BEGIN
  IDD_ABOUTBOX, DIALOG
  BEGIN
    LEFTMARGIN, 7
    RIGHTMARGIN, 210
    TOPMARGIN, 7
    BOTTOMMARGIN, 48
  END
END
#endif

//
// String Table
//

STRINGTABLE PRELOAD DISCARDABLE
BEGIN
  IDR_MAINFRAME "NoWiz\n\nNoWiz\n\n\nNoWiz.Document\nNoWiz
                 Document"
```

```
END
STRINGTABLE PRELOAD DISCARDABLE
BEGIN
  AFX_IDS_APP_TITLE       "NoWiz"
  AFX_IDS_IDLEMESSAGE     "Ready"
END
STRINGTABLE DISCARDABLE
BEGIN
  ID_INDICATOR_EXT        "EXT"
  ID_INDICATOR_CAPS       "CAP"
  ID_INDICATOR_NUM        "NUM"
  ID_INDICATOR_SCRL       "SCRL"
  ID_INDICATOR_OVR        "OVR"
  ID_INDICATOR_REC        "REC"
END
STRINGTABLE DISCARDABLE
BEGIN
  ID_FILE_NEW             "Create a new document\nNew"
  ID_FILE_OPEN            "Open an existing document\nOpen"
  ID_FILE_CLOSE           "Close the active document\nClose"
  ID_FILE_SAVE            "Save the active document\nSave"
  ID_FILE_SAVE_AS         "Save the active document with a new name\nSave As"
  ID_APP_ABOUT            "Display program information, version number and
copyrightAbout"
  ID_APP_EXIT             "Quit the application; prompts to save documentsExit"
  ID_FILE_MRU_FILE1       "Open this document"
  ID_FILE_MRU_FILE2       "Open this document"
  ID_FILE_MRU_FILE3       "Open this document"
  ID_FILE_MRU_FILE4       "Open this document"
  ID_FILE_MRU_FILE5       "Open this document"
  ID_FILE_MRU_FILE6       "Open this document"
  ID_FILE_MRU_FILE7       "Open this document"
  ID_FILE_MRU_FILE8       "Open this document"
  ID_FILE_MRU_FILE9       "Open this document"
  ID_FILE_MRU_FILE10      "Open this document"
  ID_FILE_MRU_FILE11      "Open this document"
  ID_FILE_MRU_FILE12      "Open this document"
  ID_FILE_MRU_FILE13      "Open this document"
  ID_FILE_MRU_FILE14      "Open this document"
  ID_FILE_MRU_FILE15      "Open this document"
  ID_FILE_MRU_FILE16      "Open this document"
  ID_NEXT_PANE            "Switch to the next window pane\nNext Pane"
  ID_PREV_PANE            "Switch back to the previous window pane
                           \nPrevious Pane"
  ID_WINDOW_SPLIT         "Split the active window into panes\nSplit
  ID_EDIT_CLEAR           "Erase the selection\nErase"
  ID_EDIT_CLEAR_ALL       "Erase everything\nErase All"
  ID_EDIT_COPY            "Copy the selection and put it in the Clipboard\nCopy"
```

```
  ID_EDIT_CUT             "Cut the selection and put it on the Clipboard\nCut"
  ID_EDIT_FIND            "Find the specified text\nFind"
  ID_EDIT_PASTE           "Insert Clipboard contents\nPaste"
  ID_EDIT_REPEAT          "Repeat the last action\nRepeat"
  ID_EDIT_REPLACE         "Replace specific text with different text\nReplace"
  ID_EDIT_SELECT_ALL      "Select the entire document\nSelect All"
  ID_EDIT_UNDO            "Undo the last action\nUndo"
  ID_EDIT_REDO            "Redo the previously undone action\nRedo"
END

STRINGTABLE DISCARDABLE
BEGIN
  AFX_IDS_SCSIZE          "Change the window size"
  AFX_IDS_SCMOVE          "Change the window position"
  AFX_IDS_SCMINIMIZE      "Reduce the window to an icon"
  AFX_IDS_SCMAXIMIZE      "Enlarge the window to full size"
  AFX_IDS_SCNEXTWINDOW    "Switch to the next document window"
  AFX_IDS_SCPREVWINDOW    "Switch to the previous document window"
  AFX_IDS_SCCLOSE         "Close the active window and prompts to save the
                           documents"
  AFX_IDS_SCRESTORE       "Restore the window to normal size"
  AFX_IDS_SCTASKLIST      "Activate Task List"
END

#endif

#ifndef APSTUDIO_INVOKED
//
// Generated from the TEXTINCLUDE 3 resource.
//

#define _AFX_NO_SPLITTER_RESOURCES
#define _AFX_NO_OLE_RESOURCES
#define _AFX_NO_TRACKER_RESOURCES
#define _AFX_NO_PROPERTY_RESOURCES

#if !defined(AFX_RESOURCE_DLL) || defined(AFX_TARG_ENU)
#ifdef _WIN32
LANGUAGE 9, 1
#pragma code_page(1252)
#endif
#include "NoWiz.rc2"
#include "afxres.rc"
#endif

#endif
```

This is a complicated resource script file. As you glance through the listing, you might be able to pick out the description of the application's menus, dialog boxes, string tables, and accelerators. More on these features in Chapters 9 to 11.

The NoWiz.h Header File

The NoWiz.h header file contains the class descriptions, similar to the header file used in the previous chapter.

```
#define VC_EXTRALEAN

#include <afxwin.h>
#include <afxext.h>
#include "resource.h"

class CNoWizApp : public CWinApp
{
public:
  CNoWizApp();

  //{{AFX_VIRTUAL(CNoWizApp)
  public:
  virtual BOOL InitInstance();
  //}}AFX_VIRTUAL

  //{{AFX_MSG(CNoWizApp)
  afx_msg void OnAppAbout();
  //}}AFX_MSG
  DECLARE_MESSAGE_MAP()
};

class CMainFrame : public CFrameWnd
{
protected:
  CMainFrame();
  DECLARE_DYNCREATE(CMainFrame)

public:
  //{{AFX_VIRTUAL(CMainFrame)
  virtual BOOL PreCreateWindow(CREATESTRUCT& cs);
  //}}AFX_VIRTUAL
  virtual ~CMainFrame();

protected:
  //{{AFX_MSG(CMainFrame)
  //}}AFX_MSG
  DECLARE_MESSAGE_MAP()
};

class CNoWizDoc : public CDocument
{
protected:
  CNoWizDoc();
  DECLARE_DYNCREATE(CNoWizDoc)
public:
```

```
  //{{AFX_VIRTUAL(CNoWizDoc)
  public:
  virtual BOOL OnNewDocument();
  virtual void Serialize(CArchive& ar);
 //}}AFX_VIRTUAL
  virtual ~CNoWizDoc();
protected:
  //{{AFX_MSG(CNoWizDoc)
  //}}AFX_MSG
  DECLARE_MESSAGE_MAP()
};

class CNoWizView : public CView
{
protected:
  CNoWizView();
  DECLARE_DYNCREATE(CNoWizView)

public:
  CNoWizDoc* GetDocument();
  //{{AFX_VIRTUAL(CNoWizView)
  public:
  virtual void OnDraw(CDC* pDC);
  virtual BOOL PreCreateWindow(CREATESTRUCT& cs);
  virtual void OnPaint();
  protected:
  //}}AFX_VIRTUAL
  virtual ~CNoWizView();

  protected:
  //{{AFX_MSG(CNoWizView)
  //}}AFX_MSG
  DECLARE_MESSAGE_MAP()
};

inline CNoWizDoc* CNoWizView::GetDocument()
  { return (CNoWizDoc*)m_pDocument; }
```

Compare this listing with the simple header file of the previous chapter. Things seem to be getting a bit more complicated!

The NoWiz.cpp Source Code

The following listing, named NoWiz.cpp, is the complete C++ source code for this project. Examine this listing and notice "component parts" similar to the source code in the previous chapter.

```
//
// NoWiz.cpp
// A 32-bit application for Windows 95 or Windows NT.
// This application contains, in one source code file
// and one header file, all of the equivalent code that
// will be generated by AppWizard in five separate
// source code files and five separate header files.
// Copyright (c) 1996 William H. Murray and Chris H. Pappas

#include "NoWiz.h"

BEGIN_MESSAGE_MAP(CNoWizApp, CWinApp)
  //{{AFX_MSG_MAP(CNoWizApp)
  ON_COMMAND(ID_APP_ABOUT, OnAppAbout)
  //}}AFX_MSG_MAP
  ON_COMMAND(ID_FILE_NEW, CWinApp::OnFileNew)
  ON_COMMAND(ID_FILE_OPEN, CWinApp::OnFileOpen)
END_MESSAGE_MAP()

CNoWizApp::CNoWizApp()
{
}

CNoWizApp theApp;

BOOL CNoWizApp::InitInstance()
{

  LoadStdProfileSettings();

  CSingleDocTemplate* pDocTemplate;
  pDocTemplate = new CSingleDocTemplate(
    IDR_MAINFRAME,
    RUNTIME_CLASS(CNoWizDoc),
    RUNTIME_CLASS(CMainFrame),
    RUNTIME_CLASS(CNoWizView));
    AddDocTemplate(pDocTemplate);

    CCommandLineInfo cmdInfo;
    ParseCommandLine(cmdInfo);

    if (!ProcessShellCommand(cmdInfo))
      return FALSE;

  return TRUE;
}

class CAboutDlg : public CDialog
{
public:
  CAboutDlg();

  //{{AFX_DATA(CAboutDlg)
```

```
    enum { IDD = IDD_ABOUTBOX };
    //}}AFX_DATA

    //{{AFX_VIRTUAL(CAboutDlg)
    protected:
    virtual void DoDataExchange(CDataExchange* pDX);
    //}}AFX_VIRTUAL

 protected:
   //{{AFX_MSG(CAboutDlg)
   // No message handlers
   //}}AFX_MSG
   DECLARE_MESSAGE_MAP()
};

CAboutDlg::CAboutDlg() : CDialog(CAboutDlg::IDD)
{
  //{{AFX_DATA_INIT(CAboutDlg)
  //}}AFX_DATA_INIT
}

void CAboutDlg::DoDataExchange(CDataExchange* pDX)
{
  CDialog::DoDataExchange(pDX);
  //{{AFX_DATA_MAP(CAboutDlg)
  //}}AFX_DATA_MAP
}

BEGIN_MESSAGE_MAP(CAboutDlg, CDialog)
  //{{AFX_MSG_MAP(CAboutDlg)
    // No message handlers
  //}}AFX_MSG_MAP
END_MESSAGE_MAP()

void CNoWizApp::OnAppAbout()
{
  CAboutDlg aboutDlg;
  aboutDlg.DoModal();
}

IMPLEMENT_DYNCREATE(CMainFrame, CFrameWnd)

BEGIN_MESSAGE_MAP(CMainFrame, CFrameWnd)
  //{{AFX_MSG_MAP(CMainFrame)
  //}}AFX_MSG_MAP
END_MESSAGE_MAP()

CMainFrame::CMainFrame()
{
}

CMainFrame::~CMainFrame()
```

```
{
}

BOOL CMainFrame::PreCreateWindow(CREATESTRUCT& cs)
{
  return CFrameWnd::PreCreateWindow(cs);
}

IMPLEMENT_DYNCREATE(CNoWizDoc, CDocument)

BEGIN_MESSAGE_MAP(CNoWizDoc, CDocument)
  //{{AFX_MSG_MAP(CNoWizDoc)
  //}}AFX_MSG_MAP
END_MESSAGE_MAP()

CNoWizDoc::CNoWizDoc()
{
}

CNoWizDoc::~CNoWizDoc()
{
}

BOOL CNoWizDoc::OnNewDocument()
{
  if (!CDocument::OnNewDocument())
    return FALSE;

    return TRUE;
}

void CNoWizDoc::Serialize(Curative& ar)
{
  if (ar.IsStoring())
  {
  }
  else
  {
  }
}

IMPLEMENT_DYNCREATE(CNoWizView, CView)

BEGIN_MESSAGE_MAP(CNoWizView, CView)
  //{{AFX_MSG_MAP(CNoWizView)
  ON_WM_PAINT()
  //}}AFX_MSG_MAP
END_MESSAGE_MAP()

CNoWizView::CNoWizView()
{
}
```

```
CNoWizView::~CNoWizView()
{
}

BOOL CNoWizView::PreCreateWindow(CREATESTRUCT& cs)
{
  return CView::PreCreateWindow(cs);
}

void CNoWizView::OnDraw(CDC* pDC)
{
  CNoWizDoc* pDoc = GetDocument();
  ASSERT_VALID(pDoc);
}

void CNoWizView::OnPaint()
{
  CPaintDC dc(this);

  DWORD dwVersion;
  char szVersion[25];
  int i;

  dwVersion=GetVersion();

  dc.Ellipse(10,10,210,210);
  dc.Ellipse(220,10,540,210);

  for (i=60;i>10;i-=10)
    dc.Rectangle(320-i,380-i,320+i,380+i);

if (dwVersion < 0x80000000) {
  wsprintf(szVersion,
          "This is Windows NT, Version %u.%u",
          (LOBYTE(LOWORD(dwVersion))),
          (HIBYTE(LOWORD(dwVersion))));
  dc.TextOut(210,240,szVersion,strlen(szVersion));
} else {
  wsprintf(szVersion,
          "This is Windows 95, Version %u.%u",
          (LOBYTE(LOWORD(dwVersion))),
          (HIBYTE(LOWORD(dwVersion))));
  dc.TextOut(210,240,szVersion,strlen(szVersion));
  }
}
```

Remember, these files weren't included in this chapter for you to enter and build an application. Rather, they have been included to show you how Microsoft's AppWizard generates similar code in five separate source code files.

Our NoWiz.cpp application is identical in operation and *almost* identical in actual code to the AppWizard's generated project named WithWiz. We will examine and explain each portion of the WithWiz.cpp project in the remaining section of the book.

Why and How Did They Do That?

In Chapters 5 through 7, you learned about object-oriented programming and how to develop Windows applications using the Microsoft Foundation Class library. These chapters rely heavily on the use of redundant code for establishing and registering a window. By cutting and pasting this code, you could concentrate on the new features of a particular application. This code became a boilerplate or template.

Now imagine an application where you want to incorporate file I/O capabilities, such as New, Open, or Save, or editing capabilities, such as Cut, Copy, or Paste. While these features often use a familiar menu style, that style was not part of our earlier applications. Continue to extend your thinking a little farther. Imagine creating applications with a single or multiple document interface (SDI or MDI) and object linking and embedding (OLE) features. It should be clear that there is no single piece of programming code that will allow us to pick and choose from this list of programming features.

Microsoft's AppWizard is a *dynamic* code generator. The AppWizard depends heavily on the Microsoft Foundation Class library and only generates object-oriented compatible code. The AppWizard generates, in a six-step process, a code template that will allow you to select just those features needed for your application. However, it is still up to you to write the code for your unique application.

A close relative of the AppWizard is the ClassWizard. The ClassWizard allows you to add classes or customize existing classes. The ClassWizard is used after the AppWizard generates the base code. The ClassWizard is selected from the menu.

Be warned, however, that there is a learning curve that must be overcome before you will become comfortable using these wizards. We strongly recommend that you review

Chapters 5 through 7. These are the chapters that deal with object-oriented design and the Microsoft Foundation Class library (MFC).

Why

When program developers were creating applications in the days when procedure-oriented coding was king, applications were not as complicated. That is not to say that there weren't some hefty programming files, but remember these were the days before video interfacing, security considerations (under Windows NT), and OLE. With added capabilities, program size has grown considerably.

Developers found that when, for example, OLE features were added to a project, the code size grew by thousands of lines. What they also learned was that the code was often similar between applications.

Microsoft realized that for large commercial applications, it would be a wise decision to divide code into several source code files. Thus, the AppWizard generates five source code files and five header files to start every project. As your project grows, you will likely create even more files.

How

In the previous section, we developed a single source code and single header file application to illustrate how a single source code application would be divided if it were generated by the AppWizard.

Note: *Actually, we reverse engineered the NoWiz project from information we gained from the WithWiz project discussed in the next section.*

Refer to the NoWiz.cpp source code file in the previous section. Figure 8.1 shows how that file would be divided if it were generated by the AppWizard.

In the next section, we'll generate the WithWiz project by using the AppWizard. You're going to sec almost identical code divided into five separate source code files.

Now that you know how it's done, get ready to *develop* a project without ever writing one single line of code! What is even better is that when we're ready to develop OLE projects,

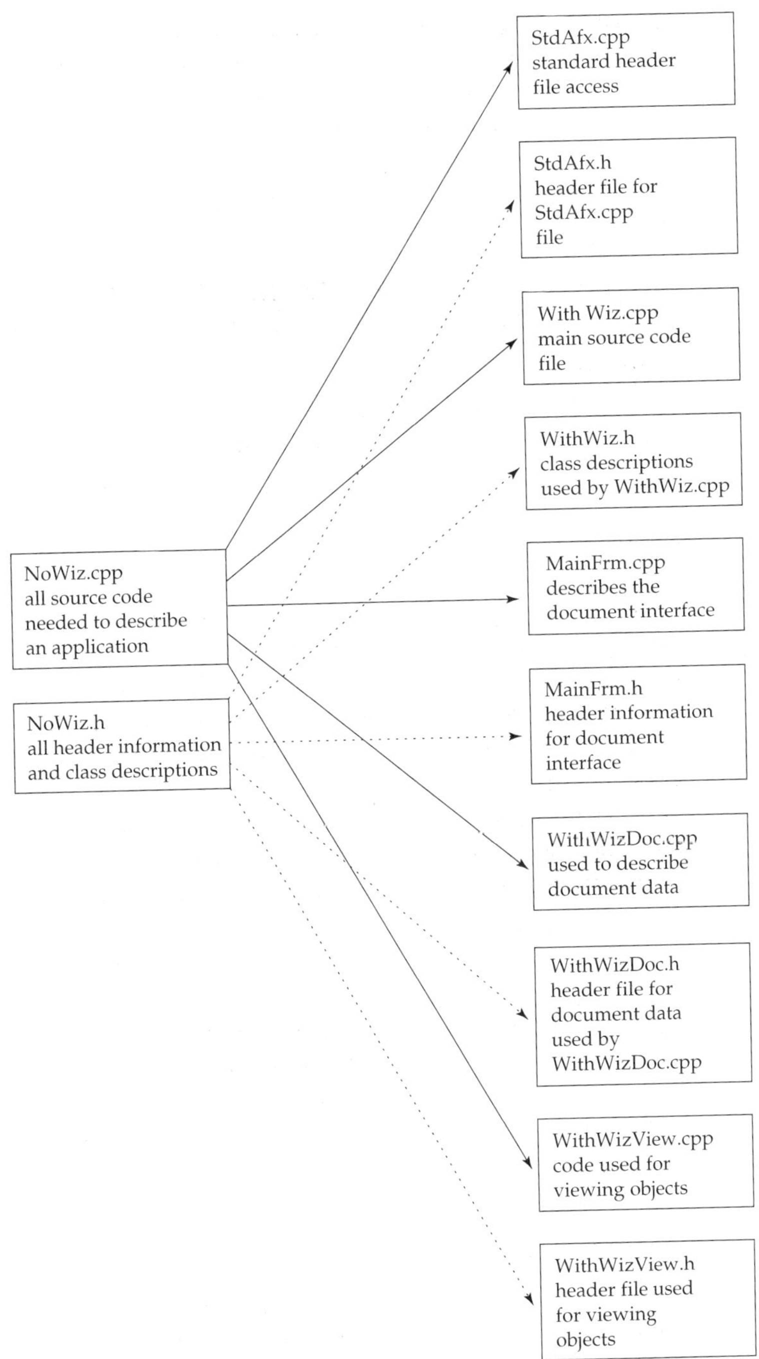

Figure 8.1: Dividing a single source code file into five separate source code components.

we'll have access to more than 20,000 programming lines of OLE code. Just remember, using the AppWizard means that it's code that you'll never have to write.

Working with the AppWizard and ClassWizard

In this section, you will learn all of the steps necessary to create a simple application named WithWiz, using the AppWizard and ClassWizard tools. In the first section, we'll discuss the six common steps that will take you through the development of code with the AppWizard. Then we'll show you how to use the ClassWizard to incorporate a WM_PAINT message handler into the AppWizard's code.

Start your Visual C++ compiler and follow along as we create the WithWiz project using this simple step-by-step approach.

The AppWizard

To create a new project and workspace, select the File menu and then the New menu item from the menu list given by the Visual C++ compiler. When this selection is made, a dialog box will appear that allows you to select a new project workspace, as shown in Figure 8.2.

Once selected, the New Project Workspace dialog box will appear. It will allow you to select the project type, name the project, set the project's platform and pick a location where the project is to be built. Figure 8.3 shows the WithWiz project and other pertinent information. Notice that the MFC AppWizard (exe) option was used as the project's type.

The first step in generating a project with the AppWizard involves making a decision on how the project will handle single, multiple or dialog-based documents. For this example, a single-document interface was desired, as shown in Figure 8.4. Use the Next pushbutton when the selection is made.

The second step is used only when database support is to be included. In this case, None is selected, as shown in Figure 8.5. Use the Next pushbutton when the selection is made.

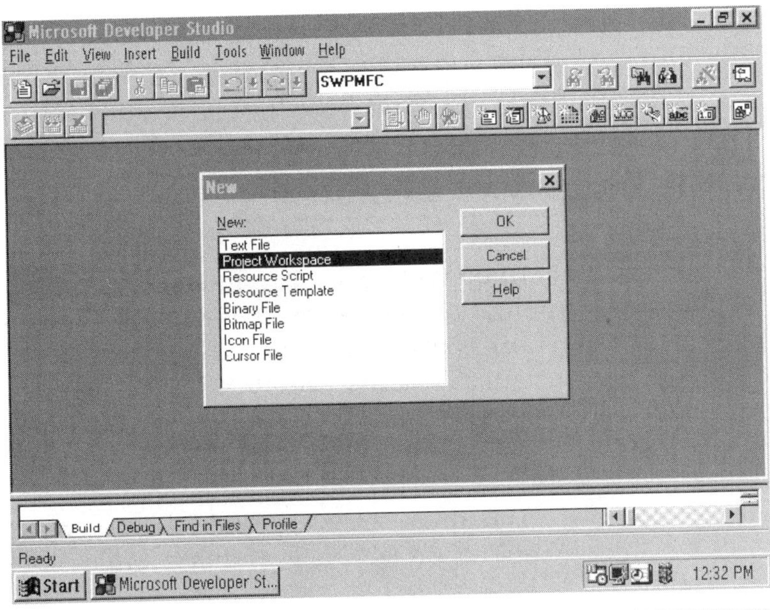

Figure 8.2: Select Project Workspace from the New dialog box.

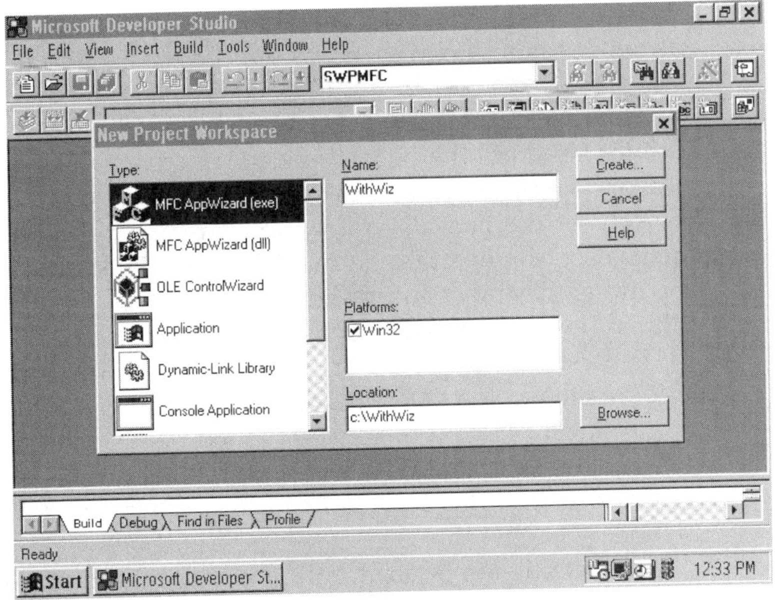

Figure 8.3: Creating a new project, named WithWiz.

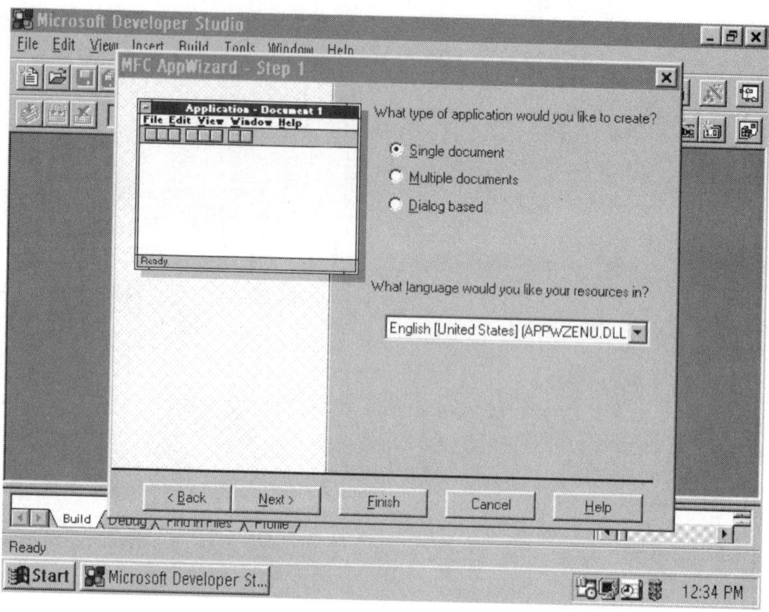

Figure 8.4: AppWizard step 1: selecting a single document interface.

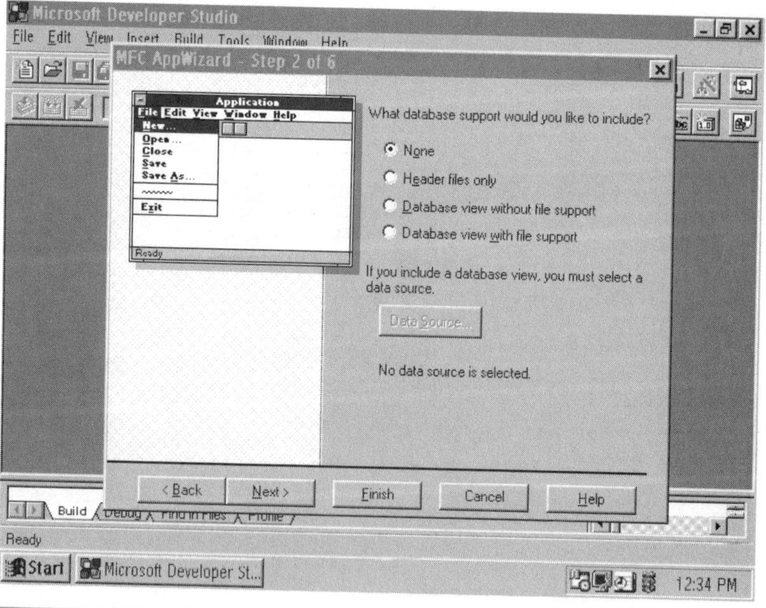

Figure 8.5: AppWizard step 2: selecting no database support.

The third step allows the developer to specify the type of OLE document and OLE support. In this example, None is selected, as shown in Figure 8.6. Use the Next pushbutton when the selection is made.

The fourth step allows programmers the opportunity to add special features to the project. For example, a toolbox or status bar could be added at this point. In the example, however, no special features are added, as shown in Figure 8.7. Use the Next pushbutton when the selection is made.

Additional features can be selected in the fifth step. For example, we'll request that no comments be generated for the source file and that a static MFC library be used. Figure 8.8 illustrates these selections. Use the Next pushbutton when the selection is made.

The sixth step lists the new classes that the AppWizard will automatically generate. These are shown in Figure 8.9. Use the Finish pushbutton when the selection is made.

The four classes that will be created for this application include **CWithWizApp, CMainFrame, CWithWizDoc,** and **CWithWizView.**

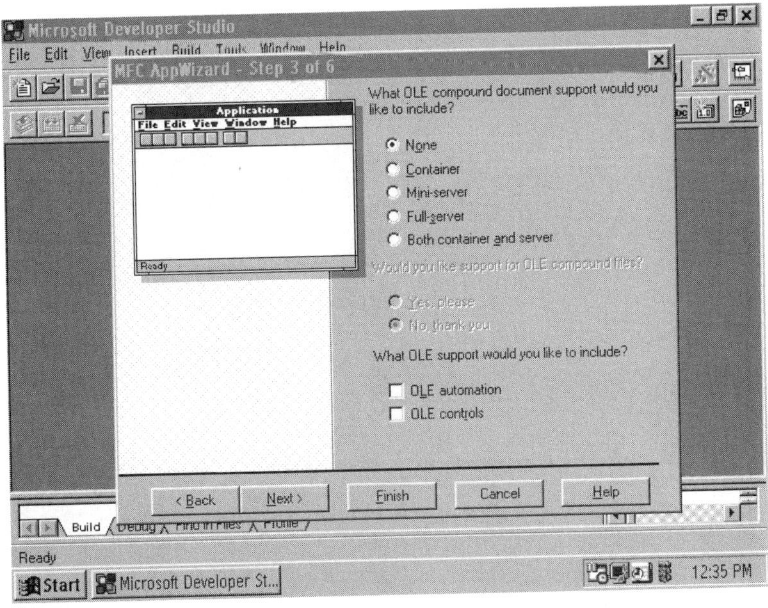

Figure 8.6: AppWizard step 3: selecting OLE documents and OLE support.

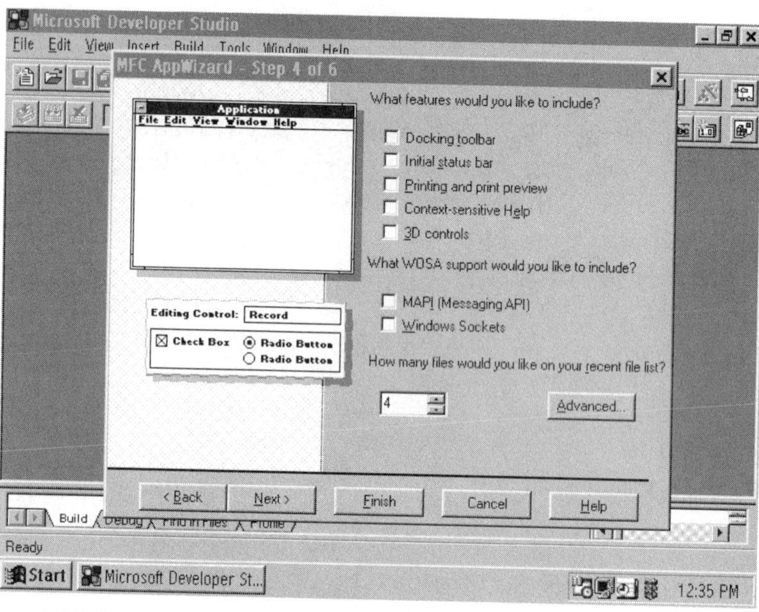

Figure 8.7: AppWizard step 4: selecting application features.

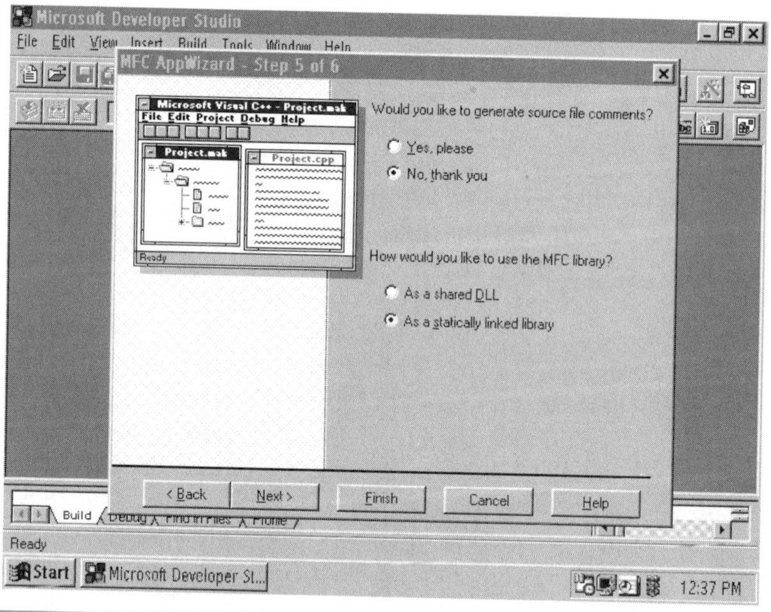

Figure 8.8: AppWizard step 5: selecting additional features for the project.

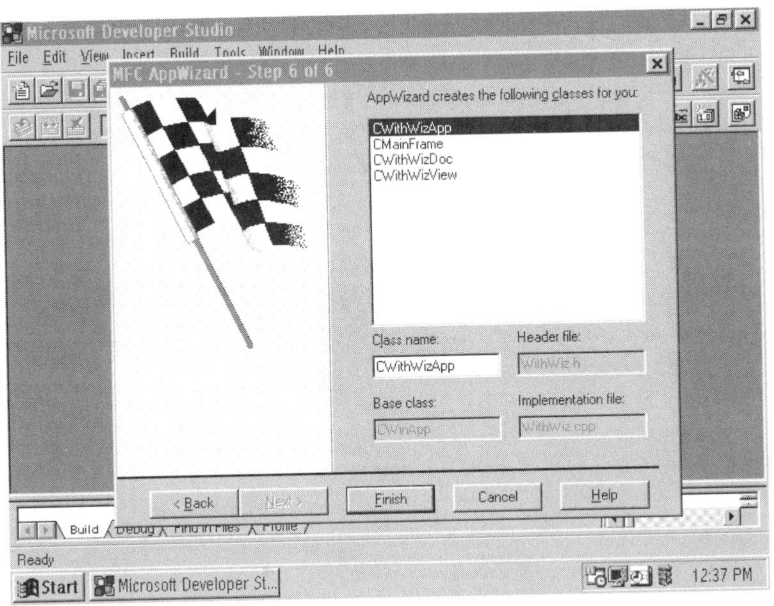

Figure 8.9: AppWizard step 6: A list of the classes that the AppWizard will generate.

If you select **CWithWizView** in the list box, the Base Class list box will expand to allow your class, **CWithWizView,** to be derived from the **CEditView, CFormView, CScrollView,** or **CView** base classes.

The **CView** class, derived from the **CWnd** class, is used to create the base for user-defined view classes. Views serve as a buffer between the document and the user and are actually a child of a frame window. Views produce an image of the document (screen, printer, etc.) and use input (keyboard, mouse, etc.) as an operation on the document.

Two other classes, just mentioned, are derived from the **CView** base class. They are **CFormView** and **CEditView**. **CFormView** describes a scrollable view. This view is based upon a dialog template resource and includes dialog box controls. **CEditView** describes a simple text editor. This class will be used in the next chapter.

This application, however, will use **CView** as the base class. As a matter of fact, all of the default classes shown in the Classes dialog box are acceptable. When the Finish pushbutton is selected, in step 6 as just described, the AppWizard will display additional information for the code it is about to generate. Figure 8.10 shows this information.

The information displayed in the previous dialog box is a summary of your previous choices. It is also your last chance to make changes before the AppWizard generates the project's code. If the options are correct, select the OK push button.

At this point, the AppWizard will generate the project code and return you to the Visual C++ compiler's edit window. You can now add features to the project by selecting the ClassWizard... menu item from the Visual C++ compiler's View menu, as shown in Figure 8.11.

This project, for example, will need to process WM_PAINT messages. A message handler must be added to the AppWizard's code by the ClassWizard.

The ClassWizard

The ClassWizard is used to generate additional code for the project. This code can be used to support the processing of

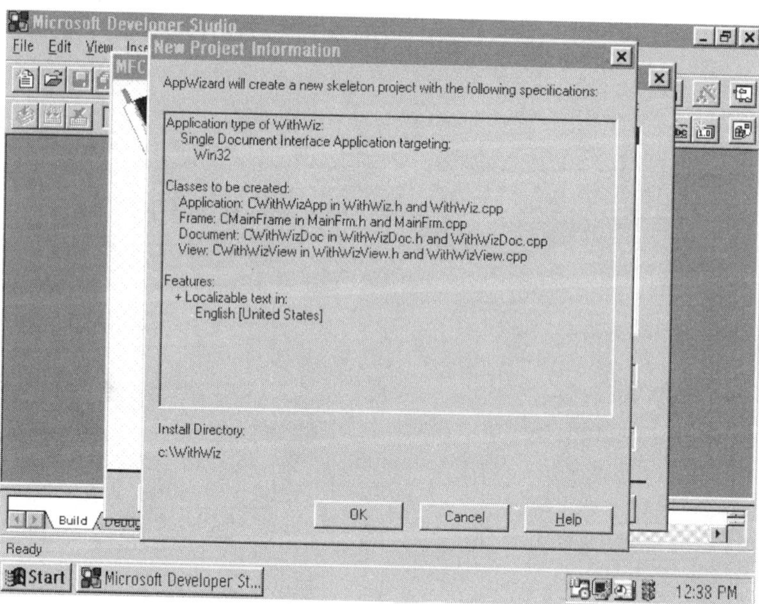

Figure 8.10: AppWizard: A summary of project information is displayed in the New Project Information dialog box.

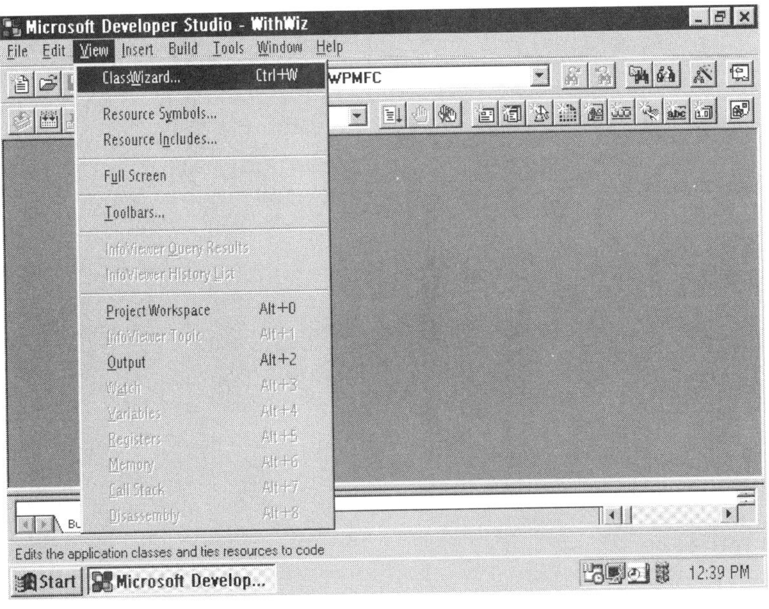

Figure 8.11: Use the ClassWizard to customize your project.

messages such as WM_MOUSEMOVE, WM_PAINT, and WM_SIZE.

The ClassWizard is selected from the Visual C++ compiler's View menu once the AppWizard has completed the code generating process. Figure 8.12 shows the initial MFC ClassWizard dialog box.

In this application, an **OnPaint()** member function will be added to our program code in order to process WM_PAINT messages. To add this support code, select **CWithWizView** in the Class Name list box. Make sure for this example that **CWithWizView** also appears in the Object IDs list box, as shown in Figure 8.12.

When **CWithWizView** is selected, a list of messages will be shown in the Messages list box, also shown in Figure 8.12.

Select the WM_PAINT message from the Messages list box. The OnPaint member function will be shown in the list of Member Functions. Select OK when this selection has been made.

The WithWizView.cpp file now contain the new code, as shown in Figure 8.13.

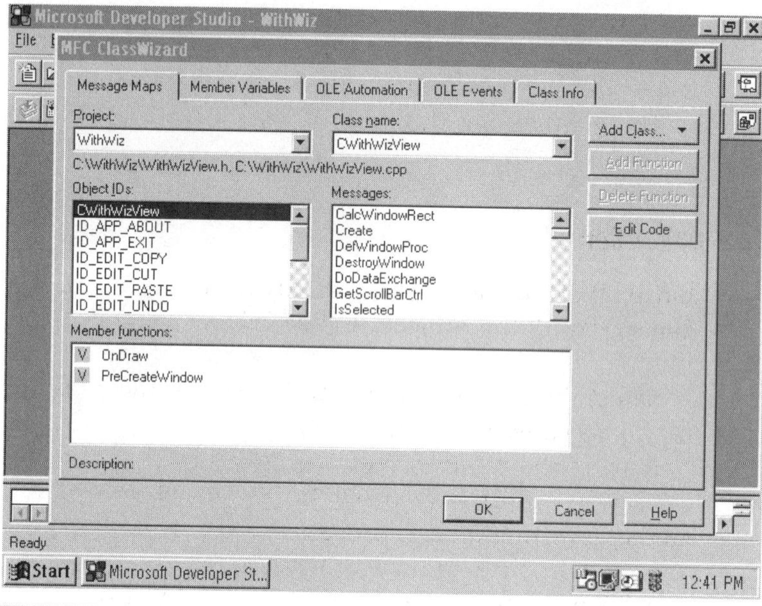

Figure 8.12: The initial MFC ClassWizard dialog box.

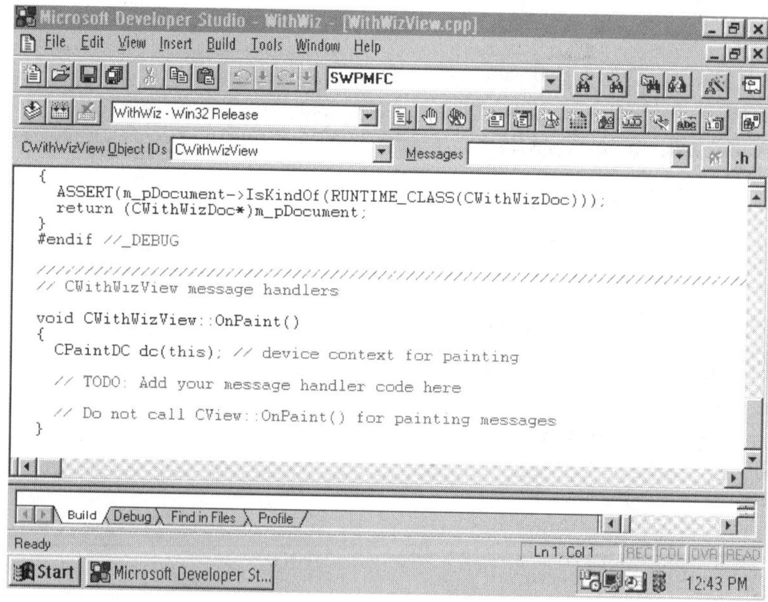

Figure 8.13: The WM_PAINT message handler code has been added to the CWithWizView.cpp file by the ClassWizard.

Now is the time to insert your application-specific code to the application. You'll see added code when this application is discussed in more detail.

The next step in the project, however, is to build the application.

Building the Application

Once all of the message handlers are added to a project, via the ClassWizard, the project can be built with the Visual C++ compiler.

Select the Rebuild All menu item from the compiler's Build menu, as shown in Figure 8.14.

During the build operation, details of the compile and link operation are displayed on the screen. Figure 8.15 shows the steps performed in this process.

Notice in particular that there are five source code files to be compiled then linked: StdAfx.cpp, WithWiz.cpp, MainFrm.cpp, WithWizDoc.cpp, and WithWizView.cpp. These files

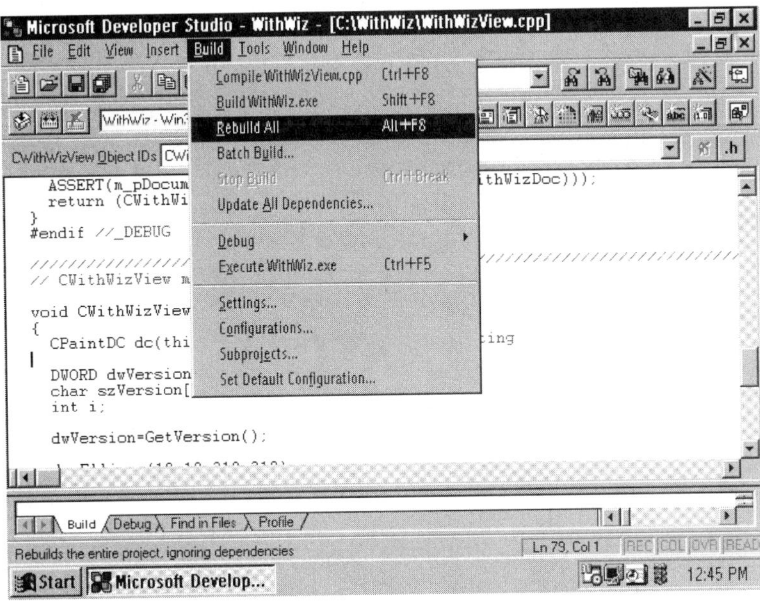

Figure 8.14: Build the project by selecting the Rebuild All menu item from the compiler's Build menu.

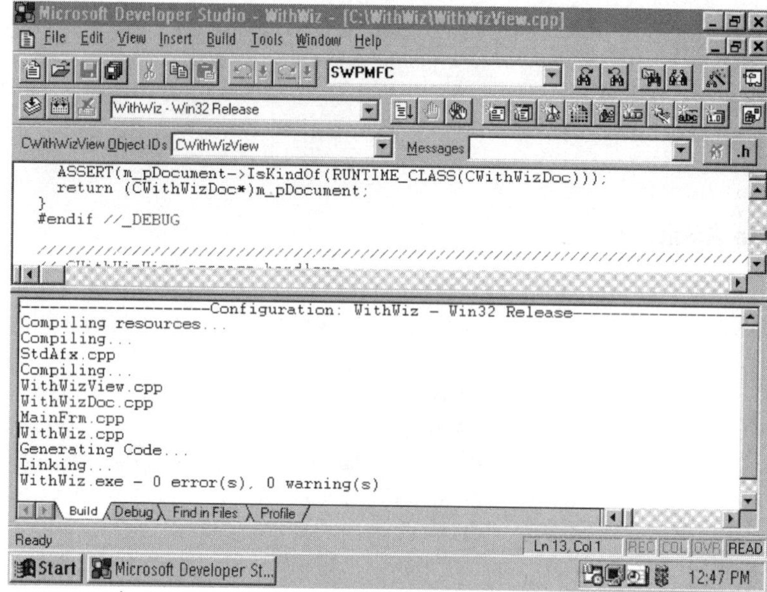

Figure 8.15: Details of the project's build process.

represent only a small portion of the total number of files involved with this project. When the build process is complete, examine the subdirectory where these files are stored. You will find more than 35 files stored in the subdirectory. There is a price to be paid for this automation.

One of the files present in the previously mentioned subdirectory is the executable file for the project. For this example, the executable file should be named WithWiz.exe. Run the application from within the Visual C++ compiler. You should see a screen similar to Figure 8.16.

In the next section, we'll investigate how the AppWizard's code actually works.

Understanding the AppWizard's Code

The AppWizard, with a little additional help from the ClassWizard, generated five important C++ files for the WithWiz project. These files were named StdAfx.cpp, WithWiz.cpp, MainFrm.cpp, WithWizDoc.cpp, and WithWizView.cpp. Each

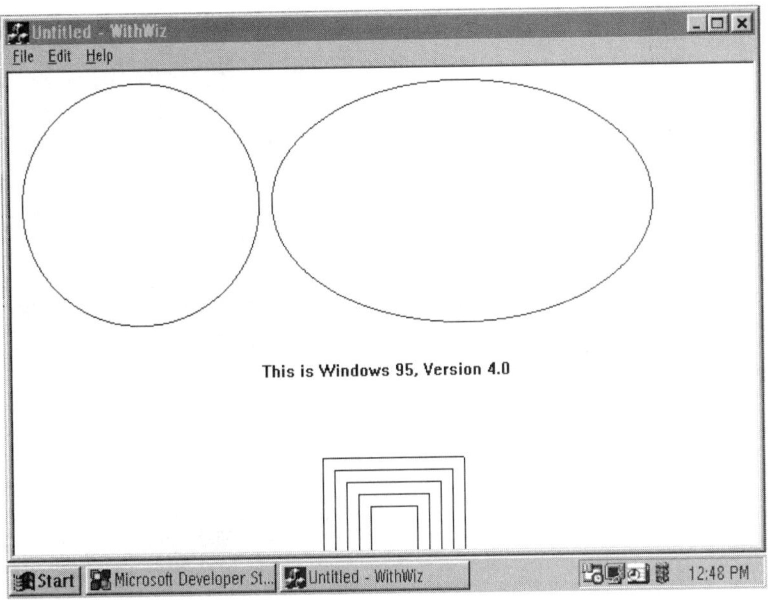

Figure 8.16: The window for the WithWiz application.

of these C++ files has an associated header file: StdAfx.h, WithWiz.h, MainFrm.h, WithWizDoc.h, and WithWizView.h. The header files contain the declarations of the specific classes in each C++ file. The purpose of each important C++ file will be examined in the following sections.

The StdAfx.cpp File

The StdAfx.cpp file is used to include standard include information. In this example, it allows access to the stdafx.h header file.

```
// stdafx.cpp : source file that includes just the standard
// includes. WithWiz.pch will be the pre-compiled header
// stdafx.obj will contain the pre-compiled type
// information

#include "stdafx.h"
```

Remember that the AppWizard is creating files in a style that can handle much larger projects than our initial WithWiz project.

The WithWiz.cpp File

The WithWiz.cpp file serves as the main file for the application. It contains the **CWithWizApp** class, which is derived from Microsoft's **CWinApp** class.

```
// WithWiz.cpp : Defines the class behaviors for the
// application.
//

#include "stdafx.h"
#include "WithWiz.h"

#include "MainFrm.h"
#include "WithWizDoc.h"
#include "WithWizView.h"

#ifdef _DEBUG
#define new DEBUG_NEW
#undef THIS_FILE static char THIS_FILE[] = __FILE__;
#endif

// CWithWizApp

BEGIN_MESSAGE_MAP(CWithWizApp, CWinApp)
  //{{AFX_MSG_MAP(CWithWizApp)
  ON_COMMAND(ID_APP_ABOUT, OnAppAbout)
  //}}AFX_MSG_MAP
  // Standard file based document commands
  ON_COMMAND(ID_FILE_NEW, CWinApp::OnFileNew)
  ON_COMMAND(ID_FILE_OPEN, CWinApp::OnFileOpen)
END_MESSAGE_MAP()

// CWithWizApp construction

CWithWizApp::CWithWizApp()
{
}

// The one and only CWithWizApp object

CWithWizApp theApp;

// CWithWizApp initialization

BOOL CWithWizApp::InitInstance()
{
  // Standard initialization

  // Load standard INI file options (including MRU)
  LoadStdProfileSettings();

  // Register document templates
```

```
    CSingleDocTemplate* pDocTemplate;
    pDocTemplate = new CSingleDocTemplate(
      IDR_MAINFRAME,
      RUNTIME_CLASS(CWithWizDoc),
      RUNTIME_CLASS(CMainFrame), // main SDI frame window
      RUNTIME_CLASS(CWithWizView));
    AddDocTemplate(pDocTemplate);

    // Parse command line for standard shell commands,
    // DDE, file open
    CCommandLineInfo cmdInfo;
    ParseCommandLine(cmdInfo);

    // Dispatch commands specified on the command line
    if (!ProcessShellCommand(cmdInfo))
      return FALSE;

      return TRUE;
  }

  // CAboutDlg dialog used for App About

  class CAboutDlg : public CDialog
  {
  public:
    CAboutDlg();

  // Dialog Data
    //{{AFX_DATA(CAboutDlg)
    enum { IDD = IDD_ABOUTBOX };
    //}}AFX_DATA

    // ClassWizard generated virtual function overrides
    //{{AFX_VIRTUAL(CAboutDlg)
    protected:
    virtual void DoDataExchange(CDataExchange* pDX);
    //}}AFX_VIRTUAL

  // Implementation
  protected:
    //{{AFX_MSG(CAboutDlg)
      // No message handlers
    //}}AFX_MSG
    DECLARE_MESSAGE_MAP()
  };

  CAboutDlg::CAboutDlg() : CDialog(CAboutDlg::IDD)
  {
    //{{AFX_DATA_INIT(CAboutDlg)
    //}}AFX_DATA_INIT }

  void CAboutDlg::DoDataExchange(CDataExchange* pDX)
```

```
{ CDialog::DoDataExchange(pDX); //{{AFX_DATA_MAP(CAboutDlg) //}}AFX_DATA_MAP }

BEGIN_MESSAGE_MAP(CAboutDlg, CDialog)
  //{{AFX_MSG_MAP(CAboutDlg)
    // No message handlers
  //}}AFX_MSG_MAP
END_MESSAGE_MAP()

// App command to run the dialog
void CWithWizApp::OnAppAbout()
{
  CAboutDlg aboutDlg;
  aboutDlg.DoModal();
}

// CWithWizApp commands
```

Our class **CWithWizApp** is derived from Microsoft's **CWinApp** class. The **CWinApp** class holds the code that initializes, runs, and terminates the application. **CWinApp** itself is derived from several other classes:

CObject→
  CCmdtarget→
    CWinThread→
      CWinApp

The message map, near the top of the previous listing, belongs to the **CWithWizApp** class. This message map specifically links the ID_APP_ABOUT, ID_FILE_NEW, and ID_FILE_OPEN messages with their member functions, **OnAppAbout(), CWinApp::OnFileNew(),** and **CWinApp::OnFileOpen()**. When you examine the listing you will also notice that a constructor, an initial instance (**InitInstance()**), and a member function (**OnAppAbout()**) are implemented. In this portion of code you will also see the use of a template for single documents. **CSingleDocTemplate** is responsible for constructing the object.

CSingleDocTemplate is derived from several other classes:

CObject→
  CCmdtarget→
    CDocTemplate→
      CSingleDocTemplate

The about dialog box is derived from the **CDialog** class. **CDialog** serves as the base class for all dialog boxes. **CDialog** is derived from several other classes:

CObject→
CCmdtarget→
CWnd→
CDialog

The lower portion of code, in the previous listing, contains a description for a message map, a constructor, and a member function, **CDialog::DoDataExchange()**.

This listing contains several place holders for user entries. Examine the listing, once again, and find the occurrence of statements such as // No message handlers.

The MainFrm.cpp File

This file contains the frame class, **CMainFrame**. This class is derived from Microsoft's **CFrameWnd** class and serves as the base class used to control all single document interface (SDI) frame features.

```
// MainFrm.cpp : implementation of the CMainFrame class
//

#include "stdafx.h"
#include "WithWiz.h"

#include "MainFrm.h"

#ifdef _DEBUG
#define new DEBUG_NEW
#undef THIS_FILE
static char THIS_FILE[] = __FILE__;
#endif

// CMainFrame

IMPLEMENT_DYNCREATE(CMainFrame, CFrameWnd)

BEGIN_MESSAGE_MAP(CMainFrame, CFrameWnd)
  //{{AFX_MSG_MAP(CMainFrame)
  //}}AFX_MSG_MAP
END_MESSAGE_MAP()

// CMainFrame construction/destruction

CMainFrame::CMainFrame()
{
}

CMainFrame::~CMainFrame()
{
}
```

```
BOOL CMainFrame::PreCreateWindow(CREATESTRUCT& cs)
{
  return CFrameWnd::PreCreateWindow(cs);
}

// CMainFrame diagnostics

#ifdef _DEBUG
void CMainFrame::AssertValid() const
{
  CFrameWnd::AssertValid();
}

void CMainFrame::Dump(CDumpContext& dc) const
{
  CFrameWnd::Dump(dc);
}

#endif //_DEBUG

// CMainFrame message handlers
```

CFrameWnd is derived from several other classes:

```
CObject→
        CCmdtarget→
                   CWnd→
                        CFrameWnd
```

Examine this listing and notice that the message map, constructor, and destructor initially contain no code. Member functions such as **AssertValid()** and **Dump()** use definitions contained in the parent class. **CMainFrame** initially contains no message handlers.

The WithWizDoc.cpp File

The WithWizDoc.cpp file contains the **CWithWizDoc** class. This class will contain code unique to your application when the application is designed to hold document data. It is also used for file loading and saving. **CWithWizDoc** is derived from Microsoft's **CDocument** class. The **CDocument** class serves as the base class for all application-specific documents.

```
// WithWizDoc.cpp : implementation of the CWithWizDoc class //

#include "stdafx.h"
#include "WithWiz.h"
```

```
#include "WithWizDoc.h"

#ifdef _DEBUG
#define new DEBUG_NEW
#undef THIS_FILE
static char THIS_FILE[] = __FILE__;
#endif

// CWithWizDoc

IMPLEMENT_DYNCREATE(CWithWizDoc, CDocument)

BEGIN_MESSAGE_MAP(CWithWizDoc, CDocument)
  //{{AFX_MSG_MAP(CWithWizDoc)
  //}}AFX_MSG_MAP
END_MESSAGE_MAP()

// CWithWizDoc construction/destruction

CWithWizDoc::CWithWizDoc()
{
}

CWithWizDoc::~CWithWizDoc()
{
}

BOOL CWithWizDoc::OnNewDocument()
{
  if (!CDocument::OnNewDocument())
  return FALSE;

  return TRUE;
}

// CWithWizDoc serialization

void CWithWizDoc::Serialize(CArchive& ar)
{
  if (ar.IsStoring())
  {
  }
  else
  {
  }
}

// CWithWizDoc diagnostics

#ifdef _DEBUG
void CWithWizDoc::AssertValid() const
{
  CDocument::AssertValid(); }
```

```
void CWithWizDoc::Dump(CDumpContext& dc) const
{
  CDocument::Dump(dc);
}
#endif //_DEBUG

// CWithWizDoc commands
```

CDocument is derived from several other classes:

CObject→
CCmdtarget→
CDocument

As you examine this listing, you will notice once again that the message map, constructor, and destructor contain no code. Several member functions can be used to provide vital document support. For example, **OnNewDocument()** uses the definition provided by the parent class to create a new document. **Serialize()** supports persistent objects. This member function is used to aid in file I/O. The member functions **AssertValid()** and **Dump()** use definitions contained in the parent class.

The WithWizView.cpp File

The WithWizView.cpp file provides the view of the document. In this implementation, our **CWithWizView** class is derived from Microsoft's **CView** class. **CView** is derived from several other classes:

CObject→
CCmdtarget→
CWnd→
CView

CView serves as the base, or parent, class for all specific views of the document's data. In otherwords, **CWithWizView** objects are used to view **CWithWizDoc** objects.

```
// WithWizView.cpp : implementation of the CWithWizView
// class
//

#include "stdafx.h"
#include "WithWiz.h"
```

```
#include "WithWizDoc.h"
#include "WithWizView.h"

#ifdef _DEBUG
#define new DEBUG_NEW
#undef THIS_FILE
static char THIS_FILE[] = __FILE__;
#endif

// CWithWizView

IMPLEMENT_DYNCREATE(CWithWizView, CView)

BEGIN_MESSAGE_MAP(CWithWizView, CView)
  //{{AFX_MSG_MAP(CWithWizView)
  //}}AFX_MSG_MAP
END_MESSAGE_MAP()

// CWithWizView construction/destruction

CWithWizView::CWithWizView()
{
}

CWithWizView::~CWithWizView()
{
}

BOOL CWithWizView::PreCreateWindow(CREATESTRUCT& cs)
{
  return CView::PreCreateWindow(cs);
}

// CWithWizView drawing

void CWithWizView::OnDraw(CDC* pDC)
{
  CWithWizDoc* pDoc = GetDocument();
  ASSERT_VALID(pDoc);
}

// CWithWizView diagnostics

#ifdef _DEBUG
void CWithWizView::AssertValid() const
{
  CView::AssertValid();
}

void CWithWizView::Dump(CDumpContext& dc) const
{
  CView::Dump(dc);
}
```

```
// non-debug version is inline
CWithWizDoc* CWithWizView::GetDocument()
{
  ASSERT(m_pDocument->IsKindOf(RUNTIME_CLASS(CWithWizDoc)));
  return (CWithWizDoc*)m_pDocument;
}
#endif //_DEBUG

// CWithWizView message handlers
```

The **OnDraw()** member function uses the pointer *pDoc* to point to the document. The member functions, **AssertValid()** and **Dump()** use definitions contained in the parent class.

Normally, the **CWithWizView** message handler area would be empty (for an initial AppWizard template). However, remember that we used the ClassWizard to add ON_WM_PAINT message handling abilities. Simple GDI graphics functions, such as those shown earlier in Chapters 4 and 7, can be inserted here.

Drawing in the Client Area The initial file generation using the AppWizard and ClassWizard produced a single document interface (SDI) application. The view class was derived from the parent class, **CView**. The ClassWizard allowed us to add the WM_PAINT message handler to this code.

The following code was added to the WithWizView.cpp file. This **OnPaint()** message handler allows us to draw in the client area.

```
// CWithWizView message handlers

void CWithWizView::OnPaint()
{
  CPaintDC dc(this);

  DWORD dwVersion;
  char szVersion[25];
  int i;

  dwVersion=GetVersion();

  dc.Ellipse(10,10,210,210);
  dc.Ellipse(220,10,540,210);

  for (i=60;i>10;i-=10)
    dc.Rectangle(320-i,380-i,320+i,380+i);

  if (dwVersion < 0x80000000) {
```

```
    wsprintf(szVersion,
            "This is Windows NT, Version %u.%u",
            (LOBYTE(LOWORD(dwVersion))),
            (HIBYTE(LOWORD(dwVersion))));
    dc.TextOut(210,240,szVersion,strlen(szVersion));
  } else {
    wsprintf(szVersion,
            "This is Windows 95, Version %u.%u",
            (LOBYTE(LOWORD(dwVersion))),
            (HIBYTE(LOWORD(dwVersion))));
    dc.TextOut(210,240,szVersion,strlen(szVersion));
    }
}
```

If you examine Figure 8.16, shown earlier, you will notice that the AppWizard also generated an application containing a menu bar with File, Edit and Help menus. Select the About option from the Help menu to view the About WithWiz dialog box shown in Figure 8.17.

Now, note that most of the other menus or menu items are not functional. Why not? It is because no additional code was added to handle those responses.

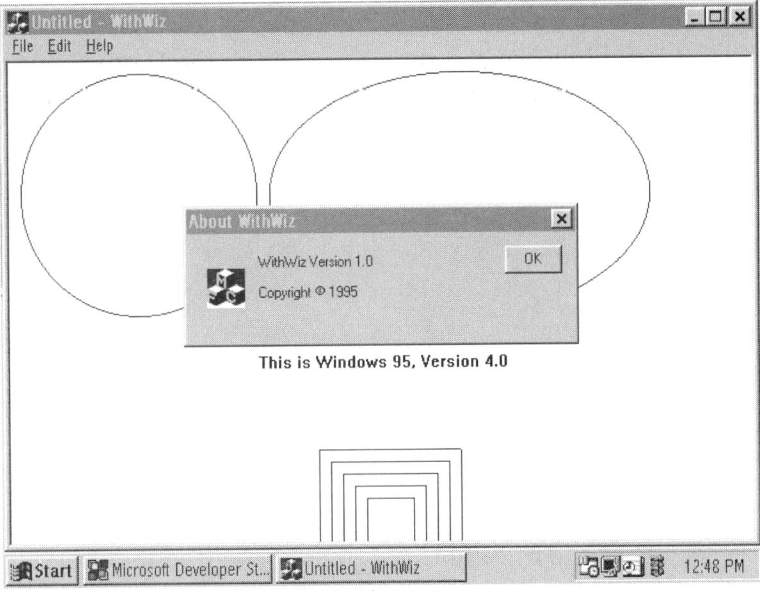

Figure 8.17: An About Box generated by the AppWizard.

It Looks the Same to Me

Have you taken the time to compare the code in the NoWiz and WithWiz projects? You'll find it almost identical, save for the fact that NoWiz contains only one source code file and WithWiz is broken into five source code files. Not only that, but if you diligently went through either the NoWiz or WithWiz projects, removing unneeded code, you would arrive at a project very similar to the application discussed in Chapter 7.

If you feel that the AppWizard has overreacted when generating project files, keep two points in mind. First, this project, in itself, is a very simple application. Secondly, most commercially designed applications have very large source code files that certainly benefit from this type of division.

In Chapters 9 through 13, we'll continue working with relatively small AppWizard projects until you have learned all of the Windows programming fundamentals, such as the use of icons, cursors, bitmaps, fonts, sound, menus, keyboard accelerators, toolbars, tooltips, dialog boxes, and various graphics primitives. By Chapter 14, you will be well prepared to venture into larger and larger projects.

Chapter 9

Adding Icon, Cursor, Bitmap, Font, and Sound Resources

In the previous chapter you learned how the AppWizard generates its dynamic template code. With a simple modification, you also learned how this template code could be modified so that the application reports the current operating system, as did the applications in Chapters 4 and 7.

The remainder of this book will be devoted to working with the code developed by the AppWizard and enhanced with the ClassWizard. In this chapter, for example, you will learn how to add important bitmap resources to the base code created by the AppWizard. The important bitmap resources include bitmaps themselves, icons, cursors, and fonts. This chapter will even show you how to create and add sound resources to your application. In Chapters 10 through 13 you will learn how to add other types of resources, such as menus, keyboard accelerators, dialog boxes, controls, graphics drawing primitives, tool bars and tooltips, and so on. Once you learn how to work with these resources, you'll be ready to build professional-quality MFC applications.

Bitmap resources are traditionally divided into three groups; icons, cursors and bitmaps. However, they are all basically the same thing—graphics images created or drawn in a graphics editor and saved in a binary format. The advantage of bitmap resources is that they can be snapped to the screen in the shortest possible time. In the following sections, you will learn how to create each of these resources and add them to a simple application. Additionally, you'll learn how to use the sound recorder to create your own custom wave (sound) files.

Microsoft Developer Studio's Bitmap Editors

The Microsoft Developer Studio contains a variety of fully integrated resource editors. In the earlier days of Windows development, most of these editors appeared as separate applications. The designer had to start the proper application to create the needed resource, such as a cursor or icon. The resource information was then merged into a resource script file (a file with a .rc file extension) and compiled with the resource compiler before being linked with the application's code.

Today, it is much easier to design, create, maintain, and implement all types of resources as a result of integrating these resource editors into the Developer Studio.

The path to creating unique resources for your application is almost always the same. To add a resource to a project that is already being developed, follow these steps:

- Choose the Insert menu from within the Developer's Studio (Visual C++ compiler).
- Select the Resource... menu item (see Figure 9.1).
- Choose the resource you wish to add from the list given in the Insert Resource dialog box (see Figure 9.2).

If you examine Figure 9.2 you'll see that the resource list includes accelerators, bitmaps, cursors, dialog boxes, icons, menus, string tables, toolbars, and versions. When you select a particular resource from this list, the Developer Studio will open the editor with the correct design criterion for designing your unique Windows resource.

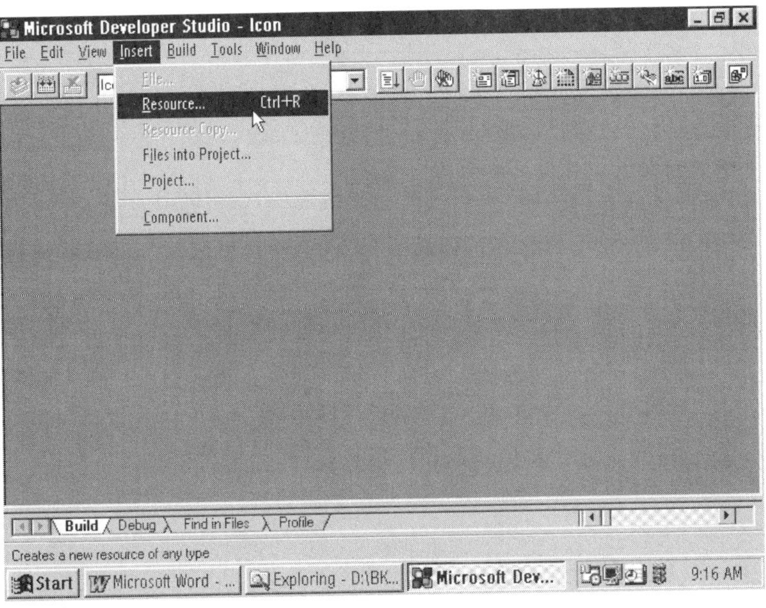

Figure 9.1: Use the Resource... menu item in the Insert menu to add a new resource to a project.

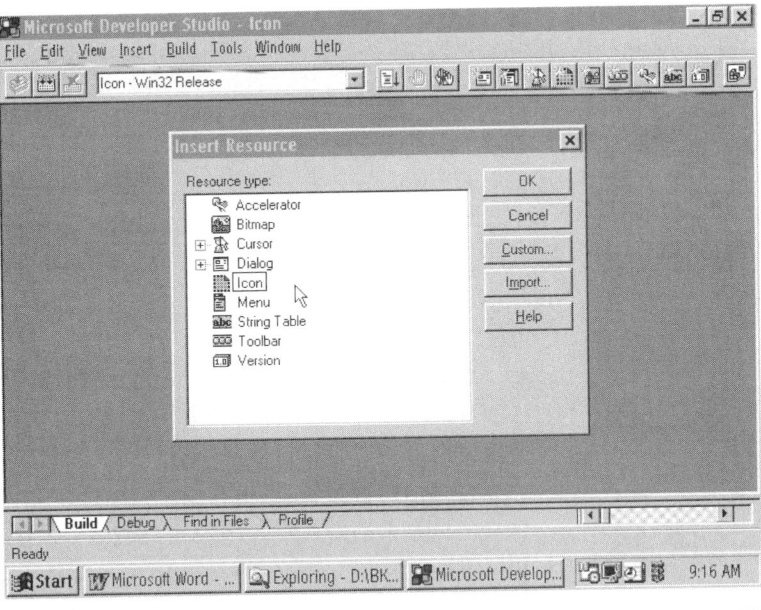

Figure 9.2: The Insert Resource dialog box permits the creation and editing of a variety of Windows resources.

In the following sections, we'll examine the steps necessary to create icons, cursors, and bitmaps.

Designing an Icon

Icons are used in Windows as small graphical reminders that applications are running or activated. Recently, they have also been employed in menus and in the title bars of applications. This is because they can also convey, in a limited way, information about the application. Icons by default have measured 32 × 32 pixels. With Windows 95, a new size standard is emerging, a 16 × 16 pixel icon.

If you follow the steps in the previous section and select an icon from the Insert Resource dialog box, you will enter a bitmap editor for iconic bitmaps. Figure 9.3 shows the initial screen for designing and editing icons.

By default, the size of the bitmap is set to 32 × 32 pixels.

Note: *While writing this book, we were provided with various beta versions of the Microsoft Developer Studio. Microsoft designers tend to change user interfaces from one version to another. Don't be surprised if the 32 × 32 pixel default suddenly becomes 16 × 16 pixels. Also, never*

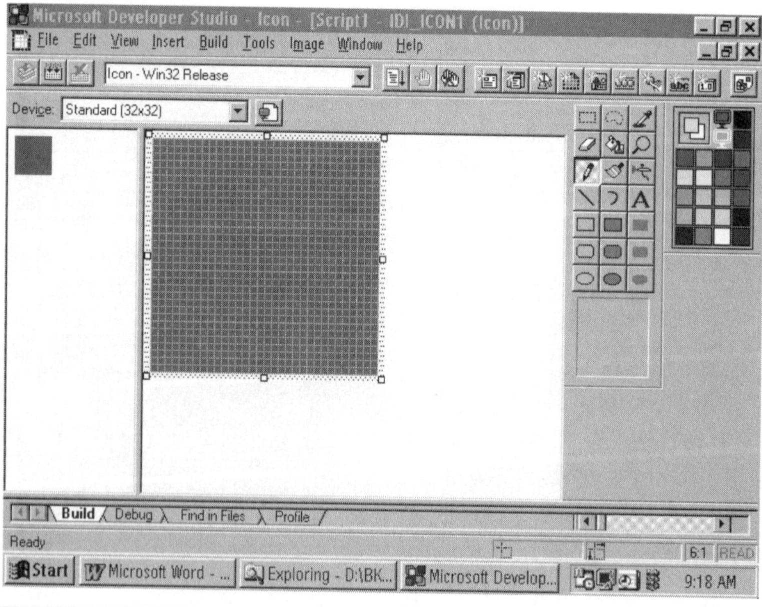

Figure 9.3: Icons are designed and edited in a simple bitmap editor.

be surprised when reading a book, if menu names or the location of menu options have been moved. This is a favorite practice of Microsoft—one which drives publishers, authors, and users a little crazy.

As you examine Figure 9.3, notice a tool box of drawing tools just to the right of the main drawing area. Likewise, a palette of 16 colors (default) is provided just to the right of the tool box. The small iconic symbol toward the left is how the icon will actually appear on the screen.

Figure 9.4 shows a completed icon designed for the Full Moon Insurance Company. Remember the icon should convey something about the application or product.

By default, the editor selects an ID value for the resource. The ID for this icon is IDI_ICON1. Can you find this ID value in the title bar?

If you are designing a Windows 95 application, you have two choices when it comes to icons. If you chose to use a 32 × 32 icon, now called a large icon, Windows 95 will automatically shrink it to 16 × 16 pixels. However, since these results are not always what you might have had in mind, the second choice is to design a 16 x 16 icon in the editor.

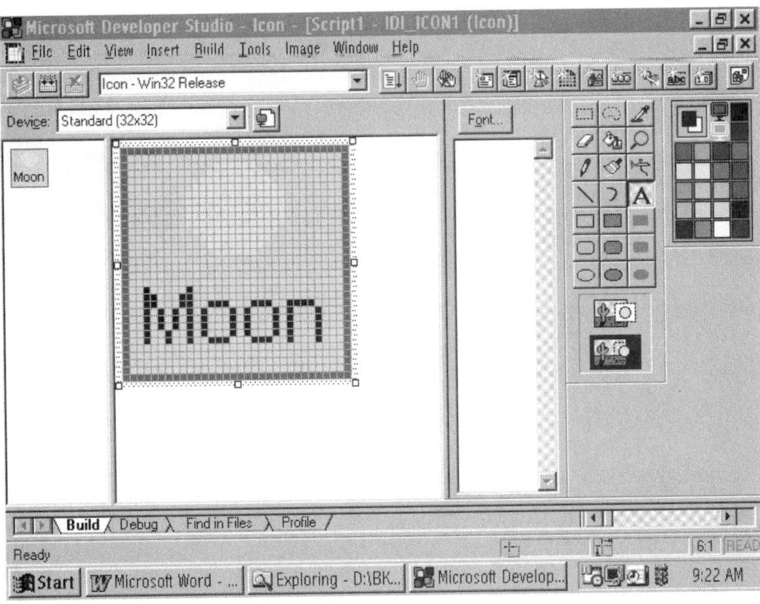

Figure 9.4: A completed 32 × 32 icon.

To design a 16 × 16 icon, use the Image menu and select the New Device Image... menu item as shown in Figure 9.5.

The New Icon Image dialog box allows you to select from a variety of icon image sizes and colors. For this example, select the Small (16 × 16) item in the list box, as shown in Figure 9.6.

If you examine Figure 9.7, you will notice that the entire drawing area has been reduced. It's a little hard to create meaningful icons in a 16 × 16 pixel drawing area, but Figure 9.7 shows a new icon designed for the Where the Wind Blows Boating Company.

That is really all there is to designing icons. If you take your time in designing meaningful and colorful icons, you can greatly enhance your finished application.

One note before leaving this section. If you find that you don't want to use the default ID value assigned to a resource by the editor, the ID value can be changed in the Properties dialog box, as shown in Figure 9.8.

The Icon Properties dialog box can be brought to the screen by double clicking on the iconic image or by selecting the Edit menu and choosing the Properties... menu item. In

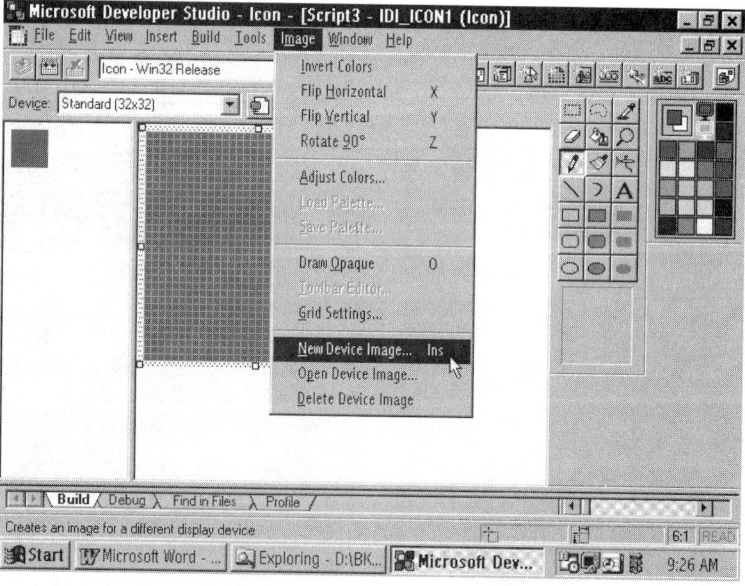

Figure 9.5: To create a 16x16 pixel icon, use the Image menu to select the New Device Image... menu item.

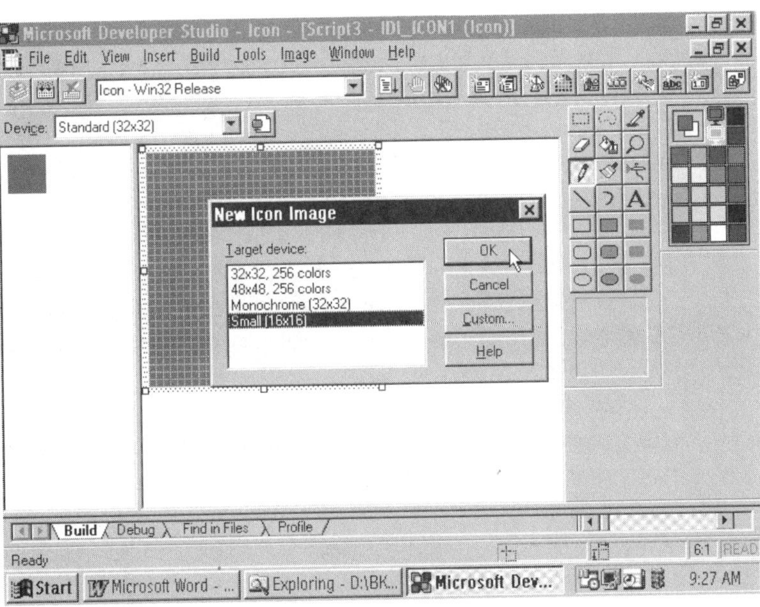

Figure 9.6: A new 16x16 icon image size is selected in the New Icon Image dialog box.

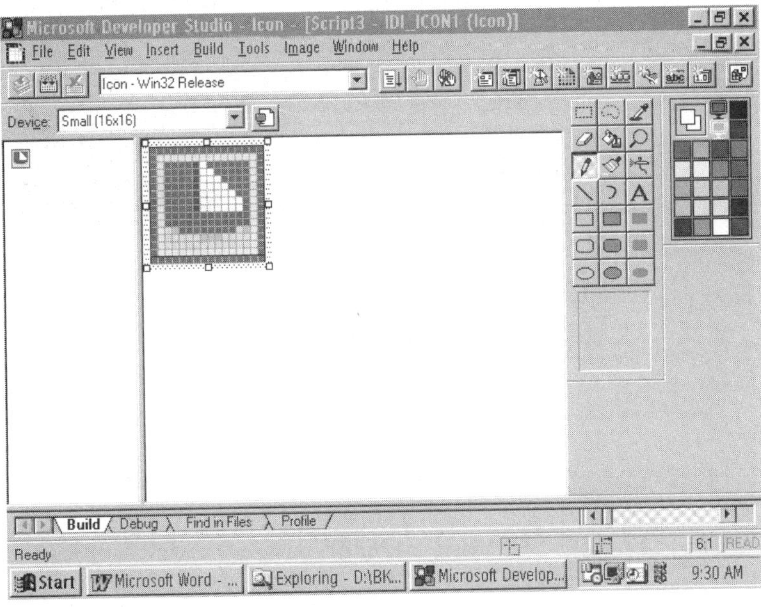

Figure 9.7: A completed 16x16 pixel icon.

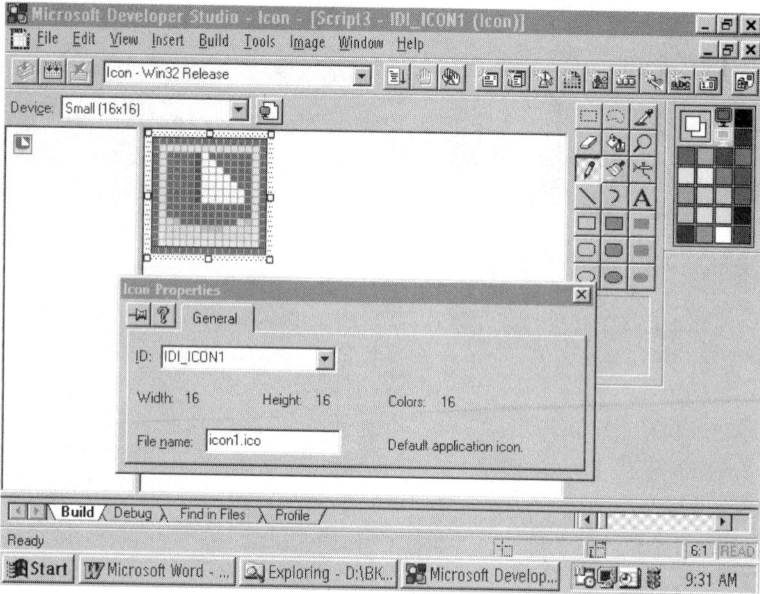

Figure 9.8: ID values and file names can be changed for a resource.

the example application for this chapter, you will find that icon resources are very easy to add to an application.

Designing a Cursor

Cursors are small graphical symbols used as pointers, prompts and reminders in Windows. Windows provides a group of stock cursors that can be selected for use or as a developer you can design your own custom cursor. The standard cursors are defined in the winuser.h header file. Here is a portion of the file showing the standard cursors.

```
#define IDC_ARROW       MAKEINTRESOURCE(32512)
#define IDC_IBEAM       MAKEINTRESOURCE(32513)
#define IDC_WAIT        MAKEINTRESOURCE(32514)
#define IDC_CROSS       MAKEINTRESOURCE(32515)
#define IDC_UPARROW     MAKEINTRESOURCE(32516)
#define IDC_SIZE        MAKEINTRESOURCE(32640)  //OBSOLETE
#define IDC_ICON        MAKEINTRESOURCE(32641)  //OBSOLETE
#define IDC_SIZENWSE    MAKEINTRESOURCE(32642)
#define IDC_SIZENESW    MAKEINTRESOURCE(32643)
#define IDC_SIZEWE      MAKEINTRESOURCE(32644)
#define IDC_SIZENS      MAKEINTRESOURCE(32645)
```

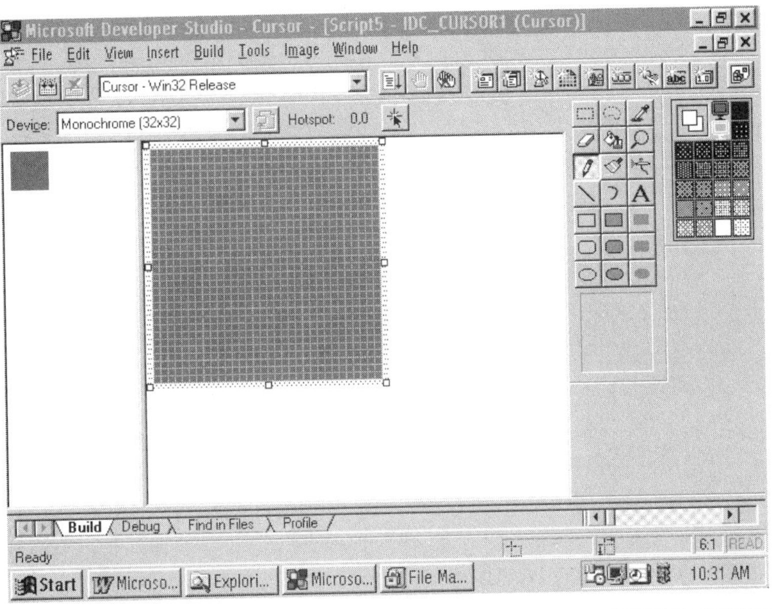

Figure 9.9: Cursors are also designed and edited in a simple bitmap editor.

```
#define IDC_SIZEALL       MAKEINTRESOURCE(32646)
#define IDC_NO            MAKEINTRESOURCE(32648) //not win3.1
#define IDC_APPSTARTING   MAKEINTRESOURCE(32650) //not win3.1
#if(WINVER >= 0x0400)
#define IDC_HELP          MAKEINTRESOURCE(32651)
#endif /* WINVER >= 0x0400 */
```

To create your own cursor, follow the steps for inserting a new resource. From the Insert Resource dialog box, you will enter a bitmap editor for cursor bitmaps. Figure 9.9 shows the initial screen for designing and editing cursors.

By default, the color and size of the bitmap is set to monochrome color and 32 × 32 pixels. The default is most likely your only choice.

Note: *At the time of this writing, to add color cursors to an application requires a modification of the Registry file. This process should be approached with caution. While we will give you the instructions for doing this, we can't help but think that it will be done automatically in the future.*

As you examine Figure 9.9, notice a tool box of drawing tools just to the right of the main drawing area. Likewise, a palette of monochrome patterns is provided just to the right of the tool box. The small cursor symbol toward the left is how the cursor will actually appear on the screen.

Figure 9.10 shows a completed cursor designed for the, you guessed it, Full Moon Insurance Company. Remember, the cursor should be useful as well as unique.

By default, the editor selects an ID value for the resource. The ID for this cursor is IDIC_CURSOR1. This value can be changed by using the Properties dialog box.

Starting with Windows NT and 95, cursors can be designed with more than two colors. However, to do this, you will most likely have to edit your system registry file. How do you know if this is necessary? Look ahead to Figure 9.11 and spot the New Device Image icon which rests between the Monochrome (32 × 32) and the word Hotspot in this figure. If the icon on your system is grayed (inactive), you must edit the Registry file. If the icon is dark (active), you will not have to edit the Registry file.

Here are the steps for editing your Registry file to add the ability to create cursors with up to 16 colors:

- Run Regedit.exe. This is probably in the C:WIN95 subdirectory.

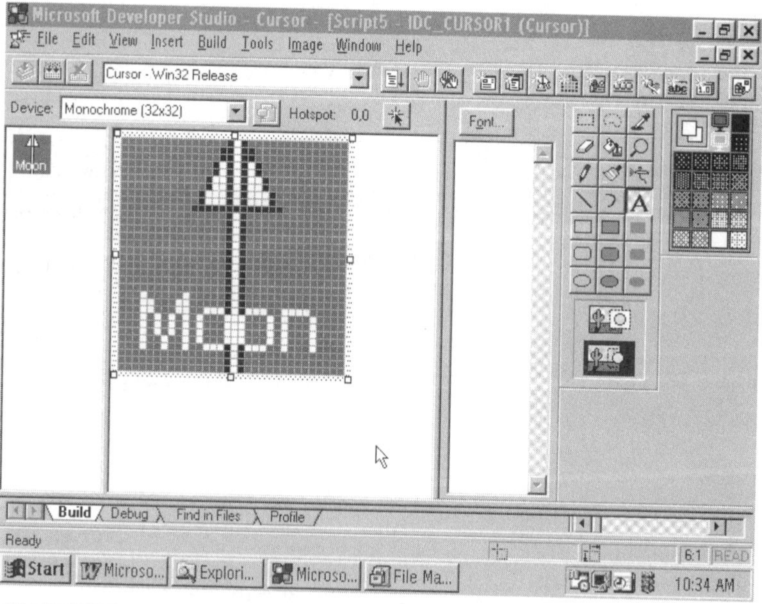

Figure 9.10: A completed monochrome 32 × 32 pixel cursor.

- Select HKEY_CURRENT_USER, then select SoftwareMicrosoftDeveloper (Developer is the name of the subdirectory where the Microsoft Developer Studio is located. SoftwareMicrosoft does NOT represent the path to that subdirectory!)
- From the Edit menu, click New and then Key. Add a key named "Cursor Devices."
- Now, using the Edit menu, click on New and then String. Add the value EGA/VGA (32 × 32).
- Use the Edit menu again and select Modify to change the string to "16,32,32" in the String Editor dialog box.
- Exit the Registry Editor and restart the Microsoft Developer Studio (your C++ compiler).
- Now, request a new cursor resource from within the Microsoft Developer Studio.

This time, the New Device Image icon should be dark (active). Click the mouse button on this icon. From the New Cursor Image dialog box, shown in Figure 9.11, select EGA/VGA (32 × 32).

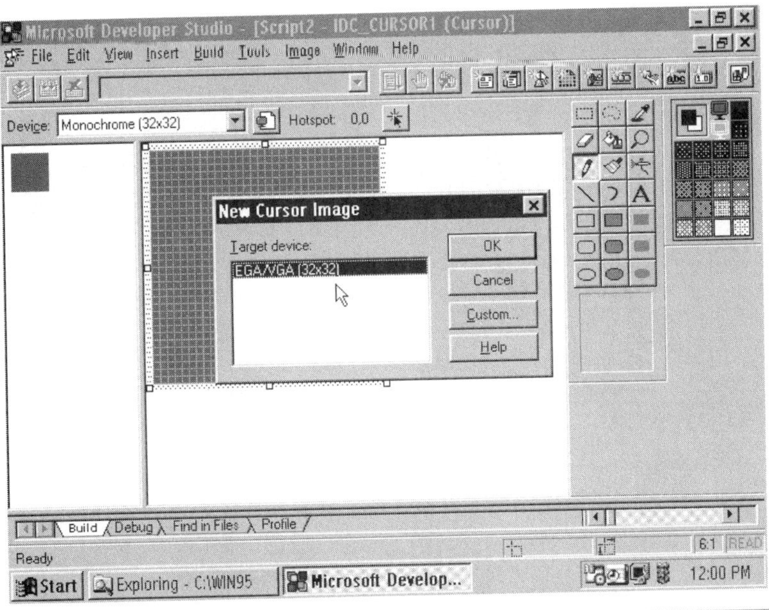

Figure 9.11: Adding color capabilities to the cursor resource editor.

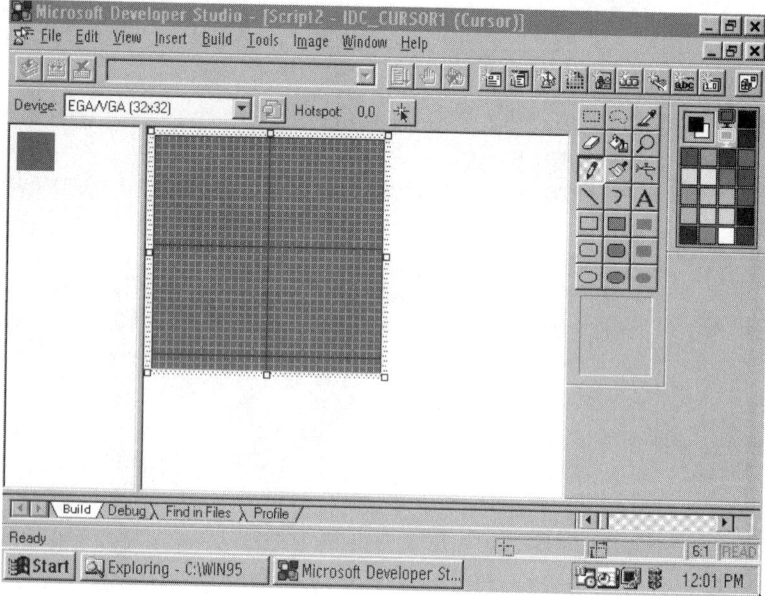

Figure 9.12: When color capabilities are added, a 16-color palette will appear.

If all goes well, your palette will change from monochrome patterns to a palette of 16 colors. The default cursor screen is shown in Figure 9.12 for colored cursors.

Figure 9.13 shows a colorful cursor designed by the new vice president of the Full Moon Insurance Company. No wonder she got the promotion!

By this point, you have probably discovered that good cursor design takes time. However, keep in mind that your product's cursor is ever-present as a consumer uses your application.

In the example application for this chapter, you will find that cursor resources are very easy to add to an application.

Designing a Bitmap

Bitmaps are resource images that vary in size from iconsized images up to whole screens. Bitmaps can be designed and created in a manner similar to icons and cursors, or in an entirely different way. For example, the Paint application supplied with Windows 95 allows images to be saved in a bitmap format. Scanners can be used to scan documents and photographs, with that information saved as a bitmap image. In other words,

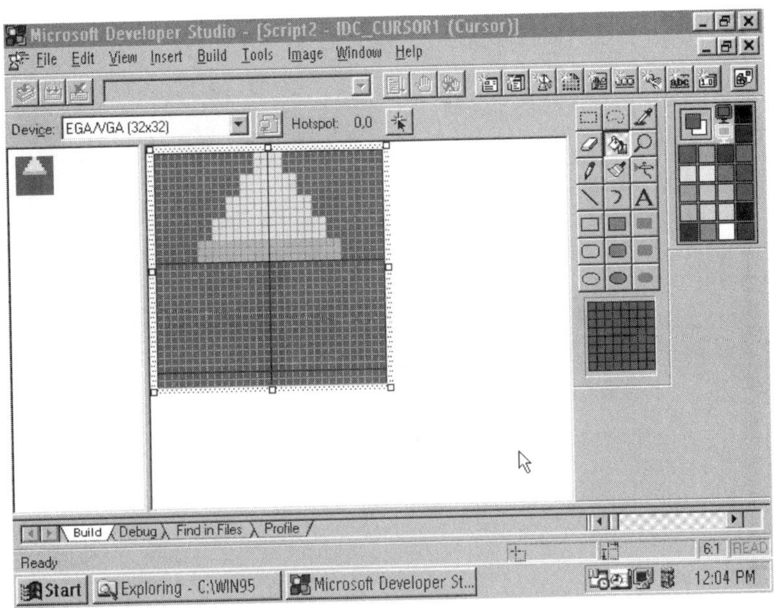

Figure 9.13: A colorful 32 × 32 pixel cursor is designed in the editor.

there are numerous sources in addition to the resource editor that will allow you to create unique bitmaps.

However, if you chose to use the resource editor to create a bitmap, just select the bitmap option from the New Resource dialog box as you have done for icons and cursors. Figure 9.14 shows the initial editing window for a new bitmap. It looks similar to the icon and cursor windows, except the drawing area is larger.

The drawing area, by default, is 54 pixels wide and 45 pixels in height. The width and height of the drawing area can be stretched with the mouse. Figure 9.15 shows a 111 × 104 pixel bitmap created with the editor. Multiple colors, shapes, and text can be added with this editor.

Notice that the ID value assigned to this resource is IDB_BITMAP1. That default value can be changed by using the Properties dialog box.

New users often have the attitude that the world is the limit when it comes to bitmap image sizes. After all, a full-screen scanned bitmap image of Aunt Martha is what you've always wanted. However, caution is in order.

For the 111 × 104 pixel bitmap we created, will need the following memory to store the image:

```
(111 × 104 × 4)/(8 bits/byte × 1024 bytes/KB) = 5.6 K bytes
```

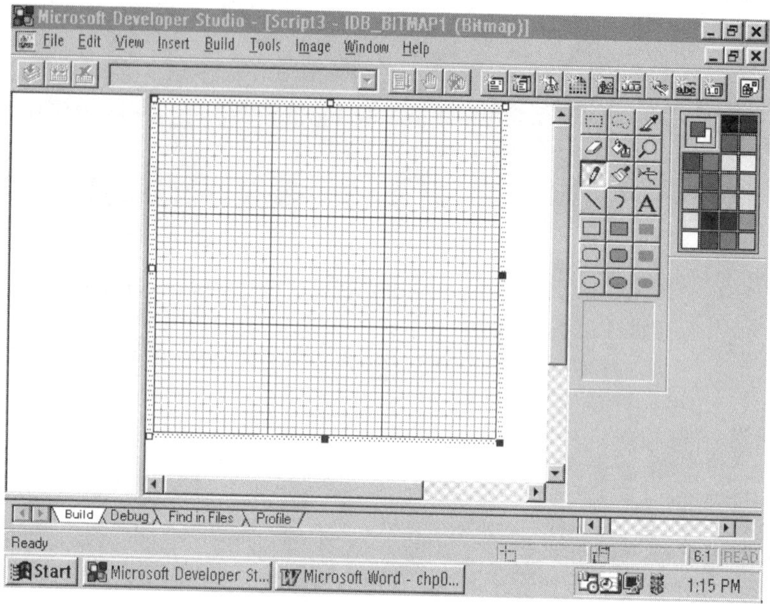

Figure 9.14: The editing window for a new bitmap resource.

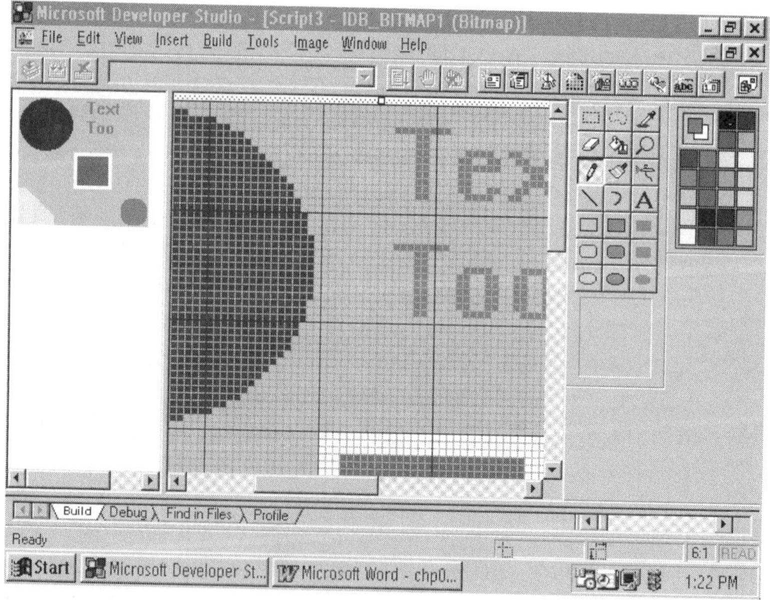

Figure 9.15: A completed 111x104 pixel bitmap image.

Note: 4 is the number of bits required to specify 16 colors.

While that doesn't seem too bad, imagine that you have a 1024 × 1024 pixel screen and you want to store Aunt Martha's picture in a 256-color bitmap.

```
(1024 × 1024 × 16)/(8 bits/byte × 1024 bytes/KB) = 2048 Kbytes or
                                                       2 Mbytes
```

You can see that disk space can become a premium very quickly when numerous bitmaps are saved.

In our example application, a scanned bitmap image will be used to illustrate Windows' ability to use external bit-mapped images.

MICROSOFT'S SOUND RECORDER

A Sound Recorder is supplied with both Windows NT and Windows 95. This recorder is most likely the easiest tool you will ever use for creating resources. The Sound Recorder is supplied with the operating system, not the Microsoft Developer Studio. You can locate it in your Windows NT Accessories Group or in your Windows 95 Multimedia Group located off of the Accessories Group.

Simple sound resources are saved as wave files with .wav file extensions. To create a sound file, start the Sound Recorder and select the File | New option. Now click on the record button when you are ready to start. The record button is the rightmost button shown in Figure 9.16.

A microphone or other audio device connected to your multimedia sound board is, necessary, of course. Recording can be stopped by clicking on the stop button. The stop button is the button with the rectangular image in Figure 9.16. If the file is what you want, save the file by selecting the File | Save option.

You can use the Edit or Effects menus to shorten your recording or add special effects, such as echo.

We'll show you how to incorporate sound resources into your application later in the chapter.

Figure 9.16: Click on the record button to record a wave file sound resource.

Font Resources

Fonts are probably one of the resources you will change frequently in your applications, but almost never create from scratch like you do icons, cursors and bitmaps. The reason is, of course, the extreme amount of time required to complete a whole family of characters and digits. Fonts are available not only from Microsoft, but also from sources such as CorelDraw.

For the brave, the Microsoft Developer Studio will permit you to install a Font Editor during the installation of the compiler. However, for our purposes, fonts supplied with the system are sufficient.

What is a font? A font is a complete set of characters of the same typeface and size, including letters, punctuation marks, and other symbols. Font sizes are measured in points. For example, a 12-point font is larger than a 10-point font. A point is the smallest unit of measure used in typography. There are 72 points in an inch.

The following font constants show the various font families. These definitions can be found in the wingdi.h header file.

```
// Font Families
#define FF_DONTCARE         (0<<4)
#define FF_ROMAN            (1<<4)
#define FF_SWISS            (2<<4)
#define FF_MODERN           (3<<4)
#define FF_SCRIPT           (4<<4)
#define FF_DECORATIVE       (5<<4)
```

Fonts are also supplied with a number of defining constants. Here is a partial listing of various font constants also found in the wingdi.h header file:

```
// Font Weights
#define FW_DONTCARE         0
#define FW_THIN             100
#define FW_EXTRALIGHT       200
#define FW_LIGHT            300
#define FW_NORMAL           400
#define FW_MEDIUM           500
#define FW_SEMIBOLD         600
#define FW_BOLD             700
#define FW_EXTRABOLD        800
#define FW_HEAVY            900

#define FW_ULTRALIGHT       FW_EXTRALIGHT
#define FW_REGULAR          FW_NORMAL
#define FW_DEMIBOLD         FW_SEMIBOLD
#define FW_ULTRABOLD        FW_EXTRABOLD
#define FW_BLACK            FW_HEAVY

#define OUT_DEFAULT_PRECIS      0
#define OUT_STRING_PRECIS       1
#define OUT_CHARACTER_PRECIS    2
#define OUT_STROKE_PRECIS       3
#define OUT_TT_PRECIS           4
#define OUT_DEVICE_PRECIS       5
#define OUT_RASTER_PRECIS       6
#define OUT_TT_ONLY_PRECIS      7
#define OUT_OUTLINE_PRECIS      8

#define CLIP_DEFAULT_PRECIS     0
#define CLIP_CHARACTER_PRECIS   1
#define CLIP_STROKE_PRECIS      2
#define CLIP_MASK               0xf
#define CLIP_LH_ANGLES          (1<<4)
#define CLIP_TT_ALWAYS          (2<<4)
#define CLIP_EMBEDDED           (8<<4)

#define DEFAULT_QUALITY         0
#define DRAFT_QUALITY           1
```

```
#define PROOF_QUALITY             2
#if(WINVER >= 0x0400)
#define NONANTIALIASED_QUALITY   3
#define ANTIALIASED_QUALITY      4
#endif /* WINVER >= 0x0400 */

#define DEFAULT_PITCH            0
#define FIXED_PITCH              1
#define VARIABLE_PITCH           2
#if(WINVER >= 0x0400)
#define MONO_FONT                8
#endif /* WINVER >= 0x0400 */

#define ANSI_CHARSET             0
#define DEFAULT_CHARSET          1
#define SYMBOL_CHARSET           2
#define SHIFTJIS_CHARSET         128
#define HANGEUL_CHARSET          129
#define GB2312_CHARSET           134
#define CHINESEBIG5_CHARSET      136
#define OEM_CHARSET              255
#if(WINVER >= 0x0400)
#define JOHAB_CHARSET            130
#define HEBREW_CHARSET           177
#define ARABIC_CHARSET           178
#define GREEK_CHARSET            161
#define TURKISH_CHARSET          162
#define THAI_CHARSET             222
#define EASTEUROPE_CHARSET       238
#define RUSSIAN_CHARSET          204

#define MAC_CHARSET              77
#define BALTIC_CHARSET           186

#define FS_LATIN1                0x00000001L
#define FS_LATIN2                0x00000002L
#define FS_CYRILLIC              0x00000004L
#define FS_GREEK                 0x00000008L
#define FS_TURKISH               0x00000010L
#define FS_HEBREW                0x00000020L
#define FS_ARABIC                0x00000040L
#define FS_BALTIC                0x00000080L
#define FS_THAI                  0x00010000L
#define FS_JISJAPAN              0x00020000L
#define FS_CHINESESIMP           0x00040000L
#define FS_WANSUNG               0x00080000L
#define FS_CHINESETRAD           0x00100000L
#define FS_JOHAB                 0x00200000L
#define FS_SYMBOL                0x80000000L
#endif /* WINVER >= 0x0400 */
```

These constants are used as parameter values for various font function calls and structures. You'll see these values used throughout this book.

The TEXTMETRIC Structure

The TEXTMETRIC structure, used in versions prior to Windows NT and Windows 95, has been redefined to include new data types. TEXTMETRIC is now associated with either TEXTMETRICA or TEXTMETRICW. TEXTMETRICW is used in Unicode applications. The NEWTEXTMETRIC structure is associated with NEWTEXTMETRICA or NEWTEXTMETRICW. NEWTEXTMETRICW is used in Unicode applications. You can find all of these structures in wingdi.h. Here is the NEWTEXTMETRICA structure.

```
struct tagNEWTEXTMETRICA
{
  LONG  tmHeight;
  LONG  tmAscent;
  LONG  tmDescent;
  LONG  tmInternalLeading;
  LONG  tmExternalLeading;
  LONG  tmAveCharWidth;
  LONG  tmMaxCharWidth;
  LONG  tmWeight;
  LONG  tmOverhang;
  LONG  tmDigitizedAspectX;
  LONG  tmDigitizedAspectY;
  BYTE  tmFirstChar;
  BYTE  tmLastChar;
  BYTE  tmDefaultChar;
  BYTE  tmBreakChar;
  BYTE  tmItalic;
  BYTE  tmUnderlined;
  BYTE  tmStruckOut;
  BYTE  tmPitchAndFamily;
  BYTE  tmCharSet;
  DWORD ntmFlags;
  UINT  ntmSizeEM;
  UINT  ntmCellHeight;
  UINT  ntmAvgWidth;
 } NEWTEXTMETRICA;
```

The last four structure members are used only by TrueType fonts. If you examine TEXTMETRICA and NEWTEXTMETRICA, you will find they are similar.

LOGFONTA Structure

In addition to the TEXTMETRIC structures just discussed, the LOGFONTA data structure is also frequently used in applications. The use of this structure makes creating logical fonts an easy process. The following is the LOGFONTA data structure:

```
struct tagLOGFONTA
{
    LONG      lfHeight;
    LONG      lfWidth;
    LONG      lfEscapement;
    LONG      lfOrientation;
    LONG      lfWeight;
    BYTE      lfItalic;
    BYTE      lfUnderline;
    BYTE      lfStrikeOut;
    BYTE      lfCharSet;
    BYTE      lfOutPrecision;
    BYTE      lfClipPrecision;
    BYTE      lfQuality;
    BYTE      lfPitchAndFamily;
    BYTE      lfFaceName[LF_FACESIZE];
} LOGFONTA;
```

The data members of this structure allow various font characteristics to be manipulated. For example, it is possible to specify the boldness of a character or its height and width.

TrueType Fonts

TrueType font technology was introduced in Windows 3.1. TrueType fonts are easy to scale. When a TrueType font is created of a particular size, information is embedded within the font's specification. This information is used to draw the lines and curves of the font. Once the character is drawn, it is converted to a bitmap. The embedded information then aids in scaling the font.

You will find that there are two important font functions: **CreatFont()** and **CreateFontIndirect()**.

CreateFont()

The **CreateFont()** function is defined in the wingdi.h header file. The syntax for this function is:

```
CreateFont(Height,Width,Escapement,
           Orientation,Weight,Italic,
           Underline,StrikeOut,
           CharSet,OutputPrecision,
           ClipPrecision,Quality,
           PitchAndFamily,Facename)
```

This font has 14 parameters. Each time a call is made to **CreateFont()**, specifications must be provided for each parameter. These parameters are discussed in Table 9.1.

Table 9.1: **CreateFont()** parameters.

Value	*Meaning*
(int) Height	Desired font height in logical units
(int) Width	Average font width in logical units
(int) Escapement	Angle (tenths of a degree) for each line written in the font
(int) Orientation	Angle (tenths of a degree) for each character's baseline
(int) Weight	Weight of font (0 to 1000); 400 is normal, 700 is bold
(byte) Italic	Italic font
(byte) Underline	Underline font
(byte) StrikeOut	Strike-through font (such a font is sometimes called a redline font)
(byte) CharSet	Character set (ANSI_CHARSET, DEFAULT_CHARSET, OEM_CHARSET, SYMBOL_CHARSET)
(byte) OutputPrecision	How closely output must match the requested specifications (OUT_CHARACTER _PRECIS, OUT_DEFAULT_PRECIS, OUT_DEVICE_PRECIS, OUT_RASTER_PRECIS, OUT_STRING_PRECIS, OUT_STROKE_PRECIS, OUT_TT_PRECIS)
(byte) ClipPrecision	How to clip characters outside of clipping range (CLIP_CHARACTER_PRECIS, CLIP_DEFAULT_PRECIS, CLIP_ENCAPSULATE, CLIP_LH_ANGLES, CLIP_STROKE_PRECIS, CLIP_MASK, CLIP_TT_ALWAYS)
(byte) Quality	How carefully the logical attributes are mapped to the physical font (DEFAULT_QUALITY, DRAFT_QUALITY, PROOF_QUALITY)

Continued on the next page.

Table 9.1: Continued

Value	*Meaning*
(byte) PitchAndFamily	Pitch and family of font (DEFAULT_PITCH, FIXED_PITCH, PROOF_QUALITY,FF_DECORATIVE, FF_DONTCARE, FF_MODERN, FF_ROMAN, FF_SCRIPT, FF_SWISS)
(lpstr) Facename	A string pointing to the name of the desired font's typeface

The **CreateFont()** function selects the logical font from the GDI's pool of physical fonts. Once the logical font is created, it can be used by any device.

CreateFontIndirect()

The **CreateFontIndirect()** function frees the programmer from parameter specifications. This function is used to create or modify a logical font. The modifications are specified in a LOGFONTA data structure. The user only needs to specify the characteristics that are to change. The syntax is for this function is:

```
HFONT CreateFontIndirect(lpLogFont)
```

Here, the parameter lpLogFont points to a LOGFONTA data structure.

Manipulating fonts is an easy task when using either the **CreateFont()** or **CreateFontIndirect()** functions. The sample application for this chapter will show you how to use the **CreateFont()** function.

Adding Resources to the AddRes Project

In this section, you'll learn how to develop a project named AddRes with the AppWizard. You'll then learn how to modify the application's base code to include a custom icon, cursor, bitmap, font, and wave (sound) resources.

You'll find that adding these resources is a snap, because the AppWizard has done all of the code writing (well, almost all) for us.

Our first task will be to generate a template for this application. Follow the steps in the next section and create a project named AddRes.

Base Code

Use the following steps to complete the base code for this project:

- Open the Microsoft Developer Studio.
- Choose the File menu and select the New menu item.
- Select Project Workspace from the New dialog box.
- From the New Project Workspace dialog box:
  Name the workspace "AddRes".

  Set the location of the workspace (for example, C:AddRes)

  Select MFC AppWizard (exe) from the list box.
- Step 1—Select a single document application type.
- Step 2—Select no database support.
- Step 3—Select none for OLE compound document support.
- Step 4—Select no additional features.
- Step 5—Do not select comments. Select a statically linked library.
- Step 6—View your settings and Finish the AppWizard process.

If the information is correct, in the New Project Information dialog box, select OK.

These are the steps you completed in Chapter 8 to create the base code for your application. Chapter 8 describes this project creation process in more detail. When the final step has been completed, as before, the AppWizard generates all of the base files needed for the AddRes project.

The AppWizard Files

The AppWizard generates numerous source code files, including AddRes.cpp, AddResDoc.cpp, MainFrame.cpp, StdAfx.cpp, and AddResView.cpp. Also generated are the associated header files and a resource script file. Of all of the base code files, only AddResView.cpp needs to be altered to include our icon, cursor, bitmap, sound and font resources. Here is the complete listing for the AddResView.cpp file. The bolded lines are lines that we added to the base code generated by the AppWizard.

```
// AddResView.cpp : implementation of the CAddResView class
//

#include "stdafx.h"
#include "AddRes.h"

#include "AddResDoc.h"
#include "AddResView.h"
#include <mmsystem.h>

static char szWave[]= "MyWav.wav";

#ifdef _DEBUG
#define new DEBUG_NEW
#undef THIS_FILE
static char THIS_FILE[] = __FILE__;
#endif

// CAddResView

IMPLEMENT_DYNCREATE(CAddResView, CView)

BEGIN_MESSAGE_MAP(CAddResView, CView)
  //{{AFX_MSG_MAP(CAddResView)
  ON_WM_SIZE()
  //}}AFX_MSG_MAP
END_MESSAGE_MAP()

// CAddResView construction/destruction

CAddResView::CAddResView()
{
}

CAddResView::~CAddResView()
{
}

BOOL CAddResView::PreCreateWindow(CREATESTRUCT& cs)
{
  return CView::PreCreateWindow(cs);
}

// CAddResView drawing

void CAddResView::OnDraw(CDC* pDC)
{
```

```
CAddResDoc* pDoc = GetDocument();
ASSERT_VALID(pDoc);

BITMAP bm;

CBitmap m_bitmap;
CFont newfont;
CFont* oldfont;

m_bitmap.LoadBitmap(IDB_BOYS);
m_bitmap.GetObject(sizeof(bm),&bm);

 CDC dcMem;
if (!dcMem.CreateCompatibleDC(pDC))
  return;
CBitmap* pBitmapOld = dcMem.SelectObject(&m_bitmap);
if (pBitmapOld == NULL)
  return;

pDC->BitBlt(0,0,bm.bmWidth,bm.bmHeight,&dcMem,0,0,SRCCOPY);
pDC->StretchBlt(bm.bmWidth,bm.bmHeight,2*bm.bmWidth,
               2*bm.bmHeight,&dcMem,0,0,bm.bmWidth,
               bm.bmHeight,SRCCOPY);

dcMem.SelectObject(pBitmapOld);

newfont.CreateFont(20,20,0,0,FW_BOLD,
                   FALSE,FALSE,FALSE,0,
                   OUT_DEFAULT_PRECIS,
                   CLIP_DEFAULT_PRECIS,
                   DEFAULT_QUALITY,
                   34,"Arial");
oldfont=pDC->SelectObject(&newfont);
pDC->TextOut(350,100,"Paul and Mark",13);
pDC->TextOut(75,300,"1980",4);

}

// CAddResView diagnostics

#ifdef _DEBUG
void CAddResView::AssertValid() const
{
  CView::AssertValid();
}

void CAddResView::Dump(CDumpContext& dc) const
{
  CView::Dump(dc);
}

CAddResDoc* CAddResView::GetDocument()
```

```
{
  ASSERT(m_pDocument->IsKindOf(RUNTIME_CLASS(CAddResDoc)));
  return (CAddResDoc*)m_pDocument;
}
#endif //_DEBUG

// CAddResView message handlers

//Allows inclusion of a unique cursor and background color
BOOL CAddResView::Create(LPCTSTR lpszClassName,
                         LPCTSTR lpszWindowName,DWORD dwStyle,
                         const RECT& rect, CWnd* pParentWnd,
                         UINT nID, CCreateContext* pContext)
{
  LPCTSTR lpszAddResClass=
    AfxRegisterWndClass(CS_HREDRAW|CS_VREDRAW,
                  LoadCursor(AfxGetInstanceHandle(),
                  MAKEINTRESOURCE(IDC_CURSOR1)),
                  (HBRUSH) CreateSolidBrush(RGB(0,255,255)),
                  NULL);

   return CWnd::Create(lpszAddResClass,lpszWindowName,
                    dwStyle,rect,pParentWnd,nID,pContext);
}

void CAddResView::OnSize(UINT nType, int cx, int cy)
{
  CView::OnSize(nType, cx, cy);

  // Play a wave file when window is resized
  sndPlaySound(szWave,SND_ASYNC);
}
```

In the following sections we examine the specific code that was added for each resource.

ADDING AN ICON

An icon resource was created using the resource editor discussed earlier in the chapter. Figure 9.17 shows this application's icon being designed.

Since the base code already supplied a default icon, no additional code is needed to incorporate a custom icon. As you leave the resource editor, save the icon resource file as AddRes.ico in the AddResRes subdirectory.

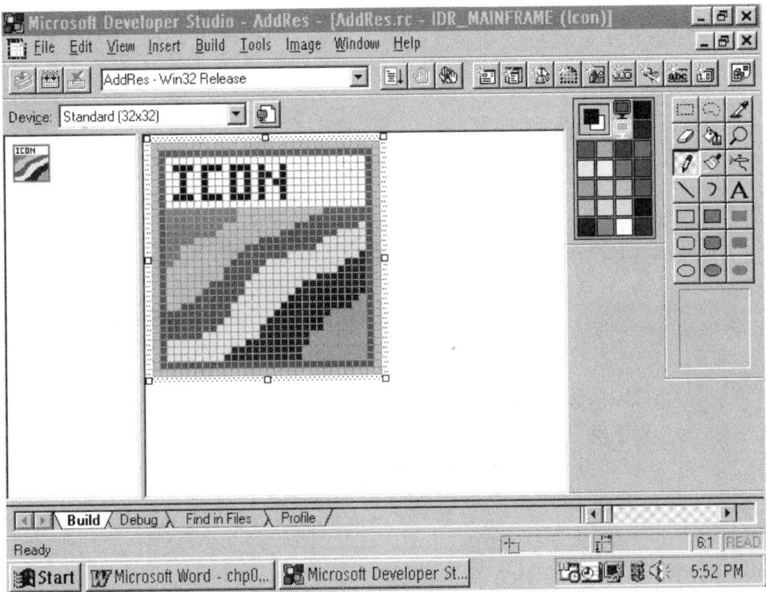

Figure 9.17: A new icon is designed for the AddRes project.

Now, check that the AddRes.rc resource script file (you might want to use the Edit editor to do this) contains the line:

```
IDR_MAINFAME ICON DISCARDABLE "resAddRes.ico"
```

When the application is built, the new icon will be used instead of the default.

Adding Sound

In order to include a sound resource, the mmsystem.h header file must be included at the start of this file. The sound resource is identified in a character string, *szWave[]*, as MyWav.wav.

```
#include <mmsystem.h>
static char szWave[]= "MyWav.wav";
```

Sound resources can be played with just a call to the **sndPlay-Sound()** function. To use this function, simply specify the wave source and SND_ASYNC or SND_SYNC. If SND_ASYNC is specified, the program will continue as the sound resource is

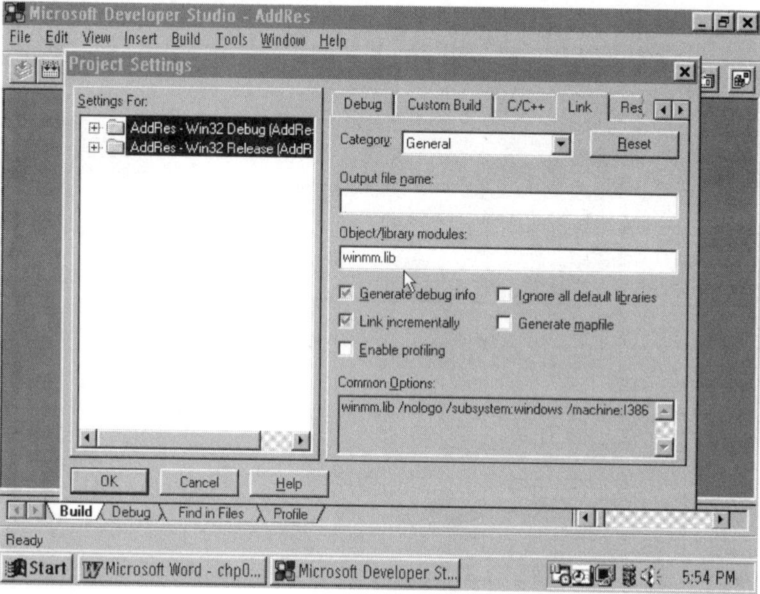

Figure 9.18: Specify winmm.lib for the linker if multimedia resources are included with the project.

played. If SND_SYNC is specified, the application will halt until the sound is completed.

```
// Play a wave file when window is resized
  sndPlaySound(szWave,SND_ASYNC);
```

Now there is just one tiny catch at this point. When you are ready to build the application, the winmm.lib must be specified for the linker, as shown in Figure 9.18.

The sound resource added to this project will sound each time the screen is resized.

Adding a Bitmap

The bitmap resource for this project was scanned and saved as boys.bmp. This is an image of two boys at the beach. In the AddRes.rc resource script file, you'll want to add the following line of code with a text editor, such as Edit:

```
IDB_BOYS BITMAP "boys.bmp"
```

Copy the bitmap resource file in the AddRes/Res subdirectory. Then use Insert Resource and the Import button to include the bitmap in the resource script.

The code for actually loading the bitmap is just a little more complicated. Here is that portion of code:

```
BITMAP bm;

CBitmap m_bitmap;

m_bitmap.LoadBitmap(IDB_BOYS);
m_bitmap.GetObject(sizeof(bm),&bm);

CDC dcMem;
if (!dcMem.CreateCompatibleDC(pDC))
  return;
CBitmap* pBitmapOld = dcMem.SelectObject(&m_bitmap);
if (pBitmapOld == NULL)
  return;

pDC->BitBlt(0,0,bm.bmWidth,bm.bmHeight,&dcMem,0,0,SRCCOPY);
pDC->StretchBlt(bm.bmWidth,bm.bmHeight,2*bm.bmWidth,
               2*bm.bmHeight,&dcMem,0,0,bm.bmWidth,
               bm.bmHeight,SRCCOPY);

dcMem.SelectObject(pBitmapOld);
```

The **LoadBitmap()** function loads the bitmap resource identified by IDB_BOYS. When the bitmap is loaded, it is attached to the CBitmap object. The first parameter specifies the number of bytes to copy into the buffer. The second parameter is a pointer to a buffer that receives the bitmap information.

The **CreateCompatibleDC()** function creates a *memory device context* that is compatible with the device given by *pDC*. A memory device context is a block of memory that represents the display surface. Images can be created here and quickly transferred to the device.

The **SelectObject()** function selects an object into the device context.

The **BitBlt()** and **StretchBlt()** functions are used to transfer the bitmap image to the screen.

pDC points to the device context where the image will be drawn. The first two parameters in this function specify the start of the bitmap image, while the third and fourth parameters give the width and height of the bitmap image. *dcMem* is the location where the bitmapped image is stored. The seventh and eighth parameters specify the upper-left coordinates of the source bitmap. The final parameter indicates the raster operation to be performed—in this case, SCRCOPY, which copies the source bitmap to the destination bitmap. You can find additional information on available raster operations with the Microsoft Developer Studio's Help resources.

The **StretchBlt()** function is similar to the **BitBlt()** function, but its parameters allow you to stretch a bitmap image to a larger size.

Adding a Font

A font is created with the **CreateFont()** function, discussed earlier in this chapter.

```
newfont.CreateFont(20,20,0,0,FW_BOLD,
                   FALSE,FALSE,FALSE,0,
                   OUT_DEFAULT_PRECIS,
                   CLIP_DEFAULT_PRECIS,
                   DEFAULT_QUALITY,
                   34,"Arial");
  oldfont=pDC->SelectObject(&newfont);
  pDC->TextOut(350,100,"Paul and Mark",13);
  pDC->TextOut(75,300,"1980",4);
```

The specifications call for an Arial TrueType font, 20 points by 20 points. The font will be bolded. All other parameters are system defaults.

Two text strings are drawn to different parts of the window with calls to the **TextOut()** function.

Using the ClassWizard

Use the ClassWizard to add a **Create()** member function to the AddResView.cpp file. The code shown in bold is the code we wrote for the member function.

```
//Allows inclusion of a unique cursor and background color
BOOL CAddResView::Create(LPCTSTR lpszClassName,
                         LPCTSTR lpszWindowName,DWORD dwStyle,
                         const RECT& rect, CWnd* pParentWnd,
                         UINT nID, CCreateContext* pContext)
```

```
{
  LPCTSTR lpszAddResClass=\
    AfxRegisterWndClass(CS_HREDRAW|CS_VREDRAW,
                 LoadCursor(AfxGetInstanceHandle(),
                 MAKEINTRESOURCE(IDC_CURSOR1)),
                 (HBRUSH) CreateSolidBrush(RGB(0,255,255)),
                 NULL);

  return CWnd::Create(lpszAddResClass,lpszWindowName,
                 dwStyle,rect,pParentWnd,nID,pContext);
}
```

This member function can be used to create a class with a unique cursor, icon and background color. Here is the syntax for the function:

```
LPCTSTR AFXAPI AfxRegisterWndClass(UINT nClassStyle,
                                   HCURSOR hCursor = 0,
                                   HBRUSH hbrBackground = 0,
                                   HICON hIcon = 0 );
```

The *nClassStyle* parameter gives class style for the window. The *hCursor* parameter gives the handle to the cursor resource. This cursor is used whenever a window of this class is created. The *hbrBackground* gives the handle to the brush that is used to paint the window. The final parameter, *hIcon,* is used to identify the icon resource that will be used when a window is created from this class. The function returns a null-terminated string with the class name.

The AddRes.rc resource script file should contain the following line of code:

```
IDC_CURSOR1 CURSOR DISCARDABLE "rescursor1.cur"
```

Figure 9.19 shows the unique cursor designed for this application.

Can you tell what the background color will be by looking at the RGB brush specification?

Building the AddRes Application

Build the AddRes executable file by using the Build and selecting the Rebuild All menu item. When a successful compilation results, execute the application from the Build menu by selecting the Execute AddRes.exe menu item.

Your results should be similar to Figure 9.20.

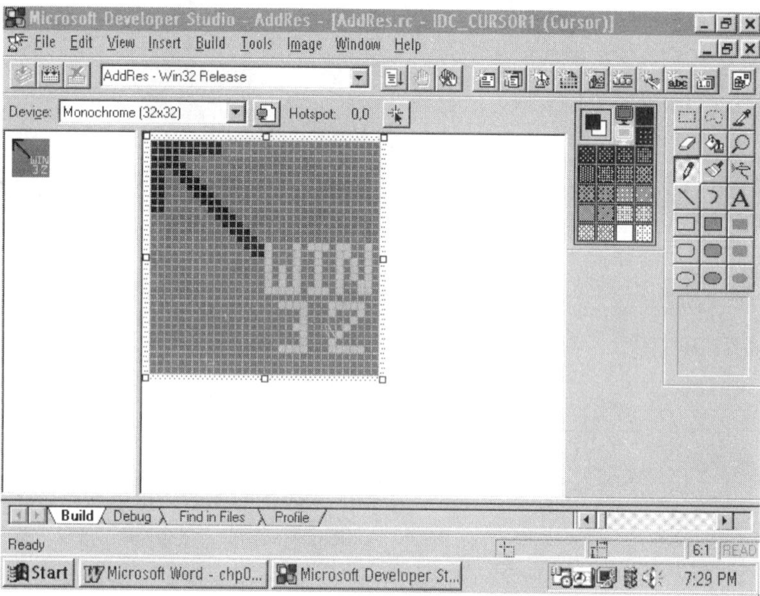

Figure 9.19: The cursor resource designed for the AddRes project.

Figure 9.20: The AddRes application showing unique resources added to the application.

You'll probably agree that resources can make an application come alive.

Note: *The base code generated by the AppWizard automatically provides a menu bar with several default popup menus. The menu items in these menus, for the most part, have not been implemented. You'll learn how to take advantage of these features as you progress through the book.*

Chapter 10

Adding Menu and Keyboard Accelerators

In the last chapter you learned how to add icon, cursor, bitmap, font, and multimedia sound resources to your application. These resources are easy to add and really help to improve the appearance of any project.

Menus and keyboard accelerators are two additional Windows resources that greatly enhance the performance of a project. Menus serve as a gateway for consistent operations from one application to another. If you use a consistent approach in menu design, users will think a new application is an old friend. Many developers consider menus the most important of all Windows resources.

Simple menus permit a user to point and click on menu items that have been predefined by the developer. Menu items allow often all users to select screen colors, object colors, sizing options, directory listings, and so on. Menu items can also serve as the interface to dialog boxes. As you'll see in the next chapter, dialog boxes are important resources because they permit interactive communications between the user and the application. Dialog boxes are used for all types of data entry, including character strings and numeric information. The proper way to access a dialog box is through a menu item.

In this chapter you will learn how to generate a base project with the AppWizard and then how to add a custom menu resource. The example application for this chapter will use a menu to allow the user to select the color of objects drawn in the client area.

Menus and Keyboard Accelerators

Before actually developing menus and keyboard accelerators for applications, you need to know what a menu is and what it looks like. You will find that both menus and keyboard accelerators are easy to create and include in any project.

What Is a Menu?

Menus, by definition, contain a list of items or names that represent options that the user can select. Selections are usually made with the mouse or a combination of keyboard keys. Menu items, the options that appear when the menu is opened, usually include simple choices. These predefined choices are used to select options or open dialog boxes and bitmaps. When a user selects a menu item, Windows automatically sends a message to the application stating which menu item was selected.

Windows draws and manages menus automatically. This feature allows menus to have a consistent appearance from one application to another. Designers and programmers create menus in the Microsoft Developer Studio as a resource. Most frequently, new menus are added to the existing menu bar created by the AppWizard. The AppWizard created a menu bar when it generated the base code for your application. This menu resource information is saved in a resource script file. Resource script files have a .rc file extension. The resource script file is compiled with the resource compiler supplied with the Microsoft Developer Studio; then combined with the application code by the linker, forming the final executable file for the project.

What Is a Keyboard Accelerator?

Keyboard accelerators are provided by Windows as an alternative method of selecting menu items. They can be used as a "hot-key" method of making menu selections. For example, a menu may allow the user to select among 12 colors, which are in turn used to set the brush color for painting closed objects. The normal technique for selecting a color choice would be to open the menu and select the menu item with the mouse. Keyboard accelerators can be used to speed up this selection process. For example, the function keys (F1 to F12) could be designated as accelerator keys and allow the user to quickly select a color without having to select the menu or menu item at all!

If a menu provides keyboard accelerators, it is common practice to list them to the right of the menu item.

BASE CODE

For the menu example in this chapter, you will need to generate base code with the AppWizard. Name the workspace MenuColor. Use the following steps to complete the project files with the AppWizard:

- Enter the Microsoft Development Studio (Visual C++ Compiler).
- Chose the File menu and select the New menu item.
- Select Project Workspace from the New dialog box.
- From the New Project Workspace dialog box:
  Name the workspace "MenuColor".

  Set the location of the workspace (for example, C:MenuColor).

  Select MFC AppWizard (exe) from the list box.
- Step 1—Select a single document application type.
- Step 2—Select no database support.
- Step 3—Select none for OLE compound document support.
- Step 4—Select no additional project features.

- Step 5—Do not select comments. Select a statically linked library.
- Step 6—View your settings and Finish the AppWizard process.

If the information is correct, in the New Project Information dialog box, select OK.

These are the steps you followed in Chapters 8 and 9. Chapter 8 describes this project creation process in more detail. When the final step has been completed as just described, the AppWizard generates all of the base files needed for the MenuColor project.

If you examine the generated files, you should find the following source code files: MainFrm.cpp, MenuColor.cpp, MenuColorDoc.cpp, MenuColorView.cpp, and StdAfx.cpp. You will also find the associated header files for these source code files, as well as a resource.h header file and a MenuColor.rc resource script file.

Changing Drawing Colors from a Menu

In this project, MenuColor, one menu will be used that will permit the user to select a new drawing color. The menu allows the user to select a new drawing color from a list of 12 predefined color choices, either directly from the menu or by using keyboard accelerators.

Designing a Menu

From the Microsoft Developer Studio, open the MenuColor.rc file. Since this is a resource script file, the Developer Studio will list all of the graphical resources already provided with this project, as shown in Figure 10.1.

As you can see from Figure 10.1, this project already has a menu resource that was added by the AppWizard. If you double-click on IDR_MAINFRAME, this menu resource will be brought to the screen, as shown in Figure 10.2.

This project will not support Edit menu items and many File menu items, so the first step will be to remove default menus and menu items not used by the project. Click on the Edit menu, as shown in Figure 10.3.

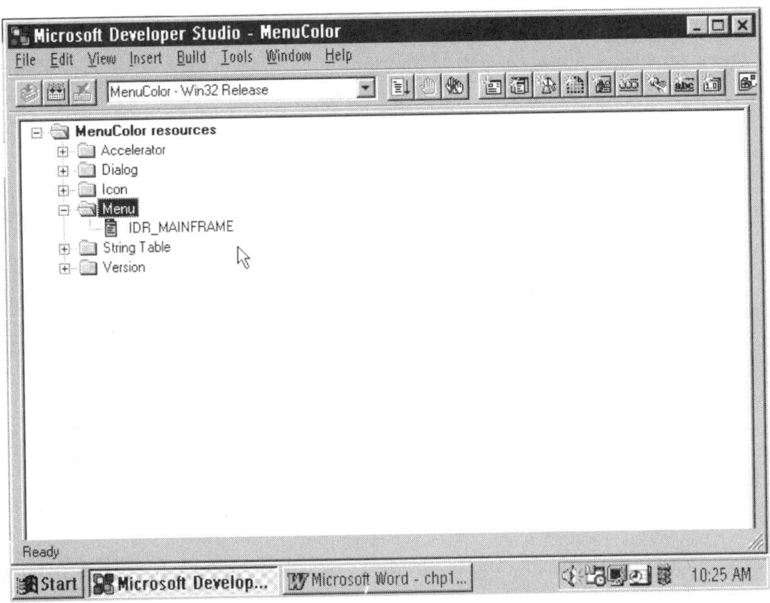

Figure 10.1: The Microsoft Developer Studio lists all project resources when the MenuColor.rc file is opened.

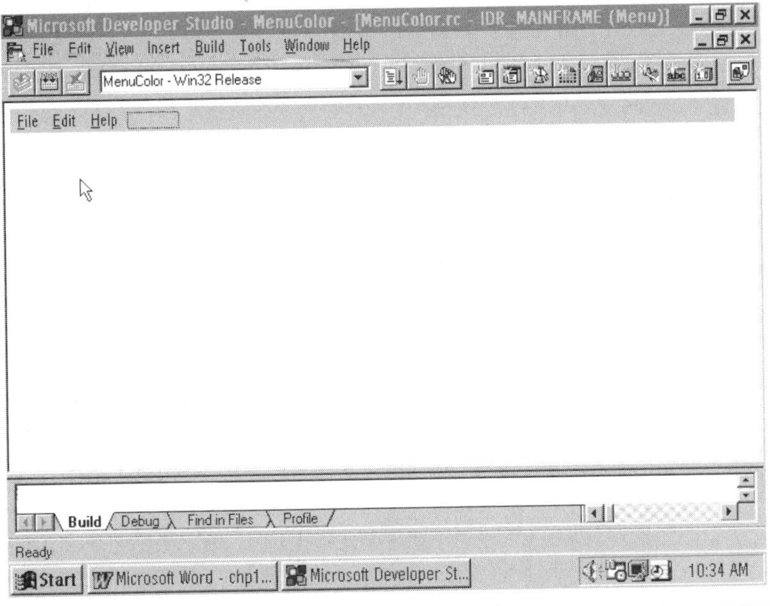

Figure 10.2: The default menu bar generated by the AppWizard.

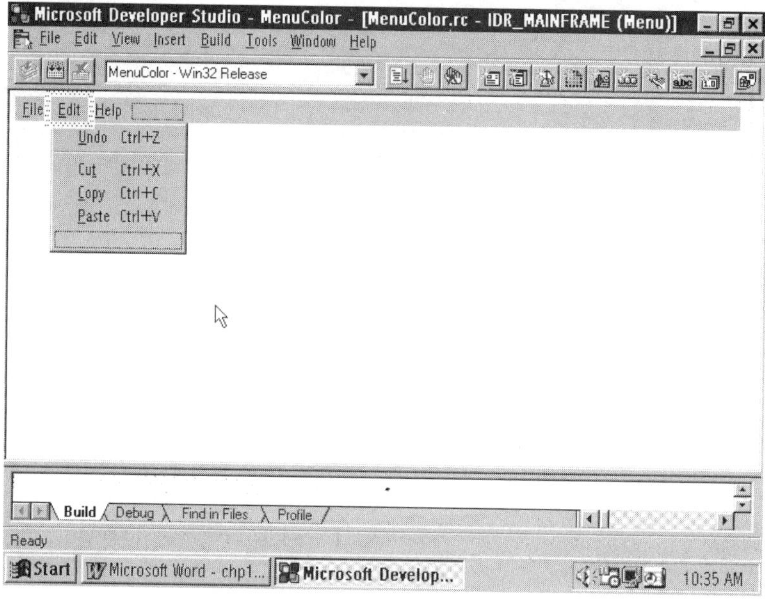

Figure 10.3: Unused default menus will be removed from this project.

If you click to open this menu's properties (right mouse button), you'll be able to cut this menu from the menu bar. Figure 10.4 shows the dialog box allowing the popup menu to be removed.

The File menu has several menu items that will not be supported. Click on File to open the menu, as shown in Figure 10.5.

Select a menu item by positioning and clicking the mouse. Use the delete key (Del) to remove the menu item from the menu.

For the File menu, remove all menu items except the Exit menu item, as shown in Figure 10.6.

To add a new menu, select the outlined rectangular shape on the menu bar, position it where you would like the new menu, and type in the menu name. Figure 10.7 shows a new menu named Colors.

When you type in the new menu name, the Menu Item Properties dialog box is opened automatically. The ampersand character (&) placed just before a letter will produce an underlined character in the resulting menu. There is no ID value associated with the menu name.

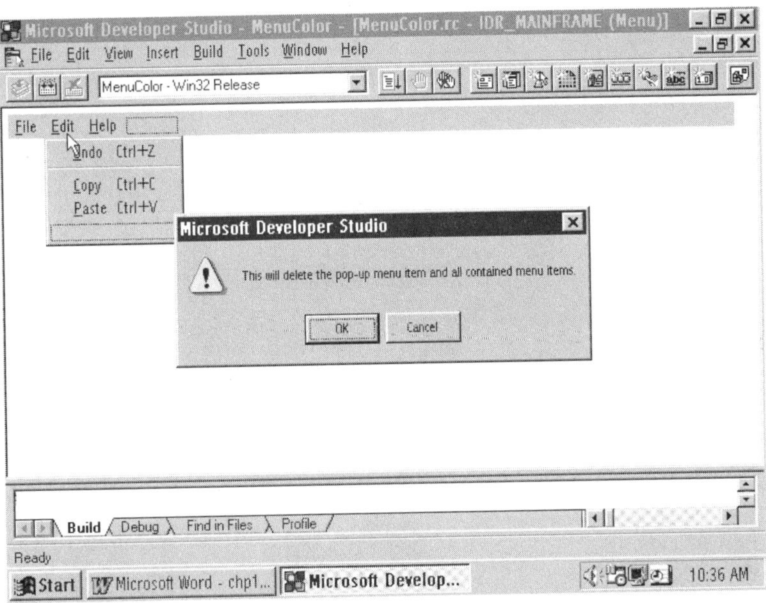

Figure 10.4: This dialog box allows the popup menu to be removed from the project.

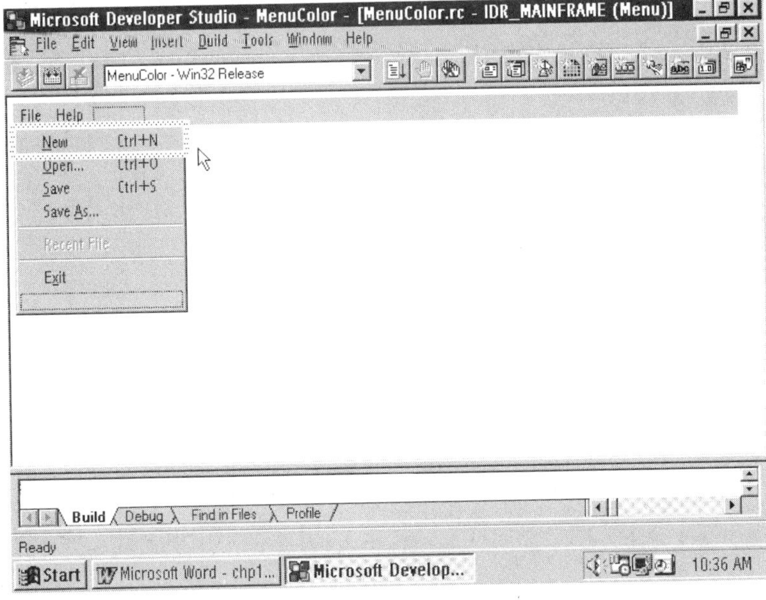

Figure 10.5: Several menu items will be removed from the File menu.

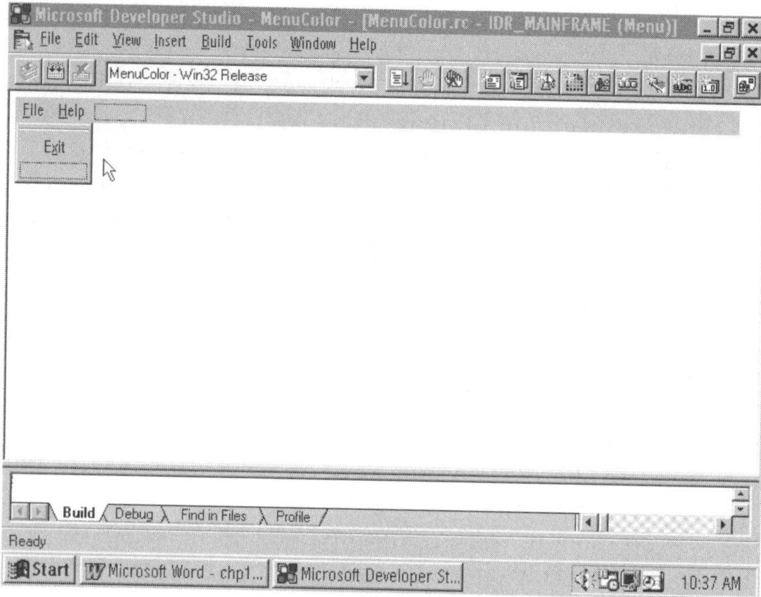

Figure 10.6: All menu items except Exit have been deleted from the File menu.

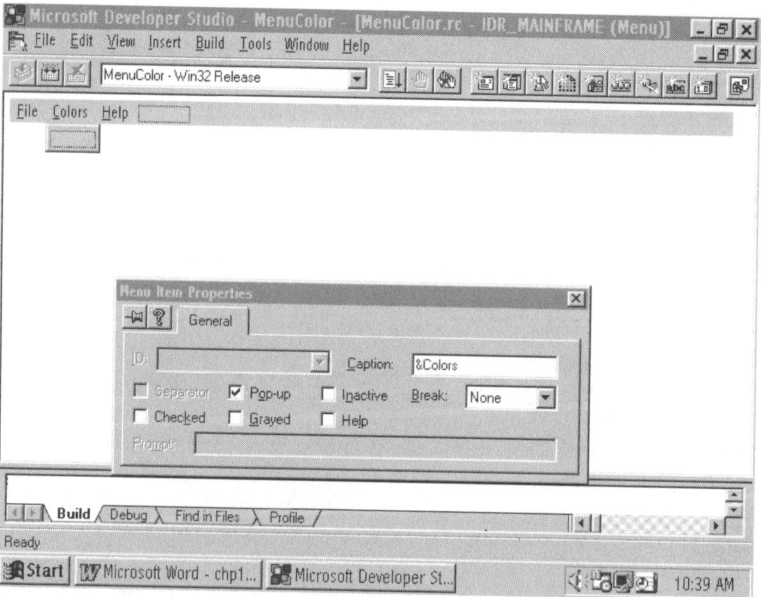

Figure 10.7: A new menu is added to the menu bar.

Now individual menu items are added to the menu. Figure 10.8 shows the first of 12 menu items.

Each time you select the outlined rectangular shape beneath the menu name, the Menu Item Properties dialog box will allow you to enter the menu item caption, ID and any special features. Notice in Figure 10.8, that the accelerator key is added to the menu caption with tF1. The t represents a tab key for the menu, and F1 will be the accelerator key corresponding to this selection. The menu item is initially checked, because this will be the default color. Note: No other menu items should have the check option set at this point. Menu items traditionally use an ID value starting with IDM (for menu). Thus, our first menu color is IDM_BLACK.

Add the remaining 11 menu items so that your menu takes on the appearance of Figure 10.9.

The menu design phase is now complete. Now it is time to add the accelerator keys. Remember, F1 through F12 shown in the previous menu are only prompts, not the implementations of the keyboard accelerators.

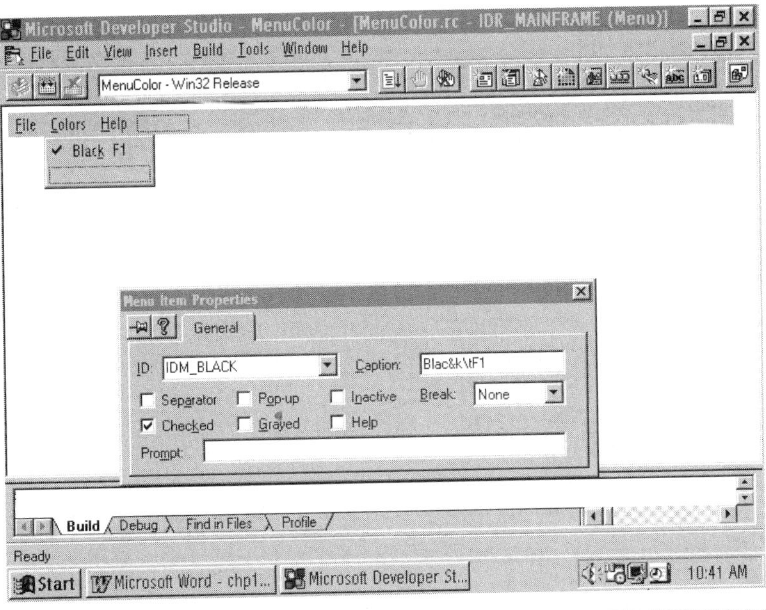

Figure 10.8: Menu items are added by selecting the outlined rectangular shape immediately under the menu name.

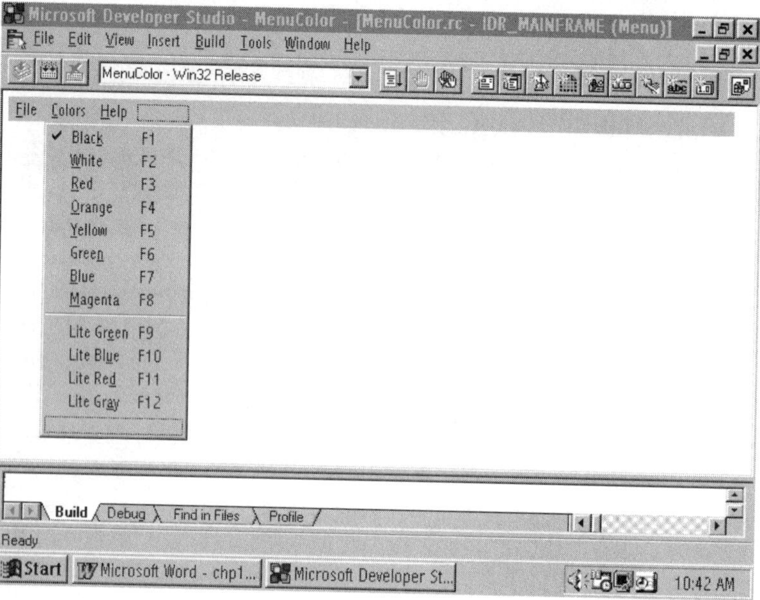

Figure 10.9: The Colors menu now contains 12 menu items and prompts for the accelerator keys.

Designing Keyboard Accelerators

Keyboard accelerators are also easy to add to a project. Return to the MenuColor.rc file and select the Accelerator item, as shown in Figure 10.10.

This project already has keyboard accelerators. The accelerator list can be opened by selecting IDR_MAINFRAME.

Figure 10.11 shows the default keyboard accelerator list produced by the AppWizard when it generated the base code for this project.

Since all file and editing options have already been removed, these keyboard accelerators are meaningless. Remove them by selecting each item and deleting it with the delete key (Del).

New keyboard accelerators can now be added to the empty list. Figure 10.12 shows the start of a new keyboard accelerator list.

To add a new key to the list, click on the outlined rectangular shape to bring up the Accel Properties dialog box. If you select the Next Key Typed button and hit the F2 function key, for example, the F2 key will now become an accelerator key. This key will be VK_F2. You must assign the ID value you want

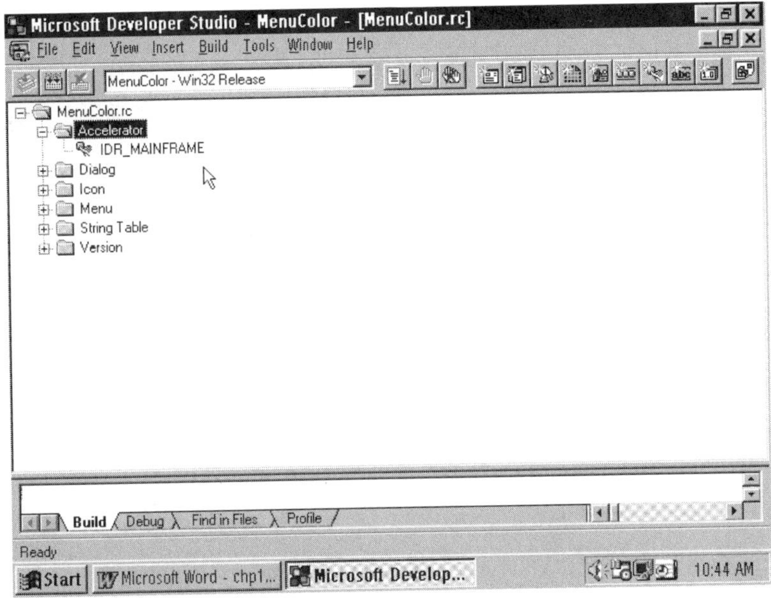

Figure 10.10: To add or alter keyboard accelerators, select the Accelerator item.

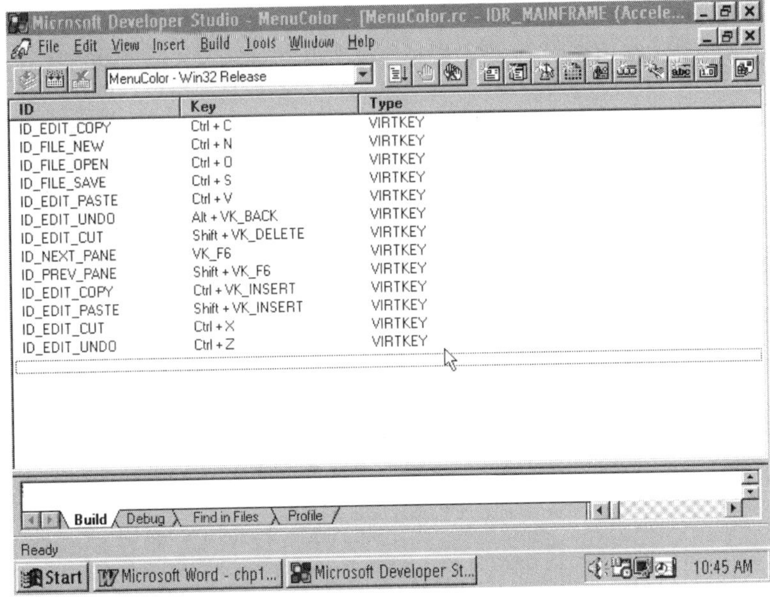

Figure 10.11: The default keyboard accelerator list generated by the AppWizard.

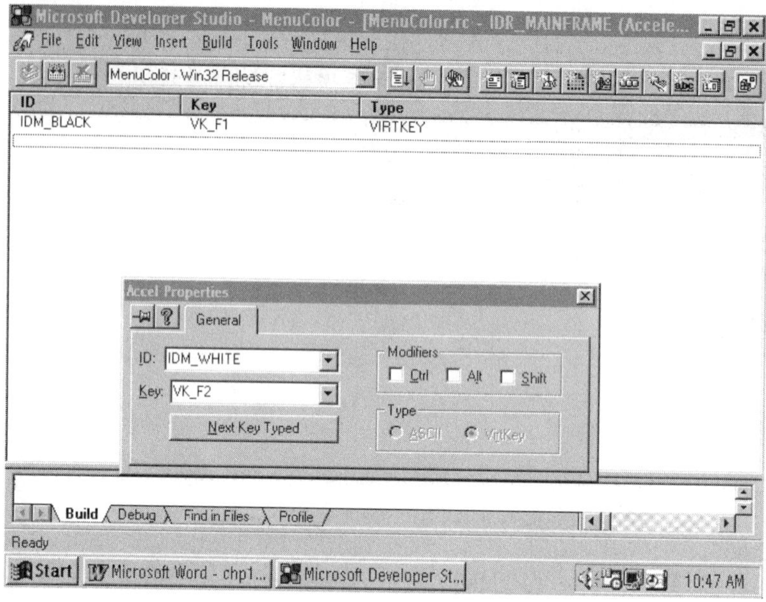

Figure 10.12: A new keyboard accelerator list being built.

associated with the key. F2 will represent the second color choice, so it is assigned the menu ID value of IDM_WHITE. All other accelerator keys are added in a similar manner.

Figure 10.13 shows the completed accelerator key list.

Why isn't the IDM_WHITE accelerator key the second key listed? The accelerator key list is maintained in alphabetical order by the Key value.

The keyboard accelerator design phase of the project is now completed.

Working with MenuColor Project Files

The AppWizard generated numerous files for this project. In the previous section, you edited the MenuColor.rc file to include a new menu, menu items, and keyboard accelerators. It is now time to alter various source code files to interact with these new resources.

The list of source code files includes MainFrm.cpp, MenuColor.cpp, MenuColorDoc.cpp, MenuColorView.cpp, and

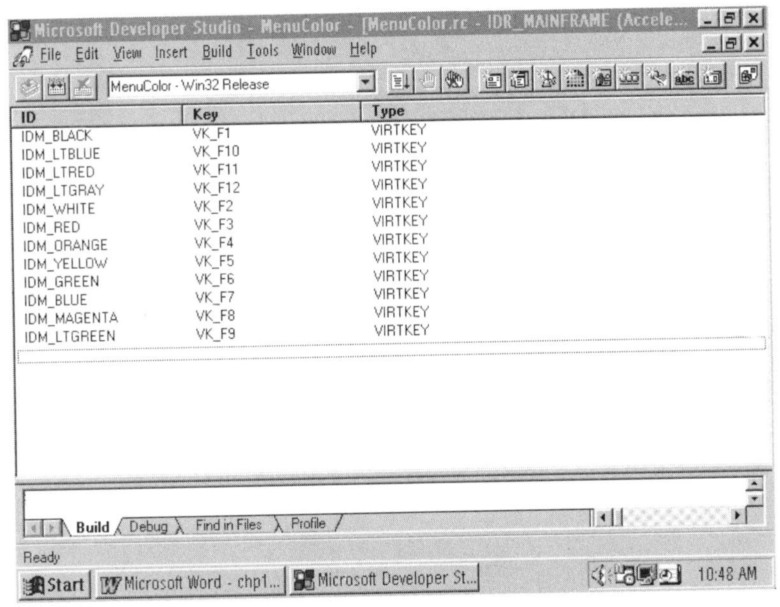

Figure 10.13: The complete accelerator key list for the MenuColor project.

StdAfx.cpp. The associated header files for these source code files are also provided. To add the new menu and keyboard accelerators will only require changes to the MenuColor.h header file and the MenuColor.cpp and MenuColorView.cpp source code files. These changes will be described in the following sections.

The MenuColor.h and MenuColor.cpp Files

The project files starting with just the name of the project, such as MenuColor, are often used to hold global values. The following listing is the complete MenuColor.h header file, showing the addition of a *ColorValue[]* variable of type COLORREF.

```
// MenuColor.h : main header file for MENUCOLOR application
//

#ifndef __AFXWIN_H__
  #error include "stdafx.h" before including file for PCH
#endif

#include "resource.h"       // main symbols

// CMenuColorApp:
```

```
// See MenuColor.cpp for the implementation of this class
//

class CMenuColorApp : public CWinApp
{
public:
  CMenuColorApp();

// Overrides
  // ClassWizard generated virtual function overrides
  //{{AFX_VIRTUAL(CMenuColorApp)
  public:
  virtual BOOL InitInstance();
  //}}AFX_VIRTUAL

// Implementation

  //{{AFX_MSG(CMenuColorApp)
  afx_msg void OnAppAbout();
  //}}AFX_MSG
  DECLARE_MESSAGE_MAP()
};

extern COLORREF NEAR ColorValue[];
```

This global reference will allow easy transfer of information between the menu items and the code implementing the color changes. These items are also often in separate files.

The definition of the *ColorValue[]* array is coded in the MenuColor.cpp source code file.

```
// MenuColor.cpp : Defines the class behaviors for the application.
//

#include "stdafx.h"
#include "MenuColor.h"

#include "MainFrm.h"
#include "MenuColorDoc.h"
#include "MenuColorView.h"

#ifdef _DEBUG
#define new DEBUG_NEW
#undef THIS_FILE
static char THIS_FILE[] = __FILE__;
#endif

// CMenuColorApp
BEGIN_MESSAGE_MAP(CMenuColorApp, CWinApp)
  //{{AFX_MSG_MAP(CMenuColorApp)
  ON_COMMAND(ID_APP_ABOUT, OnAppAbout)
  //}}AFX_MSG_MAP
```

```
  // Standard file based document commands
  ON_COMMAND(ID_FILE_NEW, CWinApp::OnFileNew)
  ON_COMMAND(ID_FILE_OPEN, CWinApp::OnFileOpen)
END_MESSAGE_MAP()

// CMenuColorApp construction
CMenuColorApp::CMenuColorApp()
{
}

// The one and only CMenuColorApp object
CMenuColorApp theApp;

// CMenuColorApp initialization
BOOL CMenuColorApp::InitInstance()
{
  // Standard initialization

  LoadStdProfileSettings();  // Load standard INI file options (including MRU)

  // Register document templates

  CSingleDocTemplate* pDocTemplate;
  pDocTemplate = new CSingleDocTemplate(
    IDR_MAINFRAME,
    RUNTIME_CLASS(CMenuColorDoc),
    RUNTIME_CLASS(CMainFrame),       // main SDI frame window
    RUNTIME_CLASS(CMenuColorView));
  AddDocTemplate(pDocTemplate);

  // Parse command line for standard shell commands, DDE, file open
  CCommandLineInfo cmdInfo;
  ParseCommandLine(cmdInfo);

  // Dispatch commands specified on the command line
  if (!ProcessShellCommand(cmdInfo))
    return FALSE;

  return TRUE;
}

// CAboutDlg dialog used for App About
class CAboutDlg : public CDialog
{
public:
  CAboutDlg();

// Dialog Data
  //{{AFX_DATA(CAboutDlg)
  enum { IDD = IDD_ABOUTBOX };
  //}}AFX_DATA

  // ClassWizard generated virtual function overrides
  //{{AFX_VIRTUAL(CAboutDlg)
```

```
  protected:
  virtual void DoDataExchange(CDataExchange* pDX);    // DDX/DDV support
  //}}AFX_VIRTUAL

// Implementation
protected:
  //{{AFX_MSG(CAboutDlg)
    // No message handlers
  //}}AFX_MSG
  DECLARE_MESSAGE_MAP()
};

CAboutDlg::CAboutDlg() : CDialog(CAboutDlg::IDD)
{
  //{{AFX_DATA_INIT(CAboutDlg)
  //}}AFX_DATA_INIT
}

void CAboutDlg::DoDataExchange(CDataExchange* pDX)
{
  CDialog::DoDataExchange(pDX);
  //{{AFX_DATA_MAP(CAboutDlg)
  //}}AFX_DATA_MAP
}

BEGIN_MESSAGE_MAP(CAboutDlg, CDialog)
  //{{AFX_MSG_MAP(CAboutDlg)
    // No message handlers
  //}}AFX_MSG_MAP
END_MESSAGE_MAP()

// App command to run the dialog
void CMenuColorApp::OnAppAbout()
{
  CAboutDlg aboutDlg;
  aboutDlg.DoModal();
}

// CMenuColorApp commands
COLORREF NEAR ColorValue[]={RGB(0,0,0),       //Black
                            RGB(255,255,255), //White
                            RGB(255,0,0),     //Red
                            RGB(255,96,0),    //Orange
                            RGB(255,255,0),   //Yellow
                            RGB(0,255,0),     //Green
                            RGB(0,0,255),     //Blue
                            RGB(255,0,255),   //Magenta
                            RGB(128,255,0),   //Lite Green
                            RGB(0,255,255),   //Lite Blue
                            RGB(255,0,159),   //Lite Red
                            RGB(180,180,180)};//Lite Gray
```

The *ColorValue[]* array holds 12 RGB color definitions. RGB values specify the amount of red, green, and blue (RGB) each color value will use. The values for each color range between 0 and 255. Thus, pure red is (255,0,0), while pure blue is (0,0,255). All other colors are specified with combinations of values, as shown in the previous listing. This global array is available to all MenuColor files.

The MenuColorView.cpp File

ClassWizard will be used to add member functions to the MenuColorView.cpp file. Open the ClassWizard from the View menu of the Microsoft Developer Studio. The Project is Menu-Color, and the Class name that we wish to work with is CMe-nuColorView, as shown in Figure 10.14.

A WM_PAINT message handler is added, as you can see in Figure 10.14. All drawing will take place when WM_PAINT messages are generated. The member function is named OnPaint.

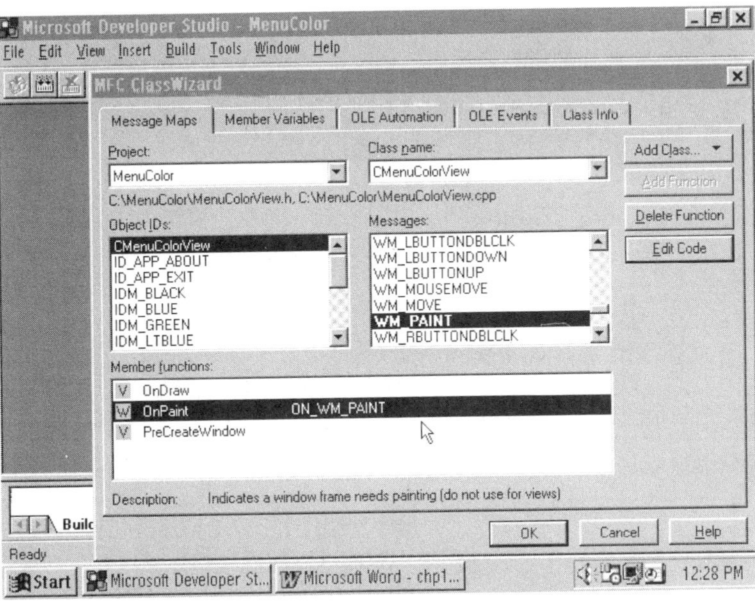

Figure 10.14: The ClassWizard is used to add member functions to the CMenuColorView class.

There are 12 menu colors. Usually you will add a separate member function for each menu choice, but this application is designed a little differently. From the MFC ClassWizard dialog box, choose the IDM_BLACK Object ID, as shown in Figure 10.15

Select the COMMAND message from the Message list box. Click on the Add Function... button to add a function for processing this information. The Add Member Function dialog box will appear with a default name for the member function. Do not use the default name. Change the name to OnColor, as shown in Figure 10.16.

Selecting a common member function name means that each color will be evaluated within the same member function. Otherwise, this application would have had member functions, each corresponding to a different color.

Now, another member function must be added to update information after a menu selection changes. In this application, the update information will be used to correctly check the menu item with a check symbol. Again, from the MFC ClassWizard dialog box, choose the IDM_BLACK Object ID, as shown in Figure 10.17.

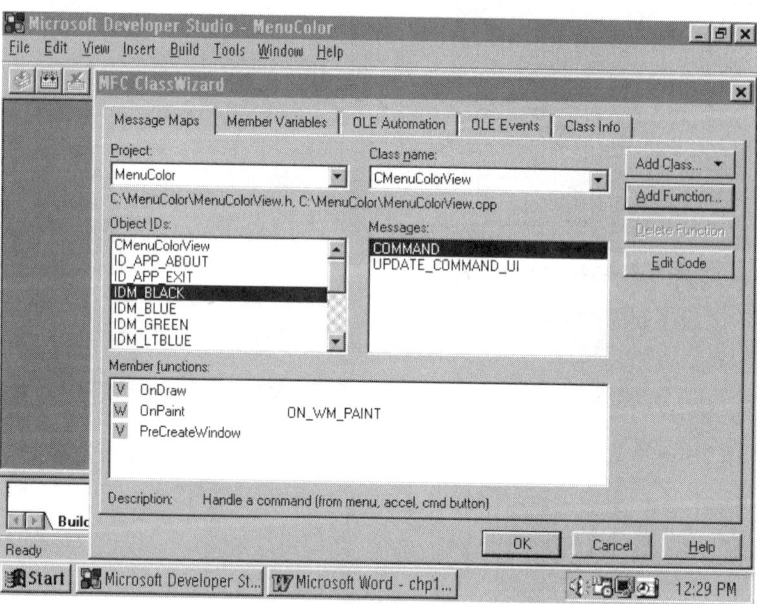

Figure 10.15: Menu items are usually processed via system commands.

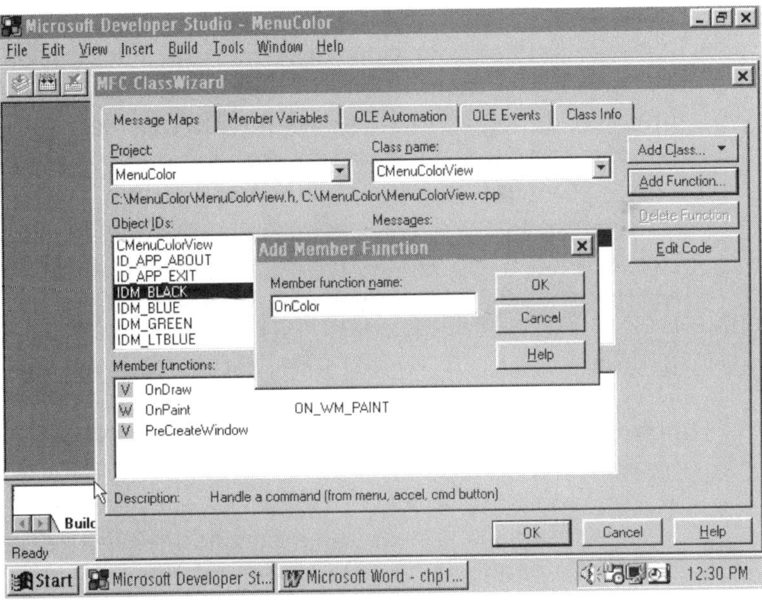

Figure 10.16: As member functions are added for each color, they will all use OnColor as the member function name.

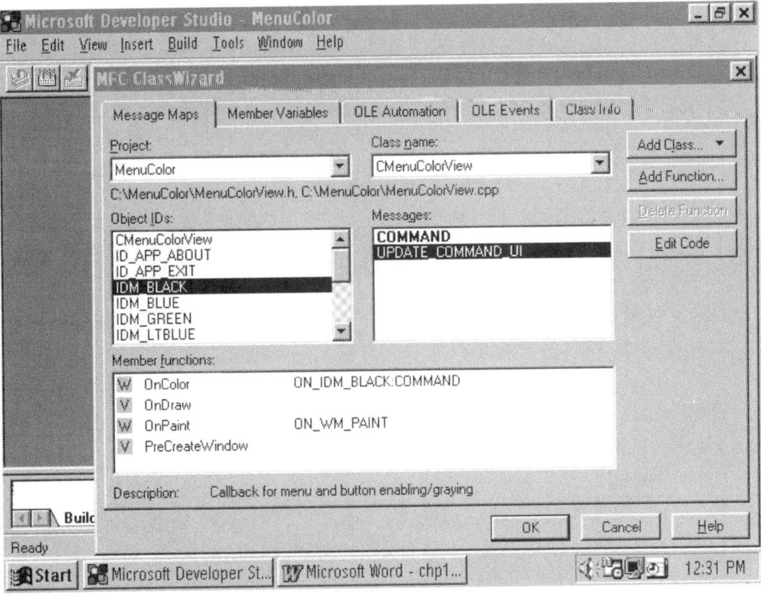

Figure 10.17: Updated information resulting from menu changes are usually processed via the UPDATE_COMMAND_UI message.

Select the UPDATE_COMMAND_UI message from the Message list box. Click on the Add Function... button to add a function for processing this information. The Add Member Function dialog box will appear with a default name for the member function. Do not use the default name. Change the name to OnUpdateColor, as shown in Figure 10.18.

Selecting a common member function name means that each time a menu item is selected, its update information will be evaluated by the same member function.

Figure 10.19 shows a partial list of all of the added member functions.

As you examine the list of member functions, notice that all menu colors use the OnColor member function. Likewise, all update messages are processed by the OnUpdateColor member function.

Once these changes are made, the ClassWizard will update the MenuColorView.cpp file. Here is a complete listing of this file.

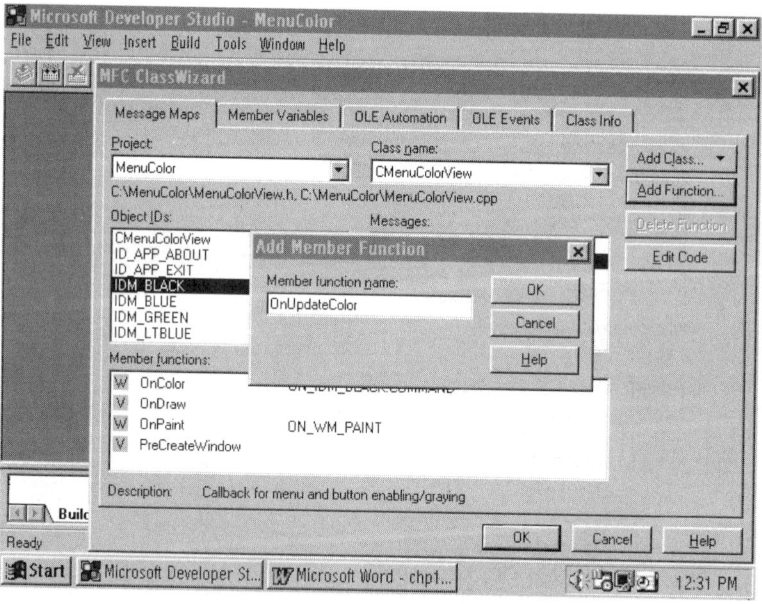

Figure 10.18: As member functions are added for each color, they will all use OnUpdateColor as the member function name.

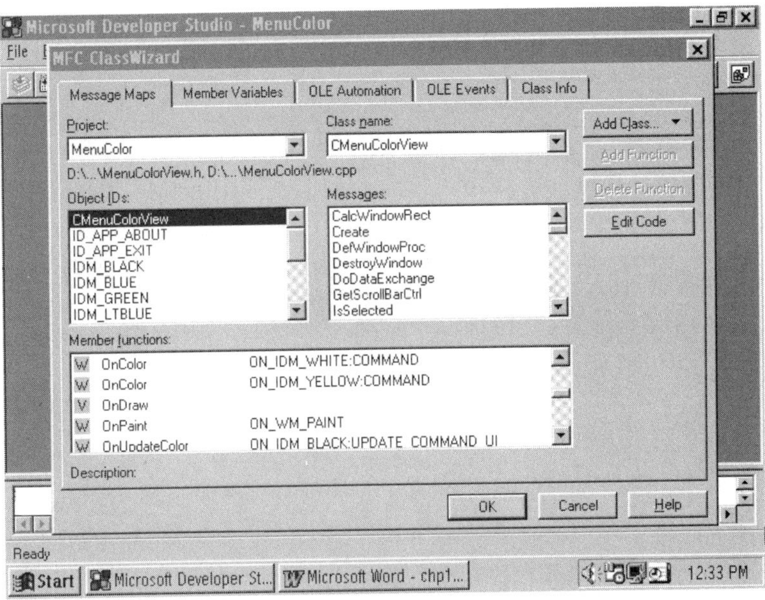

Figure 10.19: A partial view of the completed list of member functions.

```
// MenuColorView.cpp : implementation of CMenuColorView class
//

#include "stdafx.h"
#include "MenuColor.h"

#include "MenuColorDoc.h"
#include "MenuColorView.h"

#ifdef _DEBUG
#define new DEBUG_NEW
#undef THIS_FILE
static char THIS_FILE[] = __FILE__;
#endif

UINT m_nColor;
UINT m_clrBrush;

// CMenuColorView
IMPLEMENT_DYNCREATE(CMenuColorView, CView)

BEGIN_MESSAGE_MAP(CMenuColorView, CView)
  //{{AFX_MSG_MAP(CMenuColorView)
  ON_WM_PAINT()
```

```
    ON_COMMAND(IDM_BLACK, OnColor)
    ON_COMMAND(IDM_BLUE, OnColor)
    ON_COMMAND(IDM_GREEN, OnColor)
    ON_COMMAND(IDM_LTBLUE, OnColor)
    ON_COMMAND(IDM_LTGRAY, OnColor)
    ON_COMMAND(IDM_LTGREEN, OnColor)
    ON_COMMAND(IDM_LTRED, OnColor)
    ON_COMMAND(IDM_MAGENTA, OnColor)
    ON_COMMAND(IDM_ORANGE, OnColor)
    ON_COMMAND(IDM_RED, OnColor)
    ON_COMMAND(IDM_WHITE, OnColor)
    ON_COMMAND(IDM_YELLOW, OnColor)
    ON_UPDATE_COMMAND_UI(IDM_BLACK, OnUpdateColor)
    ON_UPDATE_COMMAND_UI(IDM_BLUE, OnUpdateColor)
    ON_UPDATE_COMMAND_UI(IDM_GREEN, OnUpdateColor)
    ON_UPDATE_COMMAND_UI(IDM_LTBLUE, OnUpdateColor)
    ON_UPDATE_COMMAND_UI(IDM_LTGRAY, OnUpdateColor)
    ON_UPDATE_COMMAND_UI(IDM_LTGREEN, OnUpdateColor)
    ON_UPDATE_COMMAND_UI(IDM_LTRED, OnUpdateColor)
    ON_UPDATE_COMMAND_UI(IDM_MAGENTA, OnUpdateColor)
    ON_UPDATE_COMMAND_UI(IDM_ORANGE, OnUpdateColor)
    ON_UPDATE_COMMAND_UI(IDM_RED, OnUpdateColor)
    ON_UPDATE_COMMAND_UI(IDM_WHITE, OnUpdateColor)
    ON_UPDATE_COMMAND_UI(IDM_YELLOW, OnUpdateColor)
  //}}AFX_MSG_MAP
END_MESSAGE_MAP()

// CMenuColorView construction/destruction
CMenuColorView::CMenuColorView()
{
    m_nColor = IDM_BLACK;
    m_clrBrush = RGB(0,0,0);
}

CMenuColorView::~CMenuColorView()
{
}

BOOL CMenuColorView::PreCreateWindow(CREATESTRUCT& cs)
{
  return CView::PreCreateWindow(cs);
}

// CMenuColorView drawing
void CMenuColorView::OnDraw(CDC* pDC)
{
  CMenuColorDoc* pDoc = GetDocument();
  ASSERT_VALID(pDoc);
}
```

```
// CMenuColorView diagnostics
#ifdef _DEBUG
void CMenuColorView::AssertValid() const
{
  CView::AssertValid();
}

void CMenuColorView::Dump(CDumpContext& dc) const
{
  CView::Dump(dc);
}

CMenuColorDoc* CMenuColorView::GetDocument()
{
  ASSERT(m_pDocument->IsKindOf(RUNTIME_CLASS(CMenuColorDoc)));
  return (CMenuColorDoc*)m_pDocument;
}
#endif //_DEBUG

// CMenuColorView message handlers
void CMenuColorView::OnPaint()
{
  CPaintDC dc(this); // device context for painting

  CBrush newbrush;
  CBrush* oldbrush;

  newbrush.CreateSolidBrush(m_clrBrush);
  oldbrush=dc.SelectObject(&newbrush);

  dc.Ellipse(10,10,60,60);
  dc.Ellipse(100,40,300,100);
  dc.Ellipse(20,200,50,400);
  dc.Ellipse(100,100,500,300);
}

void CMenuColorView::OnColor()
{
  m_nColor = LOWORD(GetCurrentMessage()->wParam);
  m_clrBrush = ColorValue[m_nColor - IDM_BLACK];
  InvalidateRect(NULL,TRUE);
}

void CMenuColorView::OnUpdateColor(CCmdUI* pCmdUI)
{
  pCmdUI->SetCheck(pCmdUI->m_nID==m_nColor);
}
```

The bolded lines of code were added by us during the creation of this project. All other lines were generated by the AppWizard or ClassWizard.

The first group of bolded lines identifies *m_nColor* and *m_clrBrush*. These unsigned integers will be used to identify menu items and set brush colors.

Examine the listing and notice the inclusion of ON_COMMAND and ON_UPDATE_COMMAND_UI lines for each menu color in the file's message map. These were inserted by the ClassWizard.

The class constructor is used to initialize the default brush ID and the brush color, before any menu selections are made.

```
m_nColor = IDM_BLACK;
m_clrBrush = RGB(0,0,0);
```

Several graphical shapes created with the **Ellipse()** function are drawn to the client area of the window and filled with the current brush color. These functions are handled within the **OnPaint()** member function.

```
CBrush newbrush;
CBrush* oldbrush;

newbrush.CreateSolidBrush(m_clrBrush);
oldbrush=dc.SelectObject(&newbrush);

dc.Ellipse(10,10,60,60);
dc.Ellipse(100,40,300,100);
dc.Ellipse(20,200,50,400);
dc.Ellipse(100,100,500,300);
```

The CBrush class is used for creating a new brush object. A new solid brush is created by calling the **CreateSolidBrush()** function and passing it a brush color via the *m_clrBrush* variable. Since an ellipse is a closed shape, it is automatically filled with the current brush color.

A separate member function, **OnColor()**, allows the brush color to be changed to match the menu selection.

```
m_nColor = LOWORD(GetCurrentMessage()->wParam);
m_clrBrush = ColorValue[m_nColor - IDM_BLACK];
InvalidateRect(NULL,TRUE);
```

The *wParam* value contains the menu color selection when the color is selected from the menu or by a keyboard accelerator. This value is sent as a message when the menu selection is made. The **GetCurrentMessage()** function intercepts the complete message. The color value resides in the LOWORD of the message.

The *m_nColor* value contains an integer value reflecting the menu item selected. This value is actually the ID number assigned to the color selection by the AppWizard. You can view these ID values in the resource.h header file.

Imagine that IDM_BLACK is assigned an ID value of 32771 and IDM_GREEN a value of 32776. The difference between these two numbers is 5. Five is then used as the index value into the *ColorValue[]* array. Remember the array index starts at 0, so the green color is defined in the sixth position with an index value of 5.

Once the color value is selected, it is globally available. However, the graphics colors won't change until you force a repaint of the client area. This is done with a call to the InvalidateRect() function. No handle is used, so a NULL value is specified. A TRUE value for the second parameter forces the whole client area to be repainted.

The final step is to check the selected color in the menu. If you've been programming in Windows for a while, you might be tempted to use the **CheckMenuItem()** function. However, this function has been replaced with the **SetCheck()** member function.

```
pCmdUI->SetCheck(pCmdUI->m_nID==m_nColor);
```

The framework passes the handler a pointer to a CCmdUI object when routing the update command to the handler. In this case, the object is a menu item that must be checked. A pointer is used by the update handler for calling member functions of the CCmdUI structure. Once completed, the correct menu item will be checked.

Testing the MenuColor Application

Build the executable file for this project by selecting the Rebuild All menu item from the Microsoft Developer Studio's Build menu.

Execute the MenuColor.exe file by selecting the Execute menu item also found in the Build menu.

Your results should be similar to those shown in Figure 10.20.

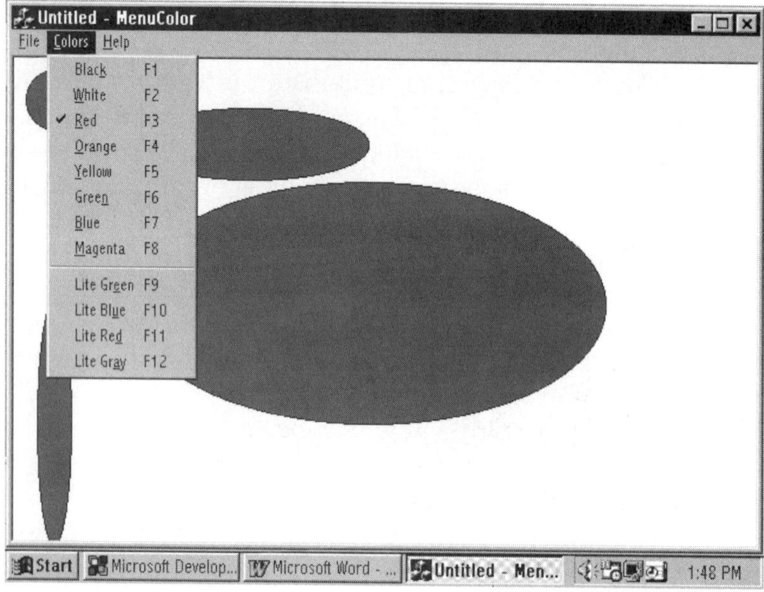

Figure 10.20: The colored graphics shapes drawn in the client area by the MenuColor application.

More Menus?

Menus are relatively easy resources to incorporate into an application. You will gain more experience developing and implementing menus as you work through the remaining chapters in this book. Remember, menus are the gateway to dialog boxes, and Chapter 11 is devoted exclusively to dialog boxes!

Chapter 11

Adding Dialog Boxes

In the last chapter you learned how to use menus and keyboard accelerators to allows a small degree of user interaction with the application. In this chapter you will learn of a more important means of allowing user interaction—the dialog box. Menus serve as the path to dialog boxes. Menu items marked with ellipses (...) indicate that the menu item will call up a dialog box. Dialog boxes, in turn, make the greatest use of Windows controls. Controls include pushbuttons, radio buttons, list boxes, edit boxes, static text boxes, and so on. The use of standard controls in a dialog box gives your application the interactive capabilities of commercially produced applications. This chapter is devoted to teaching you dialog box fundamentals, how to used standard controls, and how to pass data from dialog box resources to the application. Additional material on dialog boxes, common controls and custom controls can be found in Chapters 13 and 17.

Dialog Boxes Are Resources

Dialog boxes are child windows that pop up when a dialog box menu item is selected. Dialog boxes can range from simple About boxes to complicated data entry forms involving the use of numerous controls. When a user selects a dialog box control, such as a push button, check box, or edit box, Windows supplies the means necessary to process the message information.

Dialog boxes are created as a resource from within the Microsoft Developer Studio. When their specifications are saved, they are saved to a resource script file which uses an .rc file extension. A new dialog box resource can be created by using the Insert menu and selecting the Resource... menu item, as shown in Figure 11.1.

The Insert Resource dialog box lists possible resources that can be created in the Microsoft Developer Studio, as shown in Figure 11.2.

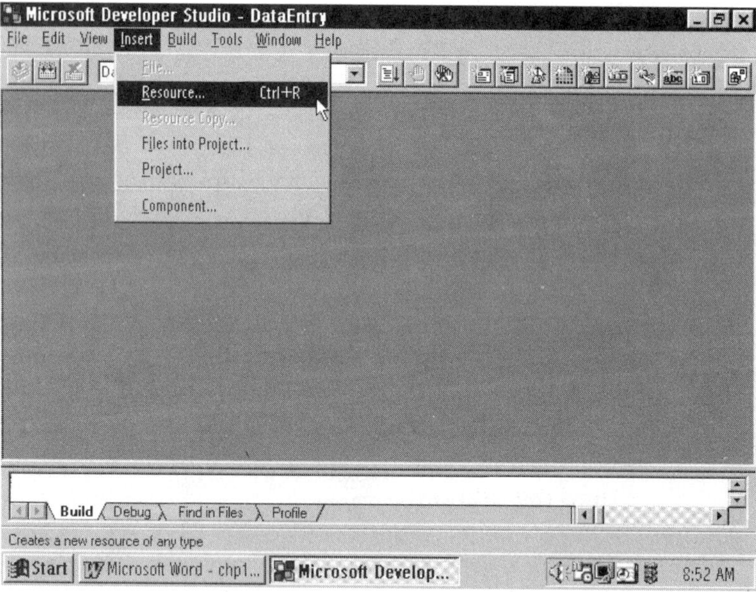

Figure 11.1: To create a dialog box, select the Resource... menu item.

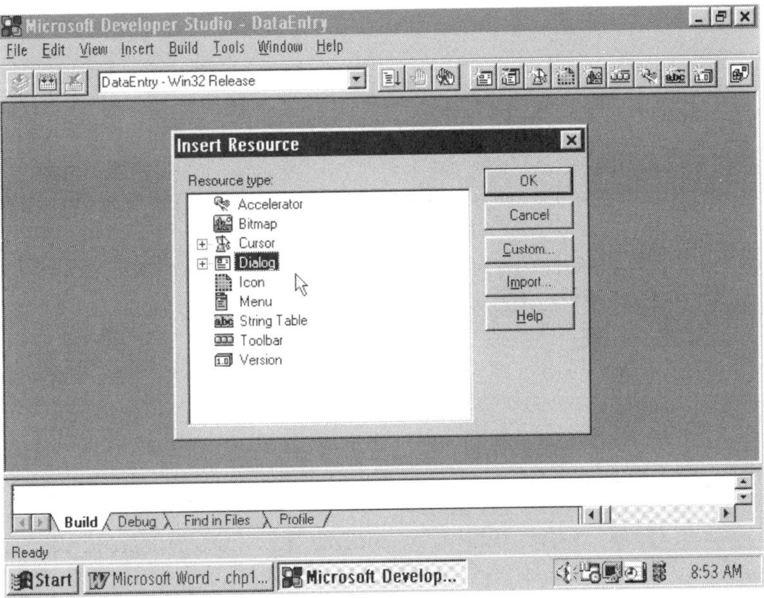

Figure 11.2: The Insert Resource dialog box lists project resources.

Select the Dialog resource type while in the Insert Resources dialog box. You will enter the dialog box editor, which provides a default dialog box, a toolbox of controls, and a toolbar of dialog box alignment items, as shown in Figure 11.3.

Examine Figure 11.3 and examine the 14 buttons in the toolbar located at the bottom of the design window. Examining the buttons from left to right, Table 11.1 describes the function of each of these buttons.

The dialog box Control toolbox is shown to the right of the default dialog box in Figure 11.3. The Control toolbox is a 3×7 grid. Cells in this grid contain small icons which represent the control. Controls can be transferred from the tool box to the dialog box under construction by placing the pointer on the control, depressing the left mouse button, and dragging the control to the dialog box.

Table 11.2 briefly names and describes each control in the toolbox. The description starts in the upper-left corner and proceeds down the column. The second column of controls is then described in the same order and finally the third column.

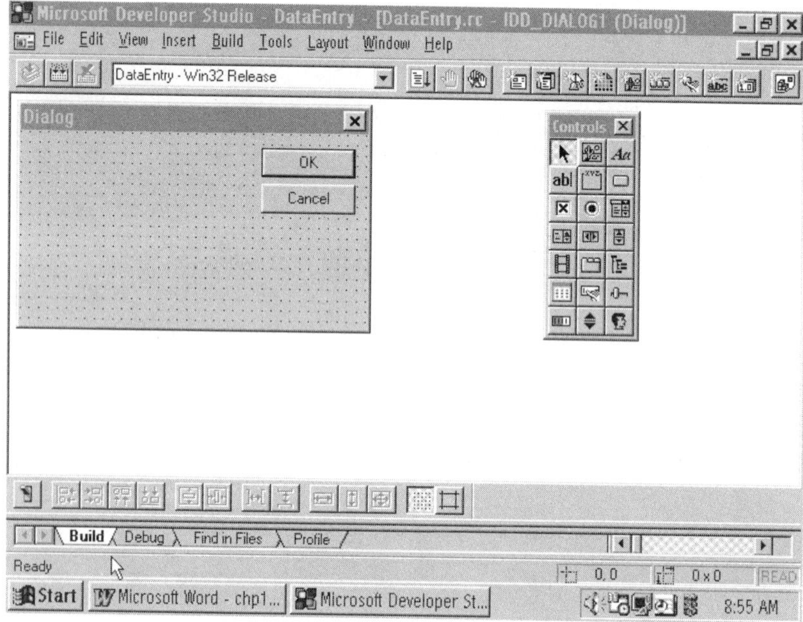

Figure 11.3: The dialog box editor provides controls and toolbar items for designing dialog boxes.

Table 11.1: Dialog Toolbar Button Functions

Button	*Function*
Test	permits developer to test dialog box.
Align Left	Allows a group of selected controls to be aligned to the left.
Align Right	Allows a group of selected controls to be aligned to the right.
Align Top	Allows a group of selected controls to be aligned to the top.
Align Bottom	Allows a group of selected controls to be aligned to the bottom.
Center Vertical	Allows a group of selected controls to be centered vertically.
Center Horizontal	Allows a group of selected controls to be centered horizontally.
Space Across	Allows a group of selected controls to be evenly spaced horizontally.
Space Down	Allows a group of selected controls to be evenly spaced vertically.
Make Same Width	Makes a group of selected controls the same width.
Make Same Height	Makes a group of selected controls the same height.
Toggle Grid	Turns the design grid on and off.
Toggle Guide	Turns the design guide on and off.

Table 11.2: Dialog Toolbox Controls

Control	*Function*
Select	Allows you to select a new control (not a control).
Edit Box	Allows text or numeric information to be entered.
Check Box	Usually used in groups to allow multiple items to be selected.
List Box	Provides a list of items, such as files, names, or options.
Animate	Allows the selected items to be animated.
List	Allows items to be listed in a sequential manner.
Progress	Allows the progress of an event, such as a file transfer, to be viewed.
Picture	Allows a picture to be placed in the dialog box.
Group Box	Allows a collection of controls to be handled as a group.
Radio Button	Allows one item in a group of items to be selected.
Horz Scroll Bar	Places a horizontal scroll bar control in dialog box.
Tab Control	Produces a set of tab controls (folders).
Hot Key	Defines hot key action.
Spin	Inserts a spin control into dialog box.
Static Text	Places text in a dialog box.
Button	A push-button control, such as OK and Cancel.
Combo Box	Places a combo box control in a dialog box.
Vertical Scroll Bar	Places a vertical scroll bar control in a dialog box.
Tree Control	Places a tree control in a dialog box.
Slider	Places a slider control in a dialog box.
Custom Control	Allows a custom control to be inserted in a dialog box.

In the next section, you'll learn additional details about the purpose and use of many of these controls.

Important Dialog Controls

New controls are frequently added to the Controls toolbox. In the following section, the most frequently used controls will be described. Other controls, such as spin, slider, and custom controls, are discussed in Chapters 13, 17, and 18.

The Button Control

The (push) Button control is a small, rounded rectangle that can also be sized. This control contains a text label. Buttons are used for making an immediate choice, such as the OK and Cancel buttons typically found on dialog boxes.

The Check Box Control

The Check Box control draws a small square box. A label is placed to the right of the rectangle. These controls are marked, or checked, by clicking the left mouse button while positioned over the control. Check box controls typically appear in groups. Groups of check boxes allow the user to check one or more features at the same time.

The Combo Box Control

The Combo Box control consists of two elements. It is a combination of a single-line edit field (also called static text control) and a list box. This control provides the ability to enter information in the edit box or scroll through the list box looking for a selection.

The Edit Box Control

The Edit Box control draws a small interactive rectangular control on the screen. Numeric or text information can be entered into this area from the keyboard. The string information can be processed as character or numeric data.

The Group Box Control

The Group Box control draws a rectangular outline within a dialog box. The outline can enclose a group of controls that are used together. For example, a group box might contain check boxes and radio buttons for setting font styles. The group box has a user-defined label on its upper-left edge.

The Hot Key Control

A key combination, defined by the designer, to quickly perform an operation. When the key combination is selected, a **WM_SETHOTKEY** message is invoked.

The List Box Control

The List Box control draws a rectangular outline with a vertical scroll bar. List boxes permit scrolling of long lists.

The Picture Control

The Picture control allows images to be inserted into a dialog box. These images are typically small, but can be expanded to fill the entire dialog box.

The Radio Button Control

The Radio Button control draws a small circle control with a label to its right. Radio button controls, like check box controls, usually appear in groups. However, only one radio button control can be selected at a given time.

The Scroll Bar Controls

The Horizontal and Vertical Scroll Bar controls draw the horizontal or vertical scroll bars for the dialog box. These controls are usually used in conjunction with another window or control that contains text or graphics information.

The Static Text Control

The Static Text control allows the insertion of labels and strings within the dialog box. These are used for titles and labels used with various controls, such as edit box controls.

Base Code

For each of the two examples in this chapter, you will need to generate the same base code with the AppWizard. Name the first workspace DataEntry. Using the following steps, complete the project files with the AppWizard.

Enter the Microsoft Development Studio (Visual C++ Compiler).

- Choose the File menu and select the New menu item.
- Select Project Workspace from the New dialog box.
- From the New Project Workspace dialog box:
  Name the workspace "DataEntry".

  Set the location of the workspace (for example, C:DataEntry).

  Select MFC AppWizard (exe) from the list box.

- Step 1—Select a single document application type.
- Step 2—Select no database support.
- Step 3—Select none for OLE compound document support.
- Step 4—Select no additional features.
- Step 5—Do not select comments. Select a statically linked library.
- Step 6—View your settings and Finish the AppWizard process.

If the information is correct, in the New Project Information dialog box, select OK.

When the final step has been completed, as just described, the AppWizard generates all of the base files needed for the DataEntry project.

You will now need to repeat the process one more time. Use the previously listed steps to create a new project workspace named Colors.

A New About Dialog Box for the DataEntry Project

When you used the AppWizard to generate the DataEntry project, described in the previous section, a default About dialog box was generated. To view and modify this About dialog box, open the DataEntry.rc file while in the Microsoft Developer Studio. You'll be able to select the About dialog box from the list of resources, as shown in Figure 11.4.

When you have selected the About dialog box for editing, the Microsoft Developer Studio will take you to the dialog editor and place the About box in the window. Figure 11.5 shows the default About dialog box designed by the AppWizard for this project.

Controls present on the dialog box can be eliminated or modified. Select the control by positioning the mouse over the control and clicking the left mouse button. Once the control is selected, it can be eliminated by pushing the delete (Del) key. Controls can be modified by clicking the right mouse button and selecting the Properties dialog box from the list of items. From the Properties dialog box, the text in the two Static Text controls can be modified, as shown in Figure 11.6.

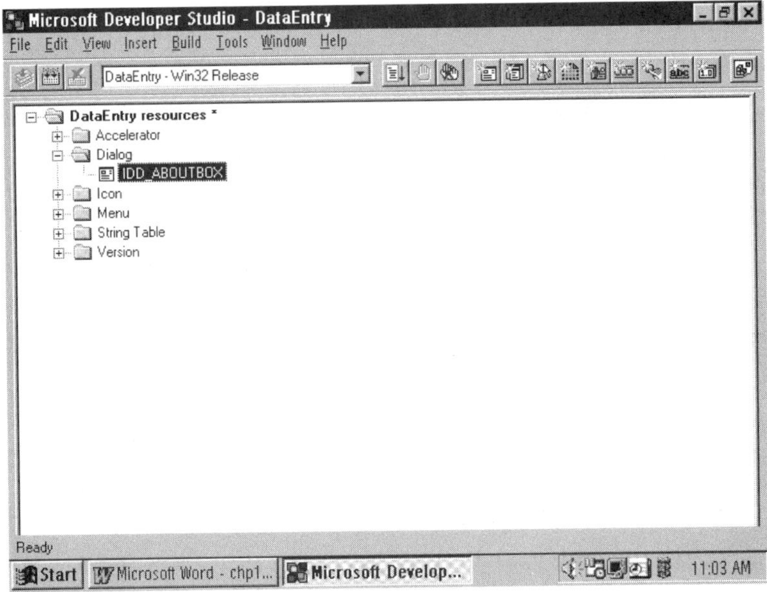

Figure 11.4: Select the IDD_ABOUTBOX item to edit the default About dialog box.

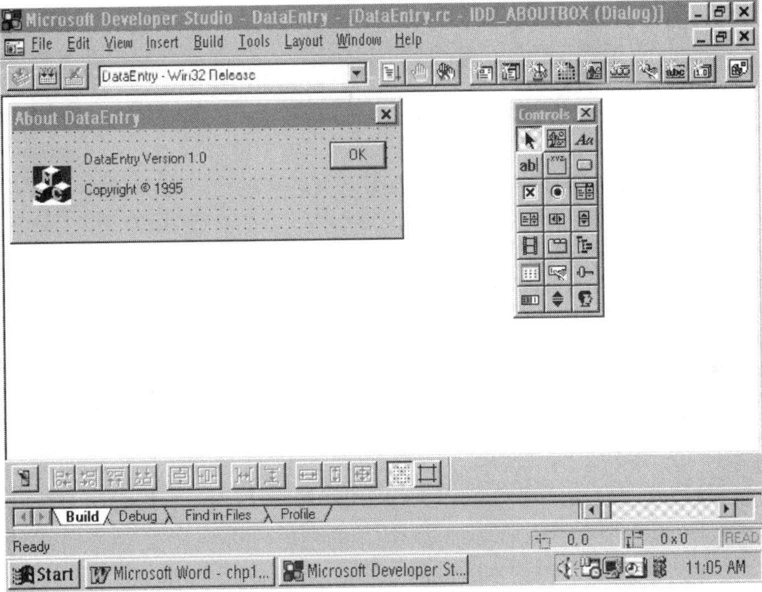

Figure 11.5: The default About dialog box generated by the AppWizard.

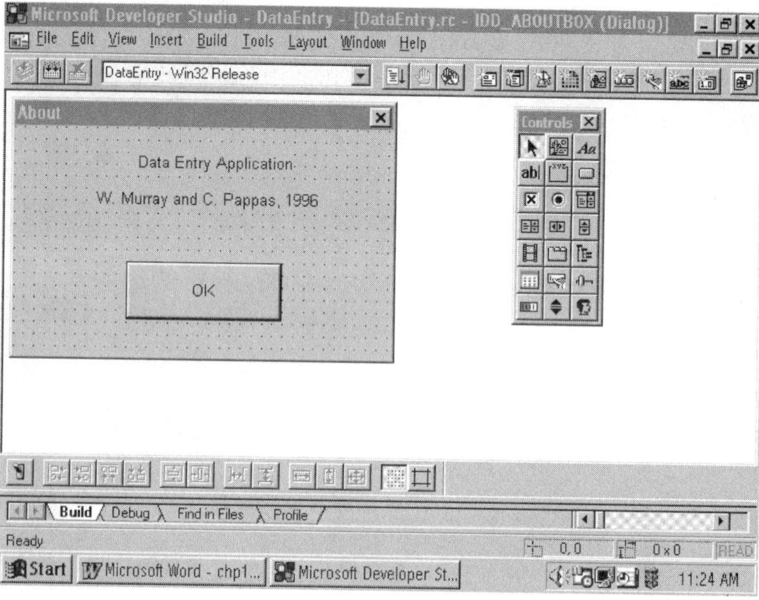

Figure 11.6: The original About dialog box is modified.

As you view Figure 11.6, also notice that the icon has been deleted, the push button moved and resized, the dialog box dimensions changed, the default font changed to an Arial TrueType font, and the static text centered horizontally.

About boxes are most used to convey information to the user concerning the application, the developers, and any copyright information. Since they are automatically added by the AppWizard, just a little editing customizes the About box for your project. What could be easier?

A Data Entry Dialog Box for the DataEntry Project

A new dialog box will be created for the DataEntry project to allow data to be entered from the keyboard. In order to reach the dialog box, a special menu will be created. The AppWizard created a default menu bar, so it will simply be a matter of opening DataEntry.rc to alter the existing menu resource. Once DataEntry.rc is opened, select the Menu resource, as shown in Figure 11.7.

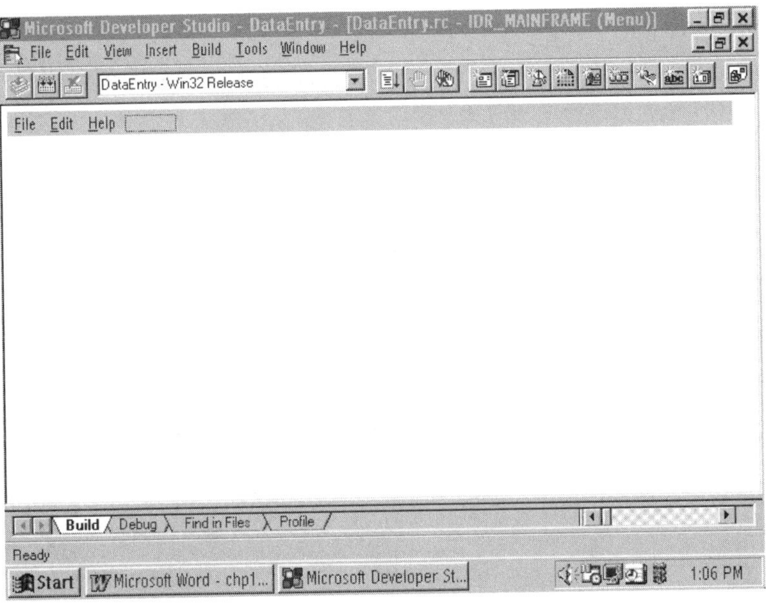

Figure 11.7: Editing the items on the default menu bar.

IDR_MAINFRAME is the ID given the menu resource. Figure 11.8 shows the modified menu bar with a new menu named Data. Data contains a menu item named Data Entry... which will allow access to a new dialog box.

If you are creating this resource while reading, now is the time to edit your menu. The Data Entry... menu item is automatically assigned an ID value. For this project it is ID_DATA_DATAENTRY.

It is now time to create an entirely new dialog box to house various data entry controls. To add an additional dialog resource, use the Insert menu and choose the Resource... menu item. The Insert Resource dialog box allows you to select the resource type. In this case, a Dialog resource is selected.

Use the default dialog box provided by the dialog editor and modify the controls so that it appears similar to Figure 11.9.

The original default dialog box was resized and the OK and Cancel push buttons moved to the new locations. Next, a group box was added and titled Shape. Two radio buttons were added to this group. One radio button is named Ellipse, and the other Rectangle. Four Static Text controls are then

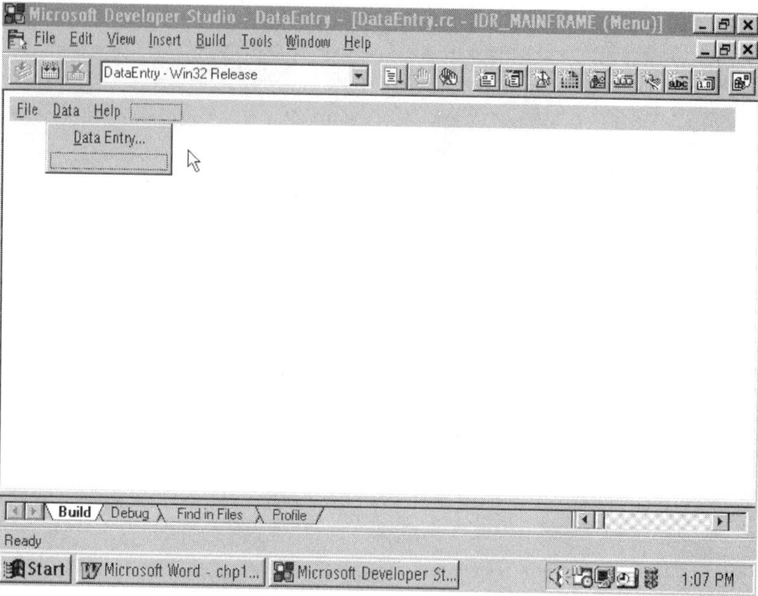

Figure 11.8: A new menu and menu item are added to the menu bar.

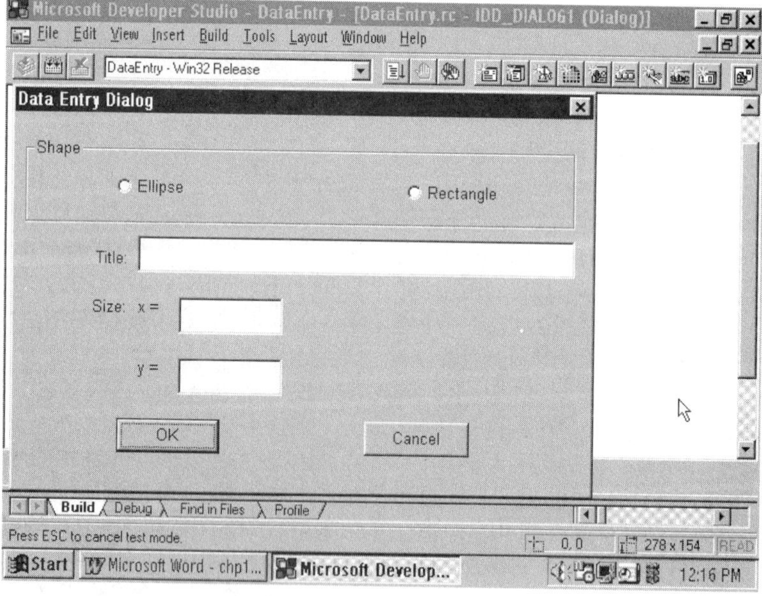

Figure 11.9: The default dialog box is modified for the DataEntry project.

added. Their titles include Title, Size, x =, and y =. Three Edit Box controls are added to allow user input. These are the white rectangles shown earlier in Figure 11.9.

In order to communicate with the dialog box and the dialog box controls, each is given a unique ID value when created. We'll use the defaults assigned by the editor for this project. The dialog box itself is assigned an ID of IDD_DIALOG1. The Ellipse radio button is assigned IDC_RADIO1, and the Rectangle radio button IDC_RADIO2. The edit box to the right of the Title text is assigned IDC_EDIT1, the next IDC_EDIT2, and the last IDC_EDIT3. These are the only controls that will be directly involved with data transfer.

Once the dialog box design has been completed, it will be necessary to create a new class to process the information from the various controls.

The MFC ClassWizard

Use the View menu and select the ClassWizard menu item. The ClassWizard will bring up the Adding a Class dialog box in order to allow you to create a new class. You can also use the Add Class push button, shown on the MFC ClassWizard dialog box in Figure 11.10.

The Create New Class dialog box is displayed, as shown in Figure 11.11, when a new class is requested.

In this application, the new class name is CDataEntry. By default, the file name containing the description of this class will then be DataEntry.cpp. Since the DataEntry.cpp file already exists, this new information will be appended to this file.

The controls included in the dialog box will require an additional member functions. Figure 11.12 shows the CDataEntry class with the **DoDataExchange()** member function already added.

The three edit controls and two radio buttons will pass information from the dialog box to the application. These controls will require member variables to assist in this transfer of information. Select the Member Variables folder to reveal a list of Control IDs used in data transfer. Select the IDC_EDIT1, IDC_EDIT2, IDC_EDIT3, IDC_RADIO1, and

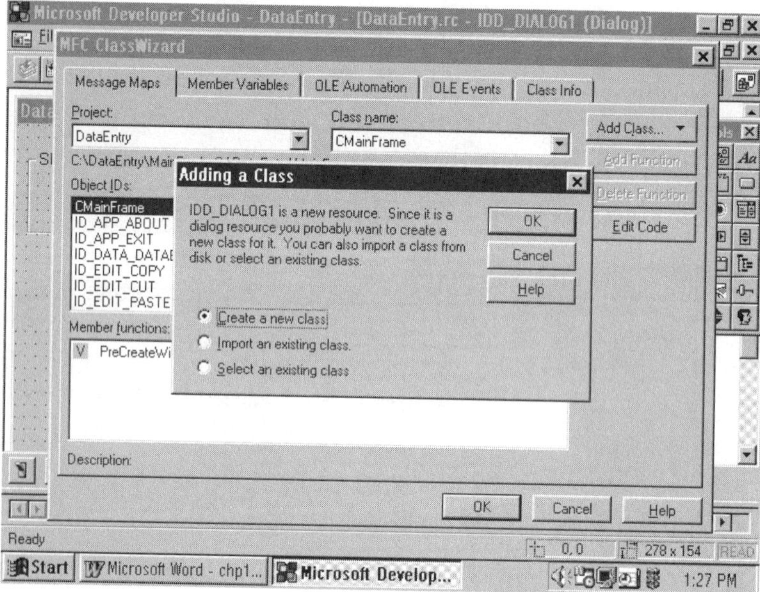

Figure 11.10: Use the Adding a Class dialog box or the MFC ClassWizard Add Class push button to add a new class to this project.

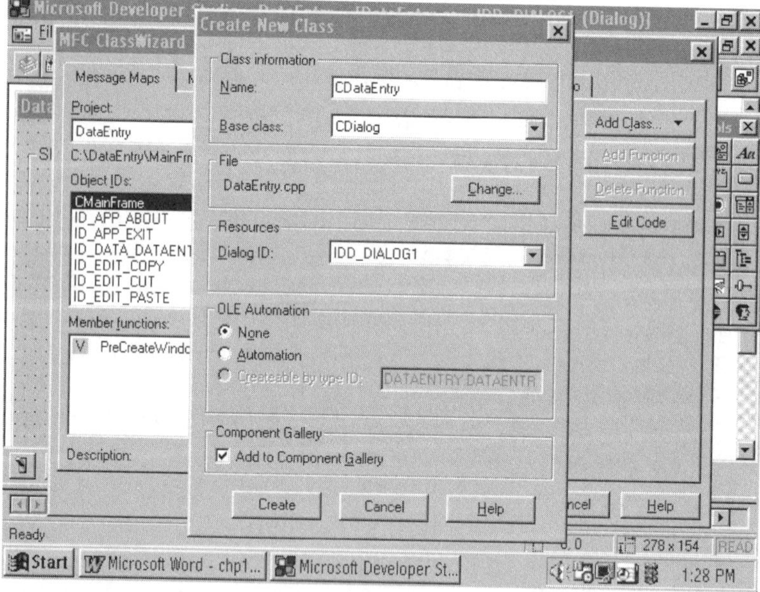

Figure 11.11: The Create New Class dialog box permits a new dialog box class to be derived from a CDialog base class.

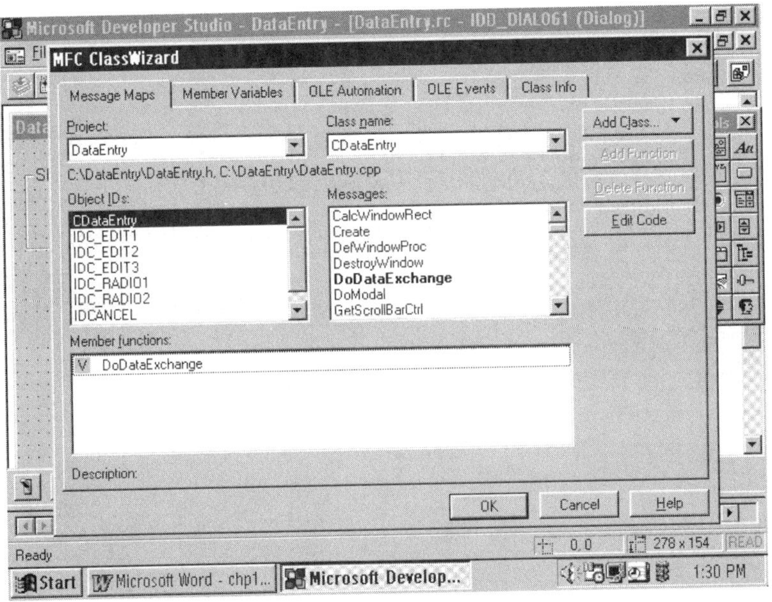

Figure 11.12: The CDataEntry class already contains a **DoDataExchange()** member function.

IDC_RADIO2 controls, one at a time, and add member variables by using the Add Variable... button. A small dialog box will permit you to name the member variable, its type and the data it will transfer. Figure 11.13 shows member variables for all five edit controls. IDC_EDIT2 is currently selected in this figure, so you can also view a preset range of acceptable values (0 to 600).

In order to be able to access the dialog box from the menu when the Data Entry... menu item is selected, a member function must also be added to the CDataEntryView class described in the DataEntryView.cpp file. Figure 11.14 shows the Object ID, the message, and the member function, **OnDataDataentry()**, that will be added by the ClassWizard.

Remember that ID_DATA_DATAENTRY is the ID value assigned to the Data Entry... menu item.

When the message handler was added to the DataEntryView.cpp file, a small amount of code had to be added to the message handler in order to process dialog box information.

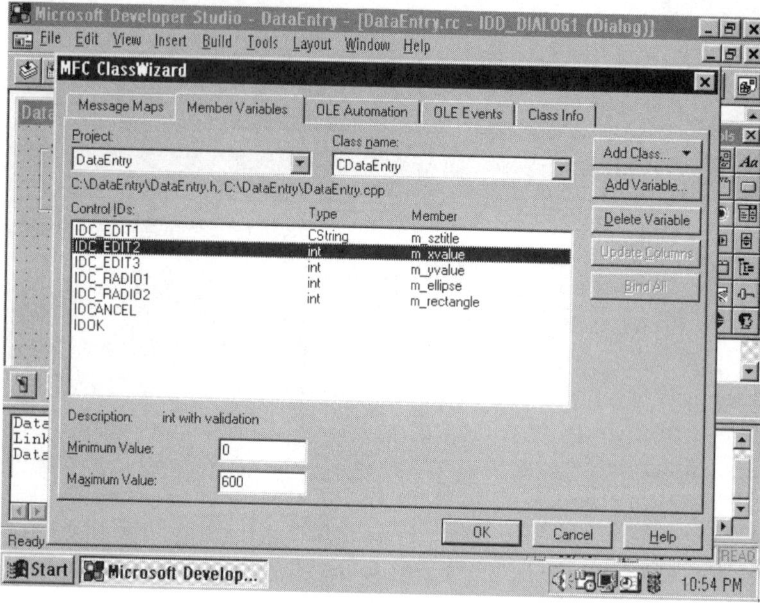

Figure 11.13: Member variables are used with each Edit Box control.

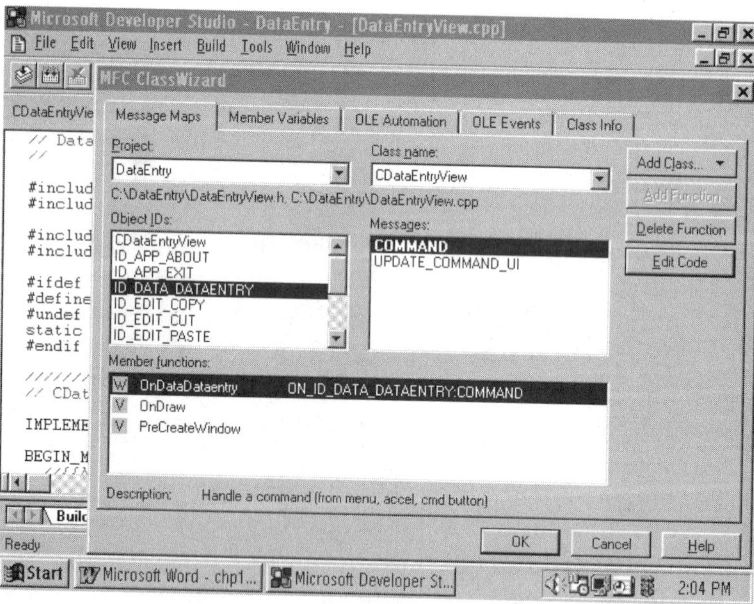

Figure 11.14: Adding a member function in CDataEntry.

```
CDataEntry dlg;
      .
      .
      .
// CDataEntryView message handlers
void CDataEntryView::OnDataDataentry()
{
  dlg.DoModal();
  InvalidateRect(NULL,TRUE);
  UpdateWindow();
}
```

The portion of code printed in bold is the actual code added to this member function's description. This allows the application to draw the dialog box when the menu selection is made.

In the next section you'll learn about the code that must be included to make this control operational.

Editing the DataEntry.cpp file

The DataEntry.cpp file contains a large amount of new code. This is a result of the member function added to the data entry dialog box in the previous section. The following listing is the complete DataEntry.cpp file.

```
// DataEntry.cpp : Defines class behaviors for application.
//

#include "stdafx.h"
#include "DataEntry.h"

#include "MainFrm.h"
#include "DataEntryDoc.h"
#include "DataEntryView.h"

#ifdef _DEBUG
#define new DEBUG_NEW
#undef THIS_FILE
static char THIS_FILE[] = __FILE__;
#endif

// CDataEntryApp
BEGIN_MESSAGE_MAP(CDataEntryApp, CWinApp)
  //{{AFX_MSG_MAP(CDataEntryApp)
  ON_COMMAND(ID_APP_ABOUT, OnAppAbout)
  //}}AFX_MSG_MAP
  // Standard file based document commands
  ON_COMMAND(ID_FILE_NEW, CWinApp::OnFileNew)
  ON_COMMAND(ID_FILE_OPEN, CWinApp::OnFileOpen)
```

```
END_MESSAGE_MAP()

// CDataEntryApp construction
CDataEntryApp::CDataEntryApp()
{
}

// The one and only CDataEntryApp object
CDataEntryApp theApp;

// CDataEntryApp initialization
BOOL CDataEntryApp::InitInstance()
{
  // Standard initialization

  LoadStdProfileSettings();
  // Register document templates

  CSingleDocTemplate* pDocTemplate;
  pDocTemplate = new CSingleDocTemplate(
    IDR_MAINFRAME,
    RUNTIME_CLASS(CDataEntryDoc),
    RUNTIME_CLASS(CMainFrame),
    RUNTIME_CLASS(CDataEntryView));
  AddDocTemplate(pDocTemplate);

  // Parse command line for standard shell commands
  CCommandLineInfo cmdInfo;
  ParseCommandLine(cmdInfo);

  // Dispatch commands specified on the command line
  if (!ProcessShellCommand(cmdInfo))
    return FALSE;

  return TRUE;
}

// CAboutDlg dialog used for App About
class CAboutDlg : public CDialog
{
public:
  CAboutDlg();

// Dialog Data
  //{{AFX_DATA(CAboutDlg)
  enum { IDD = IDD_ABOUTBOX };
  //}}AFX_DATA

  // ClassWizard generated virtual function overrides
  //{{AFX_VIRTUAL(CAboutDlg)
  protected:
  virtual void DoDataExchange(CDataExchange* pDX);
  //}}AFX_VIRTUAL
```

```
// Implementation
protected:
  //{{AFX_MSG(CAboutDlg)
    // No message handlers
  //}}AFX_MSG
  DECLARE_MESSAGE_MAP()
};

CAboutDlg::CAboutDlg() : CDialog(CAboutDlg::IDD)
{
  //{{AFX_DATA_INIT(CAboutDlg)
  //}}AFX_DATA_INIT
}

void CAboutDlg::DoDataExchange(CDataExchange* pDX)
{
  CDialog::DoDataExchange(pDX);
  //{{AFX_DATA_MAP(CAboutDlg)
  //}}AFX_DATA_MAP
}

BEGIN_MESSAGE_MAP(CAboutDlg, CDialog)
  //{{AFX_MSG_MAP(CAboutDlg)
    // No message handlers
  //}}AFX_MSG_MAP
END_MESSAGE_MAP()

// App command to run the dialog
void CDataEntryApp::OnAppAbout()
{
  CAboutDlg aboutDlg;
  aboutDlg.DoModal();
}

// CDataEntryApp commands
// CDataEntry dialog

CDataEntry::CDataEntry(CWnd* pParent /*=NULL*/)
  : CDialog(CDataEntry::IDD, pParent)
{
  //{{AFX_DATA_INIT(CDataEntry)
  m_sztitle = _T("Enter A Title");
  m_yvalue = 150;
  m_xvalue = 100;
  m_ellipse = 0;
  m_rectangle = -1;
  //}}AFX_DATA_INIT
}

void CDataEntry::DoDataExchange(CDataExchange* pDX)
{
  CDialog::DoDataExchange(pDX);
```

```
  //{{AFX_DATA_MAP(CDataEntry)
  DDX_Text(pDX, IDC_EDIT1, m_sztitle);
  DDV_MaxChars(pDX, m_sztitle, 60);
  DDX_Text(pDX, IDC_EDIT3, m_yvalue);
  DDV_MinMaxInt(pDX, m_yvalue, 0, 600);
  DDX_Text(pDX, IDC_EDIT2, m_xvalue);
  DDV_MinMaxInt(pDX, m_xvalue, 0, 600);
  DDX_Radio(pDX, IDC_RADIO1, m_ellipse);
  DDX_Radio(pDX, IDC_RADIO2, m_rectangle);
  //}}AFX_DATA_MAP
}

BEGIN_MESSAGE_MAP(CDataEntry, CDialog)
  //{{AFX_MSG_MAP(CDataEntry)
  //}}AFX_MSG_MAP
END_MESSAGE_MAP()

// CDataEntry message handlers
```

As you examine the previous listing, can you find the five member variables? The member variables are declared in the DataEntry.h header file. You'll notice that we edited the initial values for these member variables in the class constructor.

Data Exchange The **DoDataExchange()** member function uses DDX_ and DDV_ macros. DDX_ macros are used for data exchange, and DDV_ macros are used for data validation. These macros help to interface your application's variables with the various dialog box controls. DDX_ is used to represent the exchange function name. DDX_ names include DDX_Check, DDX_Control, DDX_Radio, DDX_Text, and so on. DDV_ macros are used to validate data. They make sure data is of the proper type and in the proper range. Message boxes are used to warn users of potential violations. DDV_ names include DDV_MaxChars, DDV_MinMaxInt, MinMaxUInt, and so on.

Examine the **DoDataExchange()** member function in the DataEntry.cpp file. You should note several lines with DDX_ and DDV_.

```
  .
  .
  .
DDX_Text(pDX, IDC_EDIT1, m_sztitle);
DDV_MaxChars(pDX, m_sztitle, 60);
  .
  .
  .
```

In the previous portion of code, the DDX_Text function uses the pointer to the CDataExchange object. The ID value of the control is the second parameter and the data member involved with the data exchange as the third parameter. The DDV_MaxChars checks the data member against the maximum number of characters. There are eleven DDX_ functions. The DDX_Text function is overloaded, as you can see in Table 11.3.

The direction of data exchange is controlled by the *m_bSaveAndValidate* flag. When this flag is TRUE, data transfer moves from the controls to the class member variables. When it is FALSE, data moves from the class member variables to the control.

When data exchange occurs outside the specified range, DDV_ functions will post the appropriate error messages to the system.

Editing the DataEntryView.cpp file

Information is passed from the dialog box controls and used by the functions in the DataEntryView.cpp file. Here is a complete

Table 11.3: Frequently Used DDX_ Data Exchange Functions

DDX_ Function	*Member Variable Type*
DDX_CBIndex	int
DDX_CBString	CString
DDX_CBStringExact	CString
DDX_Check	int
DDX_Control	CWnd
DDX_HexText	long
DDX_LBIndex	int
DDX_LBString	CString
DDX_LBStringExact	CString
DDX_Radio	int
DDX_Scroll	int
DDX_Text	BYTE
	ColeCurrency
	ColeDateTime
	CString
	double
	DWORD
	float
	int
	long
	short
	UINT

listing of the DataEntryView.cpp file with our code additions in a bolded font.

```
// DataEntryView.cpp : implementation of the CDataEntryView class
//

#include "stdafx.h"
#include "DataEntry.h"
#include "MainFrm.h"

#include "DataEntryDoc.h"
#include "DataEntryView.h"

CDataEntry dlg;

#ifdef _DEBUG
#define new DEBUG_NEW
#undef THIS_FILE
static char THIS_FILE[] = __FILE__;
#endif

// CDataEntryView
IMPLEMENT_DYNCREATE(CDataEntryView, CView)

BEGIN_MESSAGE_MAP(CDataEntryView, CView)
  //{{AFX_MSG_MAP(CDataEntryView)
  ON_COMMAND(ID_DATA_DATAENTRY, OnDataDataentry)
  ON_WM_PAINT()
  //}}AFX_MSG_MAP
END_MESSAGE_MAP()

// CDataEntryView construction/destruction
CDataEntryView::CDataEntryView()
{
}

CDataEntryView::~CDataEntryView()
{
}

BOOL CDataEntryView::PreCreateWindow(CREATESTRUCT& cs)
{
  return CView::PreCreateWindow(cs);
}

// CDataEntryView drawing
void CDataEntryView::OnDraw(CDC* pDC)
{
  CDataEntryDoc* pDoc = GetDocument();
  ASSERT_VALID(pDoc);
}

// CDataEntryView diagnostics
```

```
#ifdef _DEBUG
void CDataEntryView::AssertValid() const
{
  CView::AssertValid();
}

void CDataEntryView::Dump(CDumpContext& dc) const
{
  CView::Dump(dc);
}

CDataEntryDoc* CDataEntryView::GetDocument()
{
  ASSERT(m_pDocument->IsKindOf(RUNTIME_CLASS(CDataEntryDoc)));
  return (CDataEntryDoc*)m_pDocument;
}
#endif //_DEBUG

// CDataEntryView message handlers
void CDataEntryView::OnDataDataentry()
{
  dlg.DoModal();
  InvalidateRect(NULL,TRUE);
  UpdateWindow();
}

void CDataEntryView::OnPaint()
{
  CPaintDC dc(this); // device context for painting

  CBrush newbrush;
  CBrush* oldbrush;

  newbrush.CreateSolidBrush(RGB(255,255,0));
  oldbrush=dc.SelectObject(&newbrush);

  if(!dlg.m_rectangle)
    dc.Rectangle(30,30,dlg.m_xvalue,dlg.m_yvalue);
  else
    dc.Ellipse(30,30,dlg.m_xvalue,dlg.m_yvalue);

  dc.TextOut(10,10,dlg.m_sztitle,strlen(dlg.m_sztitle));

  dc.SelectObject(&newbrush);
  newbrush.DeleteObject();
}
```

This application uses two radio buttons and three edit boxes. The information returned by the radio buttons is treated as a flag in determining whether a rectangle or ellipse is drawn. The title for the figure is returned by the first edit box in a string accessed by *dlg.m_sztitle*. The size of the figure

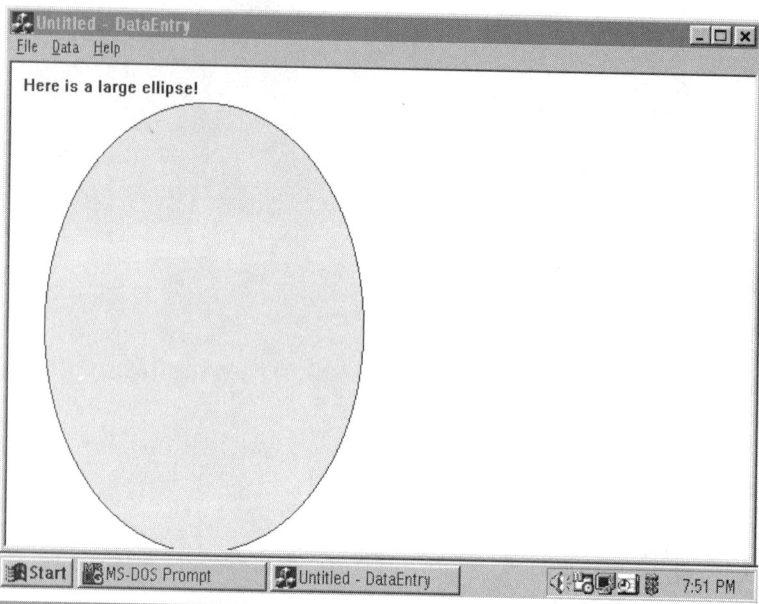

Figure 11.15: An example of the DataEntry application.

is determined by the values returned by the remaining two edit boxes. These values are returned in *dlg.m_xvalue* and *dlg.m_yvalue*.

An example of the execution of this application is shown in Figure 11.15.

Dialog boxes require a large amount of time in planning, development and implementation. Dialog boxes are literally "in the user's face" every time the application is executed.

Because certain operations, such as file selection or color selection, are common among many applications, Microsoft has designed a group of common dialog boxes for this task. The use of common dialog boxes will save hours of development time and make your applications consistent with others on the market. The common dialog approach will be discussed in the next section.

Using a Common Dialog Box

Common dialog boxes create consistent dialog box styles for operations such as color, file, font, and print selection. Each common dialog uses its own special class. The common color dialog box uses the CColorDialog class. CFileDialog, CFontDialog, and CPrintDialog correspond to the remaining classes.

Access to each common dialog box is similar, but each common dialog box uses its own group of parameters, flags, filters, and so on.

The AppWizard generates applications that can access the file and print common dialog boxes. In this section, we'll illustrate how to use the common color dialog box.

If you have been working along with the code development for this chapter, you created a workspace named Colors with the AppWizard. This code will now be modified to allow access to the common color dialog box.

Before modifying actual program code, modify the default menu so that it takes on the appearance of Figure 11.16.

Use IDC_MYCOLOR for the ID value associated with the Pick a color... menu item.

Next, use the ClassWizard to create a new class named CCustomColor which is based on the CColorDialog base class. Use the Add Class... button, as shown in Figure 11.17, to add this class.

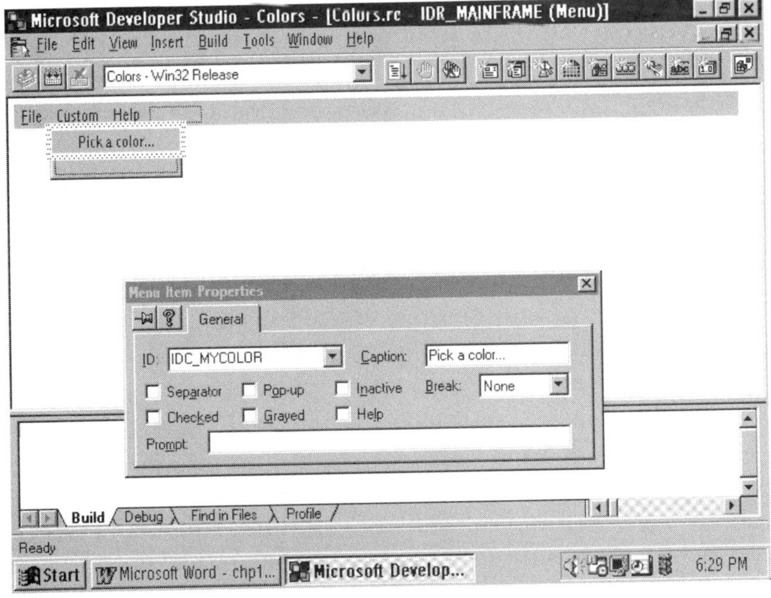

Figure 11.16: The Colors project uses a customized menu.

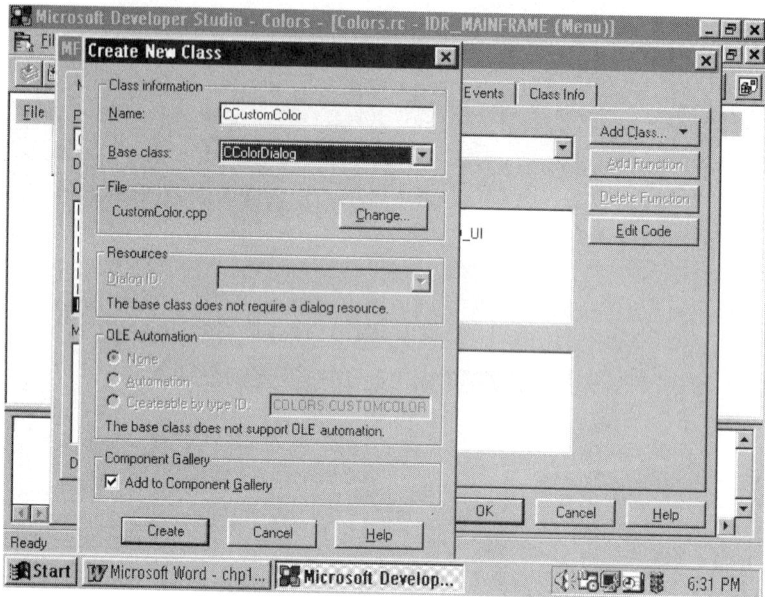

Figure 11.17: Add a class to the project based upon the CColorDialog base class.

Note: All common dialog boxes have a base class associated with them in the MFC library.

Use the ClassWizard to access the CColorsView class found in the ColorsView.cpp file. To make this application operational, we'll have to add two member functions to this class. The first member function is **OnPaint()**. Add this member function by selecting CColorsView in the Object ID list box provided by the MFC ClassWizard dialog box. Next, select WM_PAINT from the message list box. Once these selections are made, add the **OnPaint()** member function by selecting the Add Function button. The second member function is added in a similar manner. In this instance you'll want to add a member function that will respond to a command message. Choose IDC_MYCOLOR in the Object ID list box. Select COMMAND as the message from the message list box. Then add the function by selecting the Add Function button, as shown in Figure 11.18.

When this project is built, a CustomColor.cpp file will be added to support the CCustomColor class. Remember this class is based upon the CColorDialog base class. Here is a complete listing for this file.

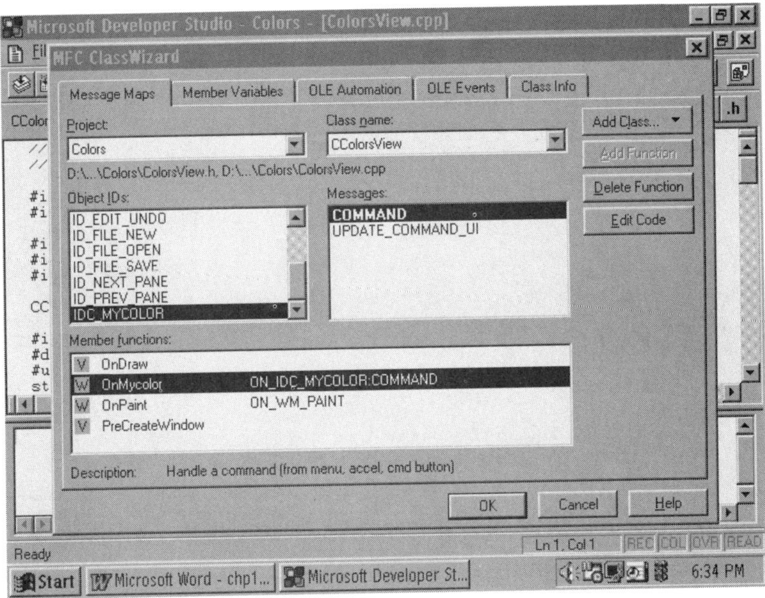

Figure 11.18: Adding the OnMycolor() member function to the project.

```
// CustomColor.cpp : implementation file
//

#include "stdafx.h"
#include "Colors.h"
#include "CustomColor.h"

#ifdef _DEBUG
#define new DEBUG_NEW
#undef THIS_FILE
static char THIS_FILE[] = __FILE__;
#endif

// CCustomColor
IMPLEMENT_DYNAMIC(CCustomColor, CColorDialog)

CCustomColor::CCustomColor(COLORREF clrInit,
                           DWORD dwFlags,
                           CWnd* pParentWnd) :
  CColorDialog(clrInit, dwFlags, pParentWnd)
{
}

BEGIN_MESSAGE_MAP(CCustomColor, CColorDialog)
  //{{AFX_MSG_MAP(CCustomColor)
  //}}AFX_MSG_MAP
END_MESSAGE_MAP()
```

This listing is fairly short because no specific message handlers were added. In order to complete this project, modifications were made to the ColorsView.cpp file. The code we added is shown in a bolded font in the following listing.

```
// ColorsView.cpp : implementation of the CColorsView class
//

#include "stdafx.h"
#include "Colors.h"

#include "ColorsDoc.h"
#include "ColorsView.h"
#include "CustomColor.h"

CColorDialog dlg;

#ifdef _DEBUG
#define new DEBUG_NEW
#undef THIS_FILE
static char THIS_FILE[] = __FILE__;
#endif

// CColorsView
IMPLEMENT_DYNCREATE(CColorsView, CView)

BEGIN_MESSAGE_MAP(CColorsView, CView)
  //{{AFX_MSG_MAP(CColorsView)
  ON_COMMAND(IDC_MYCOLOR, OnMycolor)
  ON_WM_PAINT()
  //}}AFX_MSG_MAP
END_MESSAGE_MAP()

// CColorsView construction/destruction
CColorsView::CColorsView()
{
}

CColorsView::~CColorsView()
{
}

BOOL CColorsView::PreCreateWindow(CREATESTRUCT& cs)
{
  return CView::PreCreateWindow(cs);
}

// CColorsView drawing
void CColorsView::OnDraw(CDC* pDC)
{
  CColorsDoc* pDoc = GetDocument();
  ASSERT_VALID(pDoc);
```

```
}

// CColorsView diagnostics
#ifdef _DEBUG
void CColorsView::AssertValid() const
{
  CView::AssertValid();
}

void CColorsView::Dump(CDumpContext& dc) const
{
  CView::Dump(dc);
}

CColorsDoc* CColorsView::GetDocument()
{
  ASSERT(m_pDocument->IsKindOf(RUNTIME_CLASS(CColorsDoc)));
  return (CColorsDoc*)m_pDocument;
}
#endif //_DEBUG

// CColorsView message handlers

void CColorsView::OnMycolor()
{
  dlg.DoModal();
  InvalidateRect(NULL,TRUE);
  UpdateWindow();
}

void CColorsView::OnPaint()
{
  CPaintDC dc(this);

  COLORREF mycolor;
  CBrush newbrush;
  CBrush* oldbrush;

  // Open the full dialog box
  dlg.m_cc.Flags |= CC_FULLOPEN;

  // Obtain the selected color from the dialog box
  mycolor = dlg.GetColor();

  // Pick a new brush color
  newbrush.CreateSolidBrush(mycolor);
  oldbrush=dc.SelectObject(&newbrush);

  // Pick a new text color
  dc.SetTextColor(mycolor);

  // Draw shapes and text
  dc.Rectangle(100,100,300,300);
```

```
    dc.Ellipse(400,100,600,300);
    dc.TextOut(10,320,"The color returned by the common",32);
    dc.TextOut(10,340,"color dialog box can be used to set",35);
    dc.TextOut(10,360,"brush, pen and text colors.",27);

    dc.SelectObject(&newbrush);
    newbrush.DeleteObject();
}
```

The common colors dialog box returns the color selected in the dialog box to a variable of type COLORREF. In this application, that variable is named *mycolor*. The RGB color value is easy to obtain through a call to the **GetColor()** function.

The common color dialog box can be modified by using the m_cc member function. This member function uses a CHOOSECOLOR structure, which takes on the following appearance:

```
struct {
  DWORD         lStructSize;
  HWND          hwndOwner;
  HWND          hInstance;
  COLORREF      rgbResult;
  COLORREF*     lpCustColors;
  DWORD         Flags;
  LPARAM        lCustData;
  LPCCHOOKPROC lpfnHook;
  LPCTSTR       lpTemplateName;
} CHOOSECOLOR;
```

In this structure, *lStructSize* gives the length (bytes) of the structure. The *hwndOwner* value indicates which window generated the dialog box. The *hInstance* value is a handle to a data block holding the dialog box template. The *rgbResult* value gives the color selected when the dialog box is created. Black is the initial color if this value is NULL. The *lpCustColors* pointer points to an array of 16 doublewords. Each array value maps to a custom color cell in the dialog box. The user can define custom colors within each cell. The *Flags* value give the dialog box initialization flags. These flags may be ORed together and include CC_ENABLEHOOK, CC_ENABLETEMPLATE, CC_ENABLETEMPLATEHANDLE, CC_FULLOPEN, CC_PREVENTFULLOPEN, CC_RGBINIT, and CC_SHOWHELP. Additional information for each of these flags can be found through the Microsoft Developer Studios Help screen. The *lCustData* value is used to pass data to the hook function identified by the *lpfnHook* member. The hook member is used to process messages for the dialog box. The *lpstrTemplateName* pointer points to a null-terminated string that indicates a substitute dialog box template.

If you examine the listing for the ColorsView.cpp file, you will notice that the application did change one flag value in this structure.

```
// Open the full dialog box
  dlg.m_cc.Flags |= CC_FULLOPEN;
```

Here the CC_FULLOPEN flag fully opens the common dialog box. If you examine Figure 11.19, you will see a common color dialog box in this state.

The default option is to show just the left half of the dialog box. The full view immediately allows the user to create custom colors from the dialog box options.

The color selected by the user is then used to set a brush color and text color for this application. Two simple shapes and a text message are drawn to the screen in the new color. Figure 11.20 shows a vivid blue color for the graphics figures and text (trust us).

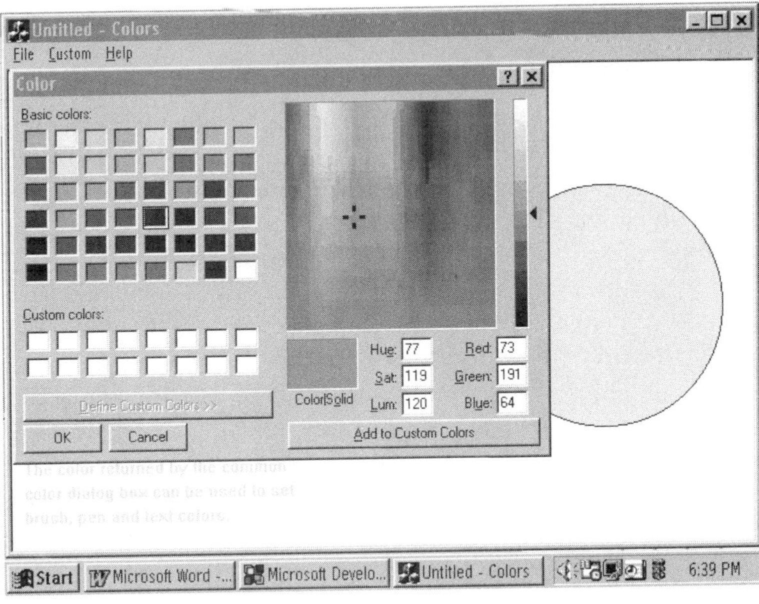

Figure 11.19: A fully opened common color dialog box.

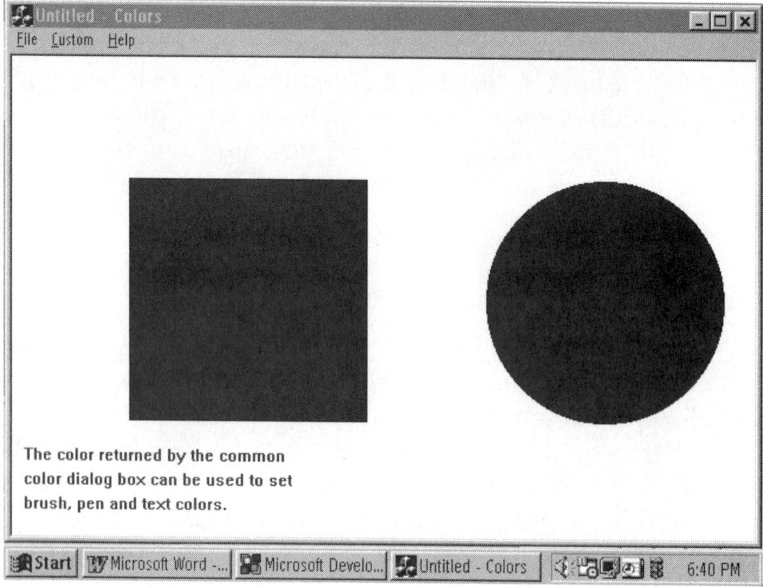

Figure 11.20: Brush and text colors can be set with the color returned by the dialog box.

More Dialog Boxes?

You'll gain even more experience with dialog boxes in the remaining chapters of this book. However, real experience is best gained by developing your own examples and working through the problems that may develop.

Chapter 12

Understanding Graphics Primitives

In the previous chapters we have used one or two graphics drawing primitives to draw a few shapes to the client area of the window. In this chapter, however, you will learn how to use a wide variety of drawing primitives. Windows provides a number of functions for drawing basic graphical shapes, such as arcs, lines, circles, and pie wedges. More complicated shapes must be constructed with the use of these basic functions, hence the name *graphics primitives*.

This chapter will also teach you how to perform fundamental operations within the graphics environment, such as changing text colors, drawing modes, and pens and brushes.

The Graphics Device Interface

The Windows code module that handles graphics instructions is called the Graphics Device Interface or simply the GDI. All graphics functions, including the drawing primitives mentioned in the last section, are contained in the GDI. In addition to providing support for all graphics functions, the GDI also supports the translation of these commands to output device drivers such as monitors, plotters, and printers. Since the GDI functions as a device-independent interface, all graphics applications will draw correctly on any properly installed graphics display, plotter, or printer.

As you progress through the material in the following sections, you will learn much of the basic terminology associated with the GDI environment.

Environments

Windows NT and Windows 95 keeps track of the software and hardware installed on a system. The GDI uses the list of installed drivers to determine how to interface with the various hardware items making up the computer system. For example, information being sent to a plotter must be handled differently from information being sent to a printer. Further differences must be taken into account, even among printers, because printers have different resolutions, color capabilities, and so on. Since Windows handles all of this interfacing in an invisible manner, Windows offers a portability unknown in the old DOS command-line environments.

The GetDeviceCaps() Function

The **GetDeviceCaps()** function can be used to obtain information concerning the hardware in a particular system. The **GetDeviceCaps()** function returns information on numerous hardware device attributes, including aspect ratios, color planes, and resolution. The syntax for this function is simple:

```
dc.GetDeviceCaps(nIndex);
```

The value *nIndex* is an integer index value used to return information on a particular item. Table 12.1 gives a description of these attributes.

Table 12.1: Device Capabilities

Index	*Meaning*	*Detail*
DRIVERVERSION	Version number	
TECHNOLOGY	DT_CHARSTREAM DT_DISPFILE DT_METAFILE DT_PLOTTER DT_RASCAMERA DT_RASDISPLAY DT_RASPRINTER	
HORZSIZE	Width of display in millimeters	
VERTSIZE	Height of display in millimeters	
HORZRES	Width of display in pixels	
VERTRES	Height of display in raster lines	
LOGPIXELSX	Number of pixels in logical inch for display width	
LOGPIXELSY	Number of pixels in logical inch for display height	
BITSPIXEL	Number of adjacent color bits/ pixel	
PLANES	Number of color planes	
NUMBRUSHES	Number of device-specific brushes	
NUMPENS	Number of device-specific pens	
NUMMARKERS	Number of device-specific mark- ers	
NUMFONTS	Number of device-specific fonts	
NUMCOLORS	Number of entries in the device color table	
ASPECTX	Relative width of device pixel	
ASPECTY	Relative height of device pixel	
ASPECTXY	Diagonal width of device pixel	

Continued on the next page.

Table 12.1: Continued

Index	*Meaning*	*Detail*
PDEVICESIZE	Size of the PDEVICE internal structure (bytes)	
CLIPCAPS	Clipping capabilities supported:	
	CP_NONE	
	CP_RECTANGLE	
	CP_REGION	
SIZEPALETTE	Number of entries in the system palette	
NUMRESERVED	Number of reserved entries in the system palette	
COLORRES	Color resolution of the device (bits/pixel)	
RASTERCAPS	Raster capabilities supported:	
	RC_BANDING	Banding
	RC_BIGFONT	Fonts larger than 64K
	RC_BITBLT	Transfers bitmaps
	RC_BITMAP64	Bitmaps larger than 64K
	RC_DEVBITS	Device bitmaps
	RC_DI_BITMAP	SetDIBits and GetDIBits support
	RC_DIBTODEV	SetDIBitsToDevice support
	RC_FLOODFILL	Flood fills supported
	RC_GDI20_OUTPUT	Windows (ver 2.0) features
	RC_GDI20_STATE	Puts a state block in device context
	RC_NONE	Raster operations not supported
	RC_OP_DX_OUTPUT	Supports dev opaque and DX array
	RC_PALETTE	Specifies a palette-based device
	RC_SAVEBITMAP	Saves bitmaps locally
	RC_SCALING	Scaling supported
	RC_STRETCHBLT	StretchBlt supported
	RC_STRETCHDIB	StretchDIBits supported
CURVECAPS	Curve capabilities the device supports:	
	CC_CHORD	Chords support
	CC_CIRCLES	Circles support
	CC_ELLIPSES	Ellipses support
	CC_INTERIORS	Interiors support
	CC_NONE	Curves support
	CC_PIE	Pie wedge support

Table 12.1: Device Capabilities

Index	*Meaning*	*Detail*
	CC_ROUNDRECT	Rectangles with rounded corners supported
	CC_STYLED	Styled borders supported
	CC_WIDE	Wide borders supported
	CC_WIDESTYLED	Wide styled borders supported
LINECAPS	Line capabilities the device supports:	
	LC_INTERIORS	Interiors supported
	LC_MARKER	Markers supported
	LC_NONE	No lines supported
	LC_POLYLINE	Polylines supported
	LC_POLYMARKER	Polymarkers supported
	LC_STYLED	Styled lines supported
	LC_WIDE	Wide lines supported
	LC_WIDESTYLED	Wide styled lines supported
POLYGONALCAPS	Polygonal capabilities the device supports:	
	PC_INTERIORS	Interiors supported
	PC_NONE	No polygons supported
	PC_POLYGON	Alternate fill polygons supported
	PC_RECTANGLE	Rectangles supported
	PC_SCANLINE	Scan lines supported
	PC_STYLED	Styled borders supported
	PC_WIDE	Wide borders supported
	PC_WIDESTYLED	Wide styled borders supported
	PC_WINDPOLYGON	Winding number fill polygons supported
TEXTCAPS	Text capabilities the device supports:	
	TC_CP_STROKE	Device can clip fonts to a pixel
	TC_CR_90	90-degree character rotation
	TC_CR_ANY	Any degree character rotation
	TC_EA_DOUBLE	Double-weight characters
	TC_IA_ABLE	Italics
	TC_OP_CHARACTER	Device can place fonts at any pixel
	TC_OP_STROKE	Device can omit any stroke of a font
	TC_RA_ABLE	Raster fonts
	TC_RESERVED	Reserved (must be zero)
	TC_SA_CONTIN	Multiples for exact scaling

Continued on the next page.

Table 12.1: Continued

Index	*Meaning*	*Detail*
	TC_SA_DOUBLE	Doubled character scaling
	TC_SA_INTEGER	Integer multiples for scaling
	TC_SF_X_YINDEP	Independent scaling X and Y direction
	C_SO_ABLE	Strikeouts
	TC_UA_ABLE	Underlining
	TC_VA_ABLE	Vector fonts
LOGPIXELSX	Pixels/inch in X direction	
LOGPIXELSY	Pixels/inch in Y direction	

As you examine Table 12.1 you will also notice that some devices, such as plotters, have the built-in capability to draw circles, ellipses, pie wedges, and so on. When these abilities are present, Windows does not have to use specific GDI routines. When the hardware device does not have these capabilities, Windows supplies the equivalent software routine through the GDI.

Windows Mapping Modes

The GDI uses the upper-left part of the window as the origin in the default mapping mode. In this mode, the X axis increases positively as you move to the right and the Y axis increases positively as you move down, as shown in Figure 12.1.

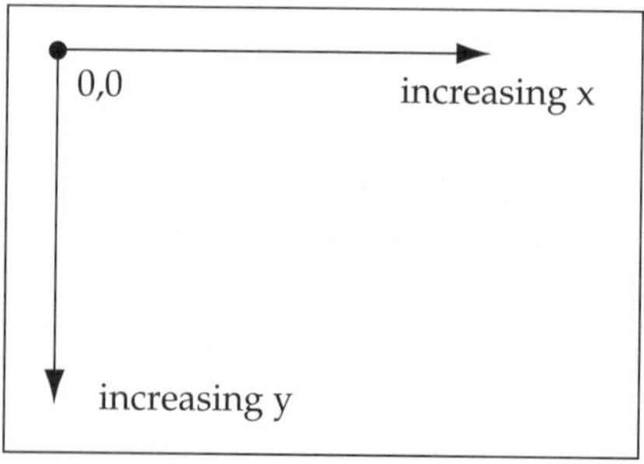

Figure 12.1: The default Windows coordinate system with the origin in the upper-left corner of the window.

This default mapping mode is called the MM_TEXT mapping mode or pixel coordinate mode. Seven additional mapping modes are available. These mapping modes allow drawing in English, metric, or user-defined units. These mapping modes will be described in the next section. The default MM_TEXT mapping mode uses 0 to 639 pixels horizontally and 0 to 479 pixels vertically when drawing on a VGA screen. If the application is then run on a system with a SVGA monitor, the GDI will adjust the window accordingly.

Mapping Modes Parameters GDI graphics functions are dependent on the mapping mode currently in use. Only the default mapping mode, MM_TEXT, measures point values in pixels. Table 12.2 lists the eight mapping modes.

You'll see how mapping modes are changes in various examples throughout this book.

Changing Mapping Modes The mapping mode can be made with a call to the **SetMapMode()** function.

```
dc.SetMapMode(fnMapMode);
```

The *fnMapMode* parameter is an integer value specified by one of the eight value types shown in Table 12.2. The function returns a type int. Remember, regardless of which mapping

Table 12.2: Eight Windows Mapping Modes

Mode	*Description*
MM_ANISOTROPIC	Arbitrary units with arbitrarily scaled axes.
MM_HIENGLISH	Logical unit mapped to 0.001 inch. Positive X is to the right, positive Y is up.
MM_HIMETRIC	Logical unit mapped to 0.01 millimeter. Positive X is to the right, positive Y is up.
MM_ISOTROPIC	Arbitrary units with equally scaled axes.
MM_LOMETRIC	Logical unit mapped to 0.1 millimeter. Positive X is to the right, positive Y is up.
MM_LOENGLISH	Logical unit mapped to 0.01 inch. Positive X is to the right, positive Y is up
MM_TEXT	Logical unit mapped to device pixel. Positive X is to the right, positive Y is down.
MM_TWIPS	Logical unit mapped to 1/20 of printer's point. Positive X is to the right, positive Y is up.

mode is used, it is the responsibility of Windows to map the logical drawing coordinates to the physical device coordinates.

Important Drawing Primitives

Windows provides an array of drawing functions for creating lines, arcs, rectangles, and so on. These graphics primitives are the building blocks of all other graphics drawing functions. Graphics primitives are the components of all Windows graphics applications.

There are numerous categories of drawing primitives. Most of these categories are composed of a single function. The most often-used categories include functions for drawing arcs, chords, circles, ellipses, lines, pie wedges, polygons, polylines, rectangles, rectangles with rounded corners, and single pixels, as well as techniques for setting cursor positions.

All drawing primitives draw with the current pen style and color and, where applicable, fill the shape with the current brush style and color. Details about pen and brush selections are included later in this chapter.

Arc() and ArcTo()

The **Arc()** function is used to draw an elliptical arc with the current pen. The arc is centered in the center of a bounding rectangle described by the points *x1,y1* and *x2,y2*, as shown in Figure 12.2.

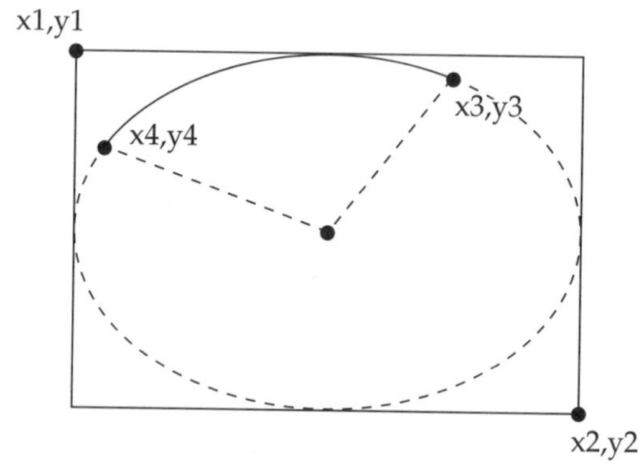

Figure 12.2: The arc is centered in a bounding rectangle.

The arc's length is described as lying between points *x3,y3* and *x4,y4*. The arc is drawn in a counterclockwise direction. The **Arc()** function does not update the coordinates of the current point. All parameters are of type int. This function returns a type BOOL.

The function can be called by supplying parameters in the following manner:

```
dc.Arc(x1,y1,x2,y2,x3,y3,x4,y4);
```

The **ArcTo()** function is similar to the **Arc()** function, except that it updates the current point.

Chord()

The **Chord()** function is similar to the **Arc()** function. The resulting Figure 12.2 is closed by a line between the two arc points *x3,y3* and *x4,y4*. The chord is drawn using the current pen. Figure 12.3 shows these points.

Since the chord is a closed figure, it is filled with the current brush color. All parameters are of type int. This function returns a type BOOL.

The function uses the following syntax:

```
dc.Chord(x1,y1,x2,y2,x3,y3,x4,y4);
```

Ellipse() (and Circle)

The **Ellipse()** function is used to draw an ellipse or a circle with the current pen. The center of the ellipse is in the center of a

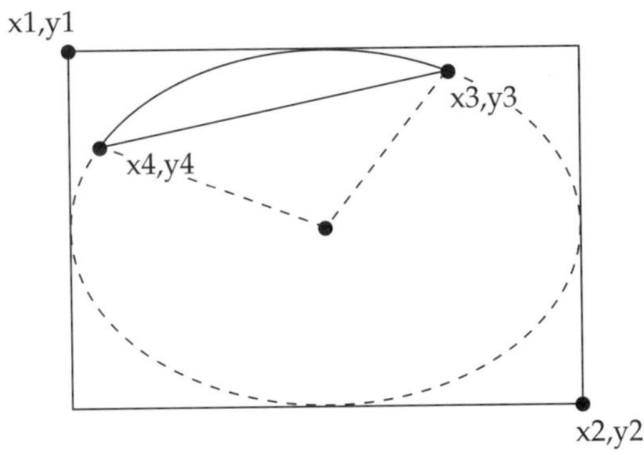

Figure 12.3: The chord is contained in a bounding rectangle.

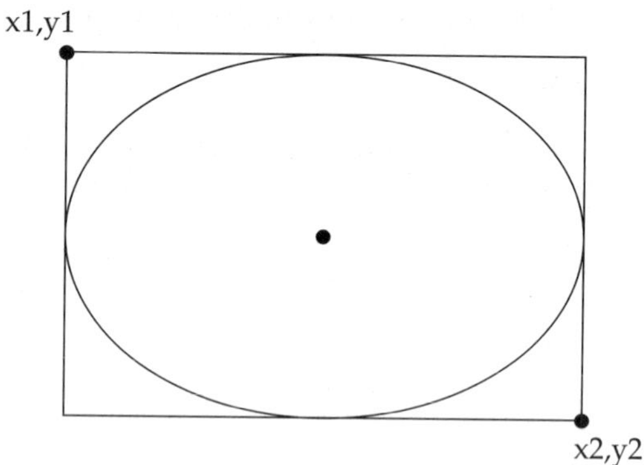

Figure 12.4: The ellipse is bounded by a rectangle.

bounding rectangle described by the points *x1,y1* and *x2,y2*, as shown in Figure 12.4.

Since the ellipse is a closed figure, it will be filled with the current brush color. All parameters are of type int. This function returns a type BOOL.

The function uses the following syntax:

```
dc.Ellipse(x1,y1,x2,y2);
```

Circles can be drawn with the **Ellipse()** function by making the bounding rectangle's points symmetric (a square).

LineTo()

The **LineTo()** function draws a line from the current point up to, but not including, the specified point with the current pen. The current point is set with the **MoveToEx()** function. The current point will be *x,y* when the function is finished. All parameters are of type int. This function returns a type BOOL.

The function uses the following syntax:

```
dc.LineTo(x,y);
```

MoveToEx()

The **MoveToEx()** function moves the current point to the specified point, and returns the original point to a data structure. The *x* and *y* values are of type int. This function returns a type BOOL. The *x* and *y* coordinates of the original point are returned in an *lpPoint* structure.

This function uses the following syntax:

```
dc.MoveToEx(x,y,lpPt);
```

If the original point's values are not required, a NULL value is inserted in the third parameter.

Pie()

The **Pie()** function is used to draw pie-shaped wedges with the current pen. The center of the elliptical pie arc is centered in a bounding rectangle described by the points *x1,y1* and *x2,y2*, as shown in Figure 12.5.

The starting and ending points of the arc are drawn counter-clockwise from points *x3,y3* to *x4,y4*. The pie wedge is filled with the current brush color because it is a closed figure. All parameters are of type int. This function returns a type BOOL.

This function uses the following syntax:

```
dc.Pie(x1,y1,x2,y2,x3,y3,x4,y4);
```

Polygon()

The **Polygon()** function draws a polygon. Polygons are specified by points which are connected by lines. The polygon is a closed shape and is drawn with the current pen and filled with the current brush color. Figure 12.6 shows an example of a polygon.

The data points for the polygon are held in an array of type POINT. The number of points in the array is an integer. This function returns a type BOOL.

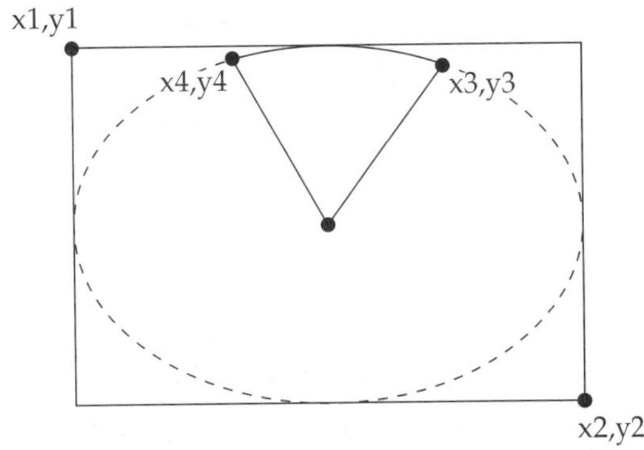

Figure 12.5: The pie slice is centered in a bounding rectangle.

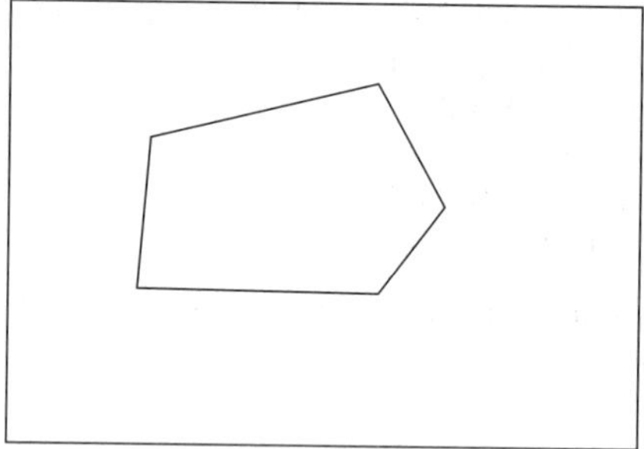

Figure 12.6: A closed polygon shape.

This function uses the following syntax:

```
dc.Polygon(pointarray,nCount);
```

Polyline() and PolylineTo()

The **Polyline()** function draws a group of connected line segments given in a type POINT array with the current pen. This function does not return the starting point. However, the **PolylineTo()** is a Win32 function that behaves like **Polyline()** and also returns the starting point. The number of data points in the array is an integer. This function returns a type BOOL.

This function uses the following syntax:

```
dc.Polyline(pointarray,nCount);
```

Rectangle()

The **Rectangle()** function draws a rectangle described by *x1,y1* and *x2,y2*. The rectangle is drawn with the current pen and filled with the current brush color because it is a closed shape. All parameters are of type int. This function returns a type BOOL.

This function uses the following syntax:

```
dc.Rectangle(x1,y1,x2,y2);
```

RoundRect()

The **RoundRect()** function draws a round-cornered rectangle described by *x1,y1* and *x2,y2* with the current pen. The values *x3* and *y3* give the width and height of the ellipse used to round the corners. The rounded rectangle is filled with the current brush color since it is a closed figure. All parameters are of type int. This function returns a type BOOL.

This function uses the following syntax:

```
dc.RoundRect(x1,y1,x2,y2,x3,y3);
```

SetPixel() and GetPixel()

The **SetPixel()** function is used to light a pixel at position *x,y*. The function uses the RGB color closest to the color requested. The *x* and *y* parameters are of type int. *crColor* is of type COLORREF. This function returns a type COLORREF.

This function uses the following syntax:

```
dc.SetPixel(x,y,crColor);
```

The **GetPixel()** function retrieves the RGB color value at the point given by *x,y* and returns it as a type COLORREF.

This function uses the following syntax:

```
pointcolor =dc.GetPixel(x,y);
```

Graphics Tools

Windows provides a number of default drawing options. Stock tools such as brush and pen styles and colors can be used, or special tools can be designed. Most GDI stock items are described in the wingdi.h header file. We recommend that you print a copy of this header file for your own use.

For example, you'll find the stock brushes and pens in Table 12.3:

Table 12.3: Stock Brushes and Pens

WHITE_BRUSH
LTGRAY_BRUSH
GRAY_BRUSH
DKGRAY_BRUSH
BLACK_BRUSH
HOLLOW_BRUSH (or NULL_BRUSH)
WHITE_PEN
BLACK_PEN
NULL_PEN

In future examples you will learn how to select brushes and pens.

Pens

Pens draw the outlines for all graphics functions. Pens have three attributes: color, style, and width. The default pen is a black pen (BLACK_PEN) drawing a solid line (PS_SOLID) one device pixel wide. Additional stock pen colors include white (WHITE_PEN) and a pen that draws in invisible ink (NULL_PEN).

The stock pen line styles are shown in Table 12.4.

Line widths are given in logical units as integer numbers. A width of 15 in the default drawing mode will draw a line 15 pixels wide. However, all pens greater than one logical unit default to either a null or a solid line drawing style.

Pens are created via the CPen class. Stock pens can be obtained with the **GetStockObject()** function. To change the pen just selected to the current pen, use the **SelectObject()** function.

```
CPen  newpen;
     .
     .
     .
newpen = dc.SelectObject(GetStockObject(WHITE_PEN));
```

A custom pen can be created and selected with the **CreatePen()** function, in conjunction with the **SelectObject()** function. The **CreatePen()** function creates a logical pen with the syntax:

```
newpen.CreatePen(nPenStyle,nWidth,rgbColor);
```

The parameter *nPenStyle* is a type int and can be specified by any of the PS_ values, for example, PS_SOLID. The value *nWidth* is of type int and is given in logical units. The *rgbColor*

Table 12.4: Table 12.4: Stock Pen Line Styles

PS_SOLID	Solid line
PS_DASH	Dashed line
PS_DOT	Dotted line
PS_DASHDOT	Dash–dot line
PS_DASHDOTDOT	Dash–dot–dot line
PS_NULL	Invisible line
PS_INSIDEFRAME	Solid rule inside a frame

value is of type COLORREF given in terms of a RGB color value. For example:

```
CPen  newpen;
CPen*  oldpen;
      .
      .
      .
newpen.CreatePen(PS_SOLID,4,RGB(0,255,0));
oldpen = dc.SelectObject(CreatePen(&newpen));
```

In this case, a pen is created and selected for drawing solid lines, four pixels wide, in a green color. Once a pen is selected, only that pen can be used to draw within the device context. To use another pen, the first pen must be deselected. This is done by calling the **DeleteObject()** function.

```
newpen.DeleteObject();
```

Stock pens should not be deleted.

Brushes

Brushes are used to fill the closed figures created with the appropriate graphics functions. Brushes have several attributes, including color, brush style, and hatch style. The default brush is a white brush (WHITE_BRUSH) that fills the object with a solid pattern (BS_SOLID). A solid brush refers to the fill pattern used by the brush. Other stock brush color choices include BLACK_BRUSH, BKGRAY_BRUSH, GRAY_BRUSH, HOLLOW_BRUSH or NULL_BRUSH, and LTGRAY_BRUSH.

The stock fill patterns used by brushes include those shown in Table 12.5.

Cross-hatching can be selected from the group of hatch patterns shown in Table 12.6.

Table 12.5: Stock Brush Fill Patterns

BS_SOLID	The fill is the color of the brush.
BS_HOLLOW	The color of the brush is ignored.
BS_HATCHED	The hatching is the color of the brush.
BS_PATTERN	The color of the brush is ignored.
BS_INDEXED	The color is selected from a color table.
BS_DIBPATTERN	The color is defined by a device-independent bitmap.

Table 12.6: Stock Brush Hatch Patterns

HS_HORIZONTAL	Horizontal hatch
HS_VERTICAL	Vertical hatch
HS_FDIAGONAL	Forward diagonal hatch
HS_BDIAGONAL	Backward diagonal hatch
HS_CROSS	+-pattern cross-hatch
HS_DIAGCROSS	x-pattern cross-hatch

You will find additional patterns described in the wingdi.h header file. Brushes are created via the CBrush class. Stock brushes can be obtained with the **GetStockObject()** function. The **SelectObject()** function changes the brush just selected to the current brush.

To create and select a custom brush, use one of the following functions: **CreateSolidBrush(), CreateHatchBrush(), CreatePatternBrush(),** or **CreateDIBPatternBrush().** Once the brush is created, it is selected with the **SelectObject()** function. Here is an example:

```
CBrush  newbrush;
CBrush* oldbrush;
     .
     .
     .
newbrush.CreateSolidBrush(RGB(0,0,255));
oldbrush = dc.SelectObject(&newbrush);
```

In this example, a solid blue brush is created and selected.

Once a brush is selected, only that brush can be used to fill objects within the current device context. To use a brush of another color or pattern, the previous brush must be deselected. This is done by calling the **DeleteObject()** function. For example:

```
newbrush.DeleteObject();
```

This function should not be used to delete stock brushes.

Changing Text Colors

The foreground and background color of text drawn to the graphics screen are easy to change. The foreground color of text can be changed with a call to the **SetTextColor()** function. For example:

```
dc.SetTextColor(RGB(255,0,0));
```

This RGB value sets the text color to red. The background color of the text block is based on the background mode and color. The background mode is either opaque or transparent. An opaque mode background color fills the space between the letters with the new color. The default is white unless the background color has been changed. In transparent mode the background color is ignored. The space between characters is not filled. The background mode is set with a call to the **SetBkMode()** function.

```
dc.SetBkMode(TRANSPARENT);
```

The background text color is set with a call to the **SetBkColor()** function.

```
dc.SetBkColor(RGB(0,0,255));
```

In this case, the background text color is set to blue.

Drawing Mode Selection

How pens and brushes are combined with objects depends upon the selected drawing mode. The **SetROP2()** function selects the drawing mode. The syntax of the function is:

```
dc.SetROP2(nDrawMode);
```

The **SetROP2()** function returns a type int. The *nDrawMode* parameter is also a type int. The value for *nDrawMode* can be any of the values shown in Table 12.7. The default value is R2_COPYPEN.

Table 12.7: Drawing Mode Values

Selected Value	*Description*
R2_BLACK	Pixel is black.
R2_COPYPEN	Pixel is pen color.
R2_MASKNOTPEN	Pixel is a combination of display and inverse of pen.
R2_MASKPEN	Pixel color is common to pen and display.
R2_MASKPENNOT	Pixel is a combination of pen color and inverse of screen.
R2_MERGENOTPEN	Pixel is display color and inverse pen color.
R2_MERGEPEN	Pixel is pen color and display color merged.
R2_MERGEPENNOT	Pixel is pen color and inverse display color merged.
R2_NOP	Pixel is unchanged.
R2_NOT	Pixel is inverse of display color.

Continued on the next page.

Table 12.7: Continued

Selected Value	*Description*
R2_NOTCOPYPEN	Pixel is inverse of pen color.
R2_NOTMASKPEN	Pixel is inverse of R2_MASKPEN.
R2_NOTMERGEPEN	Pixel is inverse of R2_MERGEOPEN color.
R2_NOTXORPEN	Pixel is inverse of R2_XORPEN.
R2_WHITE	Pixel is white.
R2_XORPEN	Pixel is combination of colors in pen and display, but not colors in both.

The default value is R2_COPYPEN.

Simple Applications Using GDI Tools and Techniques

The project developed for this chapter will put into action many of the graphics functions just discussed. This is a straightforward application designed to teach you how the various graphics primitives and drawing options can be used.

Base Code

For the project in this chapter, you will first need to generate the project's base code with the AppWizard. The workspace will be named Shapes. Use the following steps to complete the project files with the AppWizard.

- Enter the Microsoft Development Studio (Visual C++ Compiler).
- Chose the File menu and select the New menu item.
- Select Project Workspace from the New dialog box.
- From the New Project Workspace dialog box:
  Name the workspace "Shapes".

  Set the location of the workspace (for example, C:Shapes).

  Select MFC AppWizard (exe) from the list box.
- Step 1—Select a single document application type.
- Step 2—Select no database support.
- Step 3—Select none for OLE compound document support.

- Step 4—Select no additional features.
- Step 5—Do not select comments. Select a statically linked library.
- Step 6—View your settings and Finish the AppWizard process.

If the information is correct, in the New Project Information dialog box, select OK.

When the final step has been completed as just described, the AppWizard generates all of the base files needed for the Shape project.

Now before adding various GDI drawing functions, edit the menu located in the Shapes.rc file so that only a File | Exit item and an Help | About item are available, as shown in Figure 12.7.

A Variety of Graphical Shapes

When the AppWizard generated the base code for the Shapes project, it created numerous source code, header, and resource files. For example, the following source code files can be found

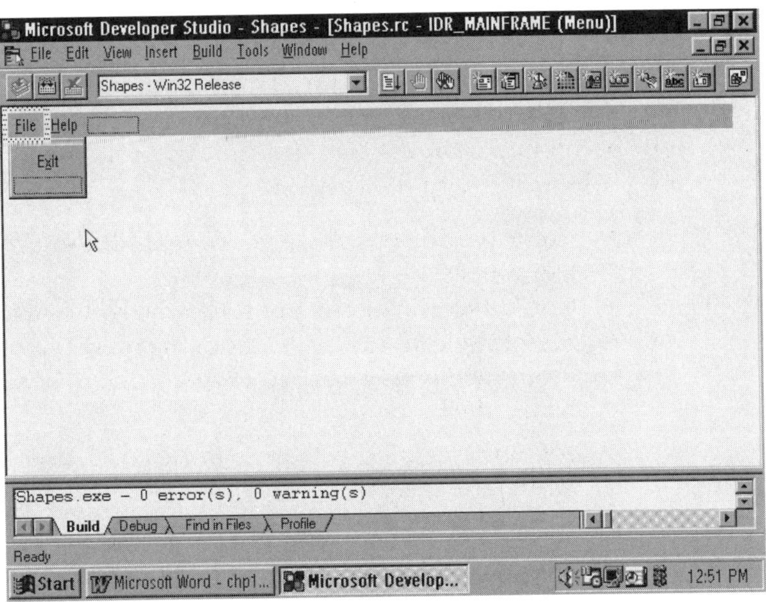

Figure 12.7: Since print and editing capabilities are not implemented, simplify the menu resources for the Shapes project.

in the Shapes subdirectory: MainFrm.cpp, Shapes.cpp, ShapesDoc.cpp, ShapesView.cpp, and StdAfx.cpp. For this example, only the ShapesView.cpp file will have to be altered to support the graphics function calls.

Open the ShapesView.cpp file. Use the Microsoft Developer Studio's View | ClassWizard... menu item to access the MFC ClassWizard dialog box, as shown in Figure 12.8.

The graphics functions will draw in the client area of the window, so we'll need to add an **OnPaint()** member function to handle WM_PAINT messages to the CShapesView class. This can be done from the ClassWizard by selecting WM_PAINT in the Message list box.

Now, you will need to enter the graphics code shown in the next listing. Only the bolded lines of code need be entered.

```
void CShapesView::OnPaint()
{
  CPaintDC dc(this); // device context for painting

  POINT polylpts[4],polygpts[5];
  int xcoord;
```

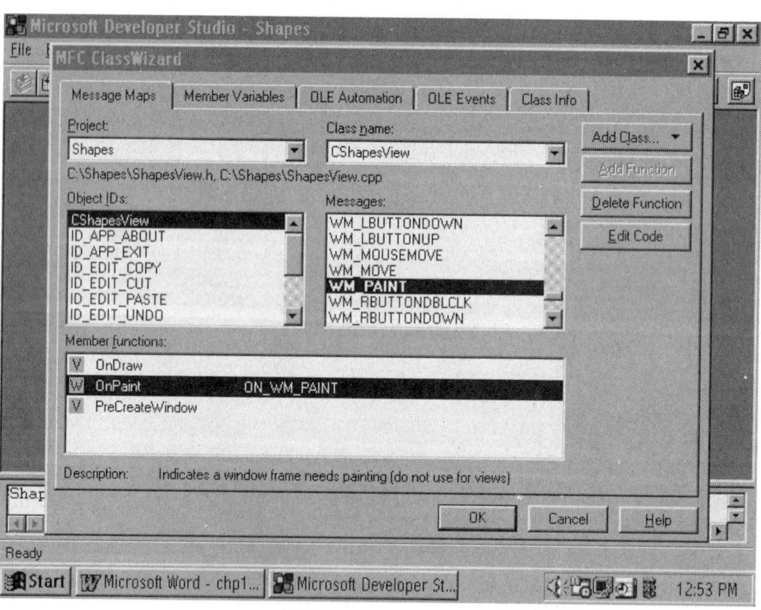

Figure 12.8: Add an OnPaint() member function to respond to WM_PAINT messages.

```
CBrush  newbrush;
CBrush* oldbrush;
CPen    newpen;
CPen*   oldpen;

// draw a diagonal line
// with a dash-dot pen
newpen.CreatePen(PS_DASHDOT,1,RGB(0,0,0));
oldpen=dc.SelectObject(&newpen);
dc.MoveTo(20,20);
dc.LineTo(100,100);
dc.TextOut(60,20,"<- diagonal line",16);
// return to default values
newpen.CreatePen(PS_SOLID,1,RGB(0,0,0));
oldpen=dc.SelectObject(&newpen);

// set several pixels on screen to red
for(xcoord=400;xcoord<450;xcoord+=5)
  dc.SetPixel(xcoord,50,0L);
dc.TextOut(460,45,"<- pixels",9);

// draw an arc
dc.Arc(25,125,175,225,175,225,100,125);
dc.TextOut(50,150,"small arc ->",12);

// drawing several lines with Polyline
polylpts[0].x=10;
polylpts[0].y=30;
polylpts[1].x=10;
polylpts[1].y=100;
polylpts[2].x=50;
polylpts[2].y=100;
polylpts[3].x=10;
polylpts[3].y=30;
dc.Polyline(polylpts,4);
dc.TextOut(10,110,"polyline",8);

// draw a chord, fill with red
newbrush.CreateSolidBrush(RGB(255,0,0));
oldbrush=dc.SelectObject(&newbrush);
dc.Chord(125,125,275,225,275,225,200,125);
dc.TextOut(280,150,"<- chord",8);

// draw an ellipse, fill with blue
newbrush.CreateSolidBrush(RGB(0,0,255));
oldbrush=dc.SelectObject(&newbrush);
dc.Ellipse(275,300,200,250);
dc.TextOut(220,265,"ellipse",7);

// draw a circle with ellipse function
// fill with green
// set text color to blue
```

```
// fill green color between letters.
newbrush.CreateSolidBrush(RGB(0,255,0));
oldbrush=dc.SelectObject(&newbrush);
dc.Ellipse(375,75,525,225);
dc.SetTextColor(RGB(0,0,255));
dc.SetBkMode(TRANSPARENT);
dc.SetBkColor(RGB(0,255,0));
dc.TextOut(435,190,"circle",6);
// return to default values
dc.SetTextColor(RGB(0,0,0));
dc.SetBkMode(OPAQUE);
dc.SetBkColor(RGB(255,255,255));

// draw a pie wedge, fill with yellow
newbrush.CreateSolidBrush(RGB(255,255,0));
oldbrush=dc.SelectObject(&newbrush);
dc.Pie(200,0,300,100,200,50,250,100);
dc.TextOut(260,80,"<- pie wedge",12);

// draw a rectangle, fill with lite blue
newbrush.CreateSolidBrush(RGB(0,255,255));
oldbrush=dc.SelectObject(&newbrush);
dc.Rectangle(25,300,150,375);
dc.TextOut(50,325,"rectangle",9);

// draw rounded rectangle, fill with gray
// change pen width to 3 and color to red
newpen.CreatePen(PS_SOLID,3,RGB(255,0,0));
oldpen=dc.SelectObject(&newpen);
newbrush.CreateSolidBrush(RGB(127,127,127));
oldbrush=dc.SelectObject(&newbrush);
dc.RoundRect(350,250,400,290,20,20);
dc.TextOut (410,270,"<--rounded rectangle",20);

// draw with Polygon, fill with a mixed color
// change pen width to 4 and color to blue
polygpts[0].x=40;
polygpts[0].y=200;
polygpts[1].x=100;
polygpts[1].y=270;
polygpts[2].x=80;
polygpts[2].y=290;
polygpts[3].x=20;
polygpts[3].y=220;
polygpts[4].x=40;
polygpts[4].y=200;
newpen.CreatePen(PS_SOLID,4,RGB(0,0,255));
oldpen=dc.SelectObject(&newpen);
```

```
    newbrush.CreateSolidBrush(RGB(127,155,55));
    oldbrush=dc.SelectObject(&newbrush);
    dc.Polygon(polygpts,5);
    dc.TextOut(80,230,"<- polygon",10);

    // de-select pen and brush
    dc.SelectObject(&newpen);
    newpen.DeleteObject();
    dc.SelectObject(&newbrush);
    newbrush.DeleteObject();
}
```

This application will make a handy reference when you want to remember how to code a particular graphics function. Examine the listing carefully, study the figure shown in Figure 12.9, and see if you can determine how each function operates.

Build the application from the Microsoft Developer Studio's Build menu, then select the Rebuild All menu item.

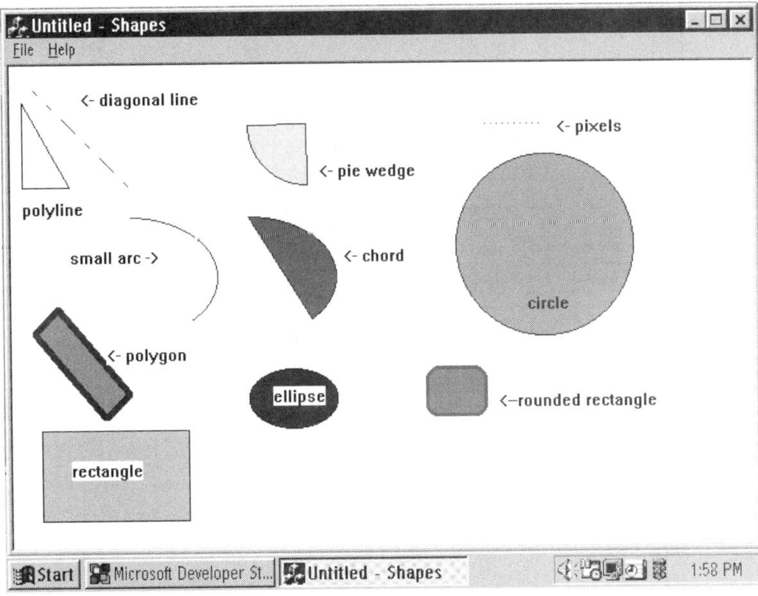

Figure 12.9: The simple graphics shapes are drawn in the client area of the window.

More Graphics Shapes?

Did you know there are even more graphics primitives then we've shown you in this chapter? Windows NT, for example, supports a whole host of graphics functions that deal with World Transformations. These functions allows the coordinate system to be rotated and scaled. By using these functions, it is possible to draw an ellipse on something other than the horizontal or vertical axis.

If you interested in these additional concepts, start first by printing the header files we suggested earlier in this chapter. The next stop is using the help engine supplied with the Microsoft Developer Studio. Finally, don't neglect Microsoft's sample programs.

Chapter 13

Common Controls

Microsoft Windows offers a variety of resources and controls. Controls such as scroll bars, push buttons, radio buttons, and so on have been available as long as Windows has been on the market. Recently, with the release of Windows 95, new emphasis has been placed on a new group of common controls. This group contains sliders, spinner buttons, toolbars, tooltips and so on.

In this chapter you will learn how to implement several common controls. If you follow the steps in each section, you'll soon be able to implement any control Windows provides.

Base Code

For each of the three examples in this chapter, you will need to generate the same base code with the AppWizard. Name the first workspace Tool. Using the following steps, complete the project files with the AppWizard.

- Enter the Microsoft Development Studio (Visual C++ Compiler).
- Chose the File menu and select the New menu item.
- Select Project Workspace from the New dialog box.
- From the New Project Workspace dialog box:
  Name the workspace "Tool".

  Set the location of the workspace (for example, C:Tool).

  Select MFC AppWizard (exe) from the list box.
- Step 1—Select a single document application type.
- Step 2—Select no database support.
- Step 3—Select none for OLE compound document support.
- Step 4—Select only the Dockable Toolbar features.
- Step 5—Do not select comments. Select a statically linked library.
- Step 6—View your settings and Finish the AppWizard process.

If the information is correct, in the New Project Information dialog box, select OK.

These are the steps you followed in Chapter 8 as you created your first AppWizard application. Chapter 8 describes this project creation process in more detail. When the final step has been completed, as described earlier, the AppWizard generates all of the base files needed for the Tool project.

You will now need to repeat the process two more times. Use the previously listed steps to create a project workspace named Intense. At Step 4, do not select any features. Finally, create a project workspace named Spin using the same process.

In the remaining sections of this chapter, we'll explain what must be added to the base code of each project workspace in order to implement a toolbar with tooltips, a slider control, and a spin button. The MFC and Windows 95 currently supports numerous common controls, as shown in Table 13.1. Windows NT will eventually incorporate these controls, too.

Table 13.1: Common Controls and Control Classes

Control	*Control Class*
Animate	CAnimateCtrl
Header	CHeaderCtrl
Hot Key	CHotKeyCtrl
Check List Box	CCheckListBox
Drag List Box	CDragListBox
List	CListCtrl
Progress	CProgressCtrl
Rich Edit	CRichEditCtrl
Slider	CSliderCtrl
Spin Button	CSpinButtonCtrl
Status Bar	CStatusBarCtrl
Tab	CTabCtrl
Tool Bar	CToolBarCtrl
Tool Tip	CToolTipCtrl
Tree	CTreeCtrl

A ToolBar Control with ToolTips

A toolbar control or object is a horizontal or vertical group or grouping of small graphical shapes. The graphical shapes are resources that are saved as a single bitmap file. When you asked the AppWizard to include a dockable toolbar, in Step 4 of the design process, a default toolbar was created. ToolTips are small "billboards" that indicated what each toolbar item does. ToolTips are automatically included with the toolbar implementation. All you have to do is supply the correct text.

The AppWizard, as you know, generates a hearty group of files. In this case, you should find MainFrm.cpp, StdAfx.cpp, Tool.cpp, ToolDoc.cpp, ToolView.cpp, and their associated header files. In addition to these files, you'll find Tool.rc and resource.h.

The code for implementing the toolbar was placed in the MainFrm.cpp file by the AppWizard. The following portion of code shows how the **OnCreate()** message handler creates, and loads the toolbar, sets the style, and enables docking.

```
int CMainFrame::OnCreate(LPCREATESTRUCT lpCreateStruct)
{
```

```
    if (CFrameWnd::OnCreate(lpCreateStruct) == -1)
      return -1;

    if (!m_wndToolBar.Create(this) ||
      !m_wndToolBar.LoadToolBar(IDR_MAINFRAME))
    {
      TRACE0("Failed to create toolbarn");
      return -1;      // fail to create
    }

    m_wndToolBar.SetBarStyle(m_wndToolBar.GetBarStyle() |
      CBRS_TOOLTIPS | CBRS_FLYBY | CBRS_SIZE_DYNAMIC);

    m_wndToolBar.EnableDocking(CBRS_ALIGN_ANY);
    EnableDocking(CBRS_ALIGN_ANY);
    DockControlBar(&m_wndToolBar);

    return 0;
}
```

For most applications, this code will not need to be modified. However, it doesn't hurt to see how the toolbar was implemented, just once.

Since this application has a toolbar in place, we'll simply edit the current bitmap to include the new graphic shapes needed for this application. You'll see how this is done in the next section of this chapter.

Augmenting the Toolbar

The Tool.rc resource file contains the resources for the application. These resources include accelerators, dialog boxes, icons, menus, string tables, toolbar and version control. For this application, we're only interested in adding images to the current toolbar.

Open the Tool.rc file from within the Microsoft Developer Studio (Visual C++ compiler) and request the Toolbar resource, as shown in Figure 13.1.

Our graphics shapes were added one at a time to the current toolbar by clicking on the blank outlined shape. This shape is shown on the extreme right of the toolbar in Figure 13.2.

The filled ellipse shape from the tool kit of shapes is used to create various colored buttons. As you can see from Figure 13.2, three buttons are in place. You now need to create a total of seven different colored buttons. The colors we used are black, blue, green, light blue, magenta, red, and yellow.

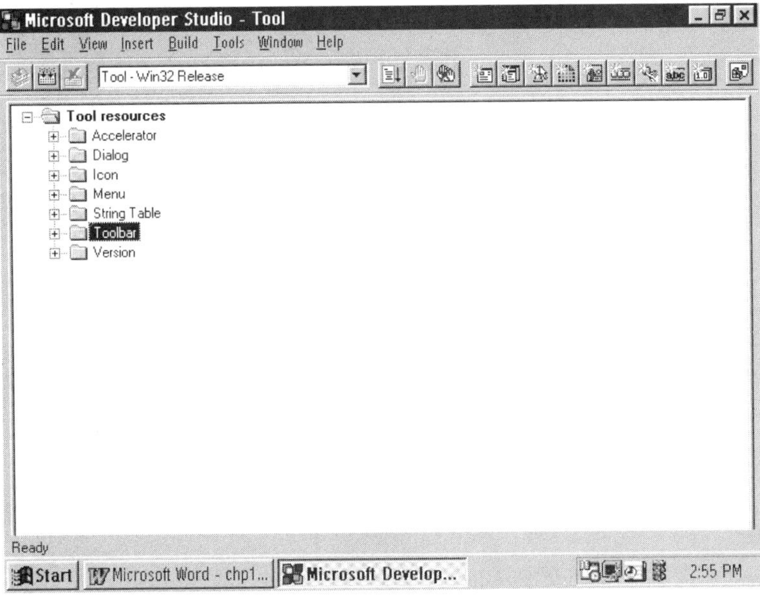

Figure 13.1: The Toolbar resource is contained in the Tool.rc file.

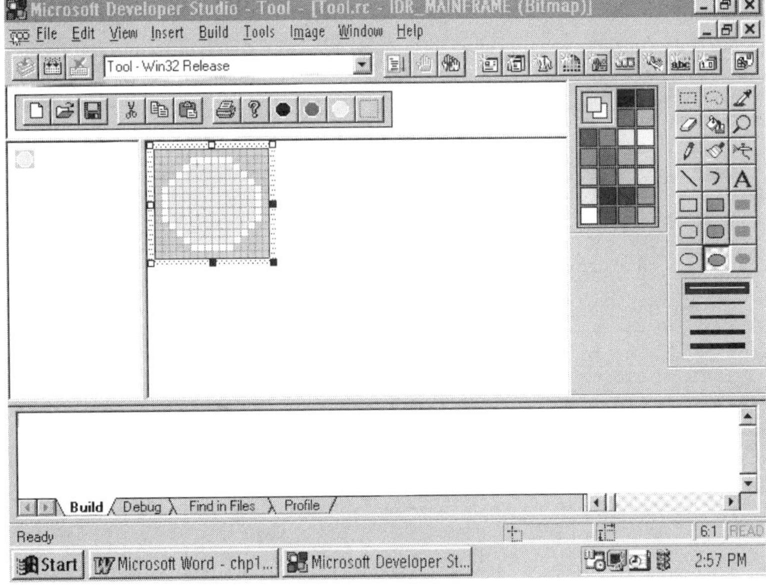

Figure 13.2: Adding a single graphics image to the toolbar.

Once the images are in place, select the black button as an example by clicking the mouse on it. Now select the Edit menu and select the Properties... menu item. You will be shown the Toolbar Button Properties dialog box, similar to Figure 13.3.

First, from within the dialog box, change the ID value to ID_BLACK. Next, change the prompt to "nBlack Brush". This is the text that will be used by tooltips. Repeat this process for the remaining six colors.

Now, the ClassWizard can be used to generate support code for these unique toolbar buttons.

The MFC ClassWizard

Select the View menu and choose the ClassWizard menu item to start the MFC ClassWizard. From the Message Maps folder, select the CToolView class name. It is into this class that the various member functions will be added. Figure 13.4 shows the options selected for adding the member function that processes the black toolbar image.

For each toolbar image, select the appropriate ID value. In this case, ID_BLACK is selected. The COMMAND Message

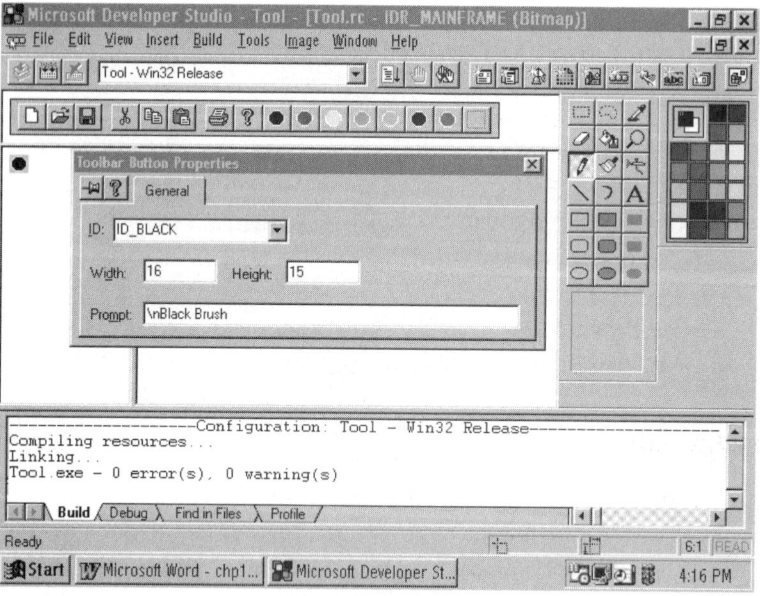

Figure 13.3: The Toolbar Button Properties dialog box.

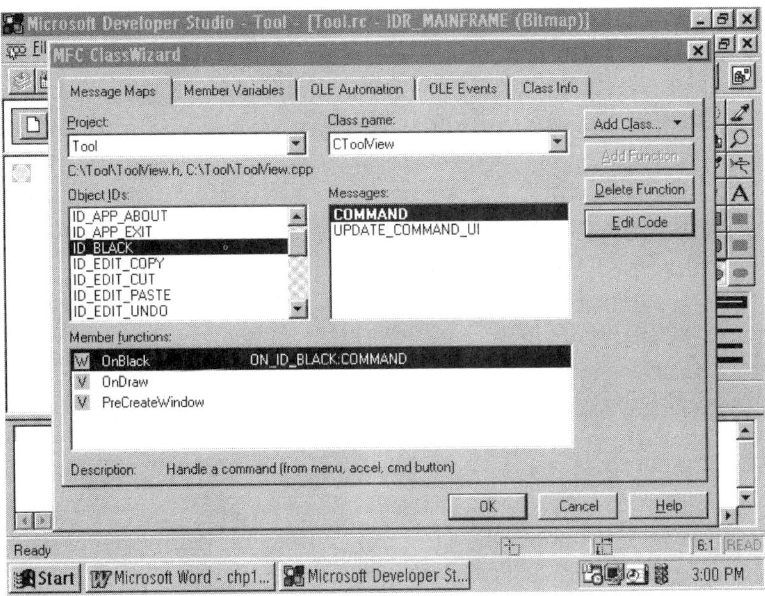

Figure 13.4: Member functions are added to the CToolView class for each toolbar image.

option is chosen. At this point, the Add Function will be functional, and the member function can be added. The member function is named **OnBlack**.

Repeat this process until you have created a member function for each of the six remaining toolbar images.

The member functions are added to the ToolView.cpp file. Figure 13.5 shows the ToolView.cpp file immediately after the **OnBlack()** member function is added.

This project will also need to respond to WM_PAINT messages, so while you have the ClassWizard opened, add an **OnPaint()** member function by selecting WM_PAINT in the Message list box while the Object ID is set to CToolView.

Code You Must Edit

You have actually completed the hardest work by simply creating the bitmap! There is some code that must be added to make the application interesting. The only file that needs to be modified is ToolView.cpp; the ClassWizard has done all of the difficult work.

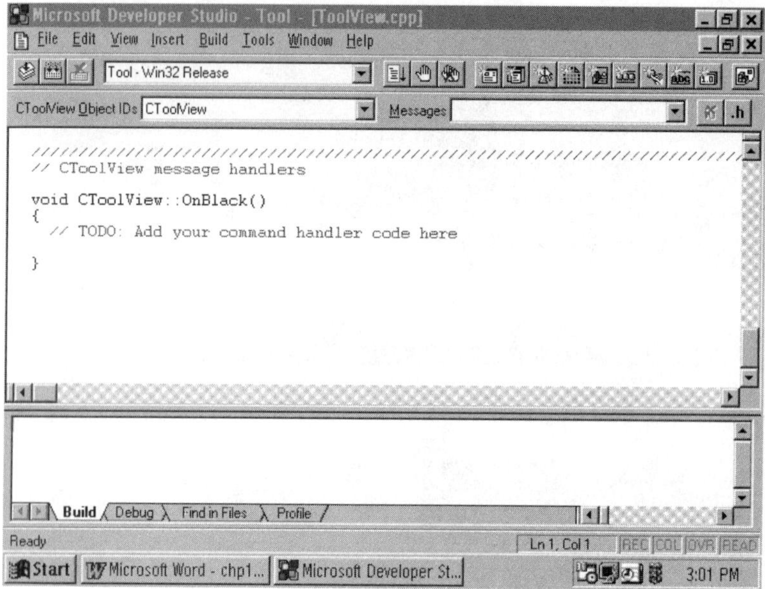

Figure 13.5: The OnBlack() member function is added to the ToolView.cpp file.

The following listing is the complete ToolView.cpp file, with our code changes shown in bold.

```
// ToolView.cpp : implementation of the CToolView class
//

#include "stdafx.h"
#include "Tool.h"

#include "ToolDoc.h"
#include "ToolView.h"

#ifdef _DEBUG
#define new DEBUG_NEW
#undef THIS_FILE
static char THIS_FILE[] = __FILE__;
#endif

CBrush newbrush;     // Prepare brush for painting
CBrush* oldbrush;

// CToolView

IMPLEMENT_DYNCREATE(CToolView, CView)

BEGIN_MESSAGE_MAP(CToolView, CView)
  //{{AFX_MSG_MAP(CToolView)
```

```
  ON_COMMAND(ID_BLACK, OnBlack)
  ON_COMMAND(ID_BLUE, OnBlue)
  ON_COMMAND(ID_GREEN, OnGreen)
  ON_COMMAND(ID_LTBLUE, OnLtblue)
  ON_COMMAND(ID_MAGENTA, OnMagenta)
  ON_COMMAND(ID_RED, OnRed)
  ON_COMMAND(ID_YELLOW, OnYellow)
  ON_WM_PAINT()
  //}}AFX_MSG_MAP
END_MESSAGE_MAP()

// CToolView construction/destruction

CToolView::CToolView()
{
}

CToolView::~CToolView()
{
}

BOOL CToolView::PreCreateWindow(CREATESTRUCT& cs)
{
  return CView::PreCreateWindow(cs);
}

// CToolView drawing

void CToolView::OnDraw(CDC* pDC)
{
  CToolDoc* pDoc = GetDocument();
  ASSERT_VALID(pDoc);
}

// CToolView diagnostics

#ifdef _DEBUG
void CToolView::AssertValid() const
{
  CView::AssertValid();
}

void CToolView::Dump(CDumpContext& dc) const
{
  CView::Dump(dc);
}

CToolDoc* CToolView::GetDocument() // non-debug is inline
{
  ASSERT(m_pDocument->IsKindOf(RUNTIME_CLASS(CToolDoc)));
  return (CToolDoc*)m_pDocument;
}
```

```
#endif //_DEBUG

// CToolView message handlers

void CToolView::OnBlack()
{
  newbrush.CreateSolidBrush(RGB(0,0,0));
  InvalidateRect(NULL,TRUE);
}

void CToolView::OnBlue()
{
  newbrush.CreateSolidBrush(RGB(0,0,255));
  InvalidateRect(NULL,TRUE);
}

void CToolView::OnGreen()
{
  newbrush.CreateSolidBrush(RGB(0,255,0));
  InvalidateRect(NULL,TRUE);
}

void CToolView::OnLtblue()
{
  newbrush.CreateSolidBrush(RGB(0,255,255));
  InvalidateRect(NULL,TRUE);
}

void CToolView::OnMagenta()
{
  newbrush.CreateSolidBrush(RGB(255,0,255));
  InvalidateRect(NULL,TRUE);
}

void CToolView::OnRed()
{
  newbrush.CreateSolidBrush(RGB(255,0,0));
  InvalidateRect(NULL,TRUE);
}

void CToolView::OnYellow()
{
  newbrush.CreateSolidBrush(RGB(255,255,0));
  InvalidateRect(NULL,TRUE);
}

void CToolView::OnPaint()
{
  CPaintDC dc(this); // device context for painting

  oldbrush=dc.SelectObject(&newbrush);
  dc.Rectangle(100,200,200,300);
```

```
    dc.Ellipse(300,100,500,400);

    dc.SelectObject(oldbrush);
    newbrush.DeleteObject();

    // Do not call CView::OnPaint() for painting messages
}
```

The toolbar is used to change brush colors when painting in the client area of the window. To illustrate this, two graphics shapes will be drawn by the **OnPaint()** member function.

Running the Application

To build this application, chose the Rebuild All menu item from the compiler's Build menu. If all goes well, the compiler will create an executable file named Tool.exe. Run Tool.exe and you should see a screen similar to Figure 13.6.

By the way, a toolbar that can be docked is one that can be dragged by the mouse to any edge of the client area. Figure 13.7 shows the toolbar on the right-hand edge of the client area.

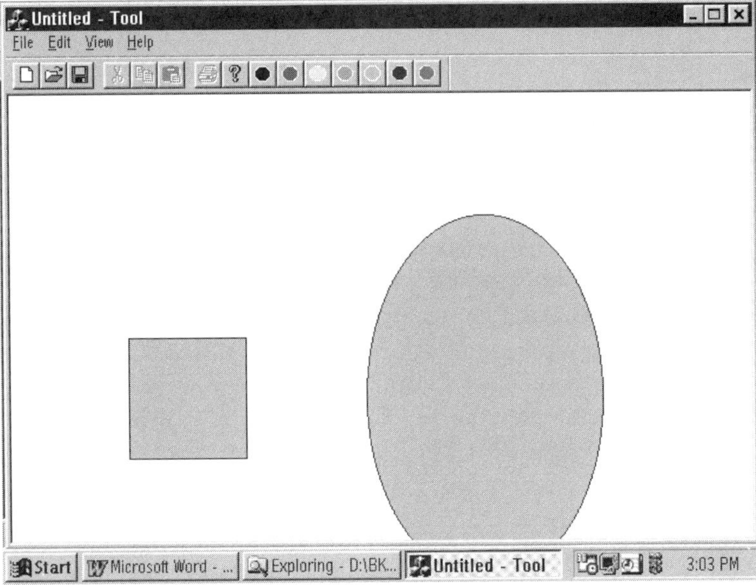

Figure 13.6: A rectangle and ellipse can be filled with any one of seven colors by selecting the color from the application's toolbar.

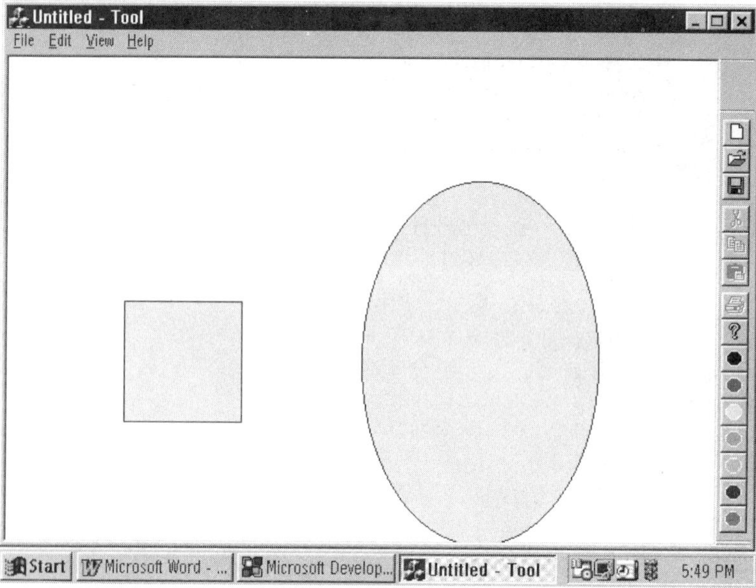

Figure 13.7: Dockable toolbars can be aligned with any edge.

What ideas do you have for a project that might include a useful toolbar with tooltips?

A Slider Control

A slider control or object allows the user to set a variety of values with a slider mechanism similar to a scroll bar. Slider controls are useful when a specific range of values or specific values are desirable. The slider control for this example is a horizontal slider that will allow the user to pick values from 0 to 50, in steps of 5.

The AppWizard generates several source code files: MainFrm.cpp, StdAfx.cpp, Intense.cpp, IntenseDoc.cpp, and IntenseView.cpp. The associated header files for these source code files and Intense.rc and resource.h are also generated.

Creating a Slider Control

The slider control will be created within a standard dialog box. The first job in this project will be to place a menu item in a menu that leads to this dialog box. Since a menu already exists for this project, simply open the Intense.rc resource file and select Menu, as shown in Figure 13.8.

IDR_MAINFRAME is the ID given the menu resource. Figure 13.9 shows a new menu, named Level, with a new menu item named Intensity. If you are working along on your computer, now is the time to add these items to the menu.

While the menu bar was generated by the AppWizard, the needed dialog box was not. To add another resource, use the Insert menu and choose the Resource... menu item, as shown in Figure 13.10.

The Insert Resource dialog box allows you to select the resource type. In this case, a dialog box is needed, as shown in Figure 13.11.

Once in the dialog box editor, design a dialog box with an OK pushbutton, edit box, and slider control. Our dialog box is shown in Figure 13.12. The cursor is pointing toward the slider control in the tool box, as you can see in the figure.

Once the dialog box has been designed, it will be necessary to create a new class to process the slider control's information.

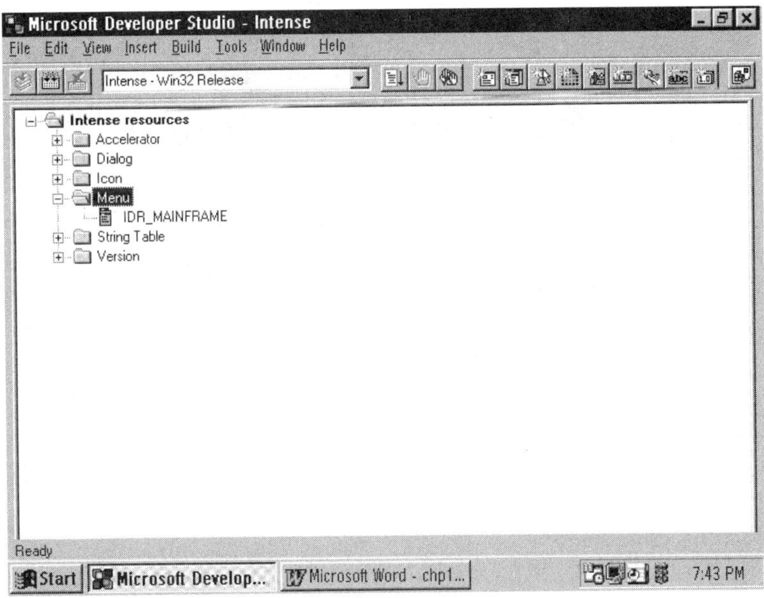

Figure 13.8: Editing the menu to add another menu item.

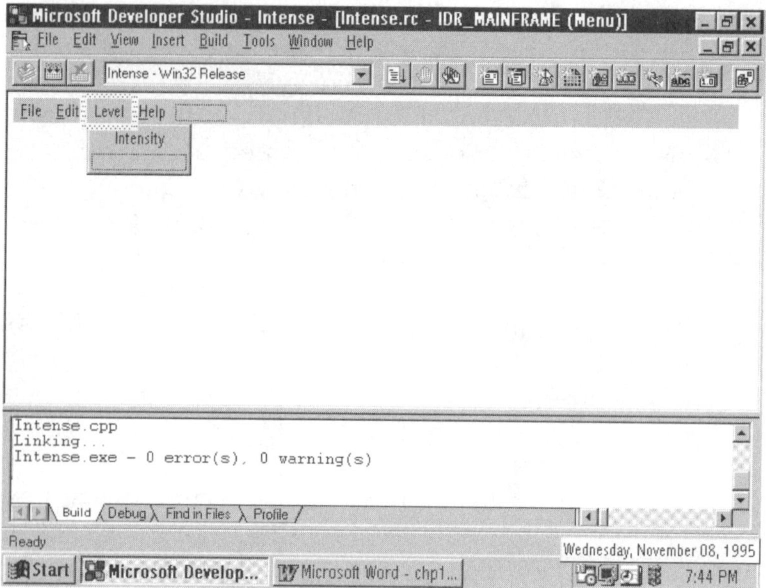

Figure 13.9: A new menu and menu item are added to the menu bar.

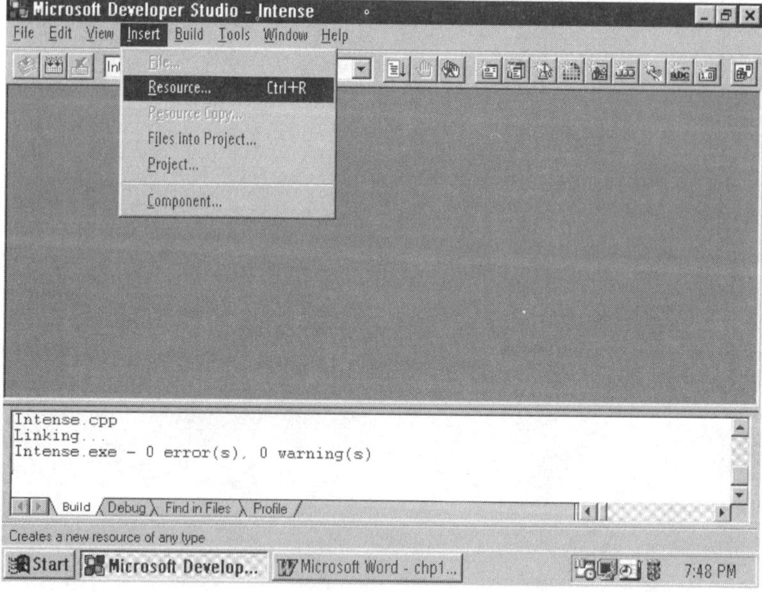

Figure 13.10: Preparing to add a new resource to the project.

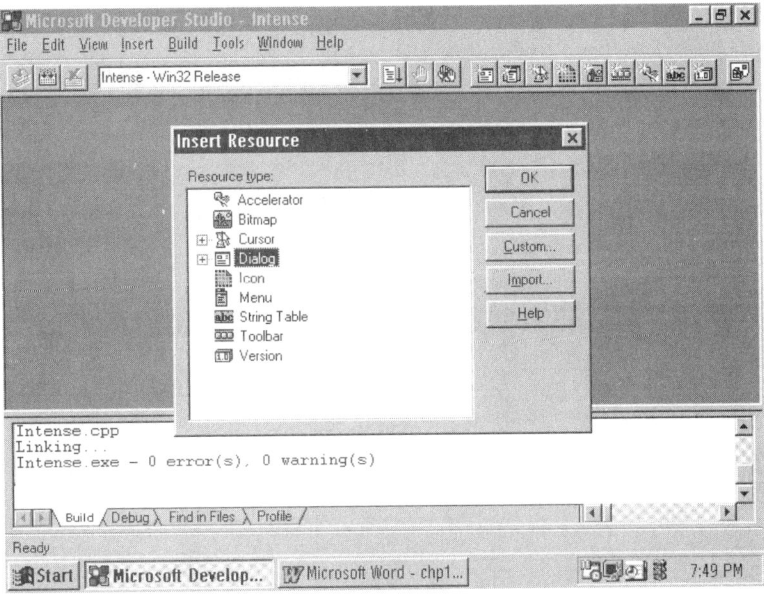

Figure 13.11: Select the Dialog item to add a new dialog box resource.

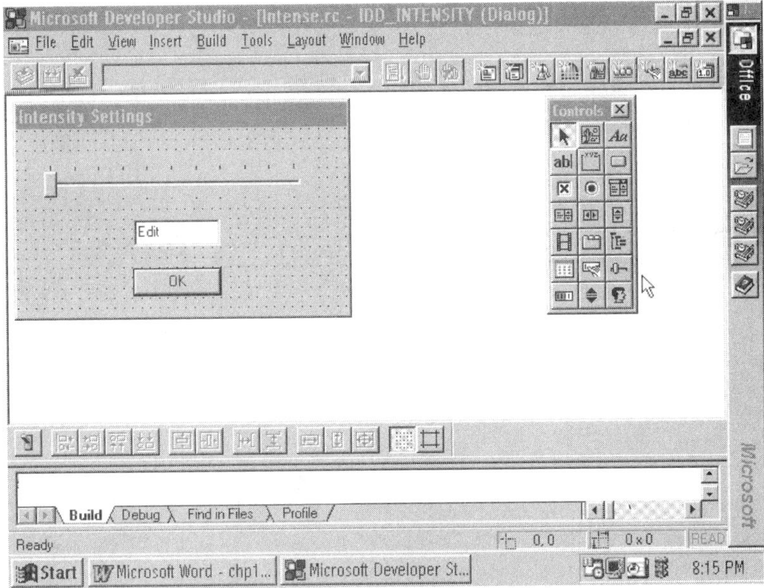

Figure 13.12: A dialog box designed with a slider control, edit box, and pushbutton.

The MFC ClassWizard

Use the compiler's View menu to select the ClassWizard. The ClassWizard has an Add Class pushbutton for generating additional classes, as shown in Figure 13.13.

When the Add Class pushbutton is selected, the Create New Class dialog box is displayed, as shown in Figure 13.14.

In this application, the new class name is CIntensityDialog. By default, the file name containing the description of this class would be IntensityDialog.cpp. However, if you view Figure 13.14 again, you will notice that both the header and implementation file names have been changed to IntDia.h and IntDia.cpp respectively.

The Slider control will need three additional member functions. These are added to CIntensityDialog from the Message list box. Examine Figure 13.15 and notice the inclusion of **DoDataExchange**, **OnHScroll**, and **OnInitDialog**. The latter two member functions respond to WM_HSCROLL scroll bar messages and WM_INITDIALOG initial dialog box messages.

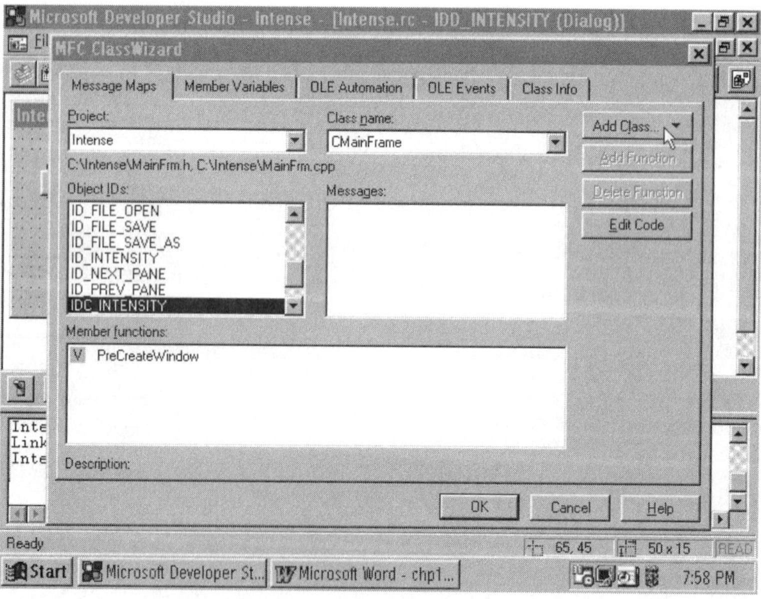

Figure 13.13: The ClassWizardís Add Class pushbutton is used to adding additional classes to the project.

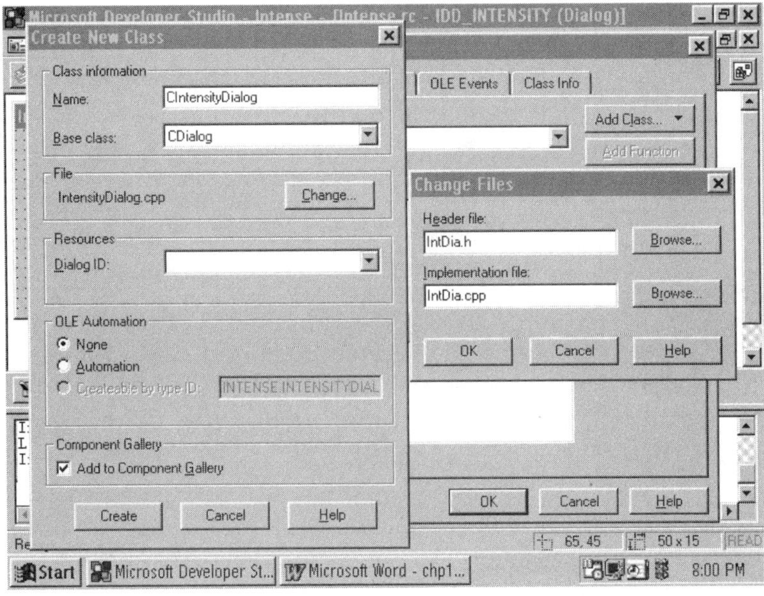

Figure 13.14: The Create New Class dialog box allows a new dialog box to be derived from a base class dialog box.

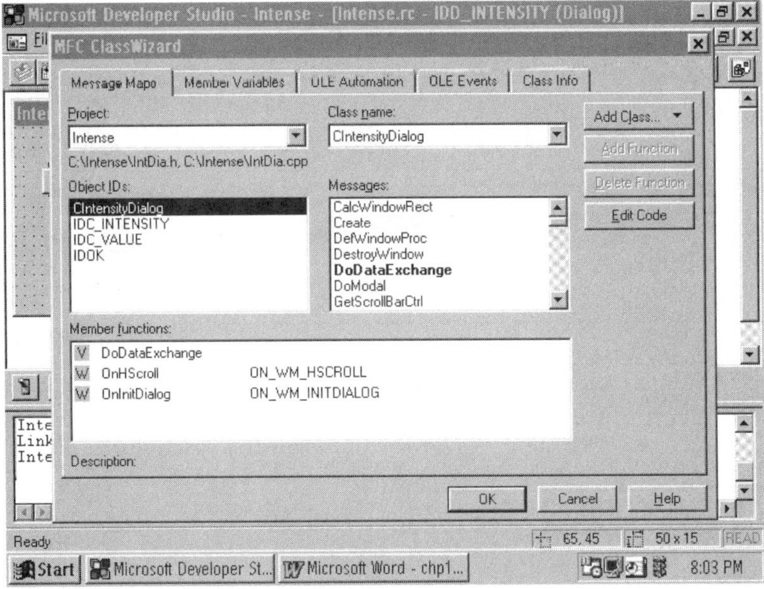

Figure 13.15: Three member functions are added to CIntensityDialog.

In order to be able to access the dialog box from the application, a member function must also be added to the CIntense-View class. This class is found in the IntenseView.cpp file. Figure 13.16 shows the Object ID, the message and the member function, **OnViewIntensity**, that will be added by the ClassWizard.

In the next section you'll learn about the code that must be included to make this control operational.

Code You Must Edit

In the last step in the previous section, a message handler was added to the IntenseView.cpp file. A small amount of code must be added to the message handler, as shown in the next listing.

```
void CIntenseView::OnViewIntensity()
{
  CIntensityDialog dlg;
  dlg.DoModal();
}
```

The portion of code printed in bold is the actual code we added to process the dialog box information.

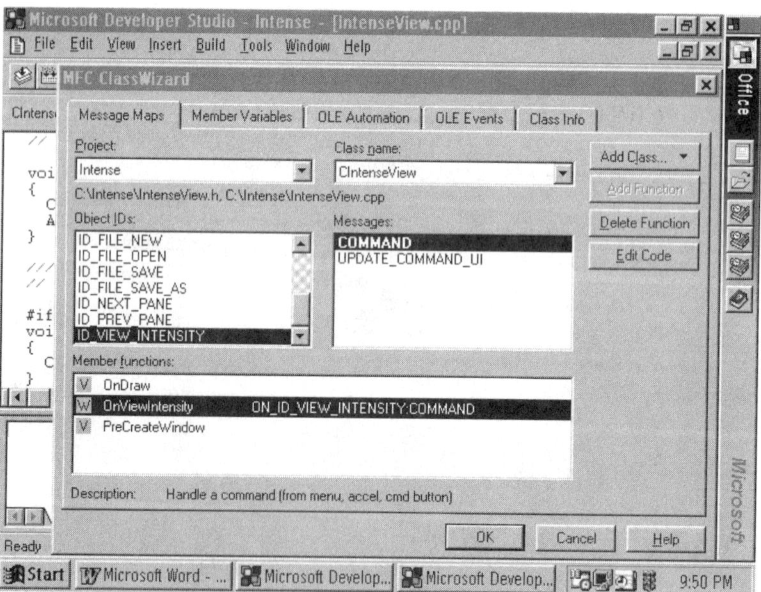

Figure 13.16: Adding a member function in CIntenseView.

It is the IntDia.cpp file that contains the largest amount of new code. This is a result of the three member functions added in the previous section. The following listing is the complete IntDia.cpp file.

```
// IntDia.cpp : implementation file
//

#include "stdafx.h"
#include "Intense.h"    // header file must be included
#include "IntDia.h"

#ifdef _DEBUG
#define new DEBUG_NEW
#undef THIS_FILE
static char THIS_FILE[] = __FILE__;
#endif

// CIntensityDialog dialog
CIntensityDialog::CIntensityDialog(CWnd* pParent /*=NULL*/)
  : CDialog(CIntensityDialog::IDD, pParent)
{
  //{{AFX_DATA_INIT(CIntensityDialog)
    // NOTE: the ClassWizard will add member init here
  //}}AFX_DATA_INIT
  m_nIntensity=0;  //initialize reading to 0
}

void CIntensityDialog::DoDataExchange(CDataExchange* pDX)
{
  CDialog::DoDataExchange(pDX);
  //{{AFX_DATA_MAP(CIntensityDialog)
    // NOTE: the ClassWizard will add DDX and DDV calls here
  //}}AFX_DATA_MAP

  CSliderCtrl* pIntensity = (CSliderCtrl*)
                              GetDlgItem(IDC_INTENSITY);

  if (pDX->m_bSaveAndValidate)
  {
    m_nIntensity = pIntensity->GetPos();
  }
  else
  {
    pIntensity->SetPos(m_nIntensity);
  }
}

BEGIN_MESSAGE_MAP(CIntensityDialog, CDialog)
  //{{AFX_MSG_MAP(CIntensityDialog)
  ON_WM_HSCROLL()
```

```
  //}}AFX_MSG_MAP
END_MESSAGE_MAP()

// CIntensityDialog message handlers
LPCTSTR pstrIntensity[] = {
  _T("5"),
  _T("10"),
  _T("15"),
  _T("20"),
  _T("25"),
  _T("30"),
  _T("35"),
  _T("40"),
  _T("45"),
};

void CIntensityDialog::OnHScroll(UINT nSBCode, UINT nPos,
                                  CScrollBar* pScrollBar)
{
  CDialog::OnHScroll(nSBCode, nPos, pScrollBar);

  int nPosition;
  int nControl = pScrollBar->GetDlgCtrlID();
  CSliderCtrl* pControl = (CSliderCtrl*)
                           GetDlgItem(nControl);

  switch (nControl)
  {
    case IDC_INTENSITY:
      ASSERT(pControl != NULL);
      nPosition = pControl->GetPos();
      GetDlgItem(IDC_VALUE)->
              SetWindowText(pstrIntensity[nPosition]);
      break;

    default:
      CDialog::OnHScroll(nSBCode, nPos, pScrollBar);
      break;
  }
  return;
}

BOOL CIntensityDialog::OnInitDialog()
{
  CDialog::OnInitDialog();

  CSliderCtrl* pIntensity = (CSliderCtrl*)
                             GetDlgItem(IDC_INTENSITY);
  pIntensity->SetRange(0, ELEMENTS(pstrIntensity)-1);
  SetDlgItemText(IDC_VALUE, pstrIntensity[0]);
```

```
    return TRUE;  // return TRUE unless focus is set to control
                  // EXCEPTION: OCX Property Pages return FALSE
}
```

Let's examine the three member functions one at a time and learn how they help provided access to this control.

DoDataExchange This member function is necessary into order to transfer information from the dialog box to the application. If you examine the CIntensityDialog implementation, you'll notice that *m_nIntensity* has been added to pass integer information. Data exchange occurs when the m_bSaveAndValidate member of the pDX object receives information from the control. The **GetPos()** function retrieves the control information for the member variables.

OnHScroll The slider control was created with the autotick feature set. This means that tick marks will be placed in the control automatically.

WM_HSCROLL messages are sent by the slider control to the application. This information is used to provide feedback to the edit box control. In other words, when the slider control is moved, the information is updated in the edit box control. You might notice in this portion of code that a pointer to the slider bar is obtained via the ID value for the control. This is because the function receives a pointer to the CScrollBar.

OnInitDialog The range or extent of the slider control's values is set with the **SetRange()** function. In this example, the range is from 0 to the number of elements in *pstrIntensity[]*–1. This member function also sets the initial value reported in the edit box control.

Running the Application

To build this application, chose the Rebuild All menu item from the compiler's Build menu. The compiler will create an executable file named Intense.exe. Run Intense.exe and you should see a screen similar to Figure 13.17.

When the range of values to be traversed is small or discrete increments are required, slider controls are always the developer's preference over scroll bars.

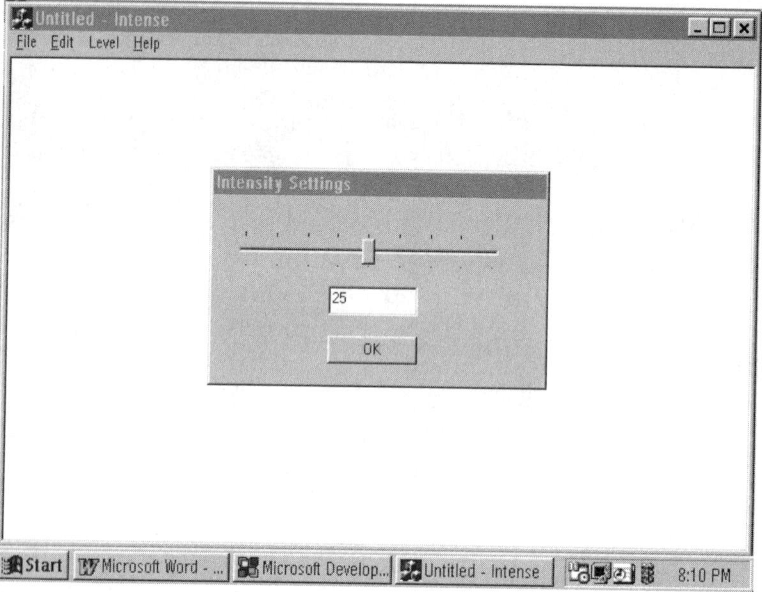

Figure 13.17: The Slider control in action.

A Spin Button Control

A Spin Button control or object allows the user to increment or decrement values with the click of an up or down button. Spin Buttons are often referred to as up and down controls. Frequently an edit box is used in conjunction with a Spin Button. When the Spin Button bonds with another control, it forms a relationship where the associated control is called a *buddy*. If the autobuddy feature is set via the control's property features, the edit box will automatically be selected if it is the first edit box control, in tab order, before the spin button.

The AppWizard will generate the following source code files: MainFrm.cpp, StdAfx.cpp, Spin.cpp, SpinDoc.cpp, and SpinView.cpp. The associated header files for these source code files and Spin.rc and resource.h are also generated. This application will used an additional source code file, but that will be discussed shortly.

Designing the Spin Button

The Spin Button control will be created within a standard dialog box. In order to reach the dialog box, a special menu will need to be created. The AppWizard created a menu, so it will simply be a matter of opening Spin.rc to alter the existing menu resource. Once Spin.rc is opened, select the Menu resource, as shown in Figure 13.18.

IDR_MAINFRAME is the ID given the menu resource. Figure 13.19 shows a new menu named Control, with a new menu item named SpinButton Control. If you are creating this resource while reading, now is the time to add these items to the menu.

It is now necessary to create an entirely new dialog box to house the spin control. To add an additional resource, use the Insert menu and choose the Resource... menu item, as shown in Figure 13.20.

The Insert Resource dialog box allows you to select the resource type. In this case, a dialog resource is needed, as shown in Figure 13.21.

Once in the dialog box editor, design a dialog box with an OK pushbutton, edit box, and spin control. Our new dialog box

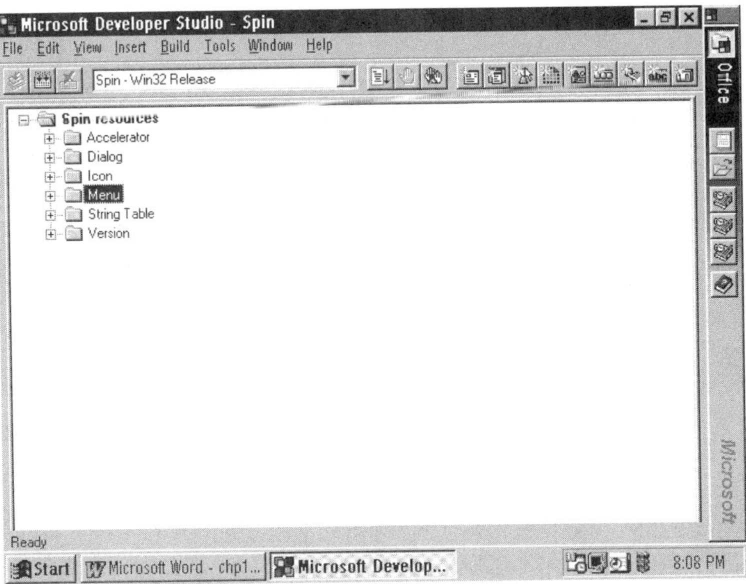

Figure 13.18: Editing the current menu to add another menu item.

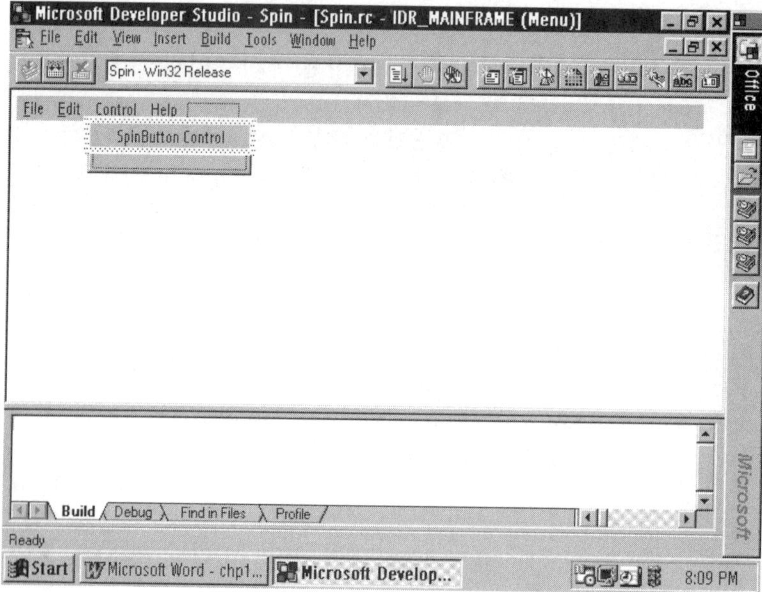

Figure 13.19: A new menu and menu item are added to the menu bar.

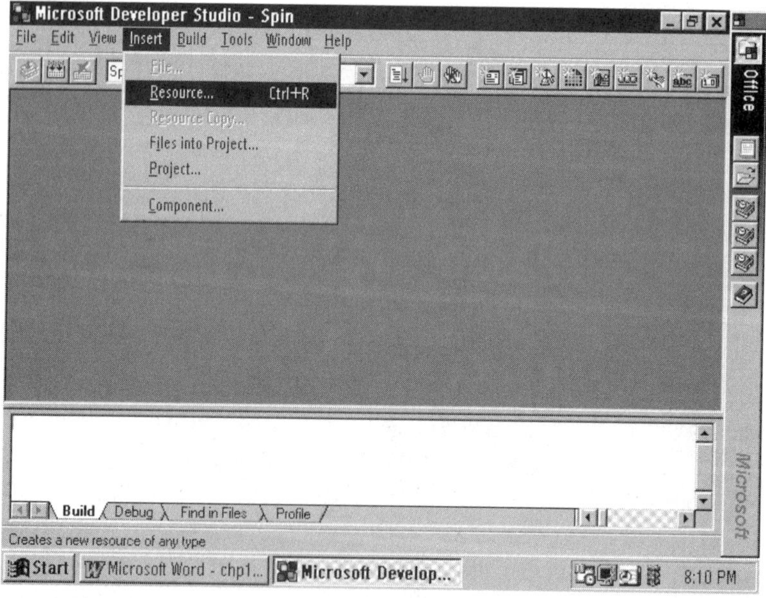

Figure 13.20: Preparing to add a new resource to the project.

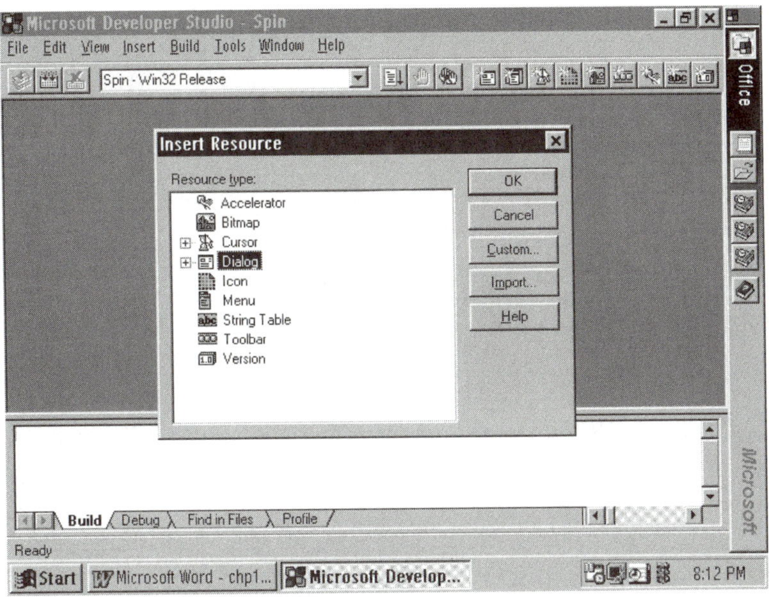

Figure 13.21: Select the Dialog item to add a new dialog box resource.

is shown in Figure 13.22. The cursor is pointing at the spin control in the tool box, as you can see in the figure.

Once the dialog box has been designed, it will be necessary to create a new class to process the spin control's information.

The MFC ClassWizard

Use the Visual C++ compiler's View menu and select the ClassWizard menu item. The ClassWizard provides an Add Class pushbutton for generating additional classes, as shown in Figure 13.23.

The Create New Class dialog box is displayed, as shown in Figure 13.24, when the Add Class pushbutton is selected,

In this application, the new class name is CSpinButDia. By default, the file name containing the description of this class is SpinButDia.cpp.

The spin button control will need two additional member functions. These are added to CSpinButDia from the Message list box. Examine Figure 13.25 and notice the inclusion of **DoDataExchange** and **OnInitDialog**. The **OnInitDialog** mem-

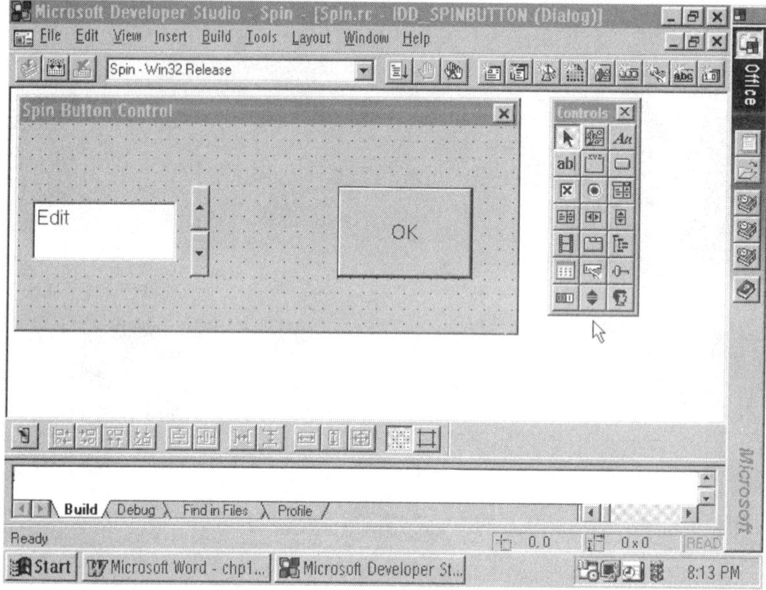

Figure 13.22: A dialog box designed with a spin control, edit box, and pushbutton.

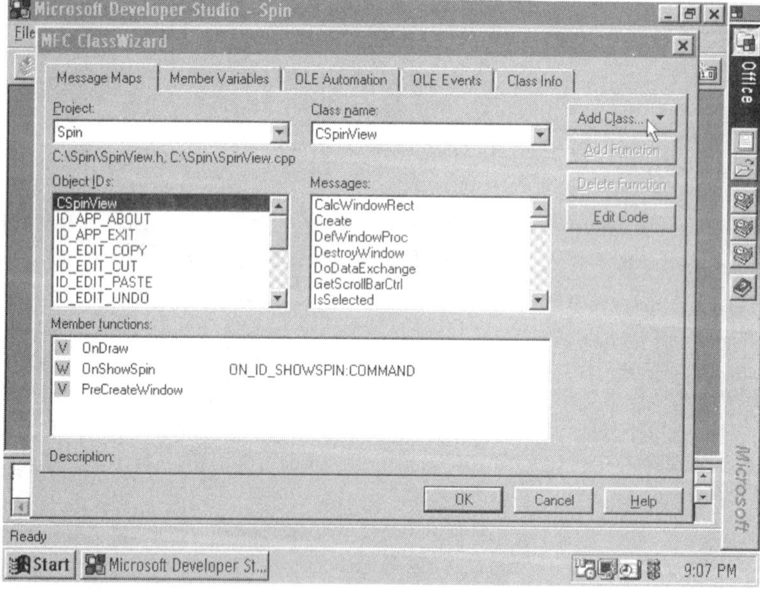

Figure 13.23: The ClassWizardís Add Class pushbutton is used when additional classes are needed by the project.

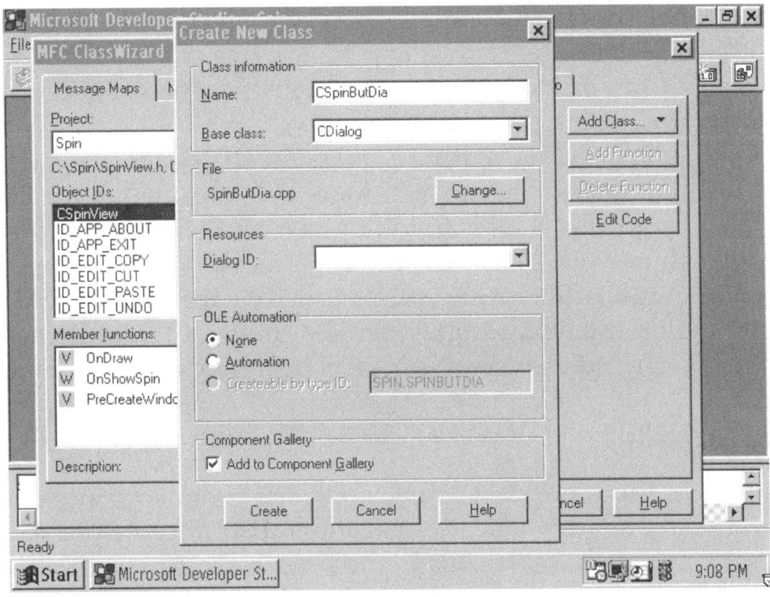

Figure 13.24: The Create New Class dialog box permits a new dialog box class to be derived from a base class dialog box class.

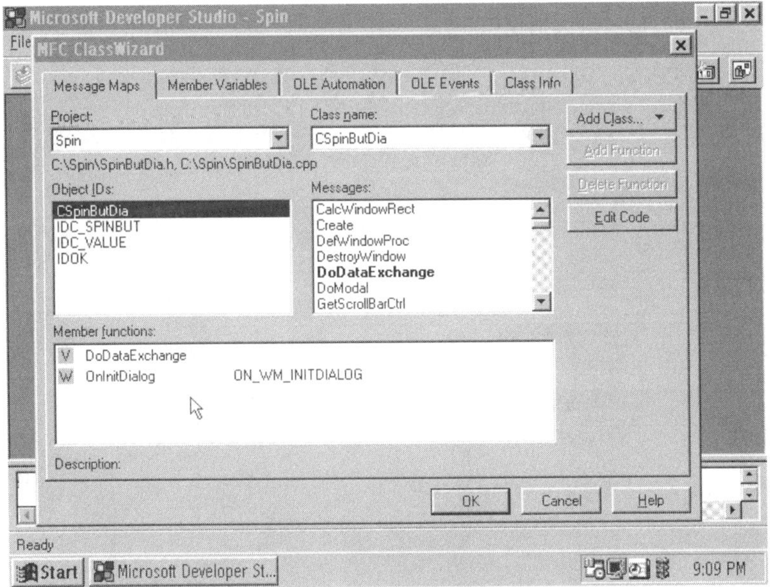

Figure 13.25: Two member functions are added to CSpinButDia.

ber function responds to a WM_INITDIALOG initial dialog box message.

You'll also want to add an integer member variable to this class named *m_nValue*.

In order to be able to access the dialog box from the application, a member function must also be added to the CSpinView class. This class is found in the SpinView.cpp file. Figure 13.26 shows the Object ID, the message and the member function, **OnShowSpin**, that will be added by the ClassWizard.

In the next section you'll learn about the code that must be included to make this control operational.

Code You Must Edit

In the previous section, a message handler was added to the SpinView.cpp file. A small amount of code must be added to the message handler in order to process dialog box information.

```
void CSpinView::OnShowSpin()
{
  CSpinButDia dlg;
  dlg.DoModal();
}
```

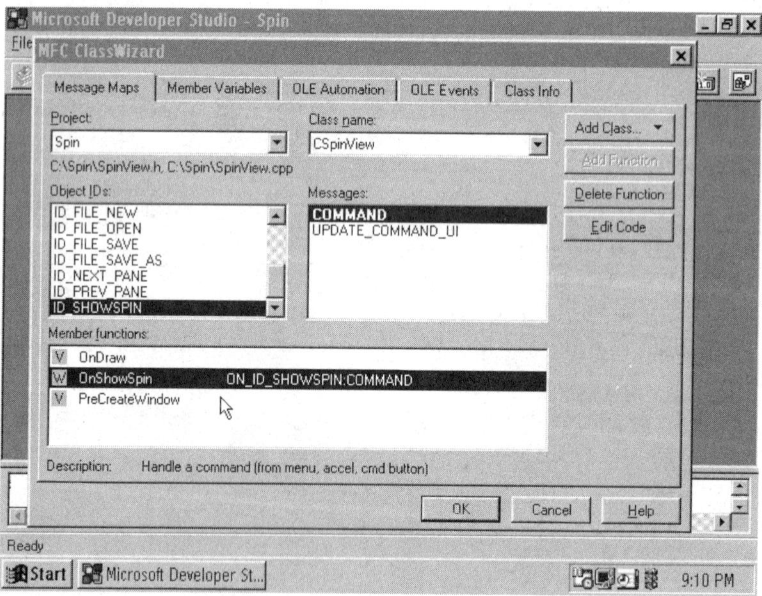

Figure 13.26: Adding a member function in CSpinView.

The portion of code printed in bold is the actual code added to this member function's description.

It is the SpinButDia.cpp file that contains the largest amount of new code. This is a result of the two member functions added in the previous section. The following listing is the complete SpinButDia.cpp file.

```
// SpinButDia.cpp : implementation file
//

#include "stdafx.h"
#include "Spin.h"
#include "SpinButDia.h"

#ifdef _DEBUG
#define new DEBUG_NEW
#undef THIS_FILE
static char THIS_FILE[] = _FILE_;
#endif

// CSpinButDia dialog

CSpinButDia::CSpinButDia(CWnd* pParent /*=NULL*/)
  : CDialog(CSpinButDia::IDD, pParent)
{
  //{{AFX_DATA_INIT(CSpinButDia)
  m_nValue = 0;
  //}}AFX_DATA_INIT
}

void CSpinButDia::DoDataExchange(CDataExchange* pDX)
{
  CDialog::DoDataExchange(pDX);
  //{{AFX_DATA_MAP(CSpinButDia)
  DDX_Text(pDX, IDC_VALUE, m_nValue);
  DDV_MinMaxInt(pDX, m_nValue, 0, 50);
  //}}AFX_DATA_MAP
}

BEGIN_MESSAGE_MAP(CSpinButDia, CDialog)
  //{{AFX_MSG_MAP(CSpinButDia)
  //}}AFX_MSG_MAP
END_MESSAGE_MAP()

// CSpinButDia message handlers

BOOL CSpinButDia::OnInitDialog()
{
  CDialog::OnInitDialog();

  CSpinButtonCtrl* pValue;
  pValue = (CSpinButtonCtrl*) GetDlgItem(IDC_SPINBUT);
```

```
    ASSERT(pValue != NULL);
    pValue->SetRange(0,50);

    return TRUE; //return TRUE unless focus set to a control
                 //EXCEPTION: OCX Property Pages return FALSE
}
```

The variable, *m_nValue,* is declared in the SpinButDia.h header file. You'll notice that it is initialized in the class constructor. This variable was added during the creation of the new class.

In the **DoDataExchange** member function you will notice the use of a DDX_ and DDV_ macro. These macros interface the variables in the dialog box with the controls. DDX_ (dialog data exchange) is used to represent the exchange function name. Typical DDX_ names include DDX_Check, DDX_Control, DDX_Radio, DDX_Text, and so on. DDV_ macros are functions used to copy data from a window to a control. DDV_ names include DDV_MaxChars, DDV_MinMaxInt, MinMaxUInt, and so on. Chapter 11 contains additional information on these macros. In this case, this code returns the information from the spin button control to the edit box control.

The **OnInitDialog** member function establishes a pointer for the CSpinButtonCtrl control, then obtains a reading from the control. Notice the use of the **SetRange()** function for limiting the spin button range to integer values between 0 and 50.

Running the Application

Choose the Rebuild All menu item from the compiler's Build menu to build this application. The compiler will create an executable file named Spin.exe. Run Spin.exe and you should see a screen similar to Figure 13.27.

Spin Button controls are useful when a small range of values is to be presented to the user.

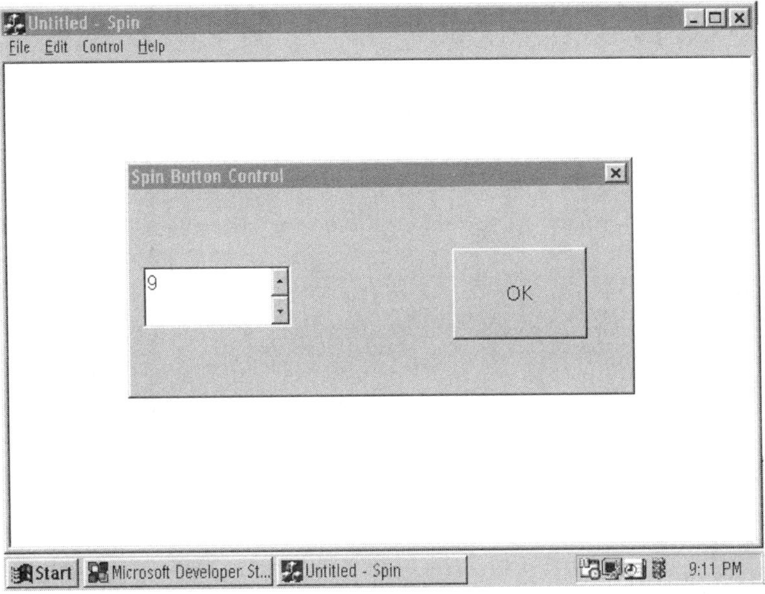

Figure 13.27: The Spin Button control in action.

MORE CONTROLS?

As you know from Table 13.1, shown earlier, the Visual C++ compiler and Windows 95 currently support a wide range of common controls. We have given you three examples in this chapter. Why not choose another control type and use the AppWizard and ClassWizard to create a working example?

Chapter 14

Complete MFC Applications

In the earlier chapters of this book, you have learned how to use the MFC "tools of the trade." These tools included the AppWizard and ClassWizard, along with various resource editors. This chapter will teach you how to use these tools to build two complete applications. One application will be a simple editor program, including complete file and print capabilities. The second will be a presentation-quality bar chart. Each of the projects will call upon skills you have developed over the past chapters.

Base Code

For each of the two projects in this chapter, you will need to generate the same base code with the AppWizard. Name the first workspace Editor. Use the following steps to complete the project files with the AppWizard.

- Enter the Microsoft Development Studio (Visual C++ Compiler).
- Chose the File menu and select the New menu item.
- Select Project Workspace from the New dialog box.
- From the New Project Workspace dialog box:
  Name the workspace "Editor".

  Set the location of the workspace (for example, C:Editor).

  Select MFC AppWizard (exe) from the list box.
- Step 1—Select a single document application type.
- Step 2—Select no database support.
- Step 3—Select none for OLE compound document support.
- Step 4—Select no extra features.
- Step 5—Do not select comments. Select a statically linked library.
- Step 6—Select CEditorView and change your Base Class to CEditView.
- Select Finish to complete the AppWizard process.
- If the information is correct, in the New Project Information dialog box, select OK.

These are the steps you learned to follow in Chapter 8. Chapter 8 describes the various project creation steps in more detail. When you have completed the final step shown above, the AppWizard will generate all of the base files needed for the Editor project.

Now, repeat the process for a workspace named BarChart. At Step 6, select the default classes as shown by the AppWizard. Then, select Finish to complete the process.

Save these BarChart files for the second example in this chapter.

A Word Processor Project

The word processor project, Editor, is very easy to create. At Step 6, you selected CEditorView in the list box. When you did this, the Base Class list box expanded, allowing you to select the CEditView base class.

Our CEditorView class will be derived from the CEditView class. CEditView describes a class that will support the development of a simple text editor. The editor will be able to print, find and replace, cut, copy, paste, clear, and undo.

Note: *The CEditView class is derived from the CView class. Its objects can be used with documents and document templates. By default, this class handles ID_FILE_PRINT, ID_EDIT_CUT, ID_EDIT_COPY, ID_EDIT_PASTE, ID_EDIT_CLEAR, ID_EDIT_UNDO, ID_EDIT_SELECT_ALL, ID_EDIT_FIND, ID_EDIT_REPLACE, and ID_EDIT_REPEAT.*

CEditView contains numerous member functions to support the previously mentioned capabilities, as shown in Table 14.1.

This application will also include an additional feature. The feature will start a clock when the application is started. At any time while working on a document, the user will be able to click the right mouse button to see the total time elapsed since the start of the current session. Now you will be able to bill your clients for the actual time spent on a project!

Table 14.1: CEditView Class Members

Function	*Operation*
FindText()	Finds a string in the given text.
GetBufferLength()	Finds the character buffer length.
GetPrinterFont()	Finds the current printer font.
GetSelectedText()	Finds the current text selection.
LockBuffer()	Locks the buffer.
OnFindNext()	Finds the next location of a given text string.
OnReplaceAll()	Replaces all occurrences of a given string with a different string.
OnReplaceSel()	Replaces the current selection.
OnTextNotFound()	If a find operation does not locate a match, this function is called.
PrintInsideRect()	Prints text in a rectangle.
SerializeRaw()	Serializes to disk as raw text.
SetPrinterFont()	Specifies a new printer font.
SetTabStops()	Specifies tab stops.
UnlockBuffer()	Unlocks the buffer.

Completing the Application

The AppWizard created the normal collection of source code, header and resource files. To this collection of files, use the ClassWizard to add a member function to the EditorView.cpp file, as shown in Figure 14.1.

With the **OnRButtonDown()** member function added, it is now time to write a little code for our elapsed time clock.

Working with the EditorView.cpp File

The following listing is the complete code for the EditorView.cpp file. Remember that our CEditorView class is derived from the MFC CEditView class.

```
// EditorView.cpp : implementation of the CEditorView class
//

#include "stdafx.h"
#include "Editor.h"

#include "EditorDoc.h"
#include "EditorView.h"
```

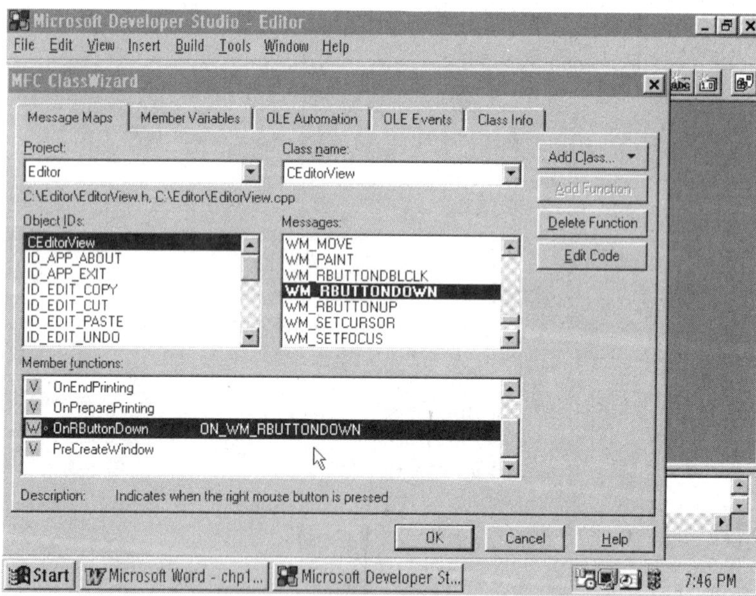

Figure 14.1: Adding an OnRButtonDown() member function to EditorView.cpp

```
#include "time.h"        //include for time functions

time_t lInitTime;

#ifdef _DEBUG
#define new DEBUG_NEW
#undef THIS_FILE
static char THIS_FILE[] = __FILE__;
#endif

// CEditorView
IMPLEMENT_DYNCREATE(CEditorView, CEditView)

BEGIN_MESSAGE_MAP(CEditorView, CEditView)
  //{{AFX_MSG_MAP(CEditorView)
  ON_WM_RBUTTONDOWN()
  //}}AFX_MSG_MAP
  // Standard printing commands
  ON_COMMAND(ID_FILE_PRINT, CEditView::OnFilePrint)
  ON_COMMAND(ID_FILE_PRINT_DIRECT, CEditView::OnFilePrint)
  ON_COMMAND(ID_FILE_PRINT_PREVIEW,
             CEditView::OnFilePrintPreview)
END_MESSAGE_MAP()

// CEditorView construction/destruction
CEditorView::CEditorView()
{
}

CEditorView::~CEditorView()
{
}

BOOL CEditorView::PreCreateWindow(CREATESTRUCT& cs)
{
  BOOL bPreCreated = CEditView::PreCreateWindow(cs);
  cs.style &= ~(ES_AUTOHSCROLL|WS_HSCROLL);

  time(&lInitTime);

  return bPreCreated;
}

// CEditorView drawing
void CEditorView::OnDraw(CDC* pDC)
{
  CEditorDoc* pDoc = GetDocument();
  ASSERT_VALID(pDoc);
}

// CEditorView printing
```

```
BOOL CEditorView::OnPreparePrinting(CPrintInfo* pInfo)
{
  // default CEditView preparation
  return CEditView::OnPreparePrinting(pInfo);
}

void CEditorView::OnBeginPrinting(CDC* pDC, CPrintInfo* pInfo)
{
  CEditView::OnBeginPrinting(pDC, pInfo);
}

void CEditorView::OnEndPrinting(CDC* pDC, CPrintInfo* pInfo)
{
  CEditView::OnEndPrinting(pDC, pInfo);
}

// CEditorView diagnostics
#ifdef _DEBUG
void CEditorView::AssertValid() const
{
  CEditView::AssertValid();
}

void CEditorView::Dump(CDumpContext& dc) const
{
  CEditView::Dump(dc);
}

CEditorDoc* CEditorView::GetDocument() // non-debug is inline
{
  ASSERT(m_pDocument->IsKindOf(RUNTIME_CLASS(CEditorDoc)));
  return (CEditorDoc*)m_pDocument;
}
#endif //_DEBUG

// CEditorView message handlers
void CEditorView::OnRButtonDown(UINT nFlags, CPoint point)
{

  char szTimeStr[30];
  time_t lPresTime;
  time(&lPresTime);

  sprintf(szTimeStr, "Elapsed Time (seconds): %06d",
          lPresTime-lInitTime);

  MessageBox(szTimeStr,"Total Elapse Time For This Session",
             MB_OK);

  CEditView::OnRButtonDown(nFlags, point);
}
```

The actual code that we added to this file is shown in a bold font. When you examine the message map, you will see that it contains ON_WM_RBUTTONDOWN, which was added by the ClassWizard, and ID_FILE_PRINT and ID_FILE_PREVIEW, which were provided when the CEditView class was selected. The constructor and destructor are empty.

The **OnDraw()** member function uses the pointer *pDoc* to point to the document. Document printing is handled by CEditorView with **OnPreparePrinting()**, **OnBeginPrinting()**, and **OnEndPrinting()**. The member functions **AssertValid()** and Dump() use definitions contained in the parent class.

The member function **OnRButtonDown()**, which handles the mouse button messages, is an easy enhancement to the application. When the user clicks the right mouse button, a small message box will pop up on the screen and display the total time, in seconds, that has elapsed since the application was started. This total time is calculated with two separate calls to the **time()** function. One call is made when the window is created, and the other whenever the right mouse button is pushed.

Figure 14.2 shows this application in action. A file has been loaded and is being edited when the user pushed the right mouse button.

Now that you see how easy this is, you might want to go back and create an editor with status bars and toolbars. In the next section, you'll learn how to create a bar chart application with menu and dialog box items.

A Bar Chart Application

The BarChart project will draw a presentation-quality bar chart in the client area of the window. This application also uses a menu and a data entry dialog box. This bar chart allows as many as 12 bars to be drawn in the client area and uses a parser routine for entering data and labels as strings of characters. You will find that this data entry approach will reduce the overall size of the dialog box and also teach you some important coding techniques.

The complete application is built with the default AppWizard files you created earlier in this chapter. These file were cre-

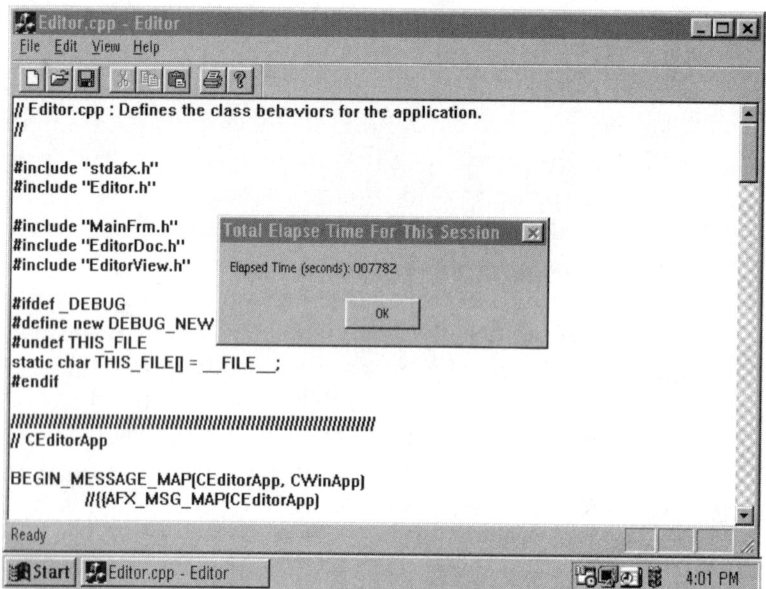

Figure 14.2: A document being edited in the Editor application.

ated in the BarChart workspace. In addition to the original group of files, the dialog box resource must be added to the BarChart.rc resource script file and a new file created for supporting the dialog box features.

A New Menu

The AppWizard generated a menu as part of the base code, so it will be necessary to edit that menu to add a new menu entry. Open the menu resource in BarChart.rc. Create a menu entry named DataEntry and a menu item named Bar_Sizes, as shown in Figure 14.3.

When you add these items, change the ID value for the Bar_Sizes menu item to IDM_INPUT. Remember, this property can be altered by using the Edit menu and selecting the Properties... menu item while Bar_Sizes is selected.

A New Dialog Box

A new dialog box resource, for data entry, must be added to the application. From the Insert menu, select the Resource menu

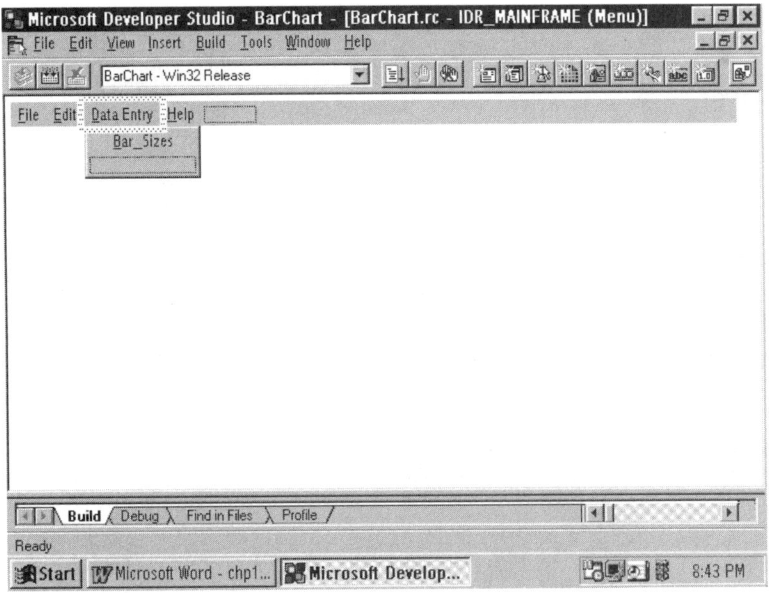

Figure 14.3: Altering the application's menu to include a new menu entry.

item. From the list of resources, select the dialog box option. Now, create a dialog box similar to the one shown in Figure 14.4.

As you can see from the figure, there are five edit boxes that will eventually be used for user input. Each edit box has an unique ID value. Use the properties option for each edit box and set the ID values to IDD_TITLE, IDD_XLABEL, IDD_YLABEL, IDD_P, and IDD_L, respectively. The dialog box itself should use IDD_BARDIALOG as its ID value. Save the new dialog box resource.

From the View menu, select ClassWizard to open the MFC ClassWizard dialog box. Select the Add Class... button to open the Create New Class dialog box, as shown in Figure 14.5.

The base class, by default, is CDialog. Our unique class name is CBarDataDialog. The only item not entered at this point is the Dialog ID. Recall that the ID for the dialog box resource is IDD_BARDIALOG, for this project. We accepted the suggested file name, BarDataDialog.cpp. Choose Create to generate this new class and file.

When you choose Create in the previous step, a new class and file will be generated and you will be returned to the MFC ClassWizard dialog box, as shown in Figure 14.6.

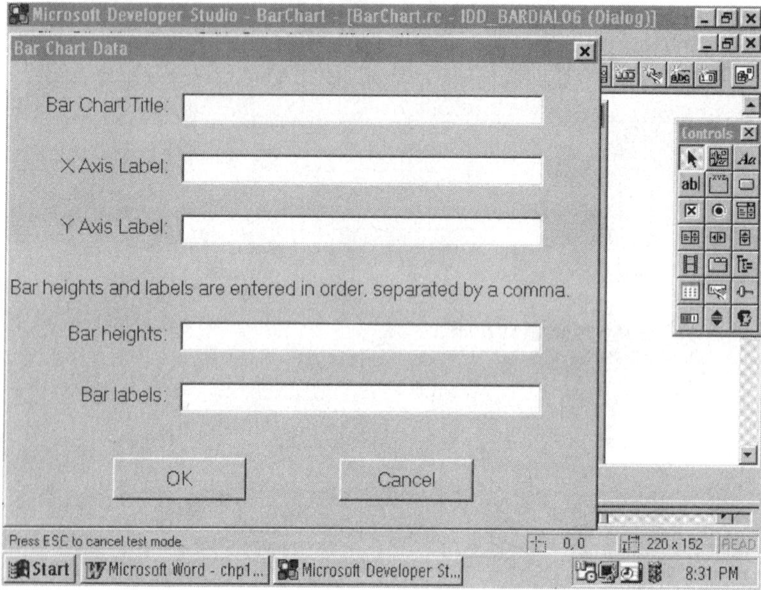

Figure 14.4: A data entry dialog box for the BarChart application.

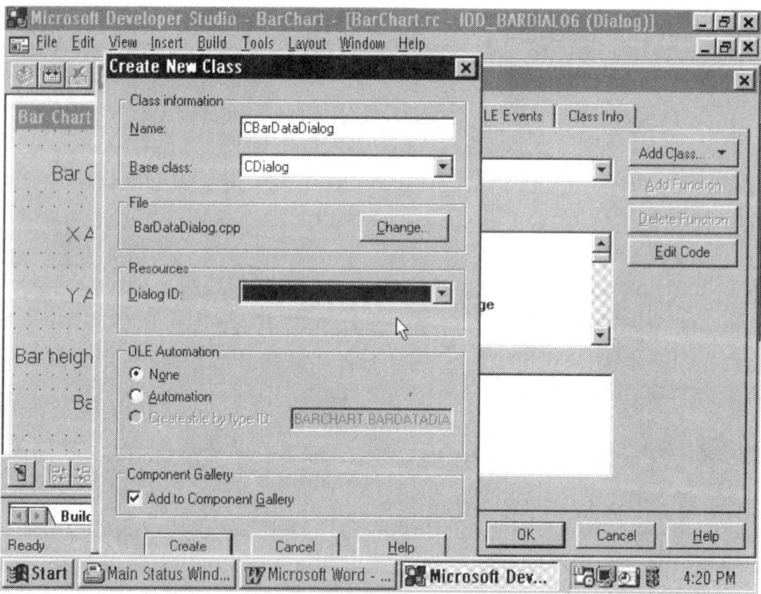

Figure 14.5: The Create New Class dialog box allows a new class to be added to the project.

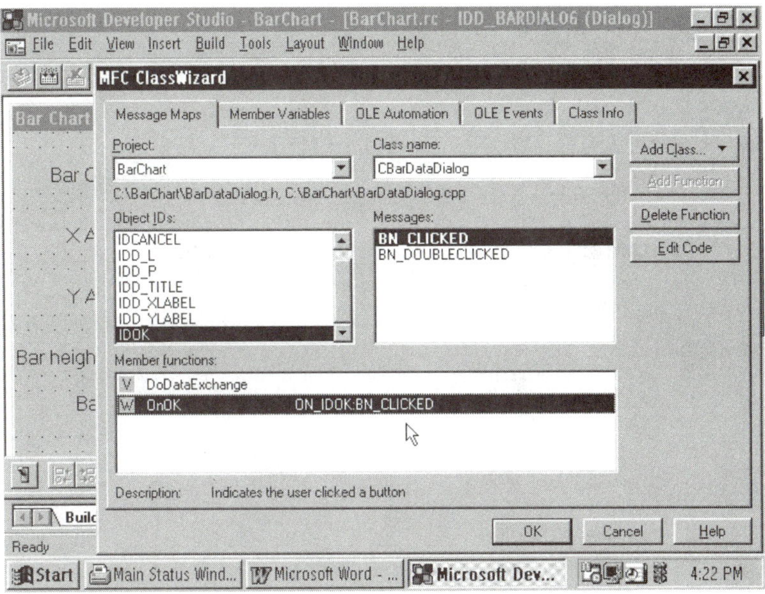

Figure 14.6: A new class has been added to the BarChart project.

Figure 14.6 shows the MFC ClassWizard dialog box after two member functions have been added: **DoDataExchange()** and **OnOK()**. These member functions provide the functionality for communicating between the dialog box and the application. The ON_IDOK:BN_CLICKED message handler will signify when it is OK to close the dialog box and process the new dialog box information.

In order to pass information to or from a dialog box, the member functions rely on member variables. Each edit box in this example will pass information to the application through a unique member variable.

To associate a member variable with an edit box ID, select the Control ID, as shown in Figure 14.7.

Once the control ID is selected, choose Add Variable... to open the Add Member Variable dialog box. Figure 14.7, you can see that this dialog box will permit you to name the member variable and to set its category and type. Most member variables start with *m_* (to denote a member variable). In this case, we expanded the name to be *m_szGLValues*. This variable is associated with the IDD_L edit box, which will return labels

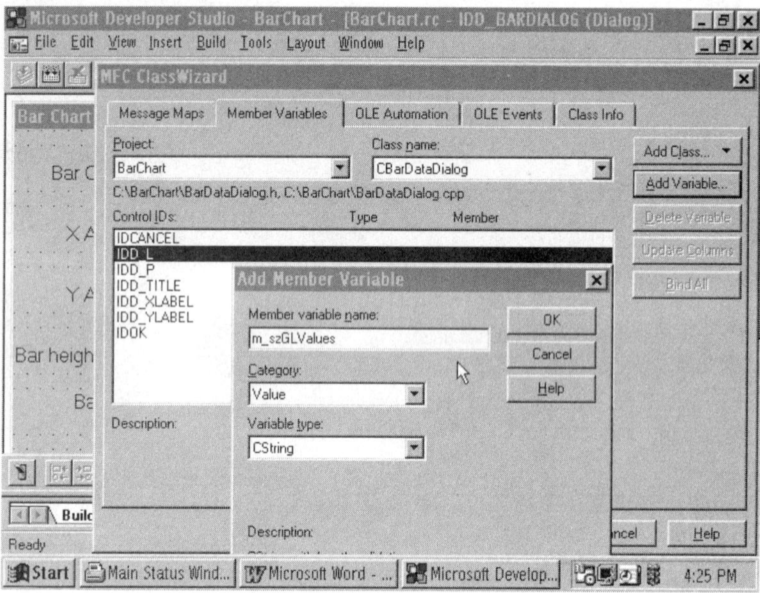

Figure 14.7: A control ID is associated with a member variable.

for the bar chart. All of the edit boxes in this example return strings. Yes, even the data points for the bar heights are returned in a string that will later be parsed.

Figure 14.8 shows the member variables we used with the edit box controls.

When you are satisfied with your variable names, select the OK pushbutton to close the MFC ClassWizard dialog box.

The following listing is the complete listing for the BarDataDialog.cpp file generated by the ClassWizard. Not a single line of this code was added directly by us.

```
// BarDataDialog.cpp : implementation file
//

#include "stdafx.h"
#include "BarChart.h"
#include "BarDataDialog.h"

#ifdef _DEBUG
#define new DEBUG_NEW
#undef THIS_FILE
static char THIS_FILE[] = __FILE__;
#endif
```

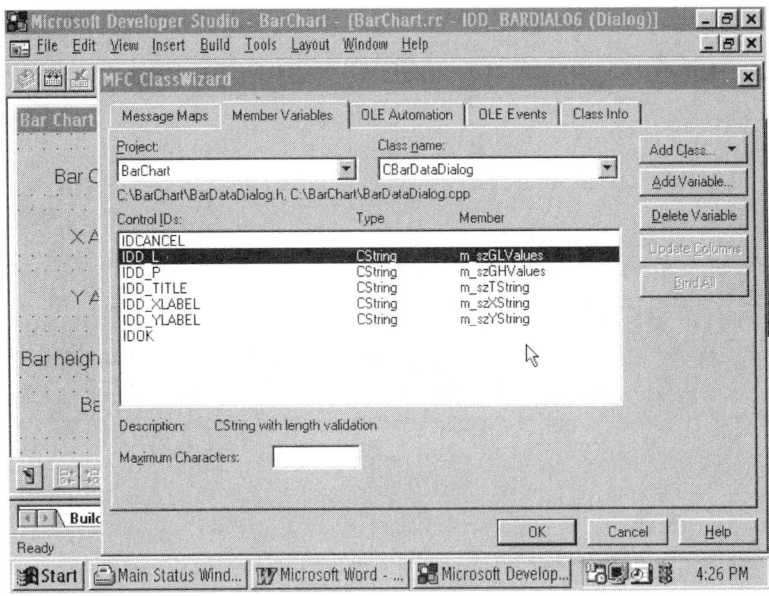

Figure 14.8: Each edit box control ID is associated with a unique member variable name.

```
// CBarDataDialog dialog
CBarDataDialog::CBarDataDialog(CWnd* pParent /*=NULL*/)
  : CDialog(CBarDataDialog::IDD, pParent)
{
  //{{AFX_DATA_INIT(CBarDataDialog)
  m_szTString = _T("");
  m_szXString = _T("");
  m_szYString = _T("");
  m_szGHValues = _T("");
  m_szGLValues = _T("");
  //}}AFX_DATA_INIT
}

void CBarDataDialog::DoDataExchange(CDataExchange* pDX)
{
  CDialog::DoDataExchange(pDX);
  //{{AFX_DATA_MAP(CBarDataDialog)
  DDX_Text(pDX, IDD_TITLE, m_szTString);
  DDX_Text(pDX, IDD_XLABEL, m_szXString);
  DDX_Text(pDX, IDD_YLABEL, m_szYString);
  DDX_Text(pDX, IDD_P, m_szGHValues);
  DDX_Text(pDX, IDD_L, m_szGLValues);
  //}}AFX_DATA_MAP
}
```

```
BEGIN_MESSAGE_MAP(CBarDataDialog, CDialog)
  //{{AFX_MSG_MAP(CBarDataDialog)
  //}}AFX_MSG_MAP
END_MESSAGE_MAP()

// CBarDataDialog message handlers
void CBarDataDialog::OnOK()
{
    CDialog::OnOK();
}
```

As you examine the previous file listing, can you see where the ClassWizard used member functions, message handlers, and member variables?

The constructor is a wonderful place to initialize member variables. However, in this example we chose not to initialize our bar chart values in the constructor. If we had the constructor might look something like the following listing:

```
CBarDataDialog::CBarDataDialog(CWnd* pParent /*=NULL*/)
  : CDialog(CBarDataDialog::IDD, pParent)
{
  //{{AFX_DATA_INIT(CBarDataDialog)
  m_szTString = _T("Bar Chart Title");
  m_szXString = _T("x-axis label");
  m_szYString = _T("y-axis label");
  m_szGHValues = _T("30,20,25,35");
  m_szGLValues = _T("#1,#2,#3,#4");
  //}}AFX_DATA_INIT
}
```

The reason we didn't initialize our bar chart via the dialog box was simply to put all of the code we entered in one file, the BarChartView.cpp file. More on this file shortly.

The **DoDataExchange()** member function is called by the framework to exchange and validate dialog data. This member function is never called directly. The **UpdateData()** member function is called instead, to initialize the various dialog box controls or retrieve data. The ClassWizard writes an overridden version of this member function. This member function contains the data map of dialog data exchange (DDX) and validation (DDV) global function calls. The code between the delimiters is automatically maintained by the ClassWizard and should not be modified directly.

```
void CBarDataDialog::DoDataExchange(CDataExchange* pDX)
{
```

```
  CDialog::DoDataExchange(pDX);
  //{{AFX_DATA_MAP(CBarDataDialog)
  DDX_Text(pDX, IDD_TITLE, m_szTString);
  DDX_Text(pDX, IDD_XLABEL, m_szXString);
  DDX_Text(pDX, IDD_YLABEL, m_szYString);
  DDX_Text(pDX, IDD_P, m_szGHValues);
  DDX_Text(pDX, IDD_L, m_szGLValues);
  //}}AFX_DATA_MAP
}
```

Exchanging data between dialog box controls and the application has been greatly simplified with MFCs dialog data exchange and dialog data validation. You might recall from our discussion in Chapter 11 that the dialog data exchange encapsulates macros for the purpose of exchanging data. Dialog data validation functions allow you to make sure valid data has been entered in your dialog box controls. As you can see from the previous listing, **DoDataExchange()** uses a pointer, pDX, to the CDataExchange object.

Each data exchange function call is of type DDX_Text, since we are exchanging string information from each edit box control. Refer to Chapter 11 for a discussion of other data exchange function names. DDX_Text is an overloaded member function and can actually accept the following types: BYTE, Cstring, double, DWORD, float, int, LONG, and UINT.

This program does not include data validation. In other words, the dialog box control will not limit string lengths directly. Hence, there are no DDV_ functions in **DoDataExchange()**.

At this point we have our dialog box ready to exchange data with our application, but we haven't created our bar chart code at this point. The bar chart code will be written in the BarChartView.cpp file described in the next section.

The BarChartView.cpp File

The BarChartView.cpp file is the standard view file created by the AppWizard. As you examine the following listing, you might wonder what has happened. Well, the bar chart application does require a little code. After all, the AppWizard can write everything for you!

Examine this code and pay particular attention to the bolded lines. These are the lines we had to write and insert ourselves.

```
// BarChartView.cpp : implementation of CBarChartView
//

#include "stdafx.h"
#include "BarChart.h"

#include "BarChartDoc.h"
#include "BarChartView.h"
#include "BarDataDialog.h"   // add for resource information

CBarDataDialog dlg;

#define maxnumber 12

int cx_Client,cy_Client;

#ifdef _DEBUG
#define new DEBUG_NEW
#undef THIS_FILE
static char THIS_FILE[] = __FILE__;
#endif

// CBarChartView
IMPLEMENT_DYNCREATE(CBarChartView, CView)

BEGIN_MESSAGE_MAP(CBarChartView, CView)
  //{{AFX_MSG_MAP(CBarChartView)
  ON_WM_SIZE()
  ON_WM_PAINT()
  ON_COMMAND(IDM_INPUT, OnInput)
  ON_WM_CREATE()
  //}}AFX_MSG_MAP
END_MESSAGE_MAP()

// CBarChartView construction/destruction
CBarChartView::CBarChartView()
{
}

CBarChartView::~CBarChartView()
{
}

BOOL CBarChartView::PreCreateWindow(CREATESTRUCT& cs)
{
  return CView::PreCreateWindow(cs);
}

// CBarChartView drawing
void CBarChartView::OnDraw(CDC* pDC)
{
  CBarChartDoc* pDoc = GetDocument();
```

```
    ASSERT_VALID(pDoc);
}

// CBarChartView diagnostics
#ifdef _DEBUG
void CBarChartView::AssertValid() const
{
    CView::AssertValid();
}

void CBarChartView::Dump(CDumpContext& dc) const
{
    CView::Dump(dc);
}

CBarChartDoc* CBarChartView::GetDocument()
{
    ASSERT(m_pDocument->IsKindOf(RUNTIME_CLASS(CBarChartDoc)));
    return (CBarChartDoc*)m_pDocument;
}
#endif //_DEBUG

// CBarChartView message handlers
void CBarChartView::OnSize(UINT nType, int cx, int cy)
{
    CView::OnSize(nType, cx, cy);

    cx_Client=cx;
    cy_Client=cy;

}

void CBarChartView::OnPaint()
{
    CPaintDC dc(this); // device context for painting

    static DWORD dwColor[12]={RGB(0,0,0),        //black
                              RGB(255,0,0),      //red
                              RGB(0,255,0),      //green
                              RGB(0,0,255),      //blue
                              RGB(255,255,0),    //yellow
                              RGB(255,0,255),    //magenta
                              RGB(0,255,255),    //cyan
                              RGB(125,125,0),    //blend 1
                              RGB(125,0,125),    //blend 2
                              RGB(0,125,125),    //blend 3
                              RGB(125,125,125),  //blend 4
                              RGB(255,255,255)}; //white

    CFont newfont;
    CFont* oldfont;
```

```
CBrush newbrush;
CBrush* oldbrush;
int i,iNBars,iBarWidth,iBarMax;
int ilenMaxLabel;
int x1,x2,y1,y2,z1,z2;
static char szLValues[80];
static char szHValues[80];
int iBarSize[maxnumber];
int iBarSizeScaled[maxnumber];
char sbuffer[10],*strptr;
char szBarLabel[12][20];
static char *n,*p;

// make copies of data for re-drawing
strcpy(szHValues,dlg.m_szGHValues);
strcpy(szLValues,dlg.m_szGLValues);

// parse string to get bar heights
iNBars=0;
i=0;
n=szHValues;
p=strtok(n,",");
while ((n!=NULL)) {
  iBarSize[i]=atoi(n);
p=strtok(NULL,",");
n=p;
  iNBars++;
i++;
}

// parse string to get bar labels
i=0;
n=szLValues;
p=strtok(n,",");
while ((n!=NULL)) {
  strcpy(szBarLabel[i],n);
p=strtok(NULL,",");
n=p;
i++;
}

iBarWidth=400/iNBars;

// Find bar with maximum height and scale
iBarMax=iBarSize[0];
for(i=0;i<iNBars;i++)
  if (iBarMax<iBarSize[i]) iBarMax=iBarSize[i];

// Convert maximum y value to a string
strptr=_itoa(iBarMax,sbuffer,10);
ilenMaxLabel=strlen(sbuffer);
```

```
// Scale bars in array. Highest bar = 270
  for (i=0;i<iNBars;i++)
    iBarSizeScaled[i]=iBarSize[i]*(270/iBarMax);

  // Create custom viewport and map mode
  dc.SetMapMode(MM_ISOTROPIC);
  dc.SetWindowExt(640,480);
  dc.SetViewportExt(cx_Client,cy_Client);
  dc.SetViewportOrg(0,0);

  // Draw text if window is large enough
  if ((cx_Client>300)&&(cy_Client>200)) {
    newfont.CreateFont(20,12,900,900,FW_NORMAL,
                       FALSE,FALSE,FALSE,
                       OEM_CHARSET,OUT_DEFAULT_PRECIS,
                       CLIP_DEFAULT_PRECIS,
                       DEFAULT_QUALITY,
                       34,
                       "Arial");
    oldfont=dc.SelectObject(&newfont);
    dc.TextOut(50,200+(strlen(dlg.m_szYString)*10/2),
               dlg.m_szYString,strlen(dlg.m_szYString));

    newfont.CreateFont(20,12,0,0,FW_NORMAL,
                       FALSE,FALSE,FALSE,OEM_CHARSET,
                       OUT_DEFAULT_PRECIS,
                       CLIP_DEFAULT_PRECIS,
                       DEFAULT_QUALITY,
                       34,
                       "Arial");
    oldfont=dc.SelectObject(&newfont);
    dc.TextOut((300-(strlen(dlg.m_szTString)*10/2)),
               15,dlg.m_szTString,strlen(dlg.m_szTString));
    dc.TextOut((300-(strlen(dlg.m_szXString)*10/2)),
               365,dlg.m_szXString,strlen(dlg.m_szXString));
    dc.TextOut((90-ilenMaxLabel*12),70,strptr,ilenMaxLabel);
  }

  // Draw coordinate axis
  dc.MoveTo(99,49);
  dc.LineTo(99,350);
  dc.LineTo(500,350);
  dc.MoveTo(99,350);

  // Initial values
  x1=100;
  y1=350;
  z1=50;
  z2=z1+15;
  x2=x1+iBarWidth;
```

```
    // Draw each bar
    for(i=0;i<iNBars;i++) {
      newbrush.CreateSolidBrush(dwColor[i]);
      oldbrush=dc.SelectObject(&newbrush);
      y2=350-iBarSizeScaled[i];
      dc.Rectangle(x1,y1,x2,y2);
      x1=x2;
      x2+=iBarWidth;

       // Draw labels
      if ((strlen(szBarLabel[0])!=0)&&(cx_Client>300)&&
          (cy_Client>200)) {
        dc.Rectangle(545,z1,560,z2);
        dc.TextOut(565,z1,szBarLabel[i],
                   strlen(szBarLabel[i]));
        z1=z2+15;
        z2+=30;
      }
    }

    // Delete objects
    if (cx_Client >= 200) {
      dc.SelectObject(oldfont);
      newfont.DeleteObject();
    }
    dc.SelectObject(&newbrush);
    newbrush.DeleteObject();

}

void CBarChartView::OnInput()
{
  dlg.DoModal();
  InvalidateRect(NULL,TRUE);
  UpdateWindow();
}

int CBarChartView::OnCreate(LPCREATESTRUCT lpCreateStruct)
{
  if (CView::OnCreate(lpCreateStruct) == -1)
    return -1;

  dlg.m_szTString = "Bar Chart Title";
  dlg.m_szXString = "x-axis label";
  dlg.m_szYString = "y-axis label";
  dlg.m_szGHValues = "30,20,25,35";
  dlg.m_szGLValues = "#1,#2,#3,#4";

  return 0;
}
```

The ClassWizard was used to add several member functions to the BarChartView.cpp file. If you examine the previous listing, you will notice **OnCreate()**, **OnInput()**, **OnPaint()**, and **OnSize()**. If you are working along on your computer, use the ClassWizard to add these member functions to your project.

Working in the View File

The BarChartView.cpp application will allow the user to create a presentation-quality bar chart in the client area of a window. Our data entry dialog box is a modal dialog box that allows the user to specify a chart title, axis labels, and the heights of up to 12 bars. The bar chart will then be scaled to fit the current window. Individual bar colors are selected from an array of predefined values.

The maximum number of bars is set to twelve by *maxnumber* at the start of the application:

```
#define maxnumbar 12
```

The number of bars can be changed, but keep in mind that a good presentation won't crowd too many bars onto a single bar chart.

In the following sections, we'll examine the role of each of the member functions to see how they contributed to the whole project.

The OnCreate() Function

If you examine the complete BarChartView.cpp listing, you will see that the **OnCreate()** member function is used to initialize the bar chart upon creation. Here is a small portion of code needed for this purpose:

```
CBarDataDialog dlg;
    .
    .
    .
  dlg.m_szTString = "Bar Chart Title";
  dlg.m_szXString = "x-axis label";
  dlg.m_szYString = "y-axis label";
  dlg.m_szGHValues = "30,20,25,35";
  dlg.m_szGLValues = "#1,#2,#3,#4";
    .
    .
    .
```

Here, *dlg* is the tag associated with the CBarDataDialog class. You will notice that all five member variables from the dialog box are being initialized. There is a default chart title and two axis labels. Notice the string of data values and bar labels.

We decided to initialize our bar chart here, instead of in the constructor of the dialog box class, because it centralizes all programmer added-code to the BarChartView.cpp file. However, the choice is yours.

When the bar chart is created, it will take on a set of initial labels and data values.

The OnSize() Function The **OnSize()** member function is used to handle WM_SIZE messages. In this application, when the size of the window is changed by the user, the graphics are sized proportionally. The window size information obtained by **OnSize()** and placed in *cxClient* and *cyClient*. This information is then available to the **OnPaint()** member function for scaling.

The OnInput() Function The **OnInput()** member function serves as our connection to the data entry dialog box.

```
    .
    .
    .
dlg.DoModal();
InvalidateRect(NULL,TRUE);
UpdateWindow();
    .
    .
    .
```

DoModal() is used to draw the modal dialog box. The function also returns the dialog box results. When the user selects, for example, the OK or Cancel pushbuttons, special message-handler member functions attempt to close the dialog box. Typically, the **OnOK()** member function will validate and update the dialog box data before closing the dialog box. The **OnCancel()** member function does not validate or update dialog box data before closing the dialog box.

Since there is always the potential for new bar chart data arriving when the dialog box is closed, the **InvalidateRect()**

and **UpdateWindow()** functions are called to ensure that the client area will be redrawn. Redrawing takes place because a WM_PAINT message is issued.

The OnPaint() Function This member function handles most of the work for the BarChart application. If you examine the complete BarChartView.cpp listing shown earlier, you will notice that bar colors are picked from the *dwColor[]* array in a sequential manner. If the bar chart has four bars, they will always be black, red, green, and blue. If the order of colors doesn't suit you, rearrange the colors in the *dwColor[]* array.

CFont and CBrush are used to allow font and brush objects to be passed to any CDC (base class for display context) member functions. A change from the default font will be necessary in order to draw the chart title and axis labels. New brushes will be used to fill the rectangular bar chart bars. The syntax for creating new font and brush objects is simple:

```
CFont newfont;
CFont* oldfont;
CBrush newbrush;
CBrush* oldbrush;
```

Recall that bar chart height data is returned via a string. Before a bar chart can be drawn, it is necessary to obtain individual bar values and then calculate how many bar values are being used. Each bar chart bar's height will be determined by parsing the *szHValues* string. The *szHValues variable* contains a copy of the string information returned by the *m_szGHValues* member variable. The number of bars will be held in the global array *iBarSize*. The following routine parses the string containing the heights of the bars.

```
// parse string to get bar heights
  iNBars=0;
  i=0;
  n=szHValues;
  p=strtok(n,",");
  while ((n!=NULL)) {
    iBarSize[i]=atoi(n);
    p=strtok(NULL,",");
    n=p;
    iNBars++;
    i++;
  }
```

In a similar manner, the next routine parses the string containing the individual bar labels.

```
// parse string to get bar labels
i=0;
n=szLValues;
p=strtok(n,",");
while ((n!=NULL)) {
  strcpy(szBarLabel[i],n);
  p=strtok(NULL,",");
  n=p;
  i++;
}
```

The parsing routines make use of the powerful **strtok()** function. Each bar chart height is saved in the *iBarSize[]* array. Likewise, each bar chart label is saved in the *szBarLabel[][]* array.

The bar count is calculated by incrementing the variable *iNBars* each time the parser finds a new bar value. The width of each bar is determined from the total number of bars. The bar chart is always drawn to the same screen width. So, the more bars contained in the bar chart, the narrower each individual bar becomes. Bar widths, *iBarWidth,* is calculated by using:

```
iBarWidth=400/iNBars;
```

The height of each bar is calculated in proportion to the tallest bar value. The tallest bar value is scaled and drawn to the same chart height regardless of its numeric value. The size of the tallest bar value is easy to find:

```
// Find bar with maximum height and scale
iBarMax=iBarSize[0];
for(i=0;i<iNBars;i++)
  if (iBarMax<iBarSize[i]) iBarMax=iBarSize[i];
```

The bar chart prints the numeric height of the tallest bar value on the vertical chart axis. The **_itoa()** macro is used to convert this numeric value to a string:

```
// Convert maximum y value to a string
strptr=_itoa(iBarMax,sbuffer,10);
ilenMaxLabel=strlen(sbuffer);
```

Once the tallest bar has been scaled, the remaining bars in the array are scaled to its value:

```
// Scale bars in array. Highest bar = 270
for (i=0;i<iNBars;i++)
  iBarSizeScaled[i]=iBarSize[i]*(270/iBarMax);
```

The mapping mode, window extent, viewport extent, and origin are set in this application with the following four function calls:

```
// Create custom viewport and map mode
  dc.SetMapMode(MM_ISOTROPIC);
  dc.SetWindowExt(640,480);
  dc.SetViewportExt(cx_Client,cy_Client);
  dc.SetViewportOrg(0,0);
```

By setting the viewport and map mode values, the graphics can be scaled to remain proportional with the window size. Notice the use of *cx_Client* and *cy_Client* in the **SetViewportExt()** function call.

Next, it is necessary to prepare several fonts for drawing titles and labels. The **CreateFont()** function uses a logical font from the GDI's pool of physical fonts that most closely matches the application's requirements. The syntax for the **CreateFont()** function is:

```
CreateFont(Height,Width,Escapement,Orientation,Weight,
           Italic,Underline,StrikeOut,CharSet,
           OutputPrecision,ClipPrecision,Quality,
           PitchAndFamily,Facename)
```

The first time **CreateFont()** is called in this application, the parameters are set to the following values:

```
Height = 20
Width  = 12
Escapement = 900
Orientation = 900
Weight = FW_NORMAL
Italic = FALSE
Underline = FALSE
StrikeOut = FALSE
CharSet = OEM_CHARSET
OutputPrecision = OUT_DEFAULT_PRECIS
ClipPrecision = CLIP_DEFAULT_PRECIS
Quality = DEFAULT_QUALITY
PitchAndFamily = 34
Facename = "Arial"
```

Windows will attempt to find a font to match these specifications. This font will be used to print a vertical string of text in the window. Notice that *Escapement* and *Orientation* are set to 900. This value represents an angle of 90.0 degrees. The *Escapement* value rotates the line of text from horizontal to vertical. The *Orientation* value rotates each character by 90.0 degrees. This is the font that is used to draw the vertical axis label.

You'll notice that the **CreateFont()** function is called a second time. This time the parameters are set to the following values:

```
Height = 20
Width  = 12
Escapement = 0
Orientation = 0
Weight = FW_NORMAL
Italic = FALSE
Underline = FALSE
StrikeOut = FALSE
CharSet = OEM_CHARSET
OutputPrecision = OUT_DEFAULT_PRECIS
ClipPrecision = CLIP_DEFAULT_PRECIS
Quality = DEFAULT_QUALITY
PitchAndFamily = 34
Facename = "Arial"
```

This is the font that will be used to draw all horizontal titles and labels.

Examine the following portion of code used to draw the vertical axis label:

```
// Draw text if window is large enough
  if ((cx_Client>300)&&(cy_Client>200)) {
    newfont.CreateFont(20,12,900,900,FW_BOLD,
                       FALSE,FALSE,FALSE,
                       OEM_CHARSET,OUT_DEFAULT_PRECIS,
                       CLIP_DEFAULT_PRECIS,
                       DEFAULT_QUALITY,
                       34,
                       "Arial");
    oldfont=dc.SelectObject(&newfont);
    dc.TextOut(50,200+(strlen(dlg.m_szYString)*10/2),
               dlg.m_szYString,strlen(dlg.m_szYString));
```

The window can be scaled, and so can our graphics. It is important to eliminate the title and labels if the fonts become too small for the user to read. Thus, a check is made on the horizontal and vertical sizes before drawing the labels.

The X and Y coordinate axes are drawn by using both the **MoveTo()** and **LineTo()** functions:

```
// Draw coordinate axis
  dc.MoveTo(99,49);
  dc.LineTo(99,350);
  dc.LineTo(500,350);
  dc.MoveTo(99,350);
```

In this application, the first bar chart bar is drawn at coordinate points 100,350 on the bar chart. These values are defined by *x1* and *y1*. The position of the first bar and its width along with all remaining bars is determined from the last drawing position and the width of each previous bar. Thus, the second X value is defined by *x2*.

```
// Initial values
  x1=100;
  y1=350;
  z1=50;
  z2=z1+15;
  x2=x1+iBarWidth;
```

Bar chart heights are retrieved from *iBarSizeScaled[]*. This scaled value is modified and saved in *y2* for use by the **Rectangle()** function. The closed rectangular shape is then filled with the current brush color. The brush color value changes with each pass through the loop. Here is the small portion of code that accomplishes this task:

```
// Draw each bar
  for(i=0;i<iNBars;i++) {
    newbrush.CreateSolidBrush(dwColor[i]);
    oldbrush=dc.SelectObject(&newbrush);
    y2=350-iBarSizeScaled[i];
    dc.Rectangle(x1,y1,x2,y2);
    x1=x2;
    x2+=iBarWidth;

    // Draw labels
    if ((strlen(szBarLabel[0])!=0)&&(cx_Client>300)&&
        (cy_Client>200)) {
      dc.Rectangle(545,z1,560,z2);
      dc.TextOut(565,z1,szBarLabel[i],
                 strlen(szBarLabel[i]));
      z1=z2+15;
      z2+=30;
    }
  }
```

A pass is made through the loop for each bar. Each time, *x1* and *x2* are updated to point to the next bar's initial position. A legend and bar label are also drawn in each pass through the loop.

Running the BarChart Application

Build the BarChart application. You should initially see a default bar chart, similar to Figure 14.9. Unique bar charts, similar to Figure 14.10, can be drawn by entering new data in the bar chart's data dialog box.

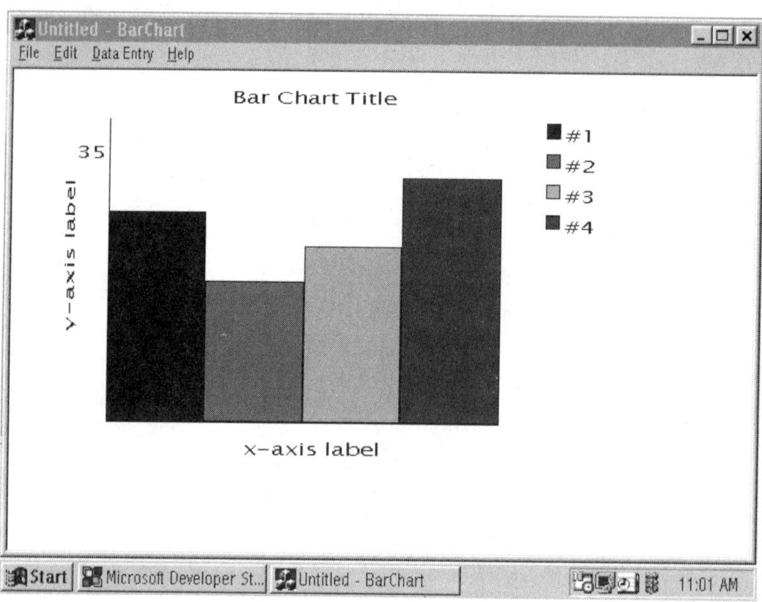

Figure 14.9: The BarChart application's default bar chart.

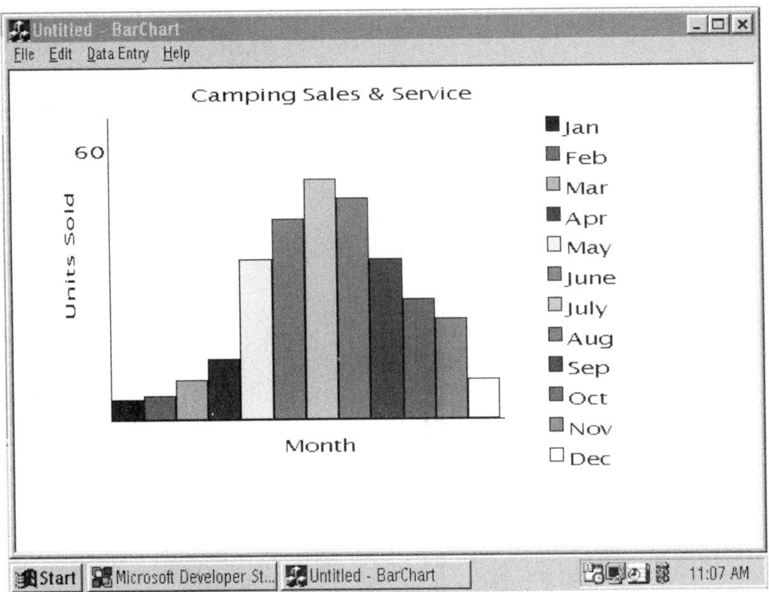

Figure 14.10: A custom bar chart created with the BarChart application.

Chapter 15

OLE Concepts

In this chapter and Chapter 16 you will learn terms, concepts, and techniques for adding OLE functionality to your AppWizard-generated programs. OLE originally stood for Object Linking and Embedding, but Microsoft has expanded its capabilities far beyond its original intentions. OLE, version 2, which is called OLE2, embraces the Component Object Model (COM) and Automation defined by Microsoft. COM provides a standard way in which Windows programming components can communicate with one another. Automation provides the glue for linking applications written with Visual C++ or Visual Basic, for example. Visual Basic has become the programming standard that reaches across all Microsoft Office products. Automation allows one application to issue commands to another application.

For this chapter and Chapter 16, we'll use the term OLE when referring to the current version of OLE. We'll examine the OLE tools shipped with the Visual C++ compiler that allow you to develop compound documents that are dynamically linked together. When applications are dynamically linked, one OLE application can use data from another OLE application.

Learning OLE terms, concepts, and techniques is one of the most daunting tasks facing programmers today. You lived through the migration from C to C++. You struggled to convert applications from a procedure-oriented approach to an object-oriented approach. You realized the understanding the MFC library is the key to your product's success. Now, you are faced with another challenge—mastering OLE.

Coding OLE applications, without the use of the MFC library, is a challenge even for the experienced programmer. Microsoft Press's *Inside OLE 2* by Kraig Brockschmidt carefully details the steps necessary for creating your own OLE applications from the ground up. Unfortunately, it took him more than 1000 pages to do the job. Others, such as writer Paul DiLascia, claim the experience is like being in OLE hell. Dilascia's first programming experience with OLE required more than 5000 lines of code.

With all of this bad news, there must be a little good news for the programmer. There is! The good news comes in two forms. First, once you learn how to write an OLE-compliant application, the code will remain virtually the same from one application to another. Secondly, if you are content with understanding OLE concepts and don't insist on understanding the details of each OLE class or function, you can use the MFC library to generate flawless code. In Chapter 16 you'll learn that its is possible to use the AppWizard to generate the base code for an OLE application in minutes instead of the weeks it would have taken you without the MFC library and associated wizards.

Understanding OLE

In its most elementary form, OLE stands for object linking and embedding. Object linking and embedding allows applications to be linked together so that object methods and data can be shared between them. This dynamic linking allows databases, spreadsheets, and word processors to share data between applications. For example, with Microsoft Office it is possible to dynamically embed an Excel spreadsheet within a Word document.

While OLE objects are not the same as C++ objects, object-oriented programming forms the foundation for OLE programming.

Objects, Files, and Data

OLE offers features that are not directly related to the common object model. These features include automation, drag-and-drop, and Visual Editing.

Recall that automation in OLE terms means that one application can issue commands to another application.

Drag-and-drop means that an object can be selected and moved from one application to another in a manner similar to cut-and-paste. Table 15.1 shows several drag-and-drop options.

Visual Editing is a feature that allows the user to edit an object while in the container application. For example, a spreadsheet could be edited if it was an object in a word-processor document.

The components that allow these features are discussed in this section.

Objects

OLE supports the Component Object Model (COM). COM is a binary specification or standard that allows two unrelated applications to communicate with each other. Once applications are connected via the COM protocol, an interface is created allowing the communications.

Table 15.1: Drag and Drop Options

Drag and Drop Action	*Meaning*
Drag and Drop + SHIFT	Move the object
Drag and Drop + CTRL	Copy the object
Drag and Drop + CTRL + SHIFT	Dynamically link the object

The COM is being used by Microsoft to replace a number of older communications techniques, such as DLLs, VIPs, and Does. COM can be instantiated through a component object library—a library that contains functions that support this instantiating. A component object is a Windows object with a unique class ID. The object's functions are contained in the library. They are used to provide an interface and can be called via a returned pointer. One of the advantages of the COM process is that the objects which are created are language independent. The library is responsible for marshaling how function calls and parameters are handled between processes.

Data

OLE allows data transfers to be made through a data object. This uniform data transfer is made by using pointers to a data object. The use of pointers makes it easier to connect the data source with the data receiver. Data objects determine how data is actually exchanged. Data transfers using drag-and-drop will appear to work the same way as data transfers via the clipboard.

Files

OLE makes use of compound files. Compound files are stream and storage objects that are used to streamline file manipulation. You can think of a single file as most closely resembling a stream object. Likewise, a file directory most closely resembles a storage object. With the use of structured storage techniques, the actual location at which data is stored on a disk is irrelevant. OLE will eventually contain a common file structure so that all files can be easily browsed.

OLE Containers and Object Embedding

Documents that are linked via the COM can hold information from a variety of unrelated sources. For example, a Word document file can contain an Excel spreadsheet and an Access database.

In the days before OLE, much of the interconnection between applications was done via the clipboard. The clipboard allowed pieces of one application to be copied, then pasted into another application. But this was a static or dead process. Once the pasting was completed, the spreadsheet or database was completely disconnected from its former application. For example, consider a spreadsheet that is connected to a electronic counting device. Imagine that the counting device is counting cell divisions in a particular type of cancer. If the spreadsheet was copied and pasted into a Word document via the clipboard, a short time later its data would no longer be correct. If you wanted to update the information in Word, you would have to erase the current spreadsheet and copy and paste the latest version back into Word. This process is clunky, static, and dead. You have only a "snapshot picture" of your information, never the information itself!

In OLE terms, the Word document described above would be called the *container*. OLE containers hold objects created by other applications, such as Microsoft Access and Excel. When applications create or provide objects to a container application, they are called *servers*. In this discussion, Access and Excel would be servers.

Let's take a look at some actual examples using various Microsoft Office components to better understand how OLE functions. In Chapter 16, you'll learn how to develop your own applications that will perform many of the same feats.

Embedding Objects

In the first example, a Windows 95 Paint object will be embedded in a Microsoft Office (Word) document. Here Word will be the container for the object and Paint will be the object's server.

Open a document in Microsoft Word. Figure 15.1 shows a Microsoft Word screen with a small portion of this chapter visible.

From the Word Insert menu, select the Object... menu item, as shown in Figure 15.1.

Selecting the Object... menu item opens the Object dialog box, as shown in Figure 15.2.

From the list box show in Figure 15.2, choose Paintbrush Picture as the object to embed. Paint will be opened automatically, as shown in Figure 15.3.

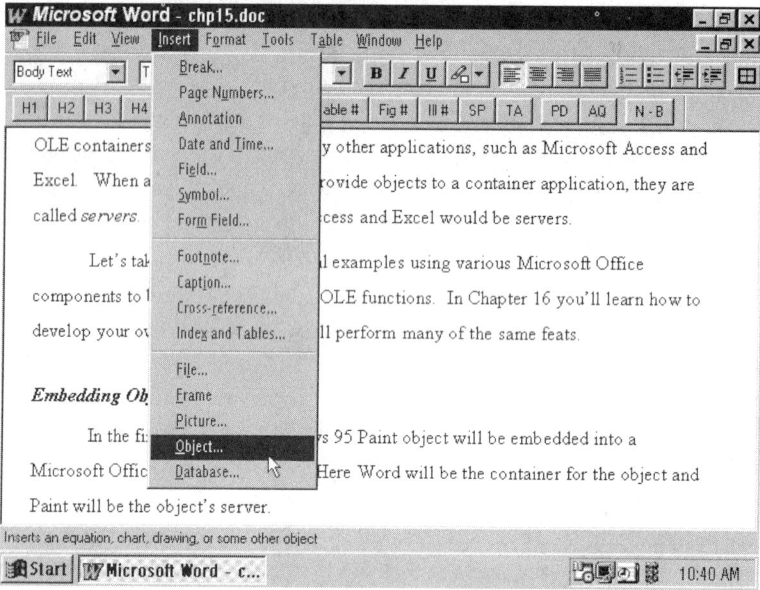

Figure 15.1: Microsoft Word will act as a container for the embedded Paint object.

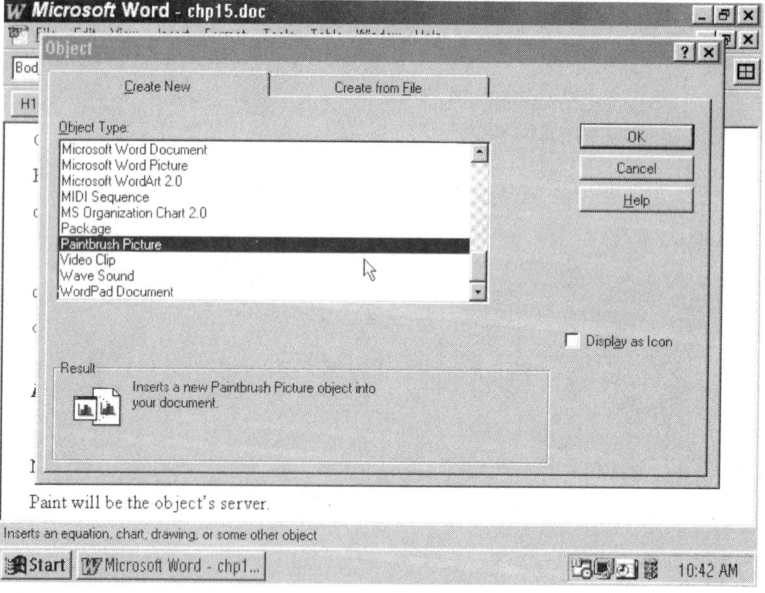

Figure 15.2: The Object dialog box shows a list of object types that your system can embed in the Word document.

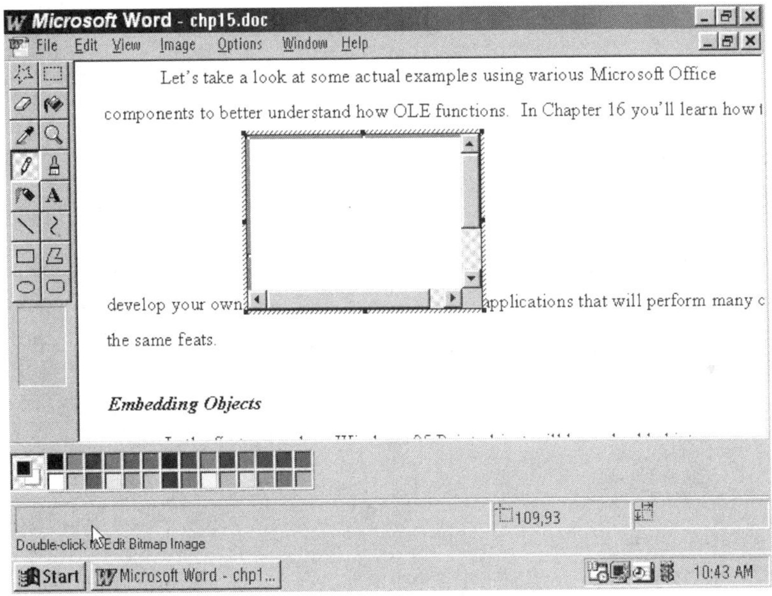

Figure 15.3: The Windows 95 Paint application is automatically started when a Paintbrush Picture is selected from the Object dialog box.

Paint places an empty drawing canvas in your Word document. This canvas can be expanded and moved in all directions.

As you examine this figure, have you noticed that the menu has changed from a Word menu to a Paint menu? We used Paint to draw a number of simple graphics shapes, as shown in Figure 15.4.

When the artwork is complete, click the right button of the mouse outside of the drawing area to return to the Word document and the Microsoft Word menu. Figure 15.5 shows the results of embedding the Paint object in the Microsoft Word document.

If you decide that the object isn't exactly the color or shape you wanted, double-click on the object and block it for editing. When the object is selected for editing, Paint is immediately opened again with the currently selected object, in place and ready for editing.

OLE and Linked Applications

The real power of OLE is in its ability to dynamically link applications. In the previous example, a graphics object was

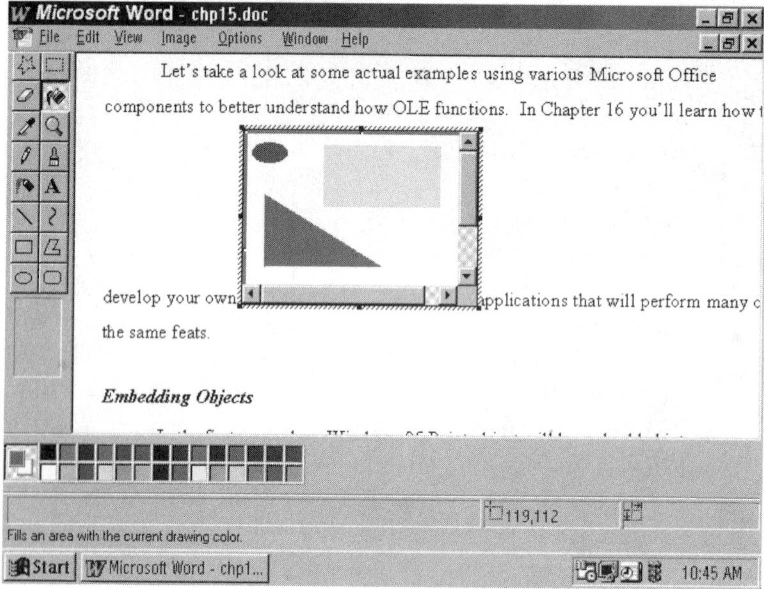

Figure 15.4: Several simple shapes are drawn by using Paint toolbox choices.

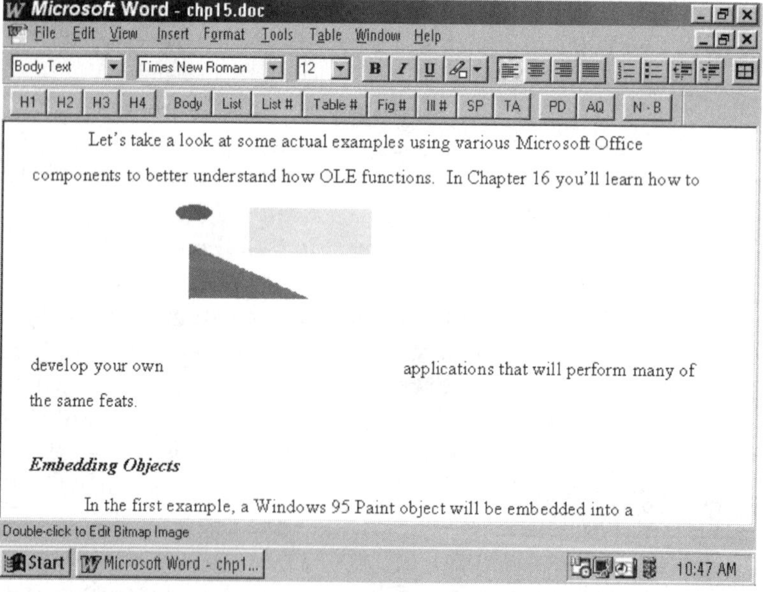

Figure 15.5: A completed Paint object embedded in a Word document.

embedded in a document. But this is nothing new; we have had that ability for a long time with just the clipboard. In this section, you'll see how OLE can be used to allow data to be instantaneously shared between a Word document and Excel spreadsheet and chart.

In past attempts to provide links between applications, the task proved difficult, and the links were usually easy to break, accidentally. OLE makes use of file monikers. File monikers prevent most of the link breakage problems encountered in the past. Monikers can be thought of as a generalization of a pathname. Monikers provide an operation for COM objects called binding. Binding is a process. First, the object named by the moniker is located. Next, the object is loaded into memory. Finally, an interface pointer is returned.

Linking

In this section you'll see how two Microsoft Office applications can share objects. A Microsoft Excel chart object will be linked to a Microsoft Word document. When data changes occur on the Excel spreadsheet, they are automatically updated in the Excel chart object embedded in the Microsoft Word document.

Start by opening both Microsoft Word and Microsoft Excel. Figure 15.6 shows a Microsoft Word document with a portion of this chapter being edited.

Figure 15.7 shows a Microsoft Excel spreadsheet with two columns of data which will be used by the ChartWizard to create a chart object.

Next, from the Excel toolbar, select the ChartWizard to begin the chart-building process. Figure 15.8 shows Step 1 of the chart-building process.

If the data range is acceptable in Step 1, select Next> to move to the next step. At Step 2, it is possible to choose the chart type, as shown in Figure 15.9.

Now, select Next> to move to Step 3. Seven different area charts are possible, as you can see in Figure 15.10.

Select the area chart style you prefer and again select the Next> push-button. At Step 4 of the chart-building process, you will be able to modify the data series used to generate the chart, as shown in Figure 15.11.

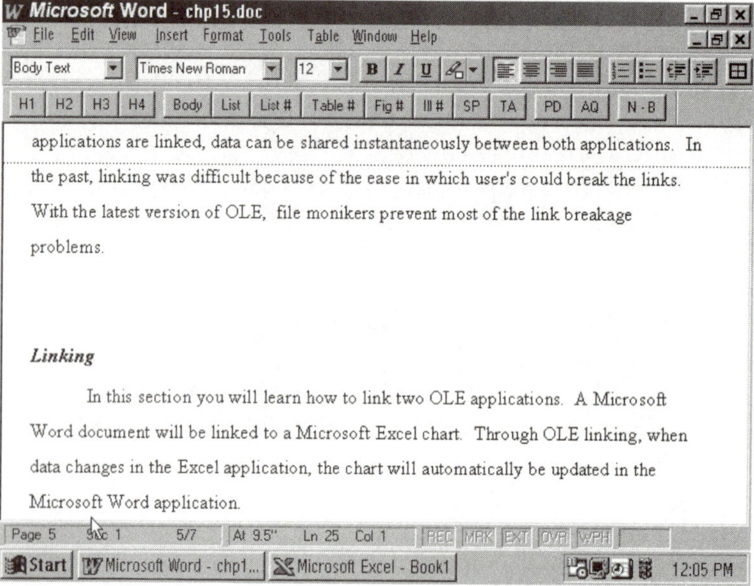

Figure 15.6: A Microsoft Word document is opened for linking.

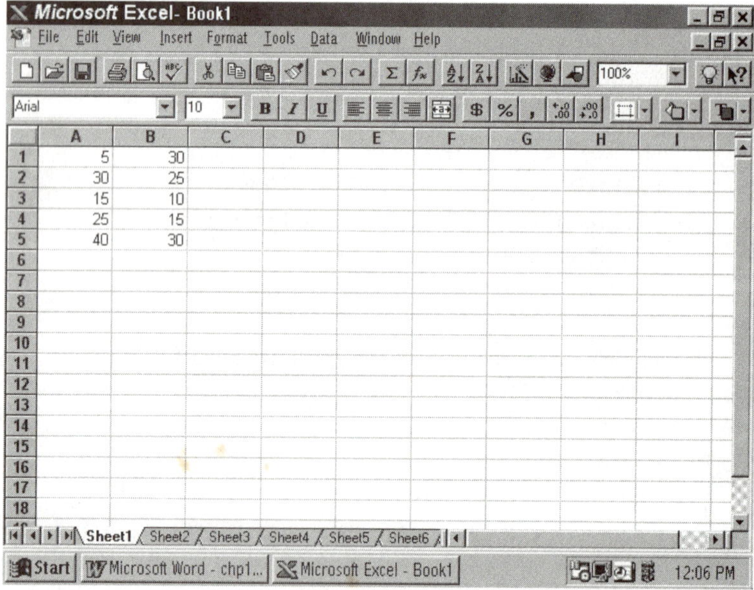

Figure 15.7: A Microsoft Excel spreadsheet is opened for creating a chart object.

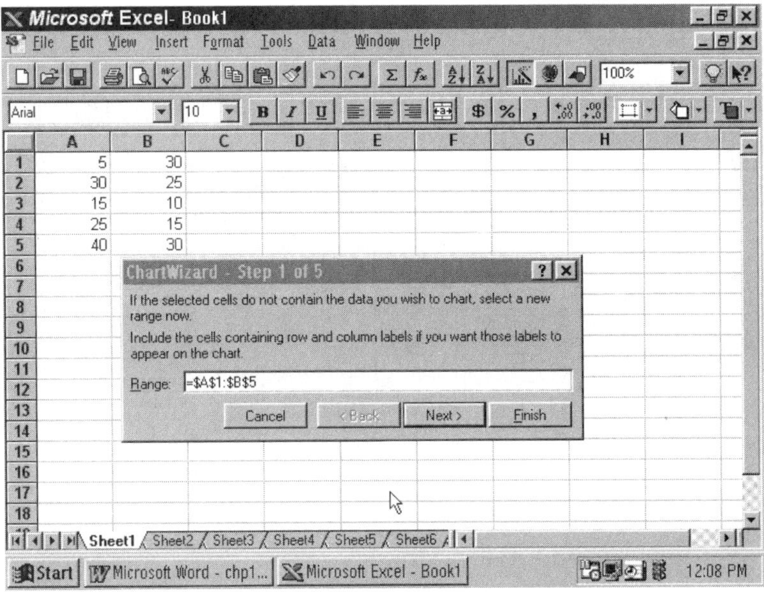

Figure 15.8: ChartWizard Step 1: Selecting the data range for the chart object.

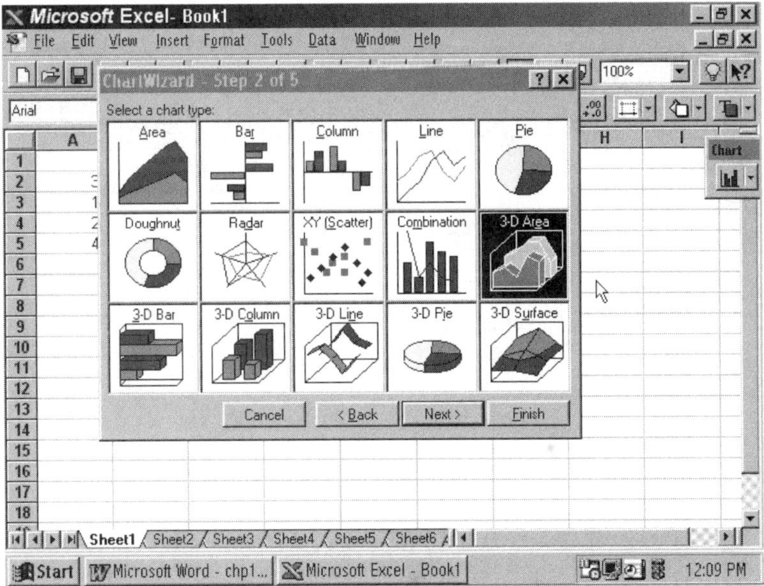

Figure 15.9: ChartWizard Step 2: Select a 3-D Area chart for this application.

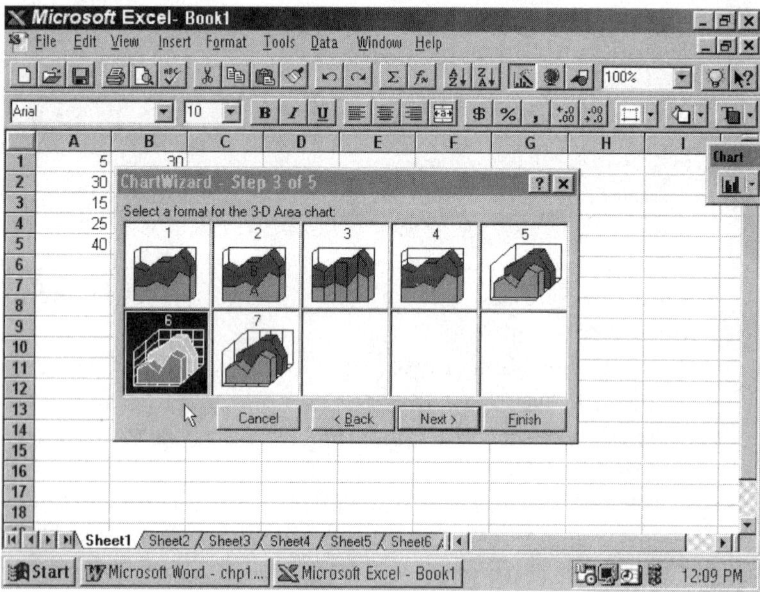

Figure 15.10: ChartWizard Step 3: Select the exact style of area chart desired.

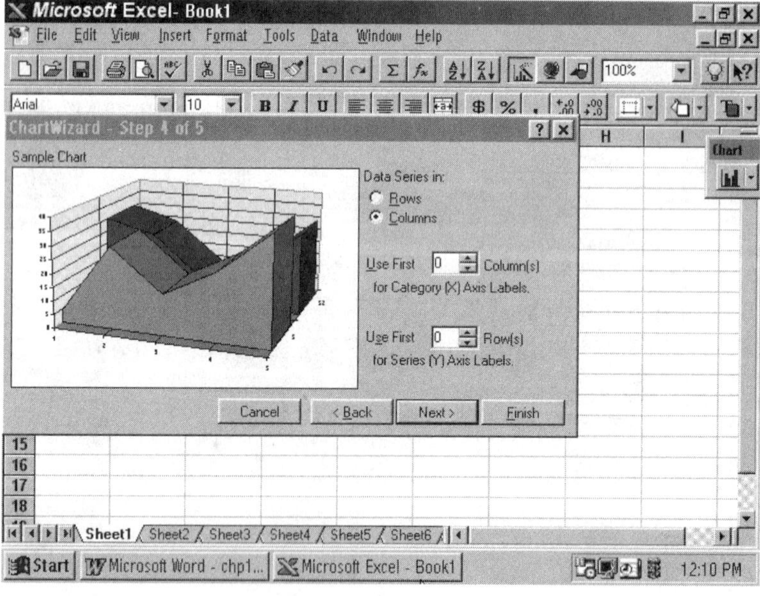

Figure 15.11: ChartWizard Step 4: Examining a sample chart.

If the sample chart is acceptable, as it is in this case, accept the defaults and choose the Next> pushbutton.

During Step 5, you can customize the chart object by adding legends, titles, and labels. We elected to add a title only, as shown in Figure 15.12.

Select Finish to view the chart under Excel. Figure 15.13 shows the finished chart. Select the Excel object by clicking on the chart, then using the Excel Edit menu to choose the Object menu item. Copy the object by electing Copy, which is also an Edit menu item.

In order to dynamically link this chart object with the Microsoft Word document, choose the Edit menu in Microsoft Word and select the Paste Special... menu item. This is shown in Figure 15.14.

From the Paste Special dialog box, select the Microsoft Excel Chart Object from the list box, while also selecting the Paste Link radio button. Figure 15.15 shows these options.

When the OK pushbutton is selected, the current Excel chart will be dynamically linked with the document, as shown in Figure 15.16.

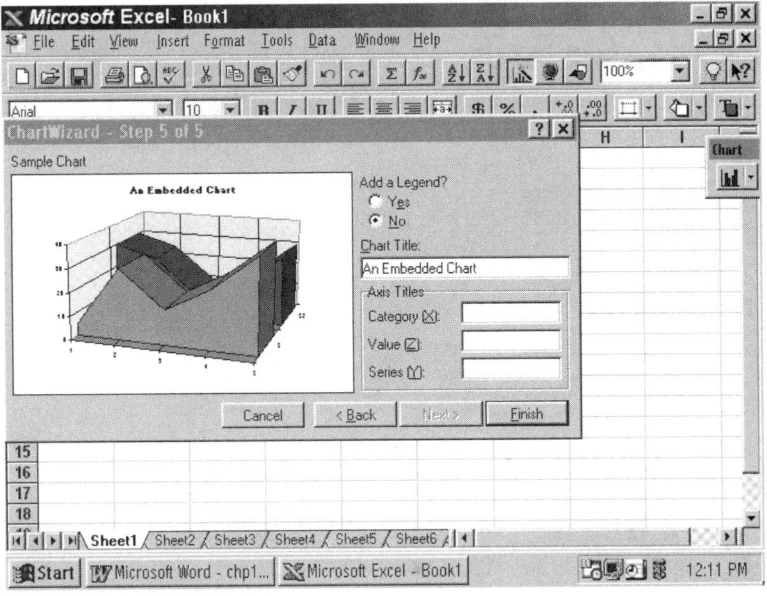

Figure 15.12: ChartWizard Step 5: Adding titles and labels to the chart object.

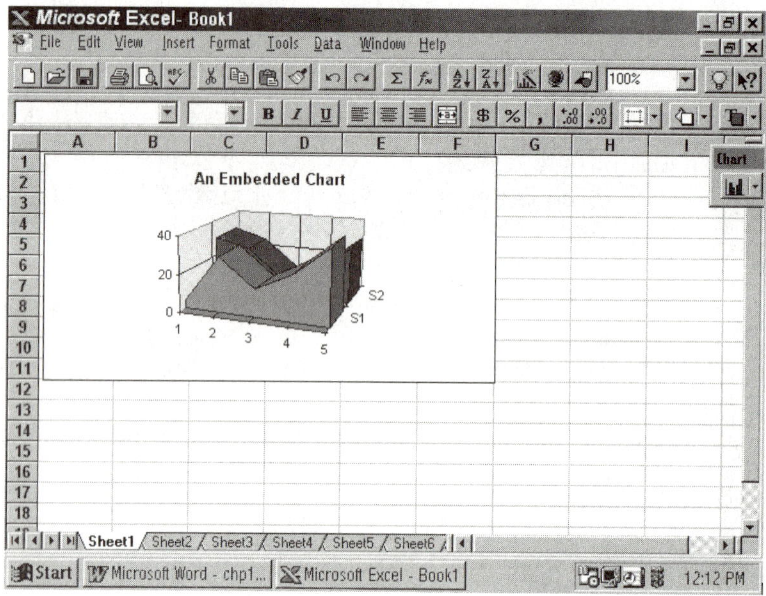

Figure 15.13: The final 3-D area chart drawn in Excel.

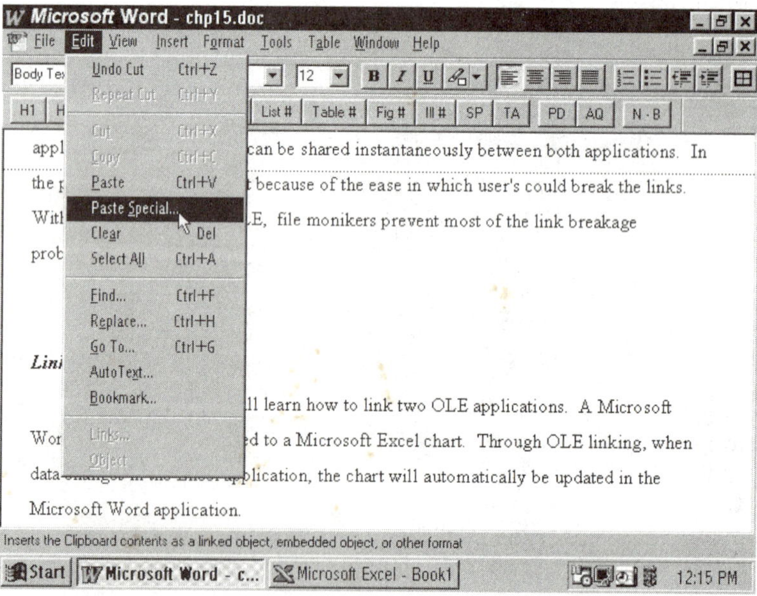

Figure 15.14: Preparing to link an Excel chart object with a Word document.

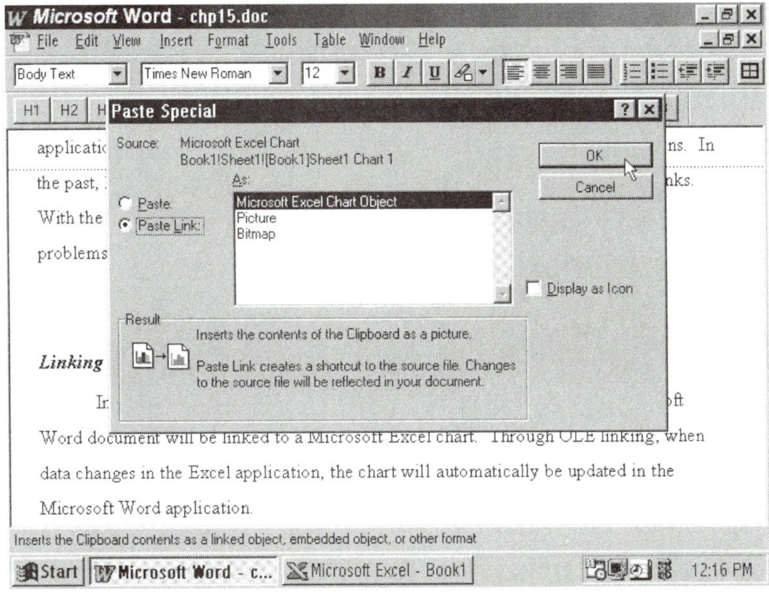

Figure 15.15: The Paste Link feature allows the chart object to be dynamically linked with the Word document.

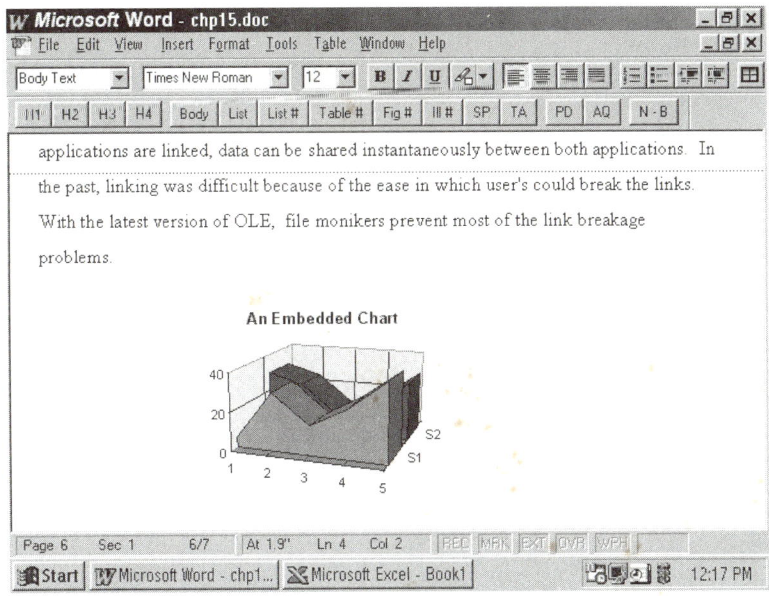

Figure 15.16: An Excel chart linked to a Word document.

To see the real magic of this dynamic linking process, return to your Excel spreadsheet and change the data in the spreadsheet. Almost instantly, the embedded chart will change to reflect the new data.

Windows 95 and Windows NT keep track of OLE objects by assigning an entry for each object in the system registry. The registry holds two identifiers: one for the object and one for the application.

Chapter 16

Developing OLE Applications

In this chapter you will learn how to use the AppWizard to generate base code that supports OLE. As you progress through this chapter, keep in mind that if you don't investigate the various OLE functions in the applications, you may never gain a full understanding of how OLE works in an object-oriented environment. One solution is to generate the program code, then study each part step by step.

The AppWizard is a great tool for developing applications with OLE features. Using the AppWizard makes implementing OLE capabilities, once so difficult, into a very easy task.

In this chapter you will learn how to develop a container project, named Contain, and a server project, named Server. The AppWizard will generate object-oriented code that takes full advantage of the MFC library.

CONTAINERS

OLE containers have implemented OLE interfaces so that the application can support the features and capabilities of both a container and an object application. The OLE container application uses two important classes. The COleDocument class manages a list of COleClientItems. The COleClientItems class manages the embedded or linked objects and the required communications between them and the application.

The container code for the Contain project is completely generated by the AppWizard. Only minor modifications were made to make this project unique.

Using The AppWizard

The AppWizard is used in the same manner it was to create the application in the previous chapters. For the Contain project, you will need to generate the base code with the AppWizard. Name the workspace Contain. Using the following steps to complete the project files with the AppWizard.

- Enter the Microsoft Development Studio (Visual C++ Compiler).
- Chose the File menu and select the New menu item.
- Select Project Workspace from the New dialog box.
- From the New Project Workspace dialog box:
  Name the workspace "Contain".

  Set the location of the workspace (for example, C:Contain).

  Select MFC AppWizard (exe) from the list box.
- Step 1—Select a single document application type.
- Step 2—Select no database support.
- Step 3—Select the OLE Container option only.
- Step 4—Select no additional features.
- Step 5—Do not select comments. Select a statically linked library.
- Step 6—View your settings and Finish the AppWizard process.

If the information is correct, in the New Project Information dialog box, select OK.

These are basically the steps you followed in Chapter 8. When the final step has been completed, as described earlier, the AppWizard generates all of the base files needed for the Contain project. The project will produce an application with a single document interface, no database options, a container option, default applications features, and no detailed file comments, etc. An additional class needed for this project will be described shortly.

Build the executable file by selecting the Rebuild All option from the compiler's Build menu. When the compile and link process is completed, you will have an executable file named Contain.exe.

AppWizard Files

The files generated by the AppWizard produce a fully working container application named Contain. When the files are generated by the AppWizard, your subdirectory will contain the following C++ files: Contain.cpp, MainFrm.cpp, ContainDoc.cpp, ContainView.cpp, StdAfx.cpp, and CntrItem.cpp. Also in this subdirectory will be a whole host of supporting header files, resource files, and so on.

In the next sections we look at just those files that have changed significantly from applications we have examined in earlier chapters.

The Contain.cpp File The Contain.cpp code is almost identical to the code used in earlier chapters. However, there is one important addition that has been bolded in the following listing.

```
// Contain.cpp : Defines the class behaviors for the application.
//

#include "stdafx.h"
#include "Contain.h"

#include "MainFrm.h"
#include "ContainDoc.h"
#include "ContainView.h"

#ifdef _DEBUG
#define new DEBUG_NEW
#undef THIS_FILE
static char THIS_FILE[] = __FILE__;
#endif
```

```
// CContainApp
BEGIN_MESSAGE_MAP(CContainApp, CWinApp)
  //{{AFX_MSG_MAP(CContainApp)
  ON_COMMAND(ID_APP_ABOUT, OnAppAbout)
    // ClassWizard will add and remove mapping macros here.
    // DO NOT EDIT these blocks of generated code!
  //}}AFX_MSG_MAP
  // Standard file based document commands
  ON_COMMAND(ID_FILE_NEW, CWinApp::OnFileNew)
  ON_COMMAND(ID_FILE_OPEN, CWinApp::OnFileOpen)
  // Standard print setup command
  ON_COMMAND(ID_FILE_PRINT_SETUP, CWinApp::OnFilePrintSetup)
END_MESSAGE_MAP()

// CContainApp construction
CContainApp::CContainApp()
{
  // TODO: add construction code here,
  // Place all significant initialization in InitInstance
}

// The one and only CContainApp object
CContainApp theApp;

// CContainApp initialization
BOOL CContainApp::InitInstance()
{
  // Initialize OLE libraries
  if (!AfxOleInit())
  {
    AfxMessageBox(IDP_OLE_INIT_FAILED);
    return FALSE;
  }

  // Standard initialization
#ifdef _AFXDLL
  Enable3dControls();
#else
  Enable3dControlsStatic();
#endif

  LoadStdProfileSettings();
  // Register the application s document templates.
  CSingleDocTemplate* pDocTemplate;
  pDocTemplate = new CSingleDocTemplate(
    IDR_MAINFRAME,
    RUNTIME_CLASS(CContainDoc),
    RUNTIME_CLASS(CMainFrame),
    RUNTIME_CLASS(CContainView));
  pDocTemplate->SetContainerInfo(IDR_CNTR_INPLACE);
```

```
    AddDocTemplate(pDocTemplate);

    // Parse command line for standard shell commands
    CCommandLineInfo cmdInfo;
    ParseCommandLine(cmdInfo);

    // Dispatch commands specified on the command line
    if (!ProcessShellCommand(cmdInfo))
      return FALSE;

    return TRUE;
}

// CAboutDlg dialog used for App About
class CAboutDlg : public CDialog
{
public:
  CAboutDlg();

// Dialog Data
  //{{AFX_DATA(CAboutDlg)
  enum { IDD = IDD_ABOUTBOX };
  //}}AFX_DATA

  // ClassWizard generated virtual function overrides
  //{{AFX_VIRTUAL(CAboutDlg)
  protected:
  virtual void DoDataExchange(CDataExchange* pDX);
  //}}AFX_VIRTUAL

// Implementation
protected:
  //{{AFX_MSG(CAboutDlg)
    // No message handlers
  //}}AFX_MSG
  DECLARE_MESSAGE_MAP()
};

CAboutDlg::CAboutDlg() : CDialog(CAboutDlg::IDD)
{
  //{{AFX_DATA_INIT(CAboutDlg)
  //}}AFX_DATA_INIT
}

void CAboutDlg::DoDataExchange(CDataExchange* pDX)
{
  CDialog::DoDataExchange(pDX);
  //{{AFX_DATA_MAP(CAboutDlg)
  //}}AFX_DATA_MAP
}

BEGIN_MESSAGE_MAP(CAboutDlg, CDialog)
```

```
  //{{AFX_MSG_MAP(CAboutDlg)
    // No message handlers
  //}}AFX_MSG_MAP
END_MESSAGE_MAP()

// App command to run the dialog
void CContainApp::OnAppAbout()
{
  CAboutDlg aboutDlg;
  aboutDlg.DoModal();
}

// CContainApp commands
```

The only real change in this file from the previous example is the insertion of this portion of OLE code:

```
// Initialize OLE libraries
  if (!AfxOleInit())
  {
    AfxMessageBox(IDP_OLE_INIT_FAILED);
    return FALSE;
  }
```

This code is responsible for initializing OLE libraries. Return to the original listing and find the remaining bolded sections. OLE supports *in-place editing.* In-place editing occurs when an object is embedded in a container and its menu replaces the container's menu. For example, if a Microsoft Word (the server) document object is embedded in Contain (the container), its menu will change to Word's.

This menu change code is handled almost automatically by the MFC library. Inplace editing is achieved by having two menu sources available: IDR_MAINFRAME and IDR_CNTR_INPLACE (the name is specific to your application). When no object is embedded in the container application, IDR_MAINFRAME is used. IDR_CNTR_INPLACE is used when an object has been embedded in the container.

The ContainDoc.cpp File container file, ContainDoc.cpp, contains more code than the equivalent file used in previous chapters. Compare this file with other document class files and see if you can spot the differences.

```
// ContainDoc.cpp : implementation of the CContainDoc class
//
```

```
#include "stdafx.h"
#include "Contain.h"

#include "ContainDoc.h"
#include "CntrItem.h"

#ifdef _DEBUG
#define new DEBUG_NEW
#undef THIS_FILE
static char THIS_FILE[] = __FILE__;
#endif

// CContainDoc
IMPLEMENT_DYNCREATE(CContainDoc, COleDocument)

BEGIN_MESSAGE_MAP(CContainDoc, COleDocument)
  //{{AFX_MSG_MAP(CContainDoc)
    // ClassWizard will add and remove mapping macros here.
    // DO NOT EDIT what you see in blocks of generated code!
  //}}AFX_MSG_MAP
  // Enable default OLE container implementation
  ON_UPDATE_COMMAND_UI(ID_EDIT_PASTE,
                       COleDocument::OnUpdatePasteMenu)
  ON_UPDATE_COMMAND_UI(ID_EDIT_PASTE_LINK,
                       COleDocument::OnUpdatePasteLinkMenu)
  ON_UPDATE_COMMAND_UI(ID_OLE_EDIT_CONVERT,
                       COleDocument::OnUpdateObjectVerbMenu)
  ON_COMMAND(ID_OLE_EDIT_CONVERT, COleDocument::OnEditConvert)
  ON_UPDATE_COMMAND_UI(ID_OLE_EDIT_LINKS,
                       COleDocument::OnUpdateEditLinksMenu)
  ON_COMMAND(ID_OLE_EDIT_LINKS, COleDocument::OnEditLinks)
  ON_UPDATE_COMMAND_UI(ID_OLE_VERB_FIRST,
                       COleDocument::OnUpdateObjectVerbMenu)
END_MESSAGE_MAP()

// CContainDoc construction/destruction
CContainDoc::CContainDoc()
{
  // Use OLE compound files
  EnableCompoundFile();

  // TODO: add one-time construction code here

}

CContainDoc::~CContainDoc()
{
}

BOOL CContainDoc::OnNewDocument()
{
```

```
    if (!COleDocument::OnNewDocument())
      return FALSE;

    // TODO: add reinitialization code here
    // (SDI documents will reuse this document)

    return TRUE;
}

// CContainDoc serialization

void CContainDoc::Serialize(CArchive& ar)
{
    if (ar.IsStoring())
    {
      // TODO: add storing code here
    }
    else
    {
      // TODO: add loading code here
    }

    // Calling base class COleDocument enables serialization
    //  of the container document s COleClientItem objects.
    COleDocument::Serialize(ar);
}

// CContainDoc diagnostics

#ifdef _DEBUG
void CContainDoc::AssertValid() const
{
    COleDocument::AssertValid();
}

void CContainDoc::Dump(CDumpContext& dc) const
{
    COleDocument::Dump(dc);
}
#endif //_DEBUG

// CContainDoc commands
```

The first significant change you should observe is the expansion of message map support for OLE operations

```
    .
    .
    .
 // Enable default OLE container implementation
  ON_UPDATE_COMMAND_UI(ID_EDIT_PASTE,
                       COleDocument::OnUpdatePasteMenu)
```

```
ON_UPDATE_COMMAND_UI(ID_EDIT_PASTE_LINK,
                     COleDocument::OnUpdatePasteLinkMenu)
ON_UPDATE_COMMAND_UI(ID_OLE_EDIT_CONVERT,
                     COleDocument::OnUpdateObjectVerbMenu)
ON_COMMAND(ID_OLE_EDIT_CONVERT, COleDocument::OnEditConvert)
ON_UPDATE_COMMAND_UI(ID_OLE_EDIT_LINKS,
                     COleDocument::OnUpdateEditLinksMenu)
ON_COMMAND(ID_OLE_EDIT_LINKS, COleDocument::OnEditLinks)
ON_UPDATE_COMMAND_UI(ID_OLE_VERB_FIRST,
                     COleDocument::OnUpdateObjectVerbMenu)
    .
    .
    .
```

The message map will now allow the implementation of the default OLE container. The function of these items is self-explanatory.

You can also see that the constructor calls the **EnableCompoundFile()** function.

```
// Use OLE compound files
  EnableCompoundFile();
```

This function is used to store the document using the compound-file format. If this function is not used, documents are stored in a *flat* nonstructured file format.

```
// Calling base class COleDocument enables serialization
  //  of the container document's COleClientItem objects.
  COleDocument::Serialize(ar);
```

The COleDocument base class permits the OLE objects to be serialized.

The ContainView.cpp File The ContainView.cpp file contains the most significant changes in order to support OLE features. When you examine the following listing, note the additions to the message map. They bring editing and printing capabilities to the project.

```
// ContainView.cpp : implementation of the CContainView class
//

#include "stdafx.h"
#include "Contain.h"

#include "ContainDoc.h"
#include "CntrItem.h"
#include "ContainView.h"
```

```
#ifdef _DEBUG
#define new DEBUG_NEW
#undef THIS_FILE
static char THIS_FILE[] = __FILE__;
#endif

// CContainView
IMPLEMENT_DYNCREATE(CContainView, CView)

BEGIN_MESSAGE_MAP(CContainView, CView)
  //{{AFX_MSG_MAP(CContainView)
    // ClassWizard will add and remove mapping macros here.
    // DO NOT EDIT these blocks of generated code!
  ON_WM_SETFOCUS()
  ON_WM_SIZE()
  ON_COMMAND(ID_OLE_INSERT_NEW, OnInsertObject)
  ON_COMMAND(ID_CANCEL_EDIT_CNTR, OnCancelEditCntr)
  //}}AFX_MSG_MAP
  // Standard printing commands
  ON_COMMAND(ID_FILE_PRINT, CView::OnFilePrint)
  ON_COMMAND(ID_FILE_PRINT_DIRECT, CView::OnFilePrint)
  ON_COMMAND(ID_FILE_PRINT_PREVIEW,CView::OnFilePrintPreview)
END_MESSAGE_MAP()

// CContainView construction/destruction
CContainView::CContainView()
{
  m_pSelection = NULL;
  // TODO: add construction code here

}

CContainView::~CContainView()
{
}

BOOL CContainView::PreCreateWindow(CREATESTRUCT& cs)
{
  return CView::PreCreateWindow(cs);
}

// CContainView drawing
void CContainView::OnDraw(CDC* pDC)
{
  CContainDoc* pDoc = GetDocument();
  ASSERT_VALID(pDoc);

  // TODO: add draw code for native data here
  // TODO: also draw all OLE items in the document
  // TODO: remove this code when final draw code is complete.

  if (m_pSelection == NULL)
```

```
 {
   POSITION pos = pDoc->GetStartPosition();
   m_pSelection = (CContainCntrItem*)pDoc->
                   GetNextClientItem(pos);
 }
 if (m_pSelection != NULL)
   m_pSelection->Draw(pDC, CRect(10, 10, 210, 210));
}

void CContainView::OnInitialUpdate()
{
  CView::OnInitialUpdate();
  m_pSelection = NULL;    // initialize selection
}

// CContainView printing
BOOL CContainView::OnPreparePrinting(CPrintInfo* pInfo)
{
  // default preparation
  return DoPreparePrinting(pInfo);
}

void CContainView::OnBeginPrinting(CDC* /*pDC*/,
                                   CPrintInfo* /*pInfo*/)
{
  // TODO: add extra initialization before printing
}

void CContainView::OnEndPrinting(CDC* /*pDC*/,
                                 CPrintInfo* /*pInfo*/)
{
  // TODO: add cleanup after printing
}

// OLE Client support and commands
BOOL CContainView::IsSelected(const CObject* pDocItem) const
{

  // TODO: implement function and test for OLE client item

  return pDocItem == m_pSelection;
}

void CContainView::OnInsertObject()
{
  // Invoke the Insert Object dialog box to get information
  //  for new CContainCntrItem object.
  COleInsertDialog dlg;
  if (dlg.DoModal() != IDOK)
    return;

  BeginWaitCursor();
```

```
    CContainCntrItem* pItem = NULL;
    TRY
    {
        // Create new item connected to this document.
        CContainDoc* pDoc = GetDocument();
        ASSERT_VALID(pDoc);
        pItem = new CContainCntrItem(pDoc);
        ASSERT_VALID(pItem);

        // Initialize the item from the dialog data.
        if (!dlg.CreateItem(pItem))
            AfxThrowMemoryException();  // any exception will do
        ASSERT_VALID(pItem);

        // If item created from class list (not from file) then launch
        //  the server to edit the item.
        if (dlg.GetSelectionType() == COleInsertDialog::createNewItem)
            pItem->DoVerb(OLEIVERB_SHOW, this);

        ASSERT_VALID(pItem);

        // As an arbitrary user interface design, this sets the selection
        //  to the last item inserted.

        // TODO: reimplement selection as appropriate for your application

        m_pSelection = pItem;   // set selection to last inserted item
        pDoc->UpdateAllViews(NULL);
    }
    CATCH(CException, e)
    {
        if (pItem != NULL)
        {
            ASSERT_VALID(pItem);
            pItem->Delete();
        }
        AfxMessageBox(IDP_FAILED_TO_CREATE);
    }
    END_CATCH

    EndWaitCursor();
}

// The following command handler provides the standard keyboard
//  user interface to cancel an in-place editing session.  Here,
//  the container (not the server) causes the deactivation.
void CContainView::OnCancelEditCntr()
{
    // Close any in-place active item on this view.
    COleClientItem* pActiveItem = GetDocument()->GetInPlaceActiveItem(this);
    if (pActiveItem != NULL)
```

```
 {
   pActiveItem->Close();
 }
 ASSERT(GetDocument()->GetInPlaceActiveItem(this) == NULL);
}

// Special handling of OnSetFocus and OnSize are required for a container
//  when an object is being edited in-place.
void CContainView::OnSetFocus(CWnd* pOldWnd)
{
  COleClientItem* pActiveItem = GetDocument()->GetInPlaceActiveItem(this);
  if (pActiveItem != NULL &&
    pActiveItem->GetItemState() == COleClientItem::activeUIState)
  {
    // need to set focus to this item if it is in the same view
    CWnd* pWnd = pActiveItem->GetInPlaceWindow();
    if (pWnd != NULL)
    {
      pWnd->SetFocus();   // don t call the base class
      return;
    }
  }

  CView::OnSetFocus(pOldWnd);
}

void CContainView::OnSize(UINT nType, int cx, int cy)
{
  CView::OnSize(nType, cx, cy);
  COleClientItem* pActiveItem = GetDocument()->
                                GetInPlaceActiveItem(this);
  if (pActiveItem != NULL)
    pActiveItem->SetItemRects();
}

// CContainView diagnostics
#ifdef _DEBUG
void CContainView::AssertValid() const
{
  CView::AssertValid();
}

void CContainView::Dump(CDumpContext& dc) const
{
  CView::Dump(dc);
}

CContainDoc* CContainView::GetDocument() // non-debug version is inline
{
  ASSERT(m_pDocument->IsKindOf(RUNTIME_CLASS(CContainDoc)));
```

```
  return (CContainDoc*)m_pDocument;
}
#endif //_DEBUG

// CContainView message handlers
```

The *m_pSelection* holds the selection to the current CContainCntrItem. For more involved applications, this simple member variable will not be sufficient, and you will have to write your own code for this purpose.

In order to handle the inserted objects for the CContainView container, the **OnDraw()** member function has been altered.

```
void CContainView::OnDraw(CDC* pDC)
{
  CContainDoc* pDoc = GetDocument();
  ASSERT_VALID(pDoc);

  // TODO: add draw code for native data here
  // TODO: also draw all OLE items in the document
  // TODO: remove this code when final draw code is complete.

  if (m_pSelection == NULL)
  {
    POSITION pos = pDoc->GetStartPosition();
    m_pSelection = (CContainCntrItem*)pDoc->
                   GetNextClientItem(pos);
  }
  if (m_pSelection != NULL)
    m_pSelection->Draw(pDC, CRect(10, 10, 210, 210));
}
```

This code places the inserted object at a predefined location, given by the **CRect()** function at 10,10 and 210,210. These values can be changed as necessary.

Other additional member functions are for manipulating the object. They include **OnInitialUpdate()**, **IsSelected()**, **OnInsertObject()**, **OnCancelEdit()**, **OnSetFocus()**, and **OnSize()**. These implementations allow selecting, inserting, canceling, and sizing of OLE objects. More code can be added to these functions.

Finally, the function **GetInPlaceActiveItem()** is used to obtain the OLE item that is presently activated, in place, in the frame window.

```
COleClientItem* pActiveItem = GetDocument()->
                              GetInPlaceActiveItem(this);
```

The CntrItem.cpp File The CntrItem.cpp file is responsible for the implementation of the **CContainContainrItem** class derived from Microsoft's **COleClientItem** class.

```
// CntrItem.cpp : implementation of the CContainCntrItem class
//

#include "stdafx.h"
#include "Contain.h"

#include "ContainDoc.h"
#include "ContainView.h"
#include "CntrItem.h"

#ifdef _DEBUG
#define new DEBUG_NEW
#undef THIS_FILE
static char THIS_FILE[] = __FILE__;
#endif

// CContainCntrItem implementation
IMPLEMENT_SERIAL(CContainCntrItem, COleClientItem, 0)

CContainCntrItem::CContainCntrItem(CContainDoc* pContainer)
  : COleClientItem(pContainer)
{
  // TODO: add one-time construction code here

}

CContainCntrItem::~CContainCntrItem()
{
  // TODO: add cleanup code here

}

void CContainCntrItem::OnChange(OLE_NOTIFICATION nCode,
                                DWORD dwParam)
{
  ASSERT_VALID(this);

  COleClientItem::OnChange(nCode, dwParam);

  // TODO: invalidate the item by calling UpdateAllViews
  //  (with hints appropriate to your application)

  GetDocument()->UpdateAllViews(NULL);
    // for now just update ALL views/no hints
}

BOOL CContainCntrItem::OnChangeItemPosition(const CRect&
                                            rectPos)
```

```
{
  ASSERT_VALID(this);

  if (!COleClientItem::OnChangeItemPosition(rectPos))
    return FALSE;

  // TODO: update any cache you may have of rectangle/extent

  return TRUE;
}

void CContainCntrItem::OnGetItemPosition(CRect& rPosition)
{
  ASSERT_VALID(this);

  // TODO: return correct rectangle (in pixels) in rPosition

  rPosition.SetRect(10, 10, 210, 210);
}

void CContainCntrItem::OnActivate()
{
    // Allow only one inplace activate item per frame
    CContainView* pView = GetActiveView();
    ASSERT_VALID(pView);
    COleClientItem* pItem = GetDocument()->
                            GetInPlaceActiveItem(pView);
    if (pItem != NULL && pItem != this)
        pItem->Close();

    COleClientItem::OnActivate();
}

void CContainCntrItem::OnDeactivateUI(BOOL bUndoable)
{
  COleClientItem::OnDeactivateUI(bUndoable);

    // Hide the object if it is not an outside-in object
    DWORD dwMisc = 0;
    m_lpObject->GetMiscStatus(GetDrawAspect(), &dwMisc);
    if (dwMisc & OLEMISC_INSIDEOUT)
        DoVerb(OLEIVERB_HIDE, NULL);
}

void CContainCntrItem::Serialize(CArchive& ar)
{
  ASSERT_VALID(this);

  COleClientItem::Serialize(ar);

  // now store/retrieve data specific to CContainCntrItem
  if (ar.IsStoring())
  {
```

```
    // TODO: add storing code here
  }
  else
  {
    // TODO: add loading code here
  }
}

// CContainCntrItem diagnostics
#ifdef _DEBUG
void CContainCntrItem::AssertValid() const
{
  COleClientItem::AssertValid();
}

void CContainCntrItem::Dump(CDumpContext& dc) const
{
  COleClientItem::Dump(dc);
}
#endif
```

The COleClientItem class is derived from other MFC base classes in the following manner:

CObject→CCmdTarget→CDocItem→COleClientItem

The COleClientItem class represents the client's portion of a connection to an embedded OLE object. Nineteen member functions for this class can be overridden. If you examine the previous listing, you will note that **OnChange()**, **OnChangeItemPosition()**, **OnDeactivateUI()**, and **OnGetItemPosition()** are implemented.

The **OnChange()** member function responds to changes brought about by the server. The variable *nCode* can take on the following values:

- OLE_CHANGED—if the item's appearance has changed
- OLE_CHANGED_STATE—if the item has changed states
- OLE_CLOSED—if the OLE item has been closed
- OLE_SAVED—if the OLE item has been saved

The **OnDeactivateUI()** member function is used to determine if current editing changes cannot be undone. This parameter is a Boolean value.

The **OnGetItemPosition()** member function references **CRect**, which in turn contains the item's position coordinates. In this instance, they are preset to 10, 10, 210 and 210. The **OnChangeItemPosition()** member function gives the item's position relative to the client area in the container.

Working with the Contain Application

The Contain project produces an application with the minimum code necessary to implement an OLE container. Minimal as it is, however, this application is fully functional.

If you haven't built the application, do it now. Execute the Contain.exe application with the Run menu item in the Build menu. Figure 16.1 shows the initial container window.

This container application can use objects from any OLE server. As an example, Microsoft Word will act as the server. To select Word, choose the container's Edit menu, as shown in Figure 16.2.

Select the Insert New Object... menu item to open the Insert Object dialog box, shown in Figure 16.3.

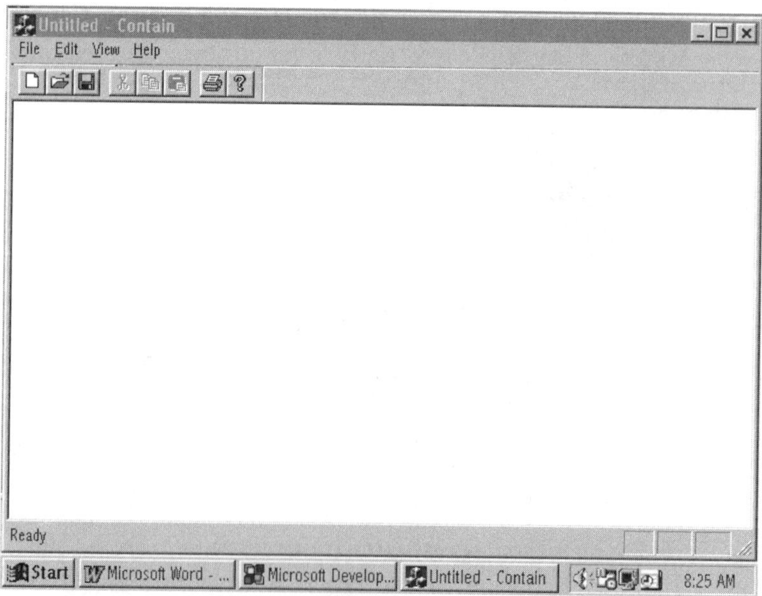

Figure 16.1: The initial container window.

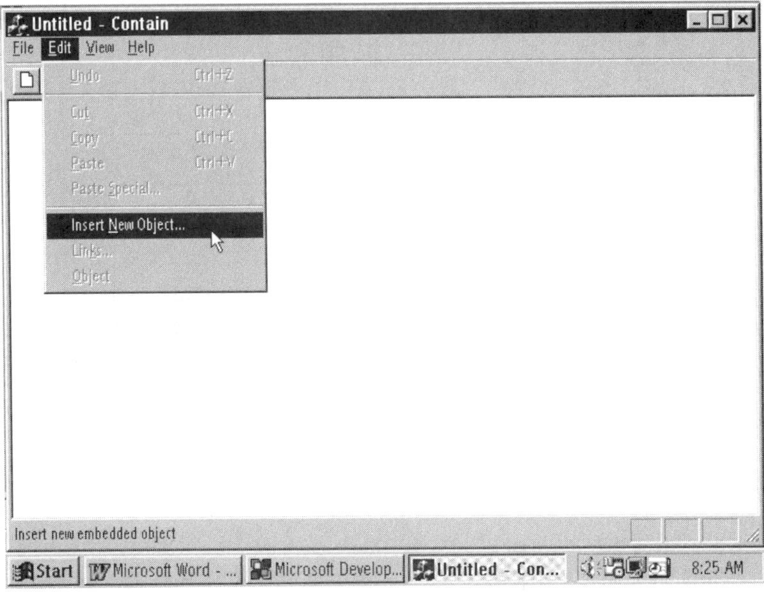

Figure 16.2: The container's Edit menu allows the insertion of OLE objects.

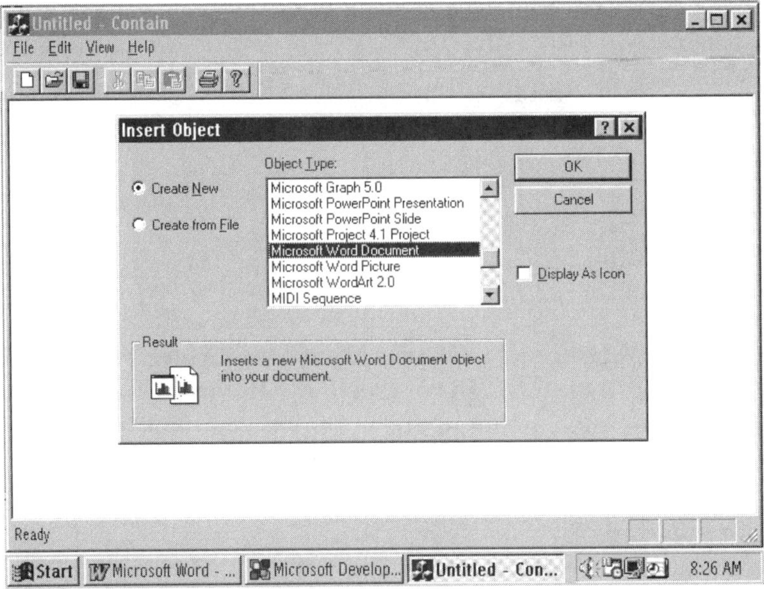

Figure 16.3: The Insert Object dialog box lists the OLE object sources for your system.

From the Insert Object dialog box, choose Microsoft Word Document as the object to embed in the container application.

Figure 16.4 shows the initial insertion of the Word object into the container document.

Notice that the window caption now reads "Untitled - Contain". This indicates that the server object has been properly embedded, but that no document has been inserted into the object.

Figure 16.5 shows that data can be entered in the embedded object which is now part of the container.

The Contain application can edit and print with full Microsoft Word capabilities as long as it contains the Word object.

Servers

The server application will be built in a manner similar to the container application. The server application is named Server and will act as a simple word processor. Just like the Microsoft Word example in the last section, this simple OLE server can be inserted into applications with OLE container abilities. Containers include Microsoft Access, Microsoft Excel, Microsoft Word, the Contain application from the last section, and so on.

Server applications built with the AppWizard will automatically do the following:

- Initialize OLE
- Obtain menu negotiation with the container
- Register themselves in the OLE registration database
- Support serialization of OLE storage streams
- Support Visual Editing
- Use an OLE class factory for creation of document objects

OLE servers are often more complicated than containers. As you work through this section, remember the AppWizard will completely generate the necessary server code. The base server code can be enhanced to provide additional features.

Using the AppWizard

The AppWizard is used in the same manner it was to create the container application in the previous section. For the

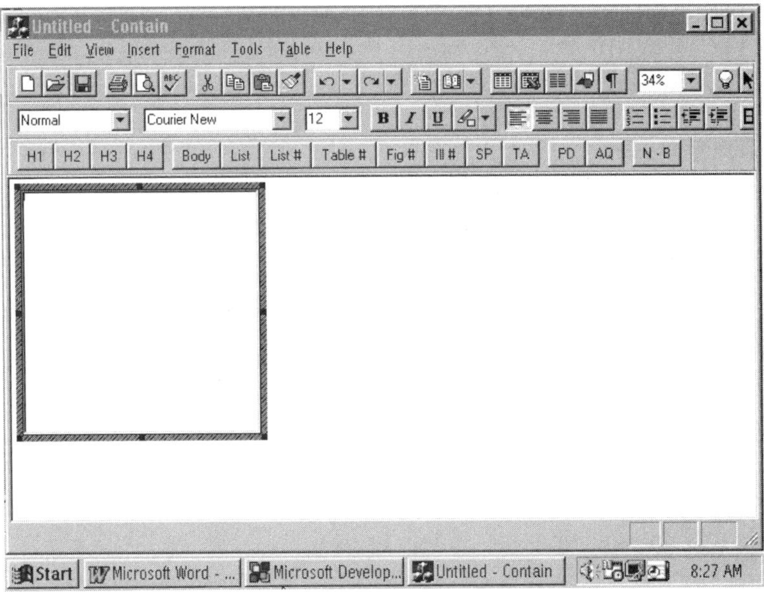

Figure 16.4: The Word server object is embedded in the Contain application's document.

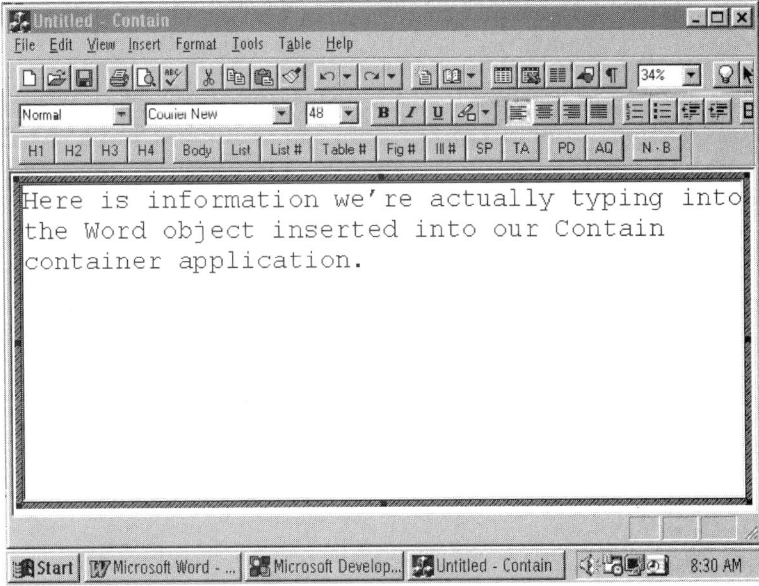

Figure 16.5: Data can be entered in the Word server object that is embedded in the Contain container application.

Server project, you will need to generate the base code with the AppWizard. Name the workspace Server. Use the following steps to complete the project files with the AppWizard.

- Enter the Microsoft Development Studio (Visual C++ Compiler).
- Chose the File menu and select the New menu item.
- Select Project Workspace from the New dialog box.
- From the New Project Workspace dialog box:
  Name the workspace "Server".

  Set the location of the workspace (for example, C:Server).

  Select MFC AppWizard (exe) from the list box.
- Step 1—Select a single document application type.
- Step 2—Select no database support.
- Step 3—Select the OLE Server option only.
- Step 4—Select no additional features.
- Step 5—Do not select comments. Select a statically linked library.
- Step 6—From the class list, select CServerView. Change the base class to CEditView for this project. Now select Finish to complete the AppWizard process.

If the information is correct, in the New Project Information dialog box, select OK.

When the final step has been completed, as described earlier, the AppWizard will generate all of the base files needed for the Server project. The project will produce an application with a single document interface, no database options, a Server option, default applications features, and no detailed file comments, etc.

Build the executable file by selecting the Rebuild All option from the compiler's Build menu. When the compile and link process is completed, you will have an executable file named Server.exe.

AppWizard Files

The files generated by the AppWizard produce a fully working server application named Server with complete editing capabilities. When the files are generated by the AppWizard, your subdirectory will contain the following C++ files: Server.cpp, MainFrm.cpp, StdAfx.cpp, ServerDoc.cpp, ServerView.cpp, SrvrItem.cpp, and IpFrame.cpp. You will also be supplied with the necessary header and resource files.

In the following section, we will examine just those files that are important to the OLE server portion of the server application.

The Server.cpp File Here is the code for the Server.cpp file.

```
// Server.cpp : Defines the class behaviors for the application.
//

#include "stdafx.h"
#include "Server.h"

#include "MainFrm.h"
#include "IpFrame.h"
#include "ServerDoc.h"
#include "ServerView.h"

#ifdef _DEBUG
#define new DEBUG_NEW
#undef THIS_FILE
static char THIS_FILE[] = __FILE__;
#endif

// CServerApp
BEGIN_MESSAGE_MAP(CServerApp, CWinApp)
  //{{AFX_MSG_MAP(CServerApp)
  ON_COMMAND(ID_APP_ABOUT, OnAppAbout)
  //}}AFX_MSG_MAP
  // Standard file based document commands
  ON_COMMAND(ID_FILE_NEW, CWinApp::OnFileNew)
  ON_COMMAND(ID_FILE_OPEN, CWinApp::OnFileOpen)
  // Standard print setup command
  ON_COMMAND(ID_FILE_PRINT_SETUP, CWinApp::OnFilePrintSetup)
END_MESSAGE_MAP()

// CServerApp construction
CServerApp::CServerApp()
{
}

// The one and only CServerApp object
CServerApp theApp;

static const CLSID clsid =
{ 0x801275c6, 0x236b, 0x11cf, { 0xaa, 0x35, 0x44, 0x45,
                                0x53, 0x54, 0x0, 0x0 } };
```

```
// CServerApp initialization
BOOL CServerApp::InitInstance()
{
  // Initialize OLE libraries
  if (!AfxOleInit())
  {
    AfxMessageBox(IDP_OLE_INIT_FAILED);
    return FALSE;
  }

  // Standard initialization

#ifdef _AFXDLL
  Enable3dControls();
#else
  Enable3dControlsStatic();
#endif

  LoadStdProfileSettings();
  // Register document templates

  CSingleDocTemplate* pDocTemplate;
  pDocTemplate = new CSingleDocTemplate(
    IDR_MAINFRAME,
    RUNTIME_CLASS(CServerDoc),
    RUNTIME_CLASS(CMainFrame),     // main SDI frame window
    RUNTIME_CLASS(CServerView));
  pDocTemplate->SetServerInfo(
    IDR_SRVR_EMBEDDED, IDR_SRVR_INPLACE,
    RUNTIME_CLASS(CInPlaceFrame));
  AddDocTemplate(pDocTemplate);
  m_server.ConnectTemplate(clsid, pDocTemplate, TRUE);

  // Parse command line for shell commands, DDE, file open
  CCommandLineInfo cmdInfo;
  ParseCommandLine(cmdInfo);

  if (cmdInfo.m_bRunEmbedded || cmdInfo.m_bRunAutomated)
  {
    COleTemplateServer::RegisterAll();

    // Application was run with /Embedding or /Automation.
    //  Don t show main window in this case.
    return TRUE;
  }

  m_server.UpdateRegistry(OAT_INPLACE_SERVER);

  // Dispatch commands specified on the command line
  if (!ProcessShellCommand(cmdInfo))
    return FALSE;

  return TRUE;
```

```
}
// CAboutDlg dialog used for App About
class CAboutDlg : public CDialog
{
public:
  CAboutDlg();

// Dialog Data
  //{{AFX_DATA(CAboutDlg)
  enum { IDD = IDD_ABOUTBOX };
  //}}AFX_DATA

  // ClassWizard generated virtual function overrides
  //{{AFX_VIRTUAL(CAboutDlg)
  protected:
  virtual void DoDataExchange(CDataExchange* pDX);
  //}}AFX_VIRTUAL

// Implementation
protected:
  //{{AFX_MSG(CAboutDlg)
    // No message handlers
  //}}AFX_MSG
  DECLARE_MESSAGE_MAP()
};

CAboutDlg::CAboutDlg() : CDialog(CAboutDlg::IDD)
{
  //{{AFX_DATA_INIT(CAboutDlg)
  //}}AFX_DATA_INIT
}

void CAboutDlg::DoDataExchange(CDataExchange* pDX)
{
  CDialog::DoDataExchange(pDX);
  //{{AFX_DATA_MAP(CAboutDlg)
  //}}AFX_DATA_MAP
}

BEGIN_MESSAGE_MAP(CAboutDlg, CDialog)
  //{{AFX_MSG_MAP(CAboutDlg)
    // No message handlers
  //}}AFX_MSG_MAP
END_MESSAGE_MAP()

// App command to run the dialog
void CServerApp::OnAppAbout()
{
  CAboutDlg aboutDlg;
  aboutDlg.DoModal();
}

// CServerApp commands
```

This server file, Server.cpp, contains interesting code in the **InitInstance()** member function. Examine the following small portion of code from the previous listing.

```
BOOL CServerApp::InitInstance()
{
    .
    .
    .
    CSingleDocTemplate* pDocTemplate;
    pDocTemplate = new CSingleDocTemplate(
      IDR_MAINFRAME,
      RUNTIME_CLASS(CServerDoc),
      RUNTIME_CLASS(CMainFrame),     // main SDI frame window
      RUNTIME_CLASS(CServerView));
    pDocTemplate->SetServerInfo(
      IDR_SRVR_EMBEDDED, IDR_SRVR_INPLACE,
      RUNTIME_CLASS(CInPlaceFrame));
    .
    .
    .
```

A document template is implemented in this portion of code in the normal manner. However, notice that immediately following this code is a call to the **SetServerInfo()** function. Document templates typically associate a document class with view and frame classes. This function call also associates menus (IDR_SRVR_EMBEDDED and IDR_SRVR_INPLACE) and an in-place frame class, CInPlaceFrame. It is because of this that the framework knows which menus and IP frame to create when the server is activated in place.

```
    .
    .
    .
if (cmdInfo.m_bRunEmbedded || cmdInfo.m_bRunAutomated)
  {
    COleTemplateServer::RegisterAll();

    // Application was run with /Embedding or /Automation.
    //  Don t show main window in this case.
    return TRUE;
  }

  m_server.UpdateRegistry(OAT_INPLACE_SERVER);
  // Dispatch commands specified on the command line
  if (!ProcessShellCommand(cmdInfo))
```

```
    return FALSE;
    .
    .
    .
```

When a server application is run as a standalone application, it is wise to update the system registry in the event that it has been damaged.

The class factory, *m_server*, is an instance of the COleTemplateServer class. This class is derived from other MFC base classes in the following manner:

CObject→CCmdTarget→COleObjectFactory→COleTemplateServer

The factory(ies) can be registered by calling the **RegisterAll()** member function. A class factory is an object used to create one or more instances of an object identified by a given class identifier. With the class factory in place, OLE libraries can create objects from other applications. Finally, **m_server.UpdateRegistry** registers the document and updates the registration database. This means that containers can now find your server application in the registration database. In this case, OAT_INPLACE_SERVER is used to provide a full server interface. OAT_SERVER is use to support just object embedding. OAT_CONTAINER is used to support links to embedded objects and OAT_DISPATCH_OBJECT makes the object IDispatch capable.

The ServerDoc.cpp File The ServerDoc.cpp file is responsible for implementing the CServerDoc class derived from Microsoft's COleServerDoc class.

```
// ServerDoc.cpp : implementation of the CServerDoc class
//

#include "stdafx.h"
#include "Server.h"

#include "ServerDoc.h"
#include "SrvrItem.h"

#ifdef _DEBUG
#define new DEBUG_NEW
#undef THIS_FILE
static char THIS_FILE[] = __FILE__;
```

```
#endif

// CServerDoc
IMPLEMENT_DYNCREATE(CServerDoc, COleServerDoc)

BEGIN_MESSAGE_MAP(CServerDoc, COleServerDoc)
  //{{AFX_MSG_MAP(CServerDoc)
  //}}AFX_MSG_MAP
END_MESSAGE_MAP()

// CServerDoc construction/destruction
CServerDoc::CServerDoc()
{
  EnableCompoundFile();

}

CServerDoc::~CServerDoc()
{
}

BOOL CServerDoc::OnNewDocument()
{
  if (!COleServerDoc::OnNewDocument())
    return FALSE;

  ((CEditView*)m_viewList.GetHead())->SetWindowText(NULL);

  return TRUE;
}

// CServerDoc server implementation
COleServerItem* CServerDoc::OnGetEmbeddedItem()
{
  CServerSrvrItem* pItem = new CServerSrvrItem(this);
  ASSERT_VALID(pItem);
  return pItem;
}

// CServerDoc serialization
void CServerDoc::Serialize(CArchive& ar)
{
  ((CEditView*)m_viewList.GetHead())->SerializeRaw(ar);
}

// CServerDoc diagnostics
#ifdef _DEBUG
void CServerDoc::AssertValid() const
{
  COleServerDoc::AssertValid();
}
void CServerDoc::Dump(CDumpContext& dc) const
{
```

```
  COleServerDoc::Dump(dc);
}
#endif //_DEBUG

// CServerDoc commands
```

The COleServerDoc class is derived from other base classes in the following manner:

CObject→CCmdTarget→CDocument→
COleDocument→COleLinkingDoc→COleServerDoc

Examine this portion of code taken from the previous listing:

```
// CServerDoc server implementation
COleServerItem* CServerDoc::OnGetEmbeddedItem()
{
  CServerSrvrItem* pItem = new CServerSrvrItem(this);
  ASSERT_VALID(pItem);
  return pItem;
}
```

This portion of code is responsible for implementing the server for the selected item. There is usually one COleServerItem used to represents the entire document during editing. If links are to be supported, then additional items must be used to represent portions of the document, rather than the whole document.

The ServerView.cpp File The ServerView.cpp file implements the CServerView class, which is derived from Microsoft's CEditView class.

```
// ServerView.cpp : implementation of the CServerView class
//

#include "stdafx.h"
#include "Server.h"

#include "ServerDoc.h"
#include "ServerView.h"

#ifdef _DEBUG
#define new DEBUG_NEW
#undef THIS_FILE
static char THIS_FILE[] = __FILE__;
#endif

// CServerView
IMPLEMENT_DYNCREATE(CServerView, CEditView)
BEGIN_MESSAGE_MAP(CServerView, CEditView)
  //{{AFX_MSG_MAP(CServerView)
```

```
  ON_COMMAND(ID_CANCEL_EDIT_SRVR, OnCancelEditSrvr)
  //}}AFX_MSG_MAP
  // Standard printing commands
  ON_COMMAND(ID_FILE_PRINT, CEditView::OnFilePrint)
  ON_COMMAND(ID_FILE_PRINT_DIRECT, CEditView::OnFilePrint)
  ON_COMMAND(ID_FILE_PRINT_PREVIEW,
            CEditView::OnFilePrintPreview)
END_MESSAGE_MAP()

// CServerView construction/destruction
CServerView::CServerView()
{
}

CServerView::~CServerView()
{
}

BOOL CServerView::PreCreateWindow(CREATESTRUCT& cs)
{
  BOOL bPreCreated = CEditView::PreCreateWindow(cs);
  cs.style &= ~(ES_AUTOHSCROLL|WS_HSCROLL);

  return bPreCreated;
}

// CServerView drawing
void CServerView::OnDraw(CDC* pDC)
{
  CServerDoc* pDoc = GetDocument();
  ASSERT_VALID(pDoc);
}

// CServerView printing
BOOL CServerView::OnPreparePrinting(CPrintInfo* pInfo)
{
  // default CEditView preparation
  return CEditView::OnPreparePrinting(pInfo);
}

void CServerView::OnBeginPrinting(CDC* pDC,CPrintInfo* pInfo)
{
  CEditView::OnBeginPrinting(pDC, pInfo);
}

void CServerView::OnEndPrinting(CDC* pDC, CPrintInfo* pInfo)
{
  CEditView::OnEndPrinting(pDC, pInfo);
}

// OLE Server support
void CServerView::OnCancelEditSrvr()
```

```
{
  GetDocument()->OnDeactivateUI(FALSE);
}

// CServerView diagnostics
#ifdef _DEBUG
void CServerView::AssertValid() const
{
  CEditView::AssertValid();
}

void CServerView::Dump(CDumpContext& dc) const
{
  CEditView::Dump(dc);
}

CServerDoc* CServerView::GetDocument()
{
  ASSERT(m_pDocument->IsKindOf(RUNTIME_CLASS(CServerDoc)));
  return (CServerDoc*)m_pDocument;
}
#endif //_DEBUG

// CServerView message handlers
```

There is just a small portion of code in the previous listing that aids in OLE support. The following piece of code highlights the command handler that supports a standard keyboard user interface to cancel an in-place editing session. It is the server that causes the deactivation.

```
// OLE Server support
void CServerView::OnCancelEditSrvr()
{
  GetDocument()->OnDeactivateUI(FALSE);
}
```

The **OnDeactivateUI()** function is used to cancel an in-place editing session. In the section discussing containers, it was used with the container for dictating deactivation.

The SrvrItem.cpp File The SrvrItem.cpp file is responsible for implementing the CServerSrvrItem class.

```
// SrvrItem.cpp : implementation of the CServerSrvrItem class
//

#include "stdafx.h"
#include "Server.h"
```

```
#include "ServerDoc.h"
#include "SrvrItem.h"
#ifdef _DEBUG
#define new DEBUG_NEW
#undef THIS_FILE
static char THIS_FILE[] = __FILE__;
#endif

// CServerSrvrItem implementation
IMPLEMENT_DYNAMIC(CServerSrvrItem, COleServerItem)

CServerSrvrItem::CServerSrvrItem(CServerDoc* pContainerDoc)
  : COleServerItem(pContainerDoc, TRUE)
{
}

CServerSrvrItem::~CServerSrvrItem()
{
}

void CServerSrvrItem::Serialize(CArchive& ar)
{
  if (!IsLinkedItem())
  {
    CServerDoc* pDoc = GetDocument();
    ASSERT_VALID(pDoc);
    pDoc->Serialize(ar);
  }
}

BOOL CServerSrvrItem::OnGetExtent(DVASPECT dwDrawAspect, CSize& rSize)
{
  if (dwDrawAspect != DVASPECT_CONTENT)
    return COleServerItem::OnGetExtent(dwDrawAspect, rSize);

  CServerDoc* pDoc = GetDocument();
  ASSERT_VALID(pDoc);

  rSize = CSize(3000, 3000);   // 3000 x 3000 HIMETRIC units

  return TRUE;
}

BOOL CServerSrvrItem::OnDraw(CDC* pDC, CSize& rSize)
{
  CServerDoc* pDoc = GetDocument();
  ASSERT_VALID(pDoc);

  pDC->SetMapMode(MM_ANISOTROPIC);
  pDC->SetWindowOrg(0,0);
  pDC->SetWindowExt(3000, 3000);

  return TRUE;
}
```

```
// CServerSrvrItem diagnostics

#ifdef _DEBUG
void CServerSrvrItem::AssertValid() const
{
  COleServerItem::AssertValid();
}

void CServerSrvrItem::Dump(CDumpContext& dc) const
{
  COleServerItem::Dump(dc);
}
#endif
```

This class is derived from the MFC COleServerItem base class in the following manner:

CObject→CCmdTarget→CDocItem→COleServerItem

Document information can be saved to the storage stream by just including **pDoc->Serialize(ar)**, as shown in the previous listing. This code redirects document information to the OLE container's storage stream.

This application handles drawing the contest aspect of the item. If other aspects are needed, the **OnGetExtent()** member function can be modified. This function is used to obtain the extent in HIMETRIC units for the entire item. The implementation returns hard-wired values of 3000 × 3000.

```
BOOL CServerSrvrItem::OnGetExtent(DVASPECT dwDrawAspect, CSize& rSize)
{
  if (dwDrawAspect != DVASPECT_CONTENT)
    return COleServerItem::OnGetExtent(dwDrawAspect, rSize);

  CServerDoc* pDoc = GetDocument();
  ASSERT_VALID(pDoc);

  rSize = CSize(3000, 3000);   // 3000 x 3000 HIMETRIC units

  return TRUE;
}
```

There is a tiny problem here as well. The mapping mode must be changed to MM_ANISOTROPIC when the **OnDraw()** member function is used.

```
BOOL CServerSrvrItem::OnDraw(CDC* pDC, CSize& rSize)
{
  CServerDoc* pDoc = GetDocument();
  ASSERT_VALID(pDoc);

  pDC->SetMapMode(MM_ANISOTROPIC);
```

```
  pDC->SetWindowOrg(0,0);
  pDC->SetWindowExt(3000, 3000);

  return TRUE;
}
```

This **OnDraw()** member function is used to draw the item. Since CDC is a metafile, the mapping mode must be MM_ANISOTROPIC. It is at this point that you can optionally set the window's origin and extent. AppWizard sets the origin at 0, 0 and the extent to 3000, 3000.

The IpFrame.cpp File The IpFrame.cpp file implements the CInPlaceFrame class. This is the class that allows Visual Editing when a server document is being edited in place.

```
// IpFrame.cpp : implementation of the CInPlaceFrame class
//

#include "stdafx.h"
#include "Server.h"

#include "IpFrame.h"

#ifdef _DEBUG
#define new DEBUG_NEW
#undef THIS_FILE
static char THIS_FILE[] = __FILE__;
#endif

// CInPlaceFrame
IMPLEMENT_DYNCREATE(CInPlaceFrame, COleIPFrameWnd)

BEGIN_MESSAGE_MAP(CInPlaceFrame, COleIPFrameWnd)
  //{{AFX_MSG_MAP(CInPlaceFrame)
  ON_WM_CREATE()
  //}}AFX_MSG_MAP
END_MESSAGE_MAP()

// CInPlaceFrame construction/destruction
CInPlaceFrame::CInPlaceFrame()
{
}

CInPlaceFrame::~CInPlaceFrame()
{
}

int CInPlaceFrame::OnCreate(LPCREATESTRUCT lpCreateStruct)
{
  if (COleIPFrameWnd::OnCreate(lpCreateStruct) == -1)
```

```
        return -1;

    if (!m_wndResizeBar.Create(this))
    {
        TRACE0("Failed to create resize barn");
        return -1;      // fail to create
    }

    m_dropTarget.Register(this);

    return 0;
}

BOOL CInPlaceFrame::OnCreateControlBars(CFrameWnd* pWndFrame,
                                        CFrameWnd* pWndDoc)
{
    m_wndToolBar.SetOwner(this);

    if (!m_wndToolBar.Create(pWndFrame) ||
        !m_wndToolBar.LoadToolBar(IDR_SRVR_INPLACE))
    {
        TRACE0("Failed to create toolbarn");
        return FALSE;
    }

    m_wndToolBar.SetBarStyle(m_wndToolBar.GetBarStyle() |
        CBRS_TOOLTIPS | CBRS_FLYBY | CBRS_SIZE_DYNAMIC);

    m_wndToolBar.EnableDocking(CBRS_ALIGN_ANY);
    pWndFrame->EnableDocking(CBRS_ALIGN_ANY);
    pWndFrame->DockControlBar(&m_wndToolBar);

    return TRUE;
}

BOOL CInPlaceFrame::PreCreateWindow(CREATESTRUCT& cs)
{
    return COleIPFrameWnd::PreCreateWindow(cs);
}

// CInPlaceFrame diagnostics
#ifdef _DEBUG
void CInPlaceFrame::AssertValid() const
{
    COleIPFrameWnd::AssertValid();
}

void CInPlaceFrame::Dump(CDumpContext& dc) const
{
    COleIPFrameWnd::Dump(dc);
}
#endif //_DEBUG

// CInPlaceFrame commands
```

This class is derived from the MFC base class **COleIP-FrameWnd** in the following manner:

CObject→CCmdTarget→CWnd→CFrameWnd→
COleIPFrameWnd

This class is also responsible for creating and placing control bars within the container application's document window. Examine this small portion of code:

```
BOOL CInPlaceFrame::OnCreateControlBars(CFrameWnd* pWndFrame,
                                        CFrameWnd* pWndDoc)
{
  m_wndToolBar.SetOwner(this);

  if (!m_wndToolBar.Create(pWndFrame) ||
    !m_wndToolBar.LoadToolBar(IDR_SRVR_INPLACE))
  {
    TRACE0("Failed to create toolbarn");
    return FALSE;
  }
    .
    .
    .
```

A call to the **SetOwner()** function insures that messages are sent to the correct application. The toolbar is loaded with a call to the **LoadToolBar()** function.

Working with the Server Application

The Server project is now ready for building and testing. Build the application in the normal manner. Select the Rebuild All menu item from the Build menu.

As an example, let's use the Contain application developed in the beginning of this chapter as the container. Start Contain in the normal manner and choose the Object... item from the Insert menu, as shown in Figure 16.6.

From the Object dialog box, choose the Server Document as the object to embed in this container. This is our server application. It was registered with the system registry during the compilation.

Figure 16.7 shows the initial insertion of the Server object into the Contain document.

Figure 16.8 shows that text can be entered in the embedded object which is now part of the Contain container.

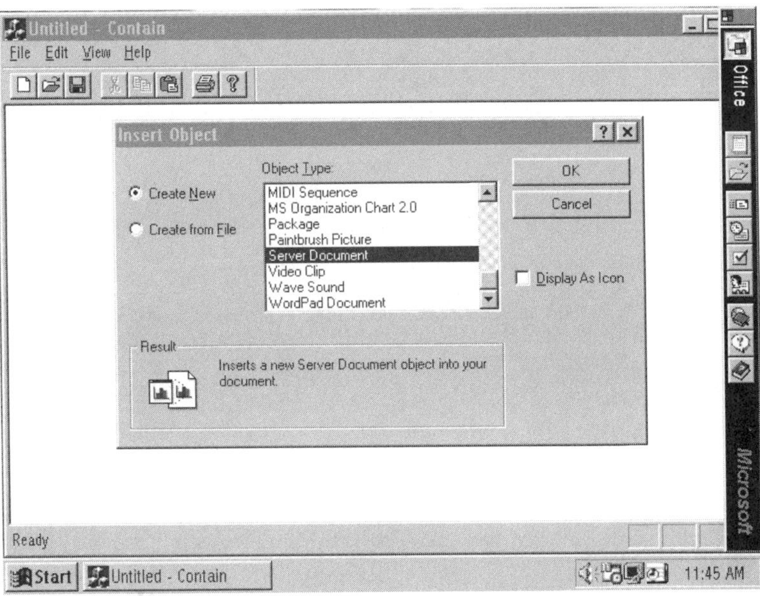

Figure 16.6: The Object dialog box lists the object sources available on your system for the Contain application.

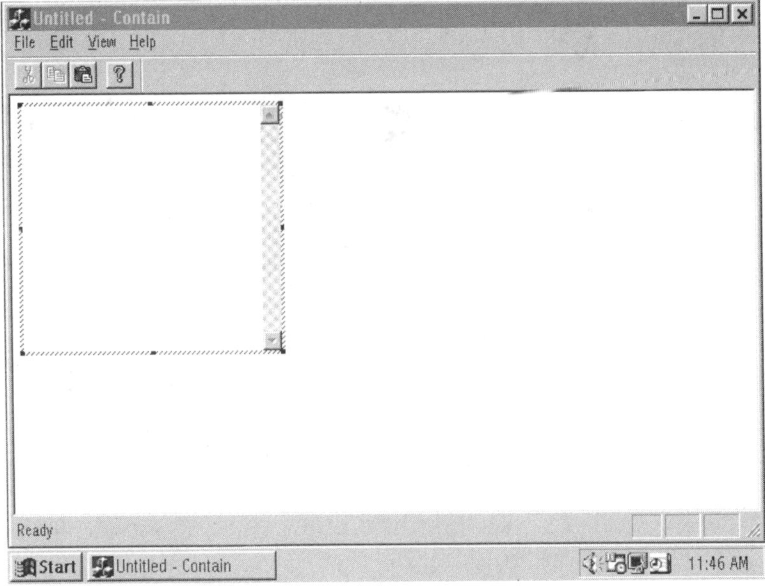

Figure 16.7: The Server object is embedded into the Contain container document.

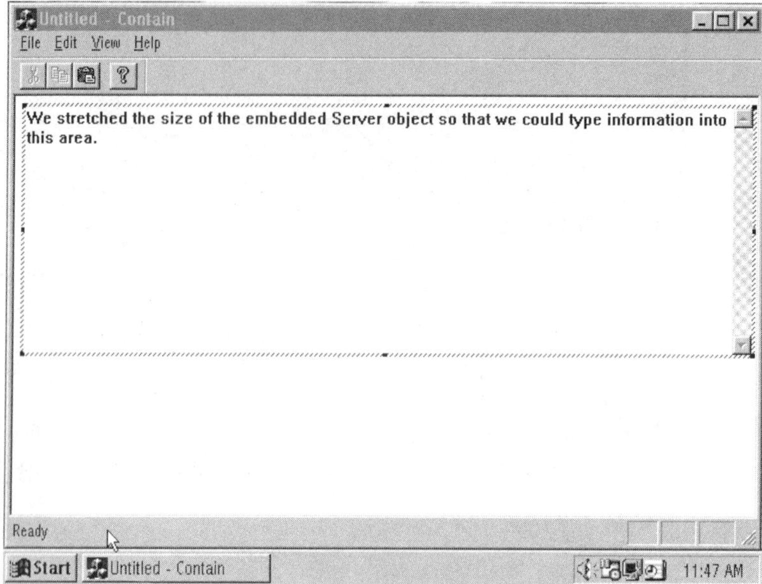

Figure 16.8: Text can be entered in the Server object that is embedded in the Contain container.

As an experiment, why not use Microsoft Word, Excel, or Access as the container? See if you can embed your Server object in one of these containers.

A Word on OLE Automation

The AppWizard permits an automation option when developing OLE containers and servers. Automation is a *programming interface*. This programming interface allows an API to be visible to OLE applications. If a Visual Basic application makes a call to your application, some mechanism must be provided to allow the Visual Basic application to know that your application has a valid automation class and exposed functions and arguments. When the automation option is selected during the design phase of creating a container or server, the protocol IDispatch will be used to provide the required visibility. When the protocol is used, a dispatch map is added to the document class for mapping virtual member functions to unique IDispatch IDs.

Chapter 17

Custom Controls

Windows divides controls into three classes: standard controls, common controls and custom controls. In Chapter 11 you learned how to use several standard controls as you developed dialog boxes. Standard controls include radio buttons, push buttons, edit boxes and list boxes. In Chapter 13 you learned how to work with a new group of controls which have become very popular since the introduction of Windows 95. These common controls include toolbars, tooltips, spin buttons and sliders. In this chapter you will be introduced to the third group of controls, OLE custom controls. The disadvantage of custom controls is the time required to design and implement them. The advantage of custom controls is that you can make any type of control you'd like. Typical custom controls include spreadsheets, word processing, calendar, grids, and so on. As a matter of fact, a whole industry has grown up around the development of commercial-quality custom controls. A good source of commercial custom controls is the Programmer's Paradise catalog. "Programmer's Paradise" can be reached at 800-445-7899.

Visual Basic was the first language that made building custom controls an easy process. These custom controls soon became known as VBX controls after their file extension (.vbx). Custom controls are actually small dynamic-link libraries (dll). A good example of a custom control might be as simple as a custom slide bar control or as complicated as a whole spreadsheet control. Figure 17.1 shows the OLE Custom Control Test Container with three custom controls: a masked edit control, a tab control, and a grid control.

C/C++ programmers initially had to obtain or create Visual Basic custom controls and then integrate them into their C/C++ applications. With the latest release of the Visual C++ compiler in the Microsoft Developer Studio, custom controls can now be directly developed for C/C++ applications. With the release of Windows NT and 95, Microsoft also saw a chance to upgrade custom controls from the original 16-bit versions to 32-bit controls. Unfortunately, the hardware-specific 16-bit custom con-

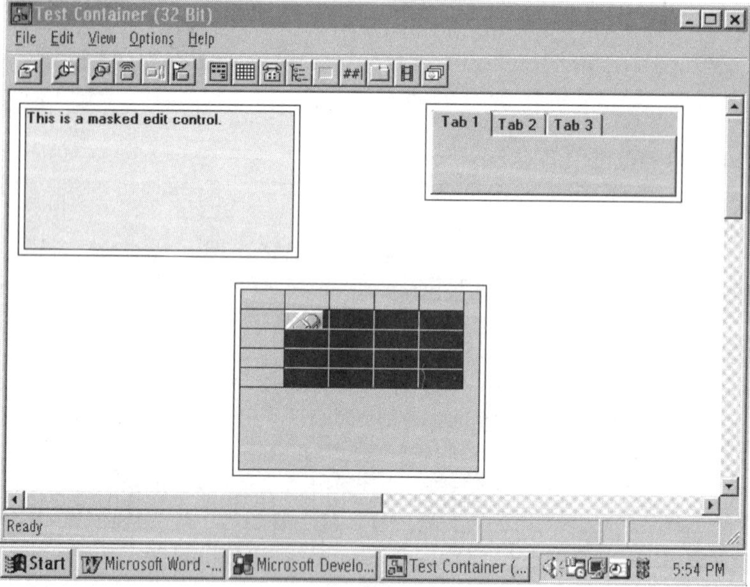

Figure 17.1: Three custom controls being tested in the OLE Custom Control Test Container.

trols would not migrate to the new 32-bit multiple-platform environments. Microsoft decided that rather than patching the specifications for the 16-bit VBX controls, it would redesign specifications to allows custom controls to work under both 16-bit and 32-bit environments. The new controls are called OLE custom controls. OLE custom controls will quickly replace older 16-bit VBX custom controls as users migrate to Windows NT and Windows 95 platforms. OLE custom controls will work in any application designed for their use. These applications include Microsoft Access, Excel, Word, PowerPoint, and the applications developed in Chapter 18 of this book.

The best news for custom control developers is that the Microsoft Developer Studio provides a control wizard to help create and integrate custom controls into your applications. The control wizard is named, naturally enough, OLE Control-Wizard. The OLE ControlWizard generates object-oriented code and makes full use of the Microsoft Foundation Class library (MFC).

The Microsoft Developer Studio also provides a special test container application for testing custom controls while they are being constructed.

While Microsoft continues to support both VBX and OLE custom controls in the 16-bit environments, we strongly recommend moving to the 32-bit arena.

OLE Custom Controls

Custom controls, after all, are just controls. They can be used in dialog boxes, for example, and placed next to standard and common controls. However, custom controls are much more difficult to design and implement. After reading this chapter and Chapter 18, you'll have a better understanding of why the commercial custom control market is flourishing.

If a custom control has not been supplied by a commercial vendor, you will be responsible for the design and implementation of the control. You must first create, write and compile the code that draws the custom control and implements all of the control's methods and so on. This custom control code will become a dynamic-link library. Custom controls use an OCX file extension instead of the DLL extension associated with dynamic-link libraries. Next, the application that is to use the custom control must interact with the control's methods, data, and so on. You must write this code as well.

OLE custom controls should be designed independently from the application in which they are to be used. Commercial vendors, for example, have no idea where a programmer will use their custom controls. Custom controls must therefore be completely re-entrant. Since OLE custom controls are really separate dynamic-linked libraries, they are not linked to the application. Thus, OLE custom controls require a separate instance of data for each use of the control. Messages are the only permissible means of communication allowed between OLE custom controls and the application.

OLE Custom Control Design Requirements

In order to create a successful OLE custom control, the control must be designed to be appealing, easy to understand, and functional. Custom controls should be as uncluttered as possible while still achieving the functionality desired.

The first step in custom control design is to decide how the control will be drawn and displayed on the screen. Talent is required to produce both attractive and functional custom controls. As a programmer, this might not be your strong suit. We've all suffered because of poor user interface designs.

OLE custom controls should be designed to take advantage of changes in control properties that result from the automation interface of the control. Property pages are often used to allow the user to change control properties at run time. Arguments are assigned OLE custom controls. These arguments help control events, set their names, and determine when they should be fired. A control's methods are defined in terms of arguments and return types. The persistence of a control's property states must be determined and implemented.

Important OLE Custom Control Files

The oldctl.h header file contains a description of structures, interfaces, type defs, and methods for OLE custom controls. This header file can be found in the msdevinclude subdirectory of your Microsoft Developer Studio. The following is a small portion of this header file, in order to give you an idea of its contents.

```
    .
    .
    .
// Typedefs for TEXTMETRIC structures
#if defined(_WIN32) && !defined(OLE2ANSI)
typedef TEXTMETRICW TEXTMETRICOLE;
#else
typedef TEXTMETRIC TEXTMETRICOLE;
#endif

typedef TEXTMETRICOLE FAR* LPTEXTMETRICOLE;
// Typedefs for interfaces
#ifdef __cplusplus
interface IOleControl;
interface IOleControlSite;
interface ISimpleFrameSite;
interface IErrorLog;
interface IPropertyBag;
interface IPersistPropertyBag;
interface IPersistStreamInit;
interface IPersistMemory;
interface IPropertyNotifySink;
interface IProvideClassInfo;
interface IProvideClassInfo2;
interface IConnectionPointContainer;
interface IEnumConnectionPoints;
interface IConnectionPoint;
interface IEnumConnections;
interface IClassFactory2;
interface ISpecifyPropertyPages;
interface IPerPropertyBrowsing;
interface IPropertyPageSite;
interface IPropertyPage;
interface IPropertyPage2;
interface IFont;
interface IFontDisp;
interface IPicture;
interface IPictureDisp;
#else
typedef interface IOleControl IOleControl;
typedef interface IOleControlSite IOleControlSite;
typedef interface ISimpleFrameSite ISimpleFrameSite;
typedef interface IErrorLog IErrorLog;
typedef interface IPropertyBag IPropertyBag;
typedef interface IPersistPropertyBag IPersistPropertyBag;
```

```
typedef interface IPersistStreamInit IPersistStreamInit;
typedef interface IPersistMemory IPersistMemory;
typedef interface IPropertyNotifySink IPropertyNotifySink;
typedef interface IProvideClassInfo IProvideClassInfo;
typedef interface IProvideClassInfo2 IProvideClassInfo2;
typedef interface IConnectionPointContainer
                  IConnectionPointContainer;
typedef interface IEnumConnectionPoints IEnumConnectionPoints;
typedef interface IConnectionPoint IConnectionPoint;
typedef interface IEnumConnections IEnumConnections;
typedef interface IClassFactory2 IClassFactory2;
typedef interface ISpecifyPropertyPages ISpecifyPropertyPages;
typedef interface IPerPropertyBrowsing IPerPropertyBrowsing;
typedef interface IPropertyPageSite IPropertyPageSite;
typedef interface IPropertyPage IPropertyPage;
typedef interface IPropertyPage2 IPropertyPage2;
typedef interface IFont IFont;
typedef interface IFontDisp IFontDisp;
typedef interface IPicture IPicture;
typedef interface IPictureDisp IPictureDisp;
#endif
     .
     .
     .
// Typedefs for structs
typedef struct tagPOINTF FAR* LPPOINTF;
typedef struct tagCONTROLINFO FAR* LPCONTROLINFO;
typedef struct tagCONNECTDATA FAR* LPCONNECTDATA;
typedef struct tagLICINFO FAR* LPLICINFO;
typedef struct tagCAUUID FAR* LPCAUUID;
typedef struct tagCALPOLESTR FAR* LPCALPOLESTR;
typedef struct tagCADWORD FAR* LPCADWORD;
typedef struct tagOCPFIPARAMS FAR* LPOCPFIPARAMS;
typedef struct tagPROPPAGEINFO FAR* LPPROPPAGEINFO;
typedef struct tagFONTDESC FAR* LPFONTDESC;
typedef struct tagPICTDESC FAR* LPPICTDESC;
     .
     .
     .
// OLEMISC_ constants
#define OLEMISC_INVISIBLEATRUNTIME  0x00000400L
#define OLEMISC_ALWAYSRUN           0x00000800L
#define OLEMISC_ACTSLIKEBUTTON      0x00001000L
#define OLEMISC_ACTSLIKELABEL       0x00002000L
#define OLEMISC_NOUIACTIVATE        0x00004000L
#define OLEMISC_ALIGNABLE           0x00008000L
#define OLEMISC_SIMPLEFRAME         0x00010000L
#define OLEMISC_SETCLIENTSITEFIRST  0x00020000L
```

```
#define OLEMISC_IMEMODE             0x00040000L
        .
        .
        .

// Property frame APIs
STDAPI OleCreatePropertyFrame(HWND hwndOwner, UINT x, UINT y,
                              LPCOLESTR lpszCaption,
                              ULONG cObjects,
                              LPUNKNOWN FAR* ppUnk,
                              ULONG cPages,
                              LPCLSID pPageClsID,
                              LCID lcid, DWORD dwReserved,
                              LPVOID pvReserved);

STDAPI OleCreatePropertyFrameIndirect(LPOCPFIPARAMS lpParams);

// Standard type APIs
STDAPI OleTranslateColor(OLE_COLOR clr, HPALETTE hpal,
                         COLORREF* lpcolorref);

STDAPI OleCreateFontIndirect(LPFONTDESC lpFontDesc,
                             REFIID riid,
                             LPVOID FAR* lplpvObj);

STDAPI OleCreatePictureIndirect(LPPICTDESC lpPictDesc,
                                REFIID riid, BOOL fOwn,
                                LPVOID FAR* lplpvObj);

STDAPI OleLoadPicture(LPSTREAM lpstream, LONG lSize,
                      BOOL fRunmode, REFIID riid,
                      LPVOID FAR* lplpvObj);

STDAPI_(HCURSOR) OleIconToCursor(HINSTANCE hinstExe,
                                 HICON hIcon);

// IPersistMemory interface
#undef  INTERFACE
#define INTERFACE IPersistMemory

DECLARE_INTERFACE_(IPersistMemory, IPersist)
{
  // IUnknown methods
  STDMETHOD(QueryInterface)(THIS_ REFIID riid,
                            LPVOID FAR* ppvObj) PURE;
  STDMETHOD_(ULONG,AddRef)(THIS) PURE;
  STDMETHOD_(ULONG,Release)(THIS) PURE;

  // IPersist methods
  STDMETHOD(GetClassID)(THIS_ LPCLSID lpClassID) PURE;

  // IPersistMemory methods
  STDMETHOD(IsDirty)(THIS) PURE;
```

```
    STDMETHOD(Load)(THIS_ LPVOID lpStream, ULONG cbSize) PURE;
    STDMETHOD(Save)(THIS_ LPVOID lpStream, BOOL fClearDirty,
                ULONG cbSize) PURE;
    STDMETHOD(GetSizeMax)(THIS_ ULONG* pcbSize) PURE;
    STDMETHOD(InitNew)(THIS) PURE;
};
```

All OLE custom controls are derived from the COleControl base class. The implementation of the COleControl class can be found in the Afxctl.h header file. This header file can be found in the msdevmfcinclude subdirectory. Examine a portion of this file in the next listing.

```
// Classes declared in this file
//CWinApp
  class COleControlModule;        // Module housekeeping .OCX

class CFontHolder;                // manipulating font obj
class CPictureHolder;             // manipulating picture obj

//CWnd
  class COleControl;              // OLE Control

//CDialog
  class COlePropertyPage;         // OLE Property page

class CPropExchange;              // for property exchange
      .
      .
      .
// COleControlModule - base class for .OCX module
//  This object is statically linked into the control.

class COleControlModule : public CWinApp
{
  DECLARE_DYNAMIC(COleControlModule)
public:
  virtual BOOL InitInstance();
  virtual int ExitInstance();
};

//  Module state macro
#define AfxGetControlModuleContext  AfxGetStaticModuleState
#define _afxModuleAddrThis AfxGetStaticModuleState()

// Connection helper functions
BOOL AFXAPI AfxConnectionAdvise(LPUNKNOWN pUnkSrc,
                               REFIID iid,
                               LPUNKNOWN pUnkSink,
                               BOOL bRefCount,
                               DWORD* pdwCookie);
```

```
BOOL AFXAPI AfxConnectionUnadvise(LPUNKNOWN pUnkSrc,
                                  REFIID iid,
                                  LPUNKNOWN pUnkSink,
                                  BOOL bRefCount,
                                  DWORD dwCookie);

// Event maps
enum AFX_EVENTMAP_FLAGS
{
  afxEventCustom = 0,
  afxEventStock = 1,
};

struct AFX_EVENTMAP_ENTRY
{
  AFX_EVENTMAP_FLAGS flags;
  DISPID dispid;
  LPCTSTR pszName;
  LPCSTR lpszParams;
};

struct AFX_EVENTMAP
{
  const AFX_EVENTMAP* lpBaseEventMap;
  const AFX_EVENTMAP_ENTRY* lpEntries;
};

#define DECLARE_EVENT_MAP()
private:
  static const AFX_DATA AFX_EVENTMAP_ENTRY _eventEntries[];
protected:
  static const AFX_DATA AFX_EVENTMAP eventMap;
  virtual const AFX_EVENTMAP* GetEventMap() const;

#define BEGIN_EVENT_MAP(theClass, baseClass)
  const AFX_EVENTMAP* theClass::GetEventMap() const
    (return &eventMap;}
  const AFX_DATADEF AFX_EVENTMAP theClass::eventMap =
    (&(baseClass::eventMap), theClass::_eventEntries};
  const AFX_DATADEF AFX_EVENTMAP_ENTRY
    theClass::_eventEntries[] =
  {
#define END_EVENT_MAP()
    (afxEventCustom, DISPID_UNKNOWN, NULL, NULL},
  };
      .
      .
      .
// Stock events
#define EVENT_STOCK_CLICK()
  (afxEventStock, DISPID_CLICK, _T("Click"), VTS_NONE},
```

```
#define EVENT_STOCK_DBLCLICK()
  (afxEventStock, DISPID_DBLCLICK, _T("DblClick"), VTS_NONE},

#define EVENT_STOCK_KEYDOWN()
  (afxEventStock, DISPID_KEYDOWN, _T("KeyDown"),
   VTS_PI2 VTS_I2},

#define EVENT_STOCK_KEYPRESS()
  (afxEventStock, DISPID_KEYPRESS, _T("KeyPress"), VTS_PI2},

#define EVENT_STOCK_KEYUP()
  (afxEventStock, DISPID_KEYUP, _T("KeyUp"), VTS_PI2 VTS_I2},

#define EVENT_STOCK_MOUSEDOWN()
  (afxEventStock, DISPID_MOUSEDOWN, _T("MouseDown"),
    VTS_I2 VTS_I2 VTS_XPOS_PIXELS VTS_YPOS_PIXELS},

#define EVENT_STOCK_MOUSEMOVE()
  (afxEventStock, DISPID_MOUSEMOVE, _T("MouseMove"),
    VTS_I2 VTS_I2 VTS_XPOS_PIXELS VTS_YPOS_PIXELS},

#define EVENT_STOCK_MOUSEUP()
  (afxEventStock, DISPID_MOUSEUP, _T("MouseUp"),
    VTS_I2 VTS_I2 VTS_XPOS_PIXELS VTS_YPOS_PIXELS},

#define EVENT_STOCK_ERROREVENT()
  (afxEventStock, DISPID_ERROREVENT, _T("Error"),
    VTS_I2 VTS_PBSTR VTS_SCODE VTS_BSTR VTS_BSTR VTS_I4
    VTS_PBOOL},
     .
     .
     .
// Macros for object factory and class ID
#define BEGIN_OLEFACTORY(class_name)
protected:
  class class_name##Factory : public COleObjectFactoryEx
  (
  public:
    class_name##Factory(REFCLSID clsid, CRuntimeClass*
      pRuntimeClass, BOOL bMultiInstance,
        LPCTSTR lpszProgID) :
        COleObjectFactoryEx(clsid, pRuntimeClass,
        bMultiInstance,
        lpszProgID) {}
    virtual BOOL UpdateRegistry(BOOL);
     .
     .
     .
// COleControl - base class for an OLE control
struct _AFXCTL_ADVISE_INFO;     // implementation class
struct _AFXCTL_UIACTIVE_INFO;   // implementation class
class COleControl : public CWnd
```

```
{
  DECLARE_DYNAMIC(COleControl)

// Constructors
public:
  COleControl();

// Operations

  // Initialization
  void SetInitialSize(int cx, int cy);
  void InitializeIIDs(const IID* piidPrimary,
                      const IID* piidEvents);

  // Invalidating
  void InvalidateControl(LPCRECT lpRect = NULL);

  // Modified flag
  BOOL IsModified();
  void SetModifiedFlag(BOOL bModified = TRUE);

  // Drawing operations
  void DoSuperclassPaint(CDC* pDC, const CRect& rcBounds);

  // Property exchange
  BOOL ExchangeExtent(CPropExchange* pPX);
  void ExchangeStockProps(CPropExchange* pPX);
  BOOL ExchangeVersion(CPropExchange* pPX,
                       DWORD dwVersionDefault,
    BOOL bConvert = TRUE);
  BOOL IsConvertingVBX();

  // Stock methods
  void Refresh();
  void DoClick();

  // Stock properties
  short GetAppearance();
  void SetAppearance(short);
  OLE_COLOR GetBackColor();
  void SetBackColor(OLE_COLOR);
  short GetBorderStyle();
  void SetBorderStyle(short);
  BOOL GetEnabled();
  void SetEnabled(BOOL);
  CFontHolder& InternalGetFont();
  LPFONTDISP GetFont();
  void SetFont(LPFONTDISP);
  OLE_COLOR GetForeColor();
  void SetForeColor(OLE_COLOR);
  OLE_HANDLE GetHwnd();
  const CString& InternalGetText();
```

```
    BSTR GetText();
    void SetText(LPCTSTR);
        .
        .
        .
protected:
    // Friend classes
    friend class COleControlInnerUnknown;
    friend class CReflectorWnd;
    friend class CControlFrameWnd;
        .
        .
        .
    // Drawing
    void DrawContent(CDC* pDC, CRect& rc);
    void DrawMetafile(CDC* pDC, CRect& rc);
    BOOL GetMetafileData(LPFORMATETC lpFormatEtc,
                         LPSTGMEDIUM lpStgMedium);
        .
        .
        .
    // Stock events
    void KeyDown(USHORT* pnChar);
    void KeyUp(USHORT* pnChar);
    void ButtonDown(USHORT iButton, UINT nFlags, CPoint point);
    void ButtonUp(USHORT iButton, UINT nFlags, CPoint point);
        .
        .
        .
// Message Maps
protected:
    //{{AFX_MSG(COleControl)
    afx_msg void OnKeyDown(UINT nChar, UINT nRepCnt, UINT nFlags);
    afx_msg void OnKeyUp(UINT nChar, UINT nRepCnt, UINT nFlags);
    afx_msg void OnChar(UINT nChar, UINT nRepCnt, UINT nFlags);
    afx_msg void OnMouseMove(UINT nFlags, CPoint point);
    afx_msg void OnLButtonDown(UINT nFlags, CPoint point);
    afx_msg void OnLButtonUp(UINT nFlags, CPoint point);
    afx_msg void OnLButtonDblClk(UINT nFlags, CPoint point);
    afx_msg void OnMButtonDown(UINT nFlags, CPoint point);
    afx_msg void OnMButtonUp(UINT nFlags, CPoint point);
    afx_msg void OnMButtonDblClk(UINT nFlags, CPoint point);
    afx_msg void OnRButtonDown(UINT nFlags, CPoint point);
    afx_msg void OnRButtonUp(UINT nFlags, CPoint point);
        .
        .
        .
```

This listing should give you an idea of how the COleControl class is derived. Spend some time examining these two header files or print a copy that you can reference in the future.

Custom Control Events

Custom control events are responses or actions triggered by the control in response to an action on the control. For example, an event might be a key press or mouse button click.

Your control class will be derived from the COleControl base class. As such it will be able to use a new map that enables messages. These custom control messages or events are then sent to the application. This application is called a control container. The application or container receives information about an event when something happens to the control—perhaps a key press. Event parameters can be used to provide additional information regarding an event.

OLE custom controls communicate with applications (containers) by firing events. Stock and custom events are provided by OLE and can be used by your custom control. Stock events are handled by the COleControl as a default. Custom events can be used to signal the application (container) when a control event has occurred—for example, when a message is received.

Custom Control Methods and Properties

In order to have interactive communications between a custom control and an application, the control must expose a set of methods (functions) and properties (interface) to the application that is using the custom control. Methods, in this case, are control functions that permit external code to alter characteristics of the custom control. These characteristics include appearance, properties and behavior. Control properties include things such as colors, text, and fonts used by the custom control.

A control's methods and properties allow the appearance and values of the control to be changed. Both methods and properties are user-defined while the custom control is being developed with the OLE ClassWizard. Stock methods, for example, are provided by the COleControl class. Custom methods can be added when additional custom features are needed for the control.

A primary interface allows early bound access to the control's methods and properties. Object methods are exposed as methods, and properties as get/set method pairs. IDispatch is used for late bound access. The application using the custom control decides which type of binding is provided the user. OLE custom controls can also provide extended properties, methods, and events.

Custom Control Persistence

Controls support persistence to streams through IPersistStream and persistence to storage through IPersistStorage. IPersistStorage is used for continued support of compound document applications. IPersistStream allows embedded controls to be saved to streams, when possible.

OLE controls use persistence to read or write property values to and from a file or stream. Applications can use persistence to store property values for the control. The property values can be retrieved later if a new instance of the control is created.

For example, the parameter PX_Bool is used to exchange a control property of type BOOL.

Custom Control Containers

Most OLE containers now provide the attributes necessary for supporting OLE custom controls. For example, the OLE container application developed in Chapter 16 will support OLE custom controls. Containers, in addition to other attributes, must provide support for events and ambient properties.

As part of the communications interface, custom controls must convert events from the user into events that can be used by the container. For each converted event, the container supplies an entry point for responding to the event. When container properties apply to all controls in a container, they are called ambient properties. For example, ambient properties might include the fonts or colors used by a custom control.

In Chapter 18 you will learn how to use the OLE ControlWizard to design a simple custom control. Then you'll learn how to test the control using the standard test container.

Chapter 18

Developing Custom Controls

Microsoft OLE custom controls are dynamic link libraries with OCX file extensions. These 32-bit OLE controls for Windows 95 and Windows NT replace the older 16-bit VBX custom controls which were developed with Microsoft's Visual Basic.

OLE custom controls are easy to design and implement by using a new wizard. This new wizard is called the ControlWizard. You can create an OLE custom control by selecting the New... menu item from the Microsoft Developer Studio's File menu. From the New Project Workspace dialog box, select the OLE ControlWizard option to begin the design process.

During the design process, the ControlWizard will create a default custom control. The default control can then be customized to the designer's specifications. During the design phase, custom controls can be tested in the Microsoft Test Container. The Test Container is a special application designed to test and allow experimenting with the control under development.

This chapter will take you step-by-step through the development of a default custom control named Clock. You'll then learn how to modify the features of this clock control and add some items that will make it unique.

CREATING A DEFAULT CUSTOM CONTROL

A step by step approach can be used for creating a custom control using the ControlWizard. Once a default custom control is developed, it can be modified by adding additional features.

Using the ControlWizard

Start the custom control design process by selecting the New... menu item from the Microsoft Developer Studio's File menu. From the New Project Workspace dialog box, select the OLE ControlWizard option to begin the design process, as shown in Figure 18.1.

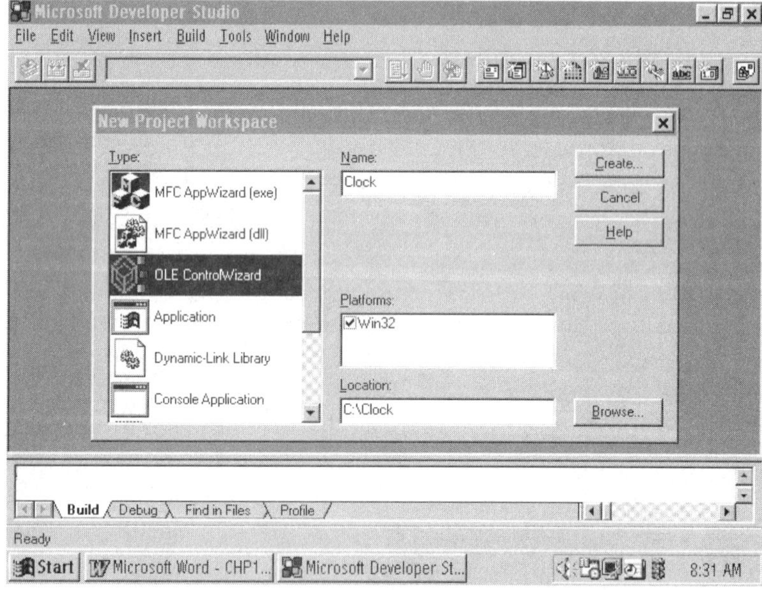

Figure 18.1: Selecting the OLE ControlWizard begins the custom control design process.

The New Project Workspace dialog box allows you to also set the project name and location. Accept these values by clicking the Create... button.

The ControlWizard will then display the first of two steps, in the control building process, as shown in Figure 18.2.

The default selections are made for step 1. The number of controls for the project is limited to one. No runtime license is generated. Comments are included with the control's code, and no help files are created. Select Next to move to step 2 of the custom control design process.

Figure 18.3 shows additional project options that can be set or modified during the custom control design process.

The defaults were again used for this control, with just one exception. The check box labeled Available in "Insert Object" dialog is checked. To complete the design process, click on the Finish button.

When the Finish button is pushed, the ControlWizard will list control information in the New Project Information dialog box, as shown in Figure 18.4.

If this information accurately reflects the custom control's design criteria, push the OK button to accept the information.

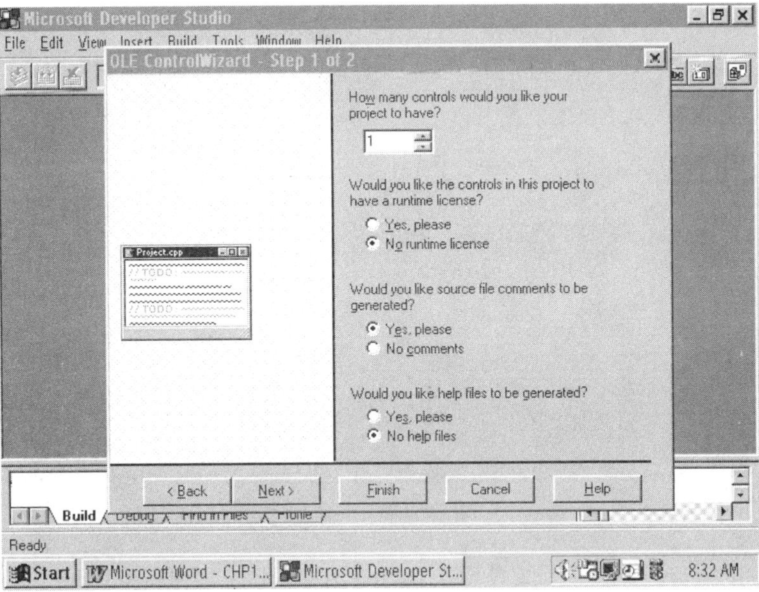

Figure 18.2: The first step, of two, in the custom control building process.

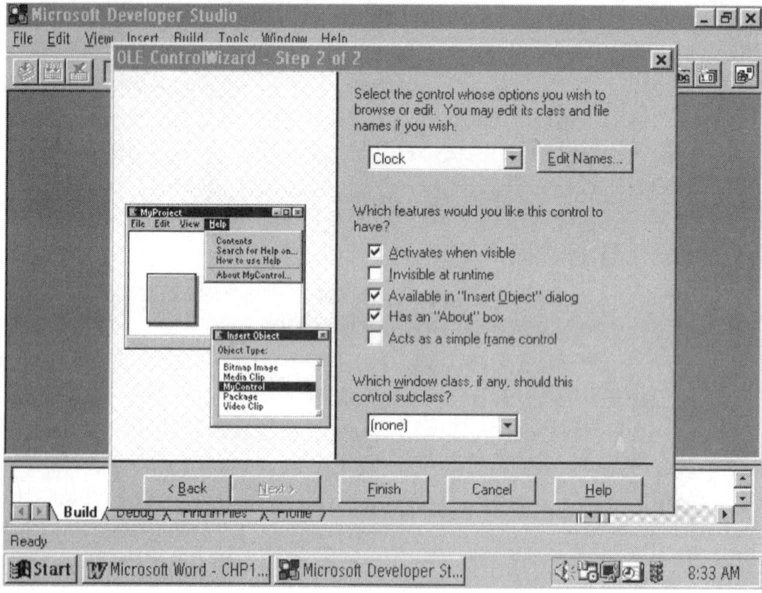

Figure 18.3: The second step, of two, in the custom control building process.

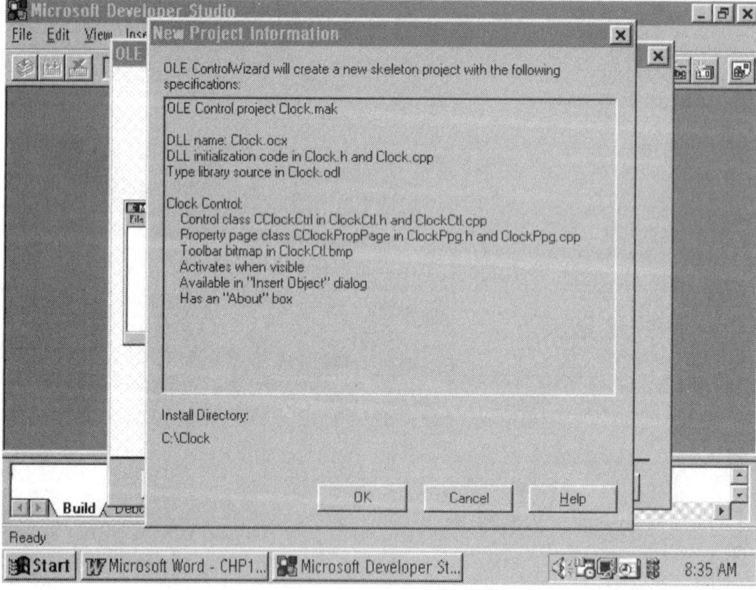

Figure 18.4: The default control's project information.

When the OK button is pushed, the ControlWizard will return you to the Microsoft Developer Studio window.

Build the default custom control by selecting the Rebuild All menu item from the Build menu.

Using the OLE Control Test Container

The Microsoft Developer Studio will build the OLE custom control and register it with the system.

At this point, we have not added any features to the default custom control generated by the ControlWizard. However, even the default control can be viewed with the use of the OLE Control Test Container. Use the Tools menu and select the OLE Control Test Container menu item, as shown in Figure 18.5.

When the OLE Control Test Container initially appears, its client area will be blank. Your custom control can be selected by using the Edit menu and selecting the Insert OLE Control... menu item, as shown in Figure 18.6.

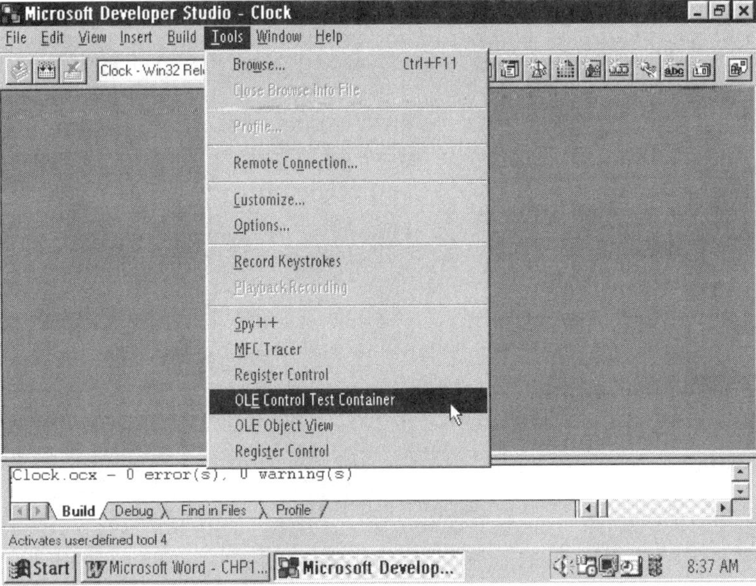

Figure 18.5: The default custom control can be examined with the OLE Control Test Container.

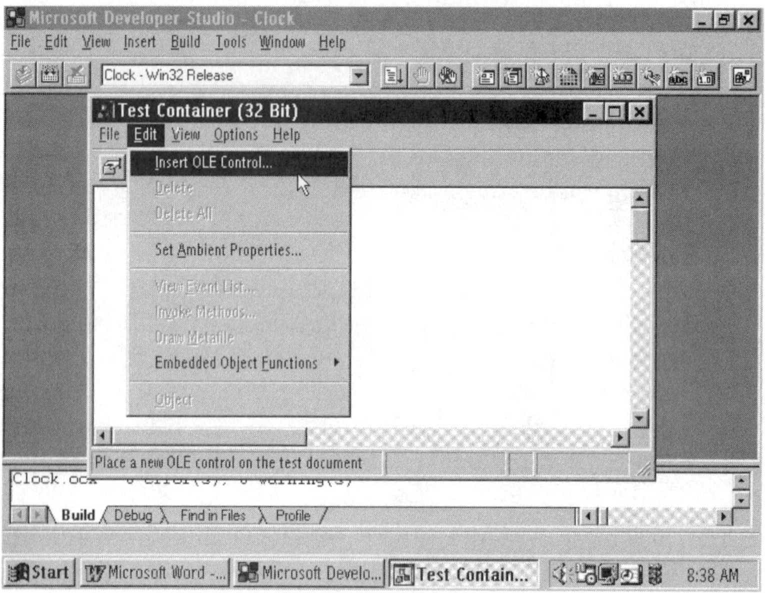

Figure 18.6: The Insert OLE Control... menu item will allow you to insert your new custom control.

When the Insert OLE Control... menu item is selected, you'll be able to select your new custom control from the Insert OLE Control dialog box. This dialog box contains a list of all registered controls, as shown in Figure 18.7.

If you examine Figure 18.7 you will notice that the Clock Control has already been selected in the list. Use the OK button to bring that control into the test container. Figure 18.8 shows the Clock control inserted into the test container.

All controls initially take on this appearance. By default, the control is an ellipse enclosed in a bounding rectangle.

Understanding the ControlWizard's Code

The ControlWizard, like the AppWizard, generates several C++ source code files for the custom controls in addition to header and resource files. In this example the source code files are named stdafx.cpp, Clock.cpp, ClockPpg.cpp, and ClockCtl.cpp.

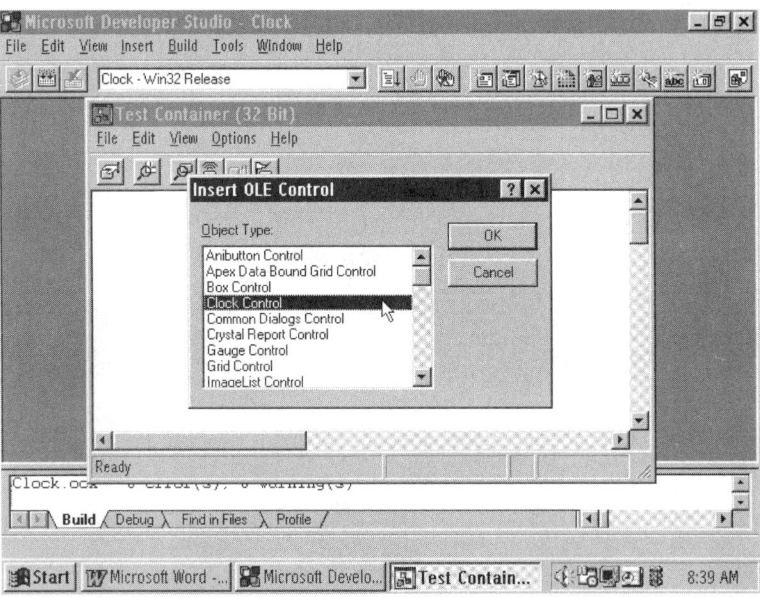

Figure 18.7: Registered controls are listed in the Insert OLE Control dialog box.

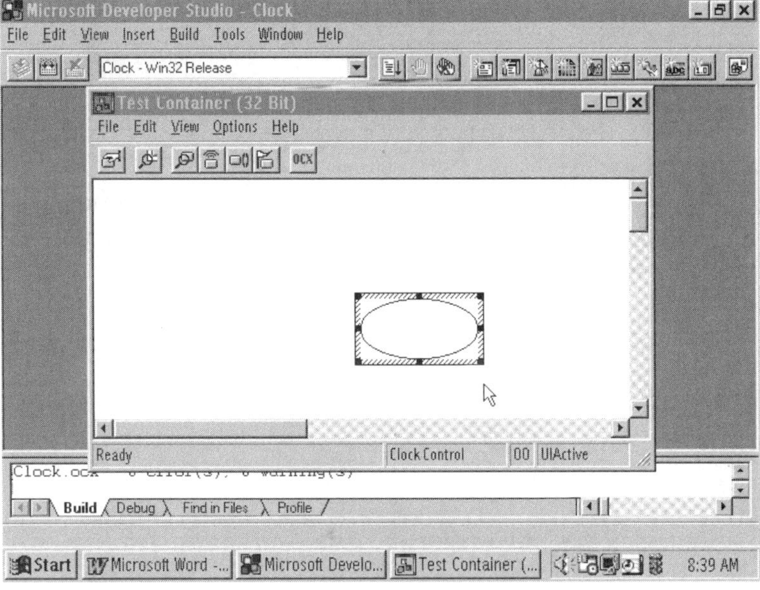

Figure 18.8: The initial Clock control is inserted into the test container.

In this section, we'll examine the role of the Clock.cpp, ClockPpg.cpp, and ClockCtl.cpp files as they relate to the default custom control.

The Clock.cpp File

This file is responsible for the implementation of the CClock-App class and the registration of the subsequent DLL code.

```
// Clock.cpp : Implement CClockApp and DLL registration.

#include "stdafx.h"
#include "Clock.h"

#ifdef _DEBUG
#define new DEBUG_NEW
#undef THIS_FILE
static char THIS_FILE[] = __FILE__;
#endif

CClockApp NEAR theApp;

const GUID CDECL BASED_CODE _tlid =
    { 0xc39b3360, 0x2c83, 0x11cf,
    { 0xaa, 0x36, 0x44, 0x45, 0x53, 0x54, 0, 0 } };
const WORD _wVerMajor = 1;
const WORD _wVerMinor = 0;

// CClockApp::InitInstance - DLL initialization

BOOL CClockApp::InitInstance()
{
  BOOL bInit = COleControlModule::InitInstance();

  if (bInit)
  {
    // TODO: Add your own module initialization code here.
  }

  return bInit;
}

// CClockApp::ExitInstance - DLL termination

int CClockApp::ExitInstance()
{
  // TODO: Add your own module termination code here.

  return COleControlModule::ExitInstance();
}

// DllRegisterServer - Adds entries to the system registry
```

```
STDAPI DllRegisterServer(void)
{
  AFX_MANAGE_STATE(_afxModuleAddrThis);

  if (!AfxOleRegisterTypeLib(AfxGetInstanceHandle(), _tlid))
    return ResultFromScode(SELFREG_E_TYPELIB);

  if (!COleObjectFactoryEx::UpdateRegistryAll(TRUE))
    return ResultFromScode(SELFREG_E_CLASS);

  return NOERROR;
}

// DllUnregisterServer - Removes entries from system registry

STDAPI DllUnregisterServer(void)
{
  AFX_MANAGE_STATE(_afxModuleAddrThis);

  if (!AfxOleUnregisterTypeLib(_tlid))
    return ResultFromScode(SELFREG_E_TYPELIB);

  if (!COleObjectFactoryEx::UpdateRegistryAll(FALSE))
    return ResultFromScode(SELFREG_E_CLASS);

  return NOERROR;
}
```

Examine the previous listing and note the four sections of code printed in a bolded font. These sections of code are responsible for DLL initialization, registration, deregistration, and termination.

Initialization The **InitInstance()** function is used to initialize all instances for this control. Notice that room is provided for additional initialization code for any code modules that are being added.

Registration The **AfxOleRegisterTypeLib()** function is used with the **UpdateRegistryAllEx()** function. When a TRUE parameter is used, all of the application's object factories are registered with the OLE system registry. Registration usually takes place when the application is first launched.

Deregistration The **AfxOleUnregisterTypeLib()** function is used with the **UpdateRegistryAllEx()** function. A FALSE parameter is passed to make sure the application's object factories are deregistered with the OLE system registry.

Termination The **ExitInstance()** function is used whenever an instance of the control is terminated. Space is provided so that any module termination code can also be added to this section.

The ClockPpg.cpp File

This file derives the CClockPropPage class from Microsoft's COlePropertyPage class. Examine the following listing.

```
// ClockPpg.cpp : Implement CClockPropPage property page.

#include "stdafx.h"
#include "Clock.h"
#include "ClockPpg.h"

#ifdef _DEBUG
#define new DEBUG_NEW
#undef THIS_FILE
static char THIS_FILE[] = __FILE__;
#endif

IMPLEMENT_DYNCREATE(CClockPropPage, COlePropertyPage)

// Message map

BEGIN_MESSAGE_MAP(CClockPropPage, COlePropertyPage)
  //{{AFX_MSG_MAP(CClockPropPage)
  // NOTE - ClassWizard will add/remove message map entries
  //    DO NOT EDIT these blocks of generated code !
  //}}AFX_MSG_MAP
END_MESSAGE_MAP()

// Initialize class factory and guid

IMPLEMENT_OLECREATE_EX(CClockPropPage,
                       "CLOCK.ClockPropPage.1",
                       0xc39b3364, 0x2c83, 0x11cf, 0xaa,
                       0x36, 0x44, 0x45, 0x53, 0x54, 0, 0)

// CClockPropPage::CClockPropPageFactory::UpdateRegistry -
// Adds or removes system registry entries for CClockPropPage

BOOL CClockPropPage::CClockPropPageFactory::
                    UpdateRegistry(BOOL bRegister)
{
  if (bRegister)
    return AfxOleRegisterPropertyPageClass
          (AfxGetInstanceHandle(), m_clsid, IDS_CLOCK_PPG);
  else
    return AfxOleUnregisterClass(m_clsid, NULL);
}
```

```
// CClockPropPage::CClockPropPage - Constructor

CClockPropPage::CClockPropPage() :
  COlePropertyPage(IDD, IDS_CLOCK_PPG_CAPTION)
{
  //{{AFX_DATA_INIT(CClockPropPage)
  // NOTE: ClassWizard will add member initialization here
  //    DO NOT EDIT these blocks of generated code !
  //}}AFX_DATA_INIT
}

// CClockPropPage::DoDataExchange
//   - Moves data between page and properties

void CClockPropPage::DoDataExchange(CDataExchange* pDX)
{
  //{{AFX_DATA_MAP(CClockPropPage)
  // NOTE: ClassWizard will add DDP, DDX, and DDV calls here
  //    DO NOT EDIT these blocks of generated code !
  //}}AFX_DATA_MAP
  DDP_PostProcessing(pDX);
}

// CClockPropPage message handlers
```

This file is mainly responsible for the registration of the property page class. The **AfxOleRegisterPropertyPageClass()** function is used to register the property page class with the registration database. When the property page class is registered, it can be used by other OLE containers that are made aware of the OLE custom control. The system registry, along with the property page name and location is updated after a call is made to this function.

You will also notice that the COlePropertyPage can use the constructor to identify the dialog template resource on which the property page is based. The string resource containing the caption is also identified. The COlePropertyPage is the class from which the CClockPropPage class is derived.

The **DoDataExchange()** function is used by the framework to exchange and validate data. In this case, its job is to move data between the page and properties of the control.

The ClockCtl.cpp File

This file is used for the actual implementation of the custom control's OLE class. In this example, that class is CClockCtrl. This is the file you will most likely spend most of your time editing. In this file, you will be able to create unique implementations of your custom control from the default custom control provided by the ControlWizard

Let's examine the specific code allotted to the default custom control. Study the following listing.

```
// ClockCtl.cpp : Implement CClockCtrl OLE control class.

#include "stdafx.h"
#include "Clock.h"
#include "ClockCtl.h"
#include "ClockPpg.h"

#ifdef _DEBUG
#define new DEBUG_NEW
#undef THIS_FILE
static char THIS_FILE[] = __FILE__;
#endif

IMPLEMENT_DYNCREATE(CClockCtrl, COleControl)

// Message map

BEGIN_MESSAGE_MAP(CClockCtrl, COleControl)
  //{{AFX_MSG_MAP(CClockCtrl)
  // NOTE - ClassWizard will add/remove message map entries
  //    DO NOT EDIT these blocks of generated code !
  //}}AFX_MSG_MAP
  ON_OLEVERB(AFX_IDS_VERB_EDIT, OnEdit)
  ON_OLEVERB(AFX_IDS_VERB_PROPERTIES, OnProperties)
END_MESSAGE_MAP()

// Dispatch map

BEGIN_DISPATCH_MAP(CClockCtrl, COleControl)
  //{{AFX_DISPATCH_MAP(CClockCtrl)
  // NOTE - ClassWizard will add/remove dispatch map entries
  //    DO NOT EDIT these blocks of generated code !
  //}}AFX_DISPATCH_MAP
  DISP_FUNCTION_ID(CClockCtrl, "AboutBox", DISPID_ABOUTBOX,
                   AboutBox, VT_EMPTY, VTS_NONE)
END_DISPATCH_MAP()

// Event map

BEGIN_EVENT_MAP(CClockCtrl, COleControl)
  //{{AFX_EVENT_MAP(CClockCtrl)
  // NOTE - ClassWizard will add/remove event map entries
  //    DO NOT EDIT these blocks of generated code !
  //}}AFX_EVENT_MAP
END_EVENT_MAP()
```

```
// Property pages

// TODO: Add more property pages as needed and increase count!
BEGIN_PROPPAGEIDS(CClockCtrl, 1)
  PROPPAGEID(CClockPropPage::guid)
END_PROPPAGEIDS(CClockCtrl)

// Initialize class factory and guid

IMPLEMENT_OLECREATE_EX(CClockCtrl, "CLOCK.ClockCtrl.1",
                       0xc39b3363, 0x2c83, 0x11cf, 0xaa,
                       0x36, 0x44, 0x45, 0x53, 0x54, 0, 0)

// Type library ID and version

IMPLEMENT_OLETYPELIB(CClockCtrl, _tlid,
                     _wVerMajor, _wVerMinor)

// Interface IDs

const IID BASED_CODE IID_DClock =
    { 0xc39b3361, 0x2c83, 0x11cf, { 0xaa, 0x36, 0x44, 0x45,
      0x53, 0x54, 0, 0 } };
const IID BASED_CODE IID_DClockEvents =
    { 0xc39b3362, 0x2c83, 0x11cf, { 0xaa, 0x36, 0x44, 0x45,
      0x53, 0x54, 0, 0 } };

// Control type information

static const DWORD BASED_CODE _dwClockOleMisc =
  OLEMISC_ACTIVATEWHENVISIBLE |
  OLEMISC_SETCLIENTSITEFIRST |
  OLEMISC_INSIDEOUT |
  OLEMISC_CANTLINKINSIDE |
  OLEMISC_RECOMPOSEONRESIZE;

IMPLEMENT_OLECTLTYPE(CClockCtrl, IDS_CLOCK, _dwClockOleMisc)

// CClockCtrl::CClockCtrlFactory::UpdateRegistry -
// Adds or removes system registry entries for CClockCtrl

BOOL CClockCtrl::CClockCtrlFactory::
                 UpdateRegistry(BOOL bRegister)
{
  if (bRegister)
    return AfxOleRegisterControlClass(
      AfxGetInstanceHandle(),
      m_clsid,
      m_lpszProgID,
      IDS_CLOCK,
      IDB_CLOCK,
      TRUE,                       // Insertable
      _dwClockOleMisc,
```

```
        _tlid,
        _wVerMajor,
        _wVerMinor);
  else
    return AfxOleUnregisterClass(m_clsid, m_lpszProgID);
}

// CClockCtrl::CClockCtrl - Constructor

CClockCtrl::CClockCtrl()
{
  InitializeIIDs(&IID_DClock, &IID_DClockEvents);

  // TODO: Initialize your control s instance data here.
}

// CClockCtrl::~CClockCtrl - Destructor

CClockCtrl::~CClockCtrl()
{
  // TODO: Cleanup your control s instance data here.
}

// CClockCtrl::OnDraw - Drawing function

void CClockCtrl::OnDraw(
      CDC* pdc, const CRect& rcBounds, const CRect& rcInvalid)
{
  // TODO: Replace with your own drawing code.
  pdc->FillRect(rcBounds,
  CBrush::FromHandle((HBRUSH)GetStockObject(WHITE_BRUSH)));
  pdc->Ellipse(rcBounds);
}

// CClockCtrl::DoPropExchange - Persistence support

void CClockCtrl::DoPropExchange(CPropExchange* pPX)
{
  ExchangeVersion(pPX, MAKELONG(_wVerMinor, _wVerMajor));
  COleControl::DoPropExchange(pPX);

  // TODO: Call PX_ functions for each custom property.

}
// CClockCtrl::OnResetState - Reset control to default state

void CClockCtrl::OnResetState()
{
  COleControl::OnResetState();  // Resets defaults

  // TODO: Reset any other control state here.
}

// CClockCtrl::AboutBox - Display an "About" box

void CClockCtrl::AboutBox()
```

```
{
  CDialog dlgAbout(IDD_ABOUTBOX_CLOCK);
  dlgAbout.DoModal();
}

// CClockCtrl message handlers
```

The message map, dispatch map, and event map are automatically created and edited by the various wizards. You will not directly edit these maps as you add features to your custom control.

Message maps are an important alternative to the switch statement used in procedure-oriented to handle messages. OLE Automation provides a means of call methods and access properties across several applications. These requests are dispatched via the dispatch map. The event map helps process custom control events, such as the click of a mouse button on the control.

This code listing shows the implementation of the OLE type library. A type library is a file or component contained in another file that holds type information. Type libraries allow OLE custom controls to exchange information concerning various properties and methods.

Class factories are used to create one or more instances of a an object identified by the CLSID (class identifier). This object implements the IClassFactory interface, which in turn is used to create additional objects of the given class.

In the following sections, the bolded sections of the previous code listing will be examined in more detail.

The *OnDraw()* Function This section of code is responsible for drawing the control's shape in the bounding rectangle.

The default shape is drawn with the **Ellipse()** function. The control is bound by the bounding rectangle specified with *rcBounds* values. The use of *rcBounds* allows the control to be sized. The default bounding rectangle area is filled with the stock WHITE_BRUSH.

Persistence Support Persistence allows an OLE control to read or write property values to and from a file or stream. An application (container) can use persistence to store property values for a custom control. Property values can then be retrieved when an instance of the control is created. For example, PX_Color is used to serialize or initialize a property of type

OLE_COLOR. The property's value is read or written to the variable referenced by *clrValue*. When *clrDefault* is used, the property's default value is accessed.

PX functions can be added for each persistent property that is included.

The About Box The ControlWizard designs a default About box. The contents of this simple dialog box can be edited to suit your project's needs. The About box uses a standard modal style.

Creating a Real Clock Control

The ClassWizard is used to modify the default custom control produced by the ControlWizard.

To build a real Clock custom control, start with the default custom control described in the previous section. Here are the features for the real Clock control:

- The Clock control will always draw a round clock face, never an ellipse.
- The Clock face will be a unique color.
- The background of the Clock control will changed to match the background of the container application using the control.
- The Clock control will respond to a mouse event within the control and report the current system time.

All of these new features can be added to the control by just working with the ClockCtl.cpp and ClockCtl.h files. In the next section, we'll add several of the new features.

Changing the Shaps, Size, and Color of the Clock

Start the Microsoft Developer Studio's ClassWizard by selecting the ClassWizard menu item from the View menu. Now follow these steps, which will allow the shape and color properties of the control to be modified:

1. Select the OLE Automation tab from within the MFC ClassWizard dialog box.
2. Select CClockCtrl from the Class name list box.

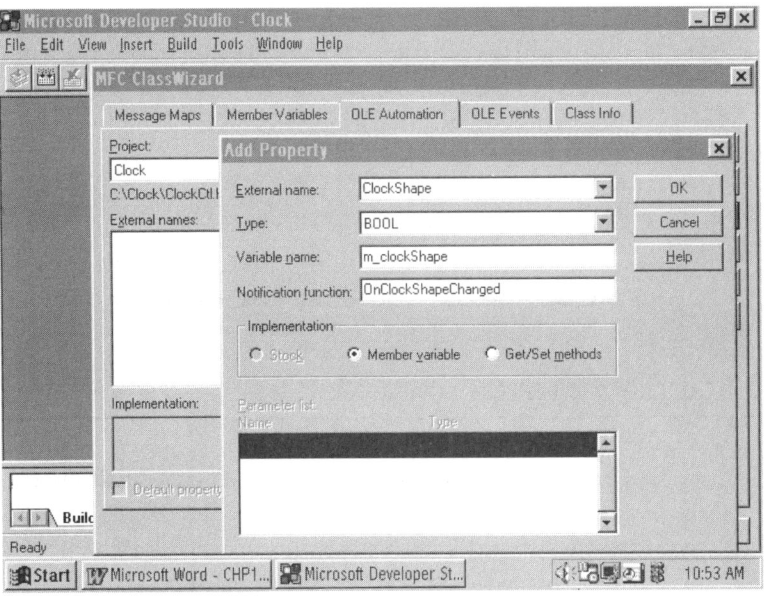

Figure 18.9: Use the Add Property dialog box to add the ClockShape property.

3. Use the Add Property button to display the Add Property dialog box (see Figure 18.9).
4. Enter the name "ClockShape" as the External name.
5. Select Member variable as the implementation.
6. Choose BOOL from the drop down Type list box. Notice that the Notification function edit control contains OnClockShapeChanged. The member variable is *m_clockShape*.
7. Accept these values with the OK button, and return to the OLE Automation tab.
8. Select the Add Property button, again, and display the Add Property dialog box.
9. In the edit control of the External name combo box, select BackColor from the drop down list of available items.
10. For an Implementation, select Stock.
11. Accept these values with the OK button, and return to the OLE Automation tab. The MFC ClassWizard dialog box should be similar to Figure 18.10.
12. Use the OK push button to accept the choices and close the ClassWizard.

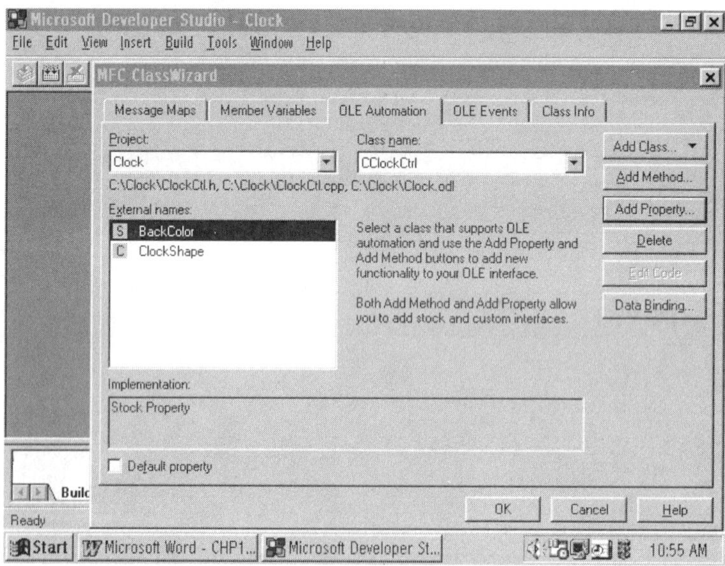

Figure 18.10: The ClassWizard will add BackColor and ClockShape properties to the project.

The ClassWizard will create the code to add the ClockShape and BackColor properties to the CClockCtrl class. The CClockCtrl class's dispatch map will be altered to accommodate the ClockShape property, and the BackColor property is added to the clock.odl library file. A declaration for the **OnClockShapeChanged()** function is added to the ClockCtl.h header file.

The previous changes are added automatically by the ClassWizard. Now, it becomes our job to write the code that reacts to these changes.

The ClockCtl.h File

A function will be written to determine the correct size of the clock face. This function will be called **GetDrawRect()**. Include the function in the ClockCtl.h file just after the destructor, as shown in the following partial listing.

```
// Implementation
 protected:
   ~CClockCtrl();
      .
      .
      .
```

```
void GetDrawRect(CRect* rc);    // Clock Size
    .
    .
    .
DECLARE_OLECREATE_EX(CClockCtrl) //Class factory and guid
```

The code for this function will be included in the ClockCtl.cpp file, shown in the next section.

The ClockCtl.cpp File

The following partial listing of the ClockCtl.cpp file shows those sections of code that must be modified. This file is identical to the default file returned by the ControlWizard, except for the bolded lines of code which add or modify control features.

```
// clockctl.cpp : Implementation of the CClockCtrl OLE
// control class.
      .
      .
      .
  CBrush* pOldBrush;
  CBrush NewBrush(TranslateColor(GetBackColor()));
  CPen* pOldPen;
  CPen NewPen;
  CRect rc = rcBounds;
  int xcenter, ycenter;

  pdc->FillRect(rcBounds, &NewBrush);
  GetDrawRect(&rc);

  NewPen.CreatePen(PS_SOLID,3,RGB(0,0,0));
  pOldPen=(CPen*)pdc->SelectObject(&NewPen);

  NewBrush.CreateSolidBrush(RGB(255,255,0));
  pOldBrush=(CBrush*)pdc->SelectObject(&NewBrush);

  pdc->Ellipse(rc);

  // Clock hands
  xcenter=(rc.right-rc.left)/2 + rc.left;
  ycenter=(rc.bottom-rc.top)/2 + rc.top;
  pdc->MoveTo(xcenter,ycenter);
  pdc->LineTo(rc.right*75/100,rc.bottom*75/100);
  pdc->MoveTo(xcenter,ycenter);
  pdc->LineTo(xcenter,rc.bottom*90/100);

  pdc->SelectObject(pOldPen);
  pdc->SelectObject(pOldBrush);
}
```

```
    .
    .
    .
void CClockCtrl::GetDrawRect(CRect* rc)
{
  // Round clock face
  int dx = rc->right - rc->left;
  int dy = rc->bottom - rc->top;
  if (dx > dy) {
    rc->left += (dx - dy) / 2;
    rc->right = rc->left + dy;
  }
  else {
    rc->top += (dy - dx) / 2;
    rc->bottom = rc->top + dx;
  }
}
```

The Clock Control's Background Color The control's background color can be set to match the container's background color with just a few lines of code.

```
CBrush  NewBrush(TranslateColor(GetBackColor()));
     .
     .
     .
pdc->FillRect(rcBounds, &NewBrush);
```

The **FillRect()** function is used to fill the bounding rectangle of the custom control with a color described by the current brush. The current brush is returned by making calls to the **TranslateColor(GetBackColor())** functions.

If this technique isn't used, and the container's background differs from the control's background color, the control will appear boxed in a rectangle of a different color.

The Clock Control's Shape and Size The clock face is drawn by using the ellipse function. The clock face is drawn and then filled with the yellow brush.

```
CBrush* pOldBrush;
CBrush NewBrush(TranslateColor(GetBackColor()));
    .
    .
    .
pdc->FillRect(rcBounds, & NewBrush);
```

```
GetDrawRect(&rc);
    .
    .
    .
NewBrush.CreateSolidBrush(RGB(255,255,0));
pOldBrush = (CBrush*)pdc->SelectObject(&NewBrush);

pdc->Ellipse(rc);
```

A test is made in order not to end up with an elliptical clock. The smaller of the X or Y extent, determined by the **GetDrawRect()** function, of the bounding rectangle is used for the diameter of the clock face. This information is passed to the **Ellipse()** function by *rc*, which holds the coordinates of the bounding rectangular area.

The clock's hands are drawn with the use of the **MoveTo()** and **LineTo()** functions.

```
xcenter = (rc.right - rc.left) / 2 + rc.left;
ycenter = (rc.bottom - rc.top) / 2 + rc.top;
pdc->MoveTo(xcenter, ycenter);
pdc->LineTo(rc.right * 75 / 100, rc.bottom * 75 / 100);
pdc->MoveTo(xcenter, ycenter);
pdc->LineTo(xcenter, rc.bottom * 90 / 100);
```

They are drawn a proportional distance from the center of the clock face.

Responding to Mouse Events

In this section, you'll learn how to make the Clock control respond to a mouse event. If the cursor is on the Clock control when the left mouse button is depressed, the Clock will change color and report the system time to the control. The color change and time information are indicators that a control "hit" has occurred.

Here are a list of steps needed to implement the "hit" features:

1. Select the OLE Automation tab from the MFC ClassWizard dialog box.
2. Select CClockCtrl from the Class name list box.
3. Select the Add Property button and display the Add Property dialog box.

4. In the edit control of the External names combo box, type HitClock.
5. For an Implementation, check to make sure Member Variable is selected.
6. Select OLE_COLOR from the Type list box and clear the Notification function edit control.
7. Close the Add Property dialog box by selection the OK button, and return to the OLE Automation tab. Your screen should look like Figure 18.11.
8. Select the Message Maps tab.
9. Select CClockCtrl from the Class name list box.
10. From the Object IDs listbox, select CClockCtrl and then view a list of messages in the Messages list box.
11. Select WM_LBUTTONDOWN from the Messages list box.
12. Choose the Add Function button.
13. Repeat this process by selecting WM_LBUTTONUP. Your screen should look like Figure 18.12.
14. Select the OK push button to accept the choices and close the ClassWizard.

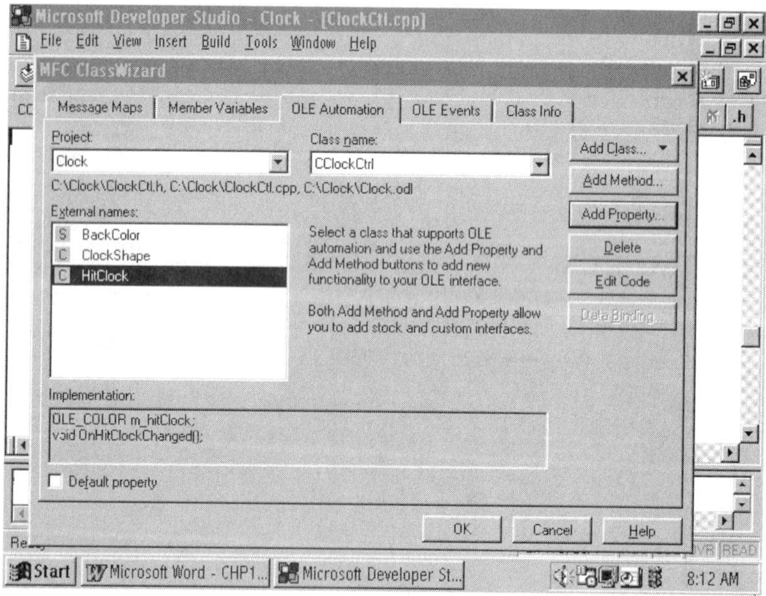

Figure 18.11: The HitClock property will allow the control to respond to a mouse event.

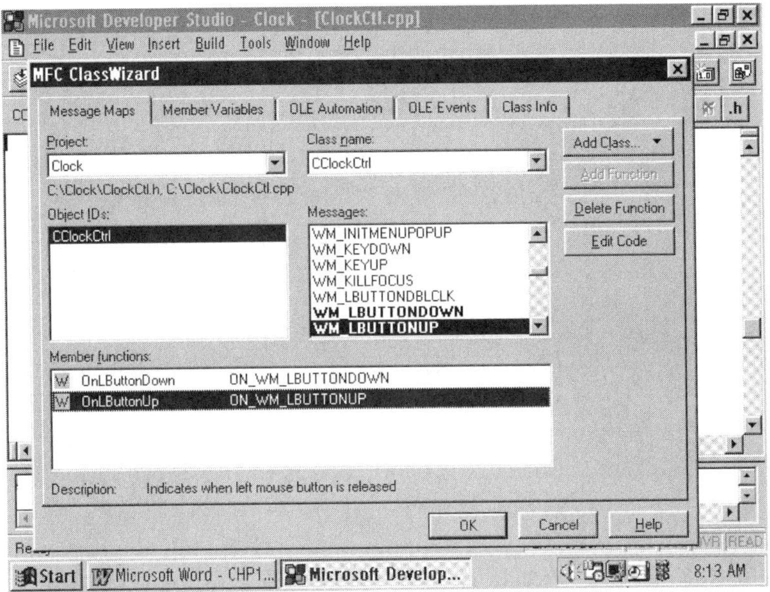

Figure 18.12: Two member functions are used to respond to mouse button events.

The ClassWizard will automatically create the code to add the HitClock property and the outlines for the above function implementations for the CClockCtrl class.

These changes are added by the ClassWizard, but we must now write the code that reacts to these events.

The ClockCtl.h Header File

Two additional insertions must be made in the header file to accommodate two functions. The first function is used to determine if a mouse event occurred within the Clock control. The second function is used to change the clock face color when a hit occurs. Insert **InFace()** and **HitClock()** just under the destructor shown in the following partial listing of the ClockCtl.h header file.

```
// Implementation
 protected:
   ~CClockCtrl();
      .
      .
      .
```

```
void GetDrawRect(CRect* rc);   // Clock Size
BOOL InFace(CPoint& point);    // Hit the Clock?
void HitClock(CDC* pdc);       // Blink the color
    .
    .
    .
DECLARE_OLECREATE_EX(CClockCtrl) //Class factory and guid
```

The code will now be added for detecting mouse clicks within the control.

The ClockCtl.cpp File

The clock face will change color when the user clicks the left mouse button within the clock face. The event notification, in part, is handled by the **DoPropExchange()** function. Here is the **DoPropExchange()** function showing the new line in a bolded font.

```
void CClockCtrl::DoPropExchange(CPropExchange* pPX)
{
    ExchangeVersion(pPX, MAKELONG(_wVerMinor, _wVerMajor));
    COleControl::DoPropExchange(pPX);

    PX_Long(pPX, _T("HitClock"), (long &)m_hitClock,
           RGB(128,128,128));
}
```

This function is responsible for initializing the *m_hitClock* member variable to a gray color. The variable *m_hitClock* must be cast to a long because it is an unsigned long value.

The ClassWizard added the **OnLButtonDown()** and **OnLButtonUp()** function outlines. The following listing shows several lines of bolded code that were added to this outline.

```
void CClockCtrl::OnLButtonDown(UINT nFlags, CPoint point)
{
    CDC* pdc;

    // Flash a color change for clock face
    if (InFace(point)) {
       pdc = GetDC();
       HitClock(pdc);
       ReleaseDC(pdc);
    }
    COleControl::OnLButtonDown(nFlags, point);
}

void CClockCtrl::OnLButtonUp(UINT nFlags, CPoint point)
```

```
{
    if (InFace(point))
        InvalidateControl();

    COleControl::OnLButtonUp(nFlags, point);
}
```

This code checks to make sure the left mouse button was clicked within the face of the clock. If it was, the **HitClock()** function will be called to change the color of the clock face from yellow to light gray and draw date and time information to the control.

When the left mouse button is released, the **OnLButtonUp()** function merely invalidates the control, forcing a repaint in the face to yellow.

The **InFace()** function is used to determine if the left mouse button was depressed within the clock face. All of the following code must be added to the end of the clockctl.cpp listing.

```
BOOL CClockCtrl::InFace(CPoint& point)
{
  CRect rc;
  GetClientRect(rc);
  GetDrawRect(&rc);

  // Find center point
  double h = (rc.right - rc.left) / 2;
  double k = (rc.bottom - rc.top) / 2;

  // Find x, y values
  double x = point.x - (rc.right + rc.left) / 2;
  double y = point.y - (rc.bottom + rc.top) / 2;

  // Ellipse equation determines location of point
  return ((x * x) / (h * h) + (y * y) / (k * k) <= 1);
}
```

This function first locates the center of the Clock control, and then determines if the hit occurred within that clock face.

If the point falls within the clock face, the **HitClock()** function is called. All of the code in the following function must be added to the end of the ClockCtl.cpp listing.

```
void CClockCtrl::HitClock(CDC* pdc)
{
  CBrush* pOldBrush;
  CBrush hitBrush(TranslateColor(m_hitClock));
  CRect rc;
  TEXTMETRIC tm;
```

```
  struct tm *date_time;
  time_t timer;

  // Fill between text
     Background mode to transparent
  pdc->SetBkMode(TRANSPARENT);

  GetClientRect(rc);
  GetDrawRect(&rc);

  pOldBrush=pdc->SelectObject(&hitBrush);
  pdc->Ellipse(rc);

  // Get time and date
  time(&timer);
  date_time=localtime(&timer);
  const CString& strtime = asctime(date_time);

  // Get Font information then print
  pdc->GetTextMetrics(&tm);
  pdc->SetTextAlign(TA_CENTER | TA_TOP);
  pdc->ExtTextOut((rc.left + rc.right)/2,
                  (rc.top + rc.bottom - tm.tmHeight)/2,
                  ETO_CLIPPED, rc, strtime,
                  strtime.GetLength()-1, NULL);

  pdc->SelectObject(pOldBrush);
}
```

The code in this function selects the gray brush, defined earlier, and repaints the entire Clock area. During this process, the system's date and time are retrieved and are drawn to the control. The date and time information replace the clock hands.

Build the Clock control from within the Microsoft Developer Studio. If your build operation is successful, you are now ready to test the new control.

The Test Container

The OLE Test Container can be used to test the Clock custom control.

To test the new control, start the Test Container and use the Edit menu to select the Insert OLE Control... menu item. When this selection is made, the new control will be available from the Insert OLE Control dialog box. Select the Clock Control item and insert the new custom control in the OLE Test Container. Figure 18.13 shows the Clock control inserted in the OLE Test Container.

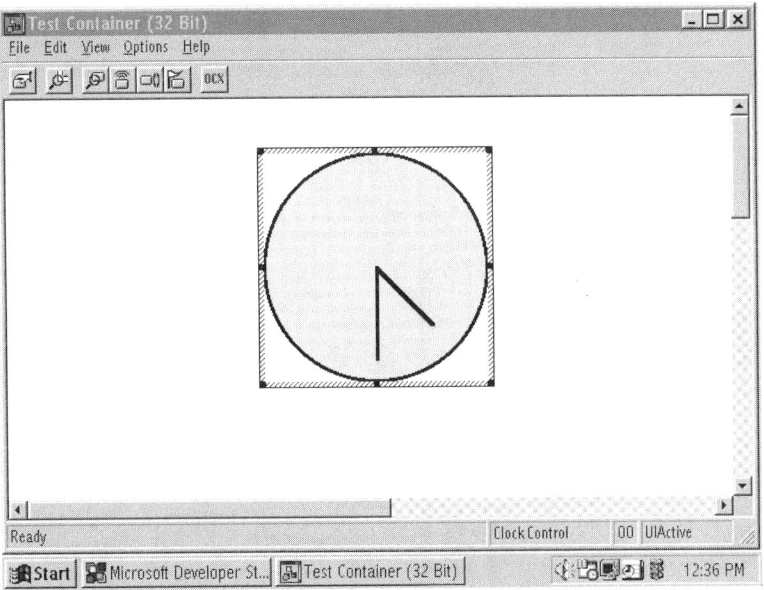

Figure 18.13: The new Clock custom control.

The OLE Test Container can be used to test several features of a new control. In Figure 18.14, you can see how the control responds to a mouse hit anywhere within the clock face.

The Test Container can also be used to view control properties. From the View menu select the Properties... menu item, as shown in Figure 18.15.

The Properties dialog box, shown in Figure 18.16, allows certain control properties to be changed. In this case, the BackColor property is changed.

Click the mouse on the Value box, once a property is selected, and display the group of colors that can be substituted for the current background color, as shown in Figure 18.17.

The BackColor value can be modified by entering a new color value in the Value box, too.

Try testing some of the Clock control's other properties.

More Custom Controls?

Custom controls, as you have learned, take a great deal of time to develop even with the use of the ControlWizard. Now you

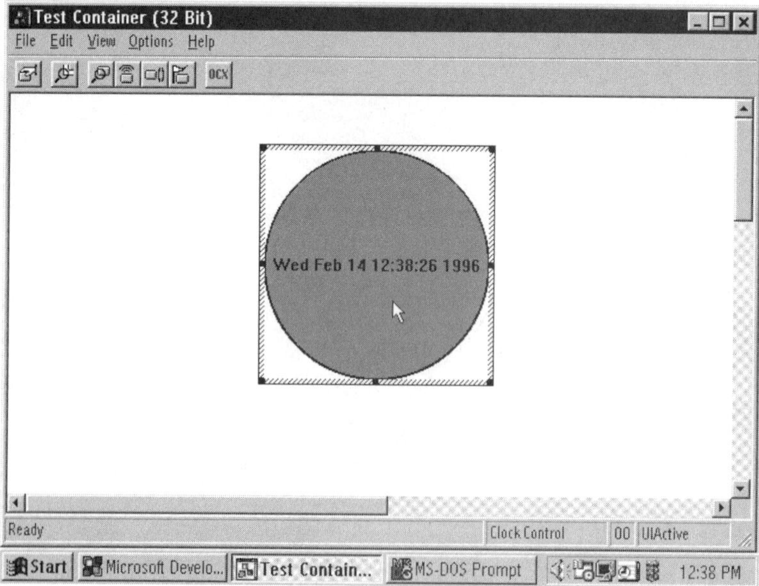

Figure 18.14: The clock face will turn gray when a mouse hit occurs within its boundaries.

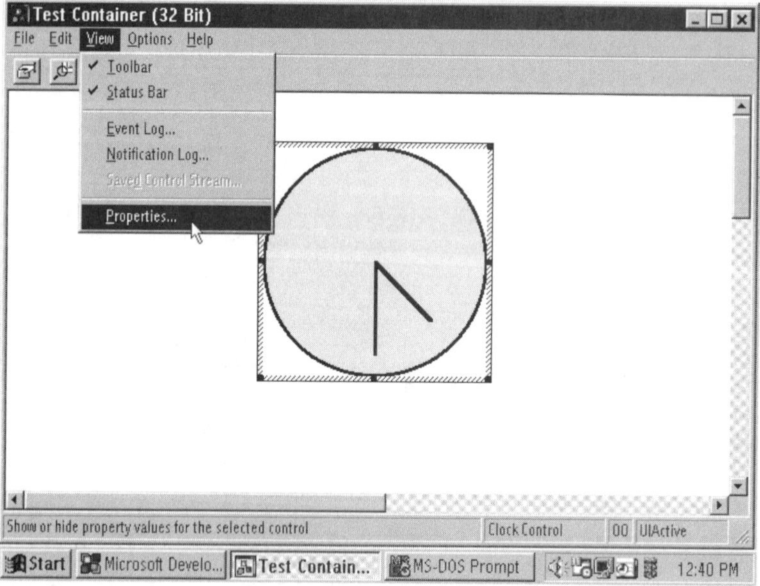

Figure 18.15: The Clock control's properties can be viewed and changed.

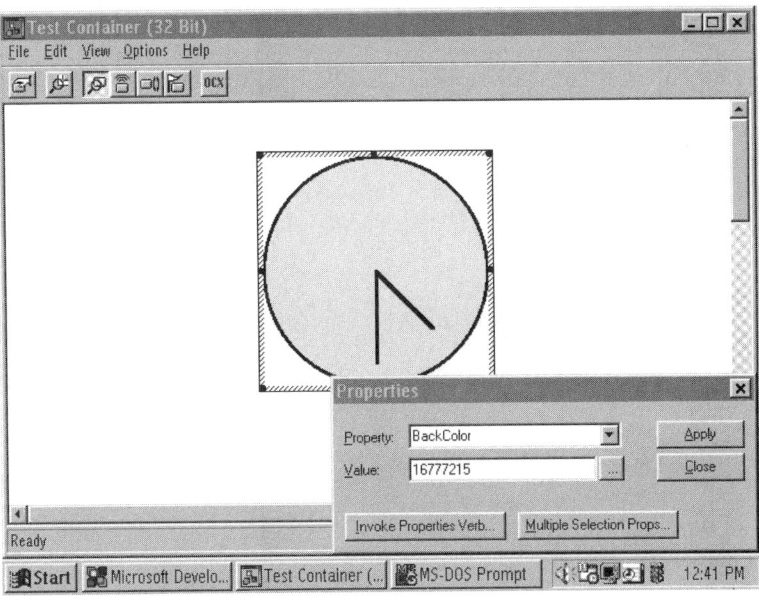

Figure 18.16: The Properties dialog box allows certain control properties to be modified.

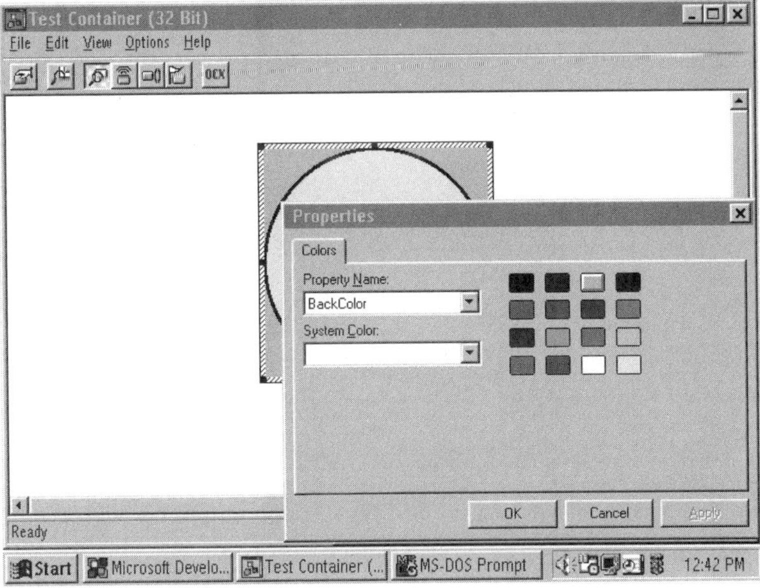

Figure 18.17: Select a new background color from this group.

can better understand why there is such a large commercial market for well-designed custom controls.

This should not discourage your development of custom controls. Sometimes there is no other solution than to develop your own custom control for a particular application.

Chapter 19

A Screen Saver Application

Windows applications introduced a major advantage over their earlier DOS counterparts - a consistent user interface. Do you remember those applications? Your word processor's menu didn't look anything like your spreadsheet's menu. The special key combinations were different from one application to another. It was, to put it mildly, a mess. But Windows changed all of that! Applications now have a consistent appearance from one application to another. If you've mastered your word processor, you can start a new spreadsheet application and feel at home with the various commands almost immediately. So where is all of this going? To the one application that does not take on a consistent appearance with other Windows applications, yet receives Microsoft's blessing. You guessed it—the screen saver.

A screen saver protects your monitor from burning the phosphor dots on the screen by blanking the screen after a predetermined amount of time. In its most elementary form, a blank screen is a black screen. However, in recent years we've come to expect more from our screen saver applications. Flying toasters, trains, stars, creatures, a scrolling marquee, and so on have become favorites. While some screen savers contained advanced features, such as password protection, all Windows screen savers have a minimal set of features that allow them to do the following. These features include:

- Produce a topmost window.
- Produce a black window without a border or menu that occupies the whole screen.
- Produce a window without a cursor.
- Draw and move an image about on the screen.

Detect mouse movement or button pushes and any keyboard actions.

Actions such as the acceptable period of inactivity or the restoration of the screen are handled by Windows, not the screen saver.

If you purchased the CD-ROM version of the Microsoft Developer Studio (Visual C++ compiler), you were supplied with a screen saver application named Saver. This screen saver is located in the d:msdev\samples\mfc\general\saver subdirectory. This is a full-bodied screen saver application complete with a dialog box for setting screen saver options and so on. The application developed in this chapter will be a bit more modest, but no less exciting, and is based on the Microsoft Saver example.

The Saucer application will blank the screen and start a little flying saucer on its journey about your screen. The colorful saucer was created as a bitmapped image. The saucer will fly about your screen in a two-dimensional journey that will last until there is either mouse or keyboard activity on your system.

Saucer Files

Design and build the basic Saucer application with the AppWizard, as you have done with applications in the previous chapters. This application will use four source code files; Saucer.cpp,

Saucerwnd.cpp, Drawwnd.cpp, and stdafx.cpp. There are also four header files associated with these source code files. If you name your application workspace Saucer, then you will end up with multiple source code files, too. The Drawwnd.cpp file is most closely associated with the view file. The Saucerwnd.cpp file corresponds to a file created for an additional class. The document file (doc) is not needed. Additionally, you'll need to create a bitmapped image of an object, like the saucer we drew. Let's look at each of the files in more detail.

Saucer.h and Saucer.cpp

The Saucer.h header file is used for the declaration of the CsaucerApp class. Note in this case that the CsaucerApp class is derived from the CWinApp class, not the CFrameWnd class as in past examples. This is because our application's window will not use a standard window frame.

```
// saucer.h : main header file for the saucer application
//

#ifndef __AFXWIN_H__
  #error include  stdafx.h  before this file for PCH
#endif

#include "resource.h"    // main symbols

// CsaucerApp:
// See saucer.cpp for the implementation of this class
//

class CsaucerApp : public CWinApp
{
public:
        CsaucerApp();

// Overrides
  // ClassWizard generated virtual function overrides
        //{{AFX_VIRTUAL(CsaucerApp)
  public:
  virtual BOOL InitInstance();
  //}}AFX_VIRTUAL

        //{{AFX_MSG(CsaucerApp)
    // NOTE - ClassWizard will add/remove member functions.
    //    DO NOT EDIT these blocks of generated code !
  //}}AFX_MSG
  DECLARE_MESSAGE_MAP()
};
```

The Saucer.cpp file implements the CsaucerApp class. You'll notice, in the following listing, that no code is added to the class constructor.

```
// saucer.cpp : Defines class behaviors for the application.
//

#include "stdafx.h"
#include "saucer.h"
#include "drawwnd.h"
#include "saucerwnd.h"

#ifdef _DEBUG
#undef THIS_FILE
static char BASED_CODE THIS_FILE[] = __FILE__;
#endif

// CsaucerApp

BEGIN_MESSAGE_MAP(CsaucerApp, CWinApp)
        //{{AFX_MSG_MAP(CsaucerApp)
    // NOTE - ClassWizard will add/remove mapping macros.
    //    DO NOT EDIT these blocks of generated code!
  //}}AFX_MSG
  ON_COMMAND(ID_HELP, CWinApp::OnHelp)
END_MESSAGE_MAP()

// CsaucerApp construction

CsaucerApp::CsaucerApp()
{
  // TODO: add construction code here,
  // Place all significant initialization in InitInstance
}

// The one and only CsaucerApp object

CsaucerApp theApp;

// CsaucerApp initialization

BOOL CsaucerApp::InitInstance()
{
  // Standard initialization

  SetRegistryKey(_T("A Screen saucer"));

  CsaucerWnd* pWnd = new CsaucerWnd;
  pWnd->Create();
  m_pMainWnd = pWnd;
  return TRUE;
}
```

The **InitInstance()** member function is used to set the registry key.

Saucerwnd.h and Saucerwnd.cpp

The saucerwnd.h header file is used for the declaration of the CsaucerWnd class. The CsaucerWnd class is derived from the CDrawWnd class. The CDrawWnd class is described in the Drawwnd.h header file.

```
// saucerwnd.h : header file
//

// CsaucerWnd window

class CsaucerWnd : public CDrawWnd
{
// Construction
public:
        CsaucerWnd();

// Attributes
public:
  CPoint m_ptLast;

// Operations
public:
  BOOL Create();

// Overrides
  // ClassWizard generated virtual function overrides
        //{{AFX_VIRTUAL(CsaucerWnd)
  //}}AFX_VIRTUAL

// Implementation
public:
        virtual ~CsaucerWnd();

  // Generated message map functions
protected:
        //{{AFX_MSG(CsaucerWnd)
  afx_msg void OnSysCommand(UINT nID, LPARAM lParam);
  afx_msg void OnDestroy();
  afx_msg BOOL OnSetCursor(CWnd* pWnd, UINT nHitTest,
                          UINT message);
  afx_msg BOOL OnNcActivate(BOOL bActive);
  afx_msg void OnActivate(UINT nState, CWnd* pWndOther,
                         BOOL bMinimized);
  afx_msg void OnActivateApp(BOOL bActive, HTASK hTask);
  afx_msg void OnMouseMove(UINT nFlags, CPoint point);
  afx_msg void OnLButtonDown(UINT nFlags, CPoint point);
  afx_msg void OnRButtonDown(UINT nFlags, CPoint point);
  afx_msg void OnKeyDown(UINT nChar, UINT nRepCnt,
                        UINT nFlags);
```

```
    afx_msg void OnSysKeyDown(UINT nChar, UINT nRepCnt,
                              UINT nFlags);
    //}}AFX_MSG
    DECLARE_MESSAGE_MAP()
};
```

The message map declaration, in the header file, indicates which events will be used to trigger the return to the normal window. As you can see from the bolded lines of code, events such as system activity, key presses, mouse movements, and mouse button activation will be used to terminate the screen saver session.

The saucerwnd.cpp file implements the CsaucerWnd class and initializes several variables within the constructor. For example, the initial bitmap position is defined here.

```
// saucerwnd.cpp : implementation file
//

#include "stdafx.h"
#include "saucer.h"
#include "drawwnd.h"
#include "saucerwnd.h"

#ifdef _DEBUG
#undef THIS_FILE
static char BASED_CODE THIS_FILE[] = __FILE__;
#endif

// CsaucerWnd

CsaucerWnd::CsaucerWnd()
{
  m_ptLast = CPoint(-1, -1);
  m_nXPos = 320;
  m_nYPos = 240;
  m_nStep = 1;
}

CsaucerWnd::~CsaucerWnd()
{
}

BEGIN_MESSAGE_MAP(CsaucerWnd, CDrawWnd)
        //{{AFX_MSG_MAP(CsaucerWnd)
  ON_WM_SYSCOMMAND()
  ON_WM_DESTROY()
  ON_WM_SETCURSOR()
  ON_WM_NCACTIVATE()
  ON_WM_ACTIVATE()
  ON_WM_ACTIVATEAPP()
  ON_WM_MOUSEMOVE()
```

```
  ON_WM_LBUTTONDOWN()
  ON_WM_RBUTTONDOWN()
  ON_WM_KEYDOWN()
  ON_WM_SYSKEYDOWN()
  //}}AFX_MSG_MAP
END_MESSAGE_MAP()

// CsaucerWnd message handlers

BOOL CsaucerWnd::Create()
{
  CRect rect(0, 0, ::GetSystemMetrics(SM_CXSCREEN),
    ::GetSystemMetrics(SM_CYSCREEN));

  return CDrawWnd::Create(WS_EX_TOPMOST, WS_VISIBLE|WS_POPUP,
                          rect, NULL, 0, NULL);
}

void CsaucerWnd::OnSysCommand(UINT nID, LPARAM lParam)
{
  if ((nID == SC_SCREENSAVE) || (nID == SC_CLOSE))
    return;
  CDrawWnd::OnSysCommand(nID, lParam);
}

void CsaucerWnd::OnDestroy()
{
  PostQuitMessage(0);
  CDrawWnd::OnDestroy();
}

BOOL CsaucerWnd::OnSetCursor(CWnd* pWnd, UINT nHitTest,
                             UINT message)
{
  SetCursor(NULL);
  return TRUE;
}

BOOL CsaucerWnd::OnNcActivate(BOOL bActive)
{
  if (!bActive)
    return FALSE;
  return CDrawWnd::OnNcActivate(bActive);
}

void CsaucerWnd::OnActivate(UINT nState, CWnd* pWndOther,
                            BOOL bMinimized)
{
  if (nState == WA_INACTIVE)
    PostMessage(WM_CLOSE);
  CDrawWnd::OnActivate(nState, pWndOther, bMinimized);
}
```

```
void CsaucerWnd::OnActivateApp(BOOL bActive, HTASK hTask)
{
  if (!bActive)
    PostMessage(WM_CLOSE);
  CDrawWnd::OnActivateApp(bActive, hTask);
}

void CsaucerWnd::OnMouseMove(UINT nFlags, CPoint point)
{
  if (m_ptLast == CPoint(-1,-1))
    m_ptLast = point;
  else if (m_ptLast != point)
    PostMessage(WM_CLOSE);
  CDrawWnd::OnMouseMove(nFlags, point);
}

void CsaucerWnd::OnLButtonDown(UINT nFlags, CPoint point)
{
  PostMessage(WM_CLOSE);
  CDrawWnd::OnLButtonDown(nFlags, point);
}

void CsaucerWnd::OnRButtonDown(UINT nFlags, CPoint point)
{
  PostMessage(WM_CLOSE);
  CDrawWnd::OnRButtonDown(nFlags, point);
}

void CsaucerWnd::OnKeyDown(UINT nChar, UINT nRepCnt,
                           UINT nFlags)
{
  PostMessage(WM_CLOSE);
  CDrawWnd::OnKeyDown(nChar, nRepCnt, nFlags);
}

void CsaucerWnd::OnSysKeyDown(UINT nChar, UINT nRepCnt,
                              UINT nFlags)
{
  PostMessage(WM_CLOSE);
  CDrawWnd::OnSysKeyDown(nChar, nRepCnt, nFlags);
}
```

As you study the previous listing, you notice that this window is designed to be a topmost window using a NULL value when calling the **SetCursor()** function.

All of the member functions used for terminating the screen saver use basically the same code. They post a WM_CLOSE window message. When the message is sent, the screen saver application will terminate until Windows once again initiates it.

Drawwnd.h and Drawwnd.cpp

The drawwnd.h header file is used for the declaration of the CDrawWnd class. You'll notice that the CDrawWnd class is derived from the CWnd class, too. A number of variables are declared in the public portion of this class. These variables will be used to set colors, step sizes, positions, and so on.

```
// drawwnd.h : header file
//

// CDrawWnd window

class CDrawWnd : public CWnd
{
// Construction
public:
  CDrawWnd(BOOL bAutoDelete = TRUE);

// Attributes
public:
  CRgn m_rgnLast;
  int m_nXSteps, m_nYSteps;
  int m_nXPos, m_nYPos;
  int m_nStep;
  LOGBRUSH m_logbrush;
  LOGBRUSH m_logbrushBlack;
  static LPCTSTR m_lpszClassName;
  void SctSpeed();
  void SetColor(COLORREF cr);

// Operations
public:

// Overrides
  // ClassWizard generated virtual function overrides
  //{{AFX_VIRTUAL(CDrawWnd)
  public:
  virtual BOOL Create(DWORD dwExStyle, DWORD dwStyle,
                    const RECT& rect, CWnd* pParentWnd,
                    UINT nID,
                    CCreateContext* pContext = NULL);
  protected:
  virtual void PostNcDestroy();
  //}}AFX_VIRTUAL

// Implementation
public:
  virtual ~CDrawWnd();
```

```
protected:
  BOOL m_bAutoDelete;

  // Generated message map functions
protected:
  //{{AFX_MSG(CDrawWnd)
  afx_msg void OnTimer(UINT nIDEvent);
  afx_msg void OnPaint();
  afx_msg int OnCreate(LPCREATESTRUCT lpCreateStruct);
  //}}AFX_MSG
  DECLARE_MESSAGE_MAP()
};
```

The drawwnd.cpp file implements the CDrawWnd class. The class constructor is used to initialize several variables, including the step size (1 unit) for the graphics, background color (black), and so on.

```
// drawwnd.cpp : implementation file
//

#include "stdafx.h"
#include "saucer.h"
#include "drawwnd.h"

#ifdef _DEBUG
#undef THIS_FILE
static char BASED_CODE THIS_FILE[] = __FILE__;
#endif

LPCTSTR CDrawWnd::m_lpszClassName = NULL;

// CDrawWnd

CDrawWnd::CDrawWnd(BOOL bAutoDelete)
{
  m_bAutoDelete = bAutoDelete;
  m_nXPos = 320;
  m_nYPos = 240;
  m_rgnLast.CreateRectRgn(0,0,0,0);

  m_nXSteps = 1;
  m_nYSteps = 1;
  m_logbrush.lbStyle = m_logbrushBlack.lbStyle = BS_SOLID;
  m_logbrush.lbHatch = m_logbrushBlack.lbHatch = 0;
  m_logbrushBlack.lbColor = RGB(0, 0, 0);
}

CDrawWnd::~CDrawWnd()
{
}
```

```
BEGIN_MESSAGE_MAP(CDrawWnd, CWnd)
  //{{AFX_MSG_MAP(CDrawWnd)
  ON_WM_TIMER()
  ON_WM_PAINT()
  ON_WM_CREATE()
  //}}AFX_MSG_MAP
END_MESSAGE_MAP()

void CDrawWnd::SetSpeed()
{
  KillTimer(1);
  VERIFY(SetTimer(1, 30, NULL) != 0);
}

void CDrawWnd::SetColor(COLORREF cr)
{
  m_logbrush.lbColor = cr;
}

// CDrawWnd message handlers

void CDrawWnd::OnTimer(UINT nIDEvent)
{
  if (nIDEvent == 1)
  {
    CClientDC dc(this);
    CRect rect;
    CBitmap m_bitmap;
    CDC dcMem;
    BITMAP bm;

    GetClientRect(&rect);
    m_bitmap.LoadBitmap(IDB_SAUCER1);
    m_bitmap.GetObject(sizeof(bm),&bm);
    m_nXPos += m_nXSteps;
    m_nYPos += m_nYSteps;

    if (!dcMem.CreateCompatibleDC(&dc))
      return;
    CBitmap* pBitmapOld = dcMem.SelectObject(&m_bitmap);
    if (pBitmapOld == NULL)
      return;

    dc.BitBlt(m_nXPos,m_nYPos,bm.bmWidth,bm.bmHeight,
              &dcMem,0,0,SRCCOPY);

    if((m_nXPos+bm.bmWidth > rect.right) ||
        (m_nXPos < rect.left))
      m_nXSteps=-m_nXSteps;

    if((m_nYPos+bm.bmHeight > rect.bottom) ||
```

```
        (m_nYPos < rect.top))
      m_nYSteps=-m_nYSteps;

    dcMem.SelectObject(pBitmapOld);
  }
  else
    CWnd::OnTimer(nIDEvent);
}

void CDrawWnd::OnPaint()
{
  CPaintDC dc(this); // device context for painting
  CRect rect;
  CBrush brush(RGB(0,0,0));

  m_rgnLast.DeleteObject();
  m_rgnLast.CreateRectRgn(0,0,0,0);
  GetClientRect(rect);
  dc.FillRect(&rect, &brush);
  // Do not call CWnd::OnPaint() for painting messages
}

int CDrawWnd::OnCreate(LPCREATESTRUCT lpCreateStruct)
{
  if (CWnd::OnCreate(lpCreateStruct) == -1)
    return -1;

  SetSpeed();

  return 0;
}

BOOL CDrawWnd::Create(DWORD dwExStyle, DWORD dwStyle,
                      const RECT& rect,
                      CWnd* pParentWnd, UINT nID,
                      CCreateContext* pContext)
{
    // Register a class with no cursor
  if (m_lpszClassName == NULL)
  {
      m_lpszClassName = AfxRegisterWndClass(CS_HREDRAW|CS_VREDRAW,
      ::LoadCursor(AfxGetResourceHandle(),
      MAKEINTRESOURCE(IDC_NULLCURSOR)));
  }

  // TODO: Add specialized code here and/or call base class
  return CreateEx(dwExStyle, m_lpszClassName, _T(""),
                  dwStyle, rect.left, rect.top,
                  rect.right - rect.left,
                  rect.bottom - rect.top,
                  pParentWnd->GetSafeHwnd(), NULL, NULL );
```

```
}

void CDrawWnd::PostNcDestroy()
{
  if (m_bAutoDelete)
    delete this;
}
```

The number of timer ticks, and hence the speed of the screen saver's animation, is controlled by the **SetTimer()** function. In this case, timer 1 is set to "tick" once every 30/1000 of a second. This value seemed just about right for this application, but it can be changed to speed up or slow down the movement of the bitmap.

The **OnTimer()** member function controls the movement of the bitmap image. The same basic code was used here that was used in Chapter 9 for retrieving and placing a bitmapped image on the screen. The real difference, of course, is in the fact that the image is being moved. Each time the **OnTimer()** function is called, the *m_nXPos* and *m_nYPos* variables are incremented by *m_nXSteps* or *m_nYSteps*.

```
m_nXPos += m_nXSteps;
m_nYPos += m_nYSteps;
```

Thus, with each timer tick, new X and Y positions are generated. The **BitBlt()** function moves the bitmap image to the new position.

```
dc.BitBlt(m_nXPos,m_nYPos,bm.bmWidth,bm.bmHeight,
          &dcMem,0,0,SRCCOPY);
```

If a collision occurs between the bitmap and any edge of the screen, the position of movement of the bitmap must be reversed. This is handled efficiently with the following portion of code.

```
if((m_nXPos+bm.bmWidth > rect.right) ||
    (m_nXPos < rect.left))
  m_nXSteps=-m_nXSteps;

if((m_nYPos+bm.bmHeight > rect.bottom) ||
    (m_nYPos < rect.top))
  m_nYSteps=-m_nYSteps;
```

The **OnPaint()** member function handles the background painting while the **Create()** member function installs the null cursor.

Notice that the return value for this class returns the **CreateEx()** values giving the extents of the rectangle used as the window.

```
return CreateEx(dwExStyle, m_lpszClassName, _T(""),
            dwStyle, rect.left, rect.top,
            rect.right - rect.left,
            rect.bottom - rect.top,
            pParentWnd->GetSafeHwnd(), NULL, NULL );
```

rect.left is the initial X-position and *rect.top* is the initial Y-position of the CWnd window. The value obtained form *rect.right - rect.left* gives the width of the CWnd in device units. Likewise, *rect.bottom – rect.top* gives the height of the CWnd in device units.

A Special Build Operation

The project settings for this application will differ from those used in other chapters. Select the Settings... menu item from the Build menu. Use the Project Settings dialog box to set the Microsoft Foundation Classes to use a shared DLL, as shown in Figure 19.1.

From the same dialog box, select the C/C++ tab, and make sure your preprocessor definitions and project options include those shown in Figure 19.2.

Finally, select the Link tab to set the final format for a screen saver file with a .scr file extension, as shown in Figure 19.3.

Build the screen saver application by selecting the Rebuild All... menu item from the Build menu.

When a successful build occurs, you will have to move the saucer.scr file to the proper Windows subdirectory. Typically, for Windows 95, this will be c:Win95system. For Windows NT, this will be c:WinNTsystem.

Running the Screen Saver

When the screen save is run, you'll see a little saucer float about the screen. Figure 19.4 shows the bitmapped image while it was being created in the resource editor.

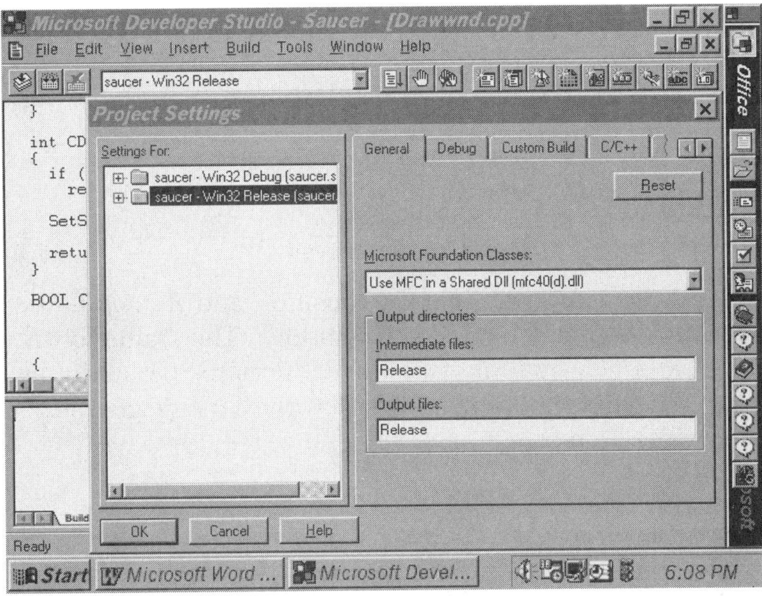

Figure 19.1: General project settings for the Saucer screen saver application.

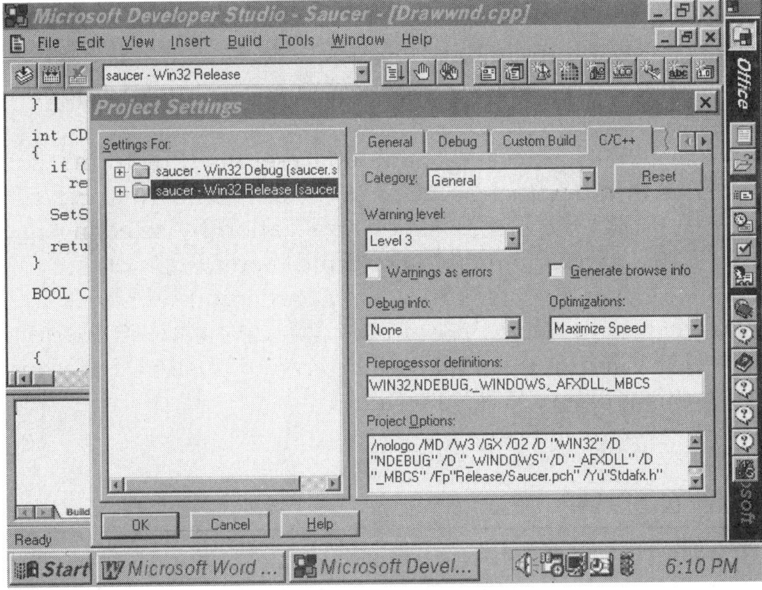

Figure 19.2: Selecting preprocessor definitions and project options for the C/C++ compiler.

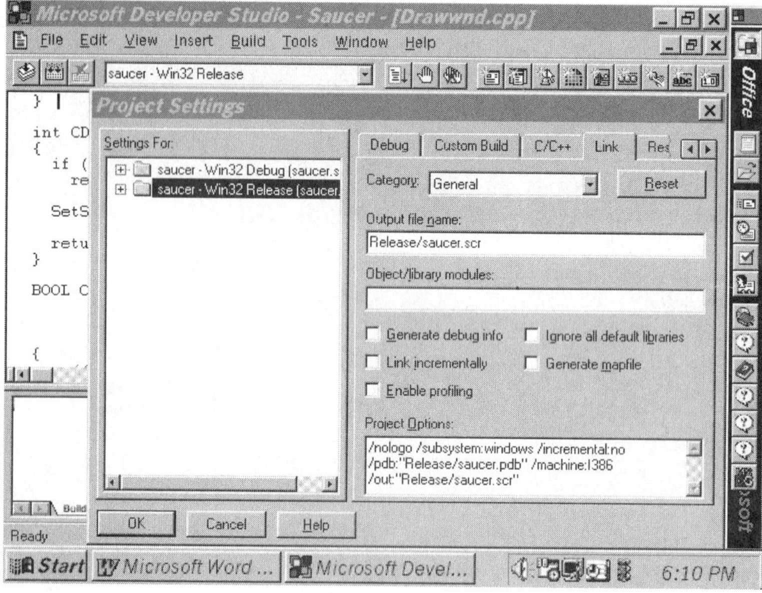

Figure 19.3: Building an .scr screen saver executable.

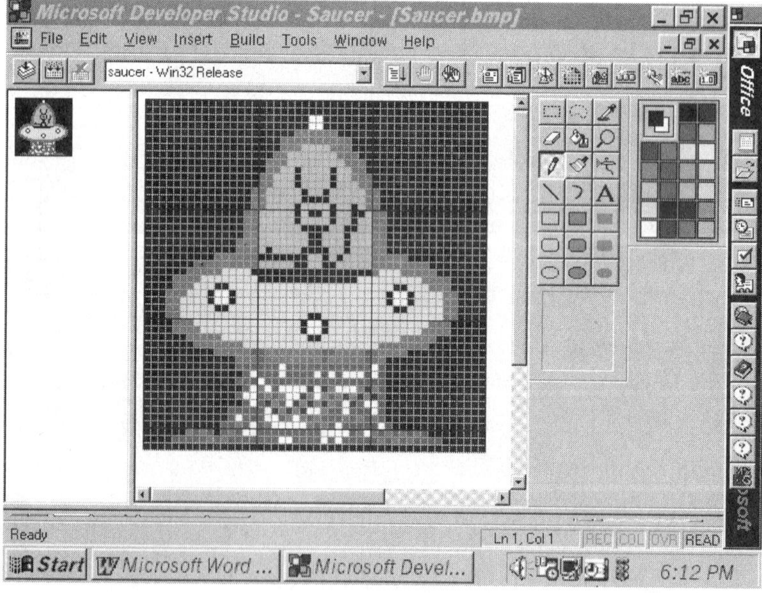

Figure 19.4: A bitmapped image for the Saucer screen saver application.

The screen saver is installed by using the SettingsControl Panel off of the Windows 95 Start menu and selecting the Display option. Then from the Display Properties dialog box, shown in Figure 19.5, the saucer screen saver is selected in the Screen Saver dialog box.

Remember, our little screen saver application does not provide all of the robust abilities that can be built into a screen saver, such as password protection and an initial settings dialog box.

MORE SCREEN SAVERS

You now have the basic program for moving any bitmapped image two-dimensionally about on the screen. Why not create your own custom bitmap and use this application, as is, as your own personal screen saver?

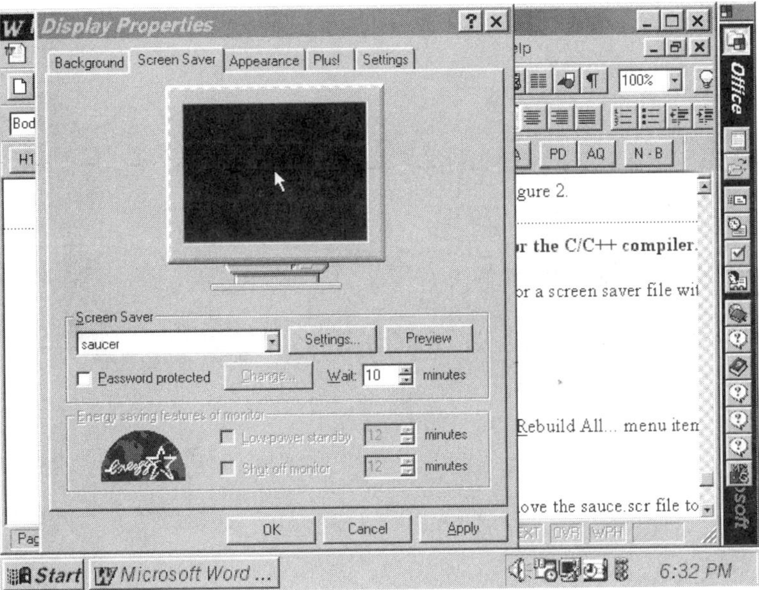

Figure 19.5: Install the saucer screen saver from the Display Properties dialog box.

INDEX

. . . (ellipses), 271
::, 124
_itoa(), 376, 382
_T, 289, 346, 372, 490
| (bitwise OR), 97
~ (tilde operator), 125
16 vs 32 bit, 13–14
16x16 icon, 214
32-Bit programming (intro), 1–22
  elements of Win 95 and NT, 5–20
    16 vs 32 bit, 13–14
    as operating system, 6–13
    beginnings, 6
    common user interface, 67
    crash management, 18
    distributed computing, 17
    DLLs, 12–13
    hardware independence, 10–12
    memory management, 8
    message-based communication, 9–10
    multiprocessing, 16–17
    open architecture, 18
    platform compatibility, 15–16
    platform independence, 14–15
    plug-and play, 12
    preemptive multitasking, 7
    queue-based input, 8–9
    scalability, 17
    security, 17–18
    virtual memory, 18–19
    Win 95 compared to Win NT, 19–20
  getting started, 20–22
    software required, 21
    system requirements, 21–22
  objects, 4–5
  reasons to develop, 3–5
32x32 icon, 214

A

about dialog box, 202
AboutBox(), 470–471
abs(), 127–128
abstract data type, 118
adding,
  bitmaps, 238–240
  fonts, 240
  icons, 236–237
  sounds, 237–238
AfxGetInstanceHandle, 241, 466
AfxMessageBox, 408
AfxOleInit, 408
AfxOleRegisterPropertyPageClass, 466–467
AfxOleRegisterTypeLib, 465
AfxOleUnregisterClass, 466
AfxOleUnregisterTypeLib, 465
AfxRegisterWndClass, 236, 241
afxwin.h, 162, 163
AngleLine(), 16
Application Program Interface (API), 150
application specific coordinates, 55
applications (Windows),
  ABSOLUTE.cpp, 127–128
  AddRes.cpp, 132–243
  BarChart.cpp, 365–387
  Clock.cpp, 458–483
  Colors.cpp, 294–302
  Contain.cpp, 406–424
  DataEntry.cpp, 277–294
  Editor.cpp, 360–365
  FRIEND.cpp, 128–131
  Intense.cpp, 338–348
  MenuColor.cpp, 247–270
  NoWiz, 172–185
  Saucer.cpp, 487–503
  Server.cpp, 424–442

Shapes.cpp, 320–326
Spin.cpp, 348–357
STACK.cpp, 132–134
Tool.cpp, 327–338
TRIGCLASS.cpp, 123–125
WinVer.cpp, 90–107
WinVerMFC.cpp, 159–168
WithWiz, 188–209
AppWizard (using), 169–210
building the application, 197–198
ClassWizard, 194–197
code generators, 170
getting started, 188–194
looks the same to me, 210
NoWiz application, 172–185
steps, 188–194
understanding code, 198–199
why and how did they do that, 185–188
WithWiz application, 188–209
arbitrary axes, 54
Arc(), 323
architecture, 137–138
arrays, 137
asctime(), 129, 482
aspect ratio, 54
ASSERT, 346
ASSERT_VALID, 432
AssertValid(), 204, 206
atoi(), 376
atol(), 129
autobuddy, 348
automation (OLE), 146, 442

B

bar chart project, 365–387
base windows class, 138–139
BEGIN_MESSAGE_MAP, 163
BeginPaint(), 54, 91, 106
BitBlt(), 235, 239, 497, 499
bitmap,
editors, 212–225
objects, 34–35
BITMAP, 235, 238–240
bitwise OR (|), 97
BOOL, 88
border, 26
brush objects, 35
brushes, 315, 317–318
BS_3STATE, 62
BS_AUTO3STATE, 61
BS_AUTOCHECKBOX, 61
BS_AUTORADIOBUTTON, 61
BS_CHECKBOX, 62
BS_DEFPUSHBUTTON, 62
BS_GROUPBOX, 62
BS_LEFTTEXT, 62
BS_OWNERDRAW, 62
BS_PUSHBUTTON, 62
BS_RADIOBUTTON, 62
BSTR, 88
buddy, 348
BUTTON class, 57
Button control styles, 61–62
BS_3STATE, 62
BS_AUTO3STATE, 61
BS_AUTOCHECKBOX, 61
BS_AUTORADIOBUTTON, 61
BS_CHECKBOX, 62
BS_DEFPUSHBUTTON, 62
BS_GROUPBOX, 62
BS_LEFTTEXT, 62
BS_OWNERDRAW, 62
BS_PUSHBUTTON, 62
BS_RADIOBUTTON, 62
Button control, 275
BYTE, 88

C

C++ **class**, 122–123
C2 security level, 18
callback function, 89, 101–105
CArchive, 146
caret objects, 31
CArray, 137
case, 91
CAsyncSocket, 145
CBitmap, 235, 497
CBrush, 267, 299, 317–318, 323, 498
CBS_AUTOHSCROLL, 65
CBS_DISABLENOSCROLL, 65
CBS_DROPDOWN, 65
CBS_HASSTRING, 65
CBS_NOINTEGRALHEIGHT, 65
CBS_OEMCONVERT, 65
CBS_OWNERDRAWFIXED, 65

CBS_SHORT, 65
CBS_SIMPLE, 65
CC_FULLOPEN, 299
CCmdTarget, 137–138
CContainCntrItem, 415
CControlBar, 139
CCreateContext, 146
CDatabase, 142
CDataExchange, 147
CDC, 144, 154–155, 235
CDialog, 140
CEditView class members, 361
CException, 143
CFile, 143
CFont, 235
CFrameWnd, 140–141
CGdiObject, 142–143, 154–155
changing Windows,
  extent, 54
  viewport, 54
Check Box control, 71–72, 276
CheckMenuItem(), 269
child,
  class, 121, 131
  windows, 272
CHOOSECOLOR structure, 300
Chord(), 323
CImageList, 142
CInPlaceFrame, 428
circle (see **Ellipse()**), 311–312
class hierarchy, 120–121, 136–137
class, 115–118, 122–123
ClassWizard, 185
client,
  area coordinates, 53
  work area, 29
ClientToScreen(), 54
CList, 144
clock custom control, 472–482
CMainframe, 428
CMainWnd(), 164
CMap, 144–145
CMenu, 145
CMultiLock, 147
CObject, 136, 152–156
COleClientItem, 417
COleControl, 454–455
COleControlModule, 464
COleDocument, 411
COleInsertDialog, 415
COleIPDFrameWindow, 440
ColeObjectFactoryEx, 465
COleServerItem, 432, 436
COLORREF, 88, 260, 299–300
Combo Box control, 276
COMBOBOX class, 58
Combobox control styles, 65–66
  CBS_AUTOHSCROLL, 65
  CBS_DISABLENOSCROLL, 65
  CBS_DROPDOWN, 65
  CBS_HASSTRING, 65
  CBS_NOINTEGRALHEIGHT, 65
  CBS_OEMCONVERT, 65
  CBS_OWNERDRAWFIXED, 65
  CBS_SHORT, 65
  CBS_SIMPLE, 65
compiler,
  options, 112–113
  project workspaces, 107–112
common controls, 327–357
  Slider Control application, 338–348
    ClassWizard, 342–344
    code you must edit, 344–347
    designing the control, 338–342
    running the application, 347–348
  Spin Button application, 348–357
    buddy, 348
    ClassWizard, 351–354
    code you must edit, 354–356
    designing the control, 348–351
    running the application, 356–357
  ToolBar application, 327–338
    augmenting the Toolbar, 330–332
    ClassWizard, 332–333
    code you must edit, 333–337
    running the application, 337–338
    ToolTips, 329–330
common dialog box application, 294–302
Component Object Model, 389, 392
compound documents, 390
constructors, 125–126
container application (OLE), 406–424
containers, 392–393
control,
  bars, 139
  box, 26

containers, 456
events, 455
control classes, 57–59, 139
BUTTON, 57
COMBOBOX, 58
EDIT, 57
LISTBOX, 58
SCROLLBAR, 58
STATIC, 59
Controls and Dialog boxes, 70–74
ControlWizard, 452–486
coordiante systems, 53–54
cosine(), 124
cout, 117, 124
CPaintDC(), 144, 162, 166, 498
CPen, 316, 323
CPropertySheet, 141
crash management, 18
Create(), 162, 164, 240–241, 439, 493
CreateCaret(), 32
CreateCompatibleDC(), 235, 239, 497
CreateDC(), 54
CreateDIBPatternBrush(), 318
CreateEx(), 498
CreateFont(), 230–232, 235, 240, 377, 383
CreateFontIndirect(), 232
CreateHatchBrush(), 318
CreatePatternBrush(), 318
CreatePen(), 316, 323
CreateRectRgn(), 498
CreateSolidBrush(), 236, 241, 267–268, 299, 318
CreateWindow(), 29, 53, 56, 73, 91, 98
CreateWindowEx(), 56
creating a window, 98–99
CRect(), 147–148, 418, 493, 481, 498
CS_HREDRAW, 90
CS_VREDRAW, 90
CServerDoc, 428
CServerView, 428, 434
CSingleDocTemplate(), 428
CSingleLock, 147
CSize, 436
CSliderCtrl, 345
CSpinButtonCtrl, 355
CString, 482
CStringList, 144
CSyncObject, 145–146
CTypedPtrArray, 147
CURRENCY, 146
cursor objects, 31
CURSOR, 241
custom control,
methods, 455–456
persistence, 456
properties, 456
custom controls, 443–486
clock custom control, 472–482
containers, 456
design requirements, 446
events, 455
important control files, 446–455
methods, 455–456
OLE custom controls, 445–446
persistence, 456
properties, 456
simple custom control, 458–472
test container, 482–483, 460–462
CView, 141, 334
CW_USEDEFAULT, 91
CWinApp, 160
CWnd, 138–139

D

Data Access Object (DAO), 142
data,
OLE, 392
exchange, 290–291
fields, 120
object, 392
types, 88
database, 142
DDE (dynamic data exchange), 39
DDV_ macros, 290, 372
DDV_MaxChars(), 290
DDX_ macros, 290–291, 372
DDX_Text(), 290
definitions, 118–119
DefWindowProc(), 92, 107
delayed binding, 13
delete, 125–126
DeleteObject(), 155
derived class, 121, 131–134
designing,
bitmaps, 222–225
cursors, 218–222
icons, 214–218

destructors, 125–126
dialog box objects, 33, 140
dialog boxes, 271–302
  as resources, 272–275
  Button control, 275
  Check Box control, 276
  Combo Box control, 276
  common dialog box application, 294–302
  data exchange, 290–291
  DDX_ data exchange functions, 291
  Edit Box control, 276
  Group Box control, 276
  Hot Key control, 276
  List Box control, 276
  Picture control, 277
  Radio Button control, 277
  Scroll Bar control, 277
  simple application, 277–294
    about dialog box, 278–280
    ClassWizard, 283–294
    data entry dialog box, 280–284
  Static Text control, 277
dialog,
  data,
    exchange (DDX), 147
    validation (DDD), 147
  toolbar function buttons, 274
  toolbox controls, 275
DispatchMessage(), 42, 91, 101
distributed computing, 17
DlgItemMessage(), 72
DLL, 12–13, 392, 445
DllRegisterServer(), 465
DockControlBar(), 330
document-centric, 4
DoDataExchange(), 203, 283, 290, 347
DoModal(), 287, 378
DoPropExchange(), 470, 480
DOS, 15
DoVerb(), 416
drag-and-drop, 391
Draw(), 415
DrawIcon(), 31
drawing,
  mode, 319–322
  objects, 142–143
Dump(), 204, 206
DWORD, 88, 91, 162
dynamic,
  code generator, 185
  data exchange (DDE), 39
  linking, 13
  type checking, 153
dynamically linked applications, 390

E

Edit Box control, 72–73, 276
EDIT class, 57
Edit control styles, 62–63
  ES_AUTOHSCROLL, 62
  ES_AUTOVSCROLL, 62
  ES_CENTER, 63
  ES_LEFT, 63
  ES_LOWERCASE, 63
  ES_MULTILINE, 63
  ES_NOHIDESEL, 63
  ES_OEMCONVERT, 63
  ES_PASSWORD, 63
  ES_READONLY, 63
  ES_RIGHT, 63
  ES_UPPERCASE, 63
  ES_WANTRETURN, 63
ELEMENTS, 346
Ellipse(), 91, 162, 267–268, 300, 323, 470
ellipses (...), 271
else, 91
embedding objects, 393–395
EnableCompoundFile(), 411–413
EnableDocking(), 330
encapsulation, 120
END_MESSAGE_MAP(), 163
endl, 124
EndPaint(), 92, 107
ES_AUTOHSCROLL, 62
ES_AUTOVSCROLL, 62
ES_CENTER, 63
ES_LEFT, 63
ES_LOWERCASE, 63
ES_MULTILINE, 63
ES_NOHIDESEL, 63
ES_OEMCONVERT, 63
ES_PASSWORD, 63
ES_READONLY, 63
ES_RIGHT, 63

ES_UPPERCASE, 63
ES_WANTRETURN, 63
exceptions, 143
ExchangeVersion(), 470, 480
ExitInstance(), 464
Extended styles, 68
  WS_EX_ACCEPTFILES, 68
  WS_EX_DLGMODALFRAME, 68
  WS_EX_NOPARENTNOTIFY, 68
  WS_EX_TOPMOST, 68
  WS_EX_TRANSPARENT, 68
ExtTextOut(), 482

F

fabs(), 127–128
FAR PASCAL, 92
file, 143
  monkiers, 397
  OLE, 392
fill patterns, 317
FillRect(), 470, 476, 498
font objects, 33–34, 226–232
for, 91
frame windows, 140–141
free store objects, 125
friend functions, 128–131
FromHandle(), 470

G

GDI (Graphical Device Interface), 37
GetBkColor(), 476
GetClientRect(), 481–482, 497
GetColor(), 299–300
GetCurrentMessage(), 267–268
GetCursorPos(), 53
GetDC(), 54, 480
GetDlgCtrlID(), 346
GetDlgItem(), 345–346
GetDocument(), 414, 417, 436
GetDrawRect(), 474, 481, 482
GetInPlaceActiveItem(), 417–418
GetMapMode(), 52
GetMessage(), 91, 100–101
GetMessagePos(), 53
GetNextClientItem(), 415
GetObject(), 235, 497
GetPos(), 345, 347
GetSelectionType(), 416
GetStartPosition(), 414
GetStockObject(), 90, 97, 470
GetSystemMetrics(), 493
GetTextMetrics(), 482
GetUpdateRect(), 107
GetVersion(), 91, 107, 162
GetWindowDC(), 53–54
GetWindowRect(), 53
Graphical,
  Device Interface (GDI), 37
  User Interface (GUI), 30
graphic object, 30
graphics primitives, 303–326
  Arc(), 310–311
  ArcTo(), 310–311
  brushes, 317–318
  Chord(), 310–311
  drawing mode, 319–322
  Ellipse(), 311–312
  environments, 304
  GetDeviceCaps(), 304–308
  GetPixel(), 315
  graphics device interface (GDI), 304
  LineTo(), 312
  mapping modes, 308–310
    MM_ANSIOTROPIC, 309
    MM_HIENGLISH, 309
    MM_HIMETRIC, 309
    MM_ISOTROPIC, 309
    MM_LOENGLISH, 309
    MM_LOMETRIC, 309
    MM_TEXT, 309
    MM_TWIPS, 309
  MoveToEx(), 312–313
  pens, 316–317
  Pie(), 313
  Polygon(), 313–314
  Polyline(), 314
  PolylineTo(), 314
  Rectangle(), 314
  RoundRect(), 314–315
  SetPixel(), 315
  simple application, 320–326
  stock,
    brushes, 315
    fill patterns, 317
    hatch patterns, 318

line styles, 316
pens, 315
text colors, 318–319
Group Box control, 276
GUI (Graphical User Interface), 30, 50

H

HAL, 15
handles, 88–89
hardware,
abstraction layer, 15
independence, 10–12
portability, 14
hatch patterns, 318
hbrBackground, 95–96
hCursor, 95
HIBYTE, 91, 162
hIconSm, 96
HIMETRIC, 437
HMENU, 145
horizontal scroll bar, 28
Hot Key control, 28, 276
Hungarian notation, 44

I

I-beam, 31
icon objects, 31
ICON, 237
IDC_ARROW, 90
IDispatch, 458
IDR_CNTR_INPLACE, 408
IDR_MAINFRAME, 248, 254, 408
IDR_SRVR_INPLACE, 439
if, 91
inheritance, 121
initial window characteristics, 56–69
InitialInstance(),164–165, 430
in-place editing, 410
instances, 120
interface pointer, 397
InvalidateRect(), 106, 267, 287
iostream.h, 124, 127
IPersistentStorage, 458
IPersistentStream, 458

K

key elements, 116–118
keyboard accelerator,
definition, 247
design, 254–256
KillTimer(), 77–78

L

language and approach, 85–87
late binding, 122
LBS_DISABLENOSCROLL, 63
LBS_EXTENDEDSEL, 63
LBS_HASSTRINGS, 64
LBS_MULTICOLUMN, 64
LBS_MULTIPLESEL, 64
LBS_NOINTEGRALHEIGHT, 64
LBS_NOREDRAW, 64
LBS_NOTIFY, 64
LBS_OWNERDRAWFIXED, 64
LBS_OWNERDRAWVARIABLE, 64
LBS_SORT, 64
LBS_STANDARD, 64
LBS_USETABSTOPS, 64
LBS_WANTKEYBOARDINPUT, 65
line styles, 316
LineTo(), 323
link breakage problems, 397
linked applications (OLE), 395–404
List Box control, 72, 276
LISTBOX class, 58
Listbox control styles, 63–65
LBS_DISABLENOSCROLL, 63
LBS_EXTENDEDSEL, 63
LBS_HASSTRINGS, 64
LBS_MULTICOLUMN, 64
LBS_MULTIPLESEL, 64
LBS_NOINTEGRALHEIGHT, 64
LBS_NOREDRAW, 64
LBS_NOTIFY, 64
LBS_OWNERDRAWFIXED, 64
LBS_OWNERDRAWVARIABLE, 64
LBS_SORT, 64
LBS_STANDARD, 64
LBS_USETABSTOPS, 64
LBS_WANTKEYBOARDINPUT, 65
lists, 144
LoadBitmap(), 235, 239, 497
LoadCursor(), 90, 236, 241
LoadToolBar(), 330, 439–440
LOBYTE, 91, 162
localtime(), 129, 482

LOGBRUSH, 495
LOGFONTA structure, 230
logical,
  coordinate units, 51, 54
  units, 54
LONG, 88
LOWORD, 91, 162, 267
LPARAM, 37–38, 88
LPCRECT, 88
LPCSTR, 88
LPCTSTR, 88
LPSTR, 88
LPTSTR, 88
LPVOID, 88
LRESULT, 88
ltoa(), 129

M

m_, 372, 480
m_bSaveAndValidate, 345
m_wndToolBar, 330
main(), 124
MAKELONG, 480
mapping modes, 51–53
maps, 144–145
math.h, 124, 127
maximize box, 27
member,
  data, 120
  functions, 120
  device context, 239
memory management, 8, 78–79
menu and keyboard accelerators, 245–270
  AppWizard files, 256–269
  keyboard accelerator,
    definition, 247
    design, 254–256
  menu,
    definition, 246–247
    design, 248–254
  simple application, 247–270
  testing application, 269
menu bar, 28
menu,
  definition, 246–247
  design, 248–254
menus, 145
message,
  based communication, 9–10
  box objects, 32
  loop, 100–101
  map, 202
  priority, 41
  resources, 38–39
  types, 38
MessageBox(), 32, 364
messages, 118
methods, 118, 120
MFC,
  design techniques, 151
  key featuers, 152
  Parent Class Hierarchy, 156–158
Microsoft Foundation Class (MFC) Library, 135–148
minimize box, 27
MM_ANISOTROPIC, 52–54, 436
MM_HIENGLISH, 52–53
MM_HIMETRIC, 52–53
MM_ISOTROPIC, 52–54
MM_LOENGLISH, 52–53
MM_LOMETRIC, 51–53
MM_MAX, 52
MM_MAX_FIXEDSCALE, 52
MM_MIN, 52
MM_TEXT, 52–53
MM_TWIPS, 52–53
mmsystem.h, 234, 237
monkiers, 397
MoveTo(), 323
MoveWindow(), 53
MSG, 89
multiple inheritance, 121
multiprocessing, 16–17

N

new, 125–126, 163
normal type checking, 153
NULL, 93
null-terminated string, 93

O

object, 120
  linking and embedding (OLE), 389
  model, 146
Object-Oriented concepts, 115–168

and C++, 118
architecture, 137–138
arrays, 137
automation, 146
base windows class, 138–139
C++ **class**, 122–123
CArchive, 146
CArray, 137
CAsyncSocket, 145
CCmdTarget, 137–138
CControlBar, 139
CCreateContext, 146
CDatabase, 142
CDataExchange, 147
CDC, 144
CDialog, 140
CException, 143
CFile, 143
CFrameWnd, 140–141, 163
CGdiObject, 142–143
CImageList, 142
class hierarchy, 120–121, 136–137
CList, 144
CMap, 144–145
CMenu, 145
CMultiLock, 147
CObject, 136, 152–156
constructors, 125–126
control,
  bars, 139
  classes, 139
CPropertySheet, 141
CSingleLock, 147
CSyncObject, 145–146
CTypedPtrArray, 147
CView, 141
CWnd, 138–139
database, 142
definitions, 118–119
derived class, 131–134
destructors, 125–126
dialog boxes, 140
drawing objects, 142–143
encapsulation, 120
exceptions, 143
file, 143
frame windows, 140–141
friend functions, 128–131
graphics, 144
HMENU, 145
inheritance, 121
key elements, 116–118
lists, 144
maps, 144–145
menus, 145
MFC,
  design techniques, 151
  key featuers, 152
Microsoft Foundation Class (MFC) Library, 135–148
object model, 146
OLE automation, 146
overloading class member functions, 127–128
parent class hierarchy, 156–159
polymorphism, 121
property sheets, 141
serialization, 146
simple,
  C++ class, 123–125
  MFC application, 159–168
sockets, 145
structures, 146
support, 147
switching to MFC, 150–151
synchronization, 145–147
tab dialog objects, 141
typed templates, 147
types, 147–148
type-safe wrappers, 147
view classes, 141
virtual functions, 122
vs. procedure-oriented, 116
wrappers, 148
objects, 4–5
  OLE, 391–392
OCX, 445
OLE,
  automation, 146
  custom controls, 445–446
OLE applications, 405–442
  container, 406–424
    AppWizard files, 407–422
    working with the application, 422–424
  server, 424–442

AppWizard files, 424–440
working with the application, 440–442
OLE concepts, 389–404
containers, 392–393
data, 392
embedding objects, 393–395
files, 392
linked applications, 395–404
objects, 391–392
understanding OLE, 390–391
OLE_COLOR, 472
OLE2, 389
ON_COMMAND(), 414
ON_UPDATE_COMMAND_UI(), 411
ON_WM_PAINT(), 163
ON_WM_SETFOCUS(), 414
ON_WM_SIZE(), 414
OnAppAbout(), 202
OnCancelEditCntr(), 413
OnCancelEditSrvr(), 434
OnChange(), 421
OnChangeItemPosition(), 422
OnColor(), 268
OnCreate(), 329, 379–380
OnDeactivateUI(), 421, 435
OnDraw(), 208, 418, 436–438, 470–471
OnEditConvert(), 411
OnFileOpen(), 202
OnFilePrint(), 413
OnFilePrintPreview(), 413
OnGetEmbeddedItem(), 432
OnGetExtent(), 436–437
OnGetItemPosition(), 422
OnHScroll(), 346–347
OnInitDialog(), 356
OnInput(), 380
OnInsertObject(), 413
OnLButtonDown(), 480
OnLButtonUp(), 480
OnNewDocument(), 206
OnPaint(), 161–162, 165–166, 208, 296, 322, 381–386, 498
OnRButtonDown(), 365
OnShowSpin(), 354
OnSize(), 380
OnTimer(), 499
OnUpdateColor(), 264
OnUpdateEditLinksMenu(), 411
OnUpdateObjectVerbMenu(), 411
OnUpdatePasteLinkMenu(), 411
OnUpdatePasteManu(), 411
open architecture, 18
operating system control, 79–80
OS/2, 15
overloading class member functions, 127–128

P

PAINTSTRUCT, 89, 91
parent class, 121, 131
hierarchy, 156–159
Paste Link feature, 403
pDX, 345
pen objects, 35, 315–317
persistence, 153
physical coordinates, 51
Picture control, 277
Pie(), 324
platform,
compatibility, 15–16
independence, 14–15
plug-and play, 12
POINT, 322
Polygon(), 325
Polyline(), 323
polymorphism, 121
POSITION, 88
PostMessage(), 42
PostQuitMessage(), 92
printf(), 117
private, 120, 123
visibility, 125
procedure-oriented, 85–113
compiler,
options, 112–113
project workspaces, 107–112
data types, 88
handles, 88–89
language and approach, 85–87
programming elements, 87–88
simple application, 89–107
callback function, 101–105
creating a window, 98–99
DefWindowProc(), 107
DispatchMesage(), 101

GetMessage(), 100–101
message loop, 100–101
showing a window, 99–100
TranslateMessage(), 101
updating a window, 99–100
window messages, 102–105
Windows class, 93–98
WinMain(), 92–93
WM_DESTROY, 107
WM_PAINT, 105–107
WNDCLASSEX, 94–96
WinMain(), 89
processing messages, 39–40
programming elements, 49–83
application specific coordinates, 55
changing the,
extent, 54
viewport, 54
Controls and Dialog boxes, 70–74
check-box controls, 71–72
edit box controls, 72–73
list box controls, 72
push-button controls, 71
radio-button controls, 71
scroll bar controls, 73–74
static controls, 71
coordiante systems, 53–54
initial window characteristics, 56–69
logical units, 54
mapping modes, 51–53
memory management, 78–79
operating system control, 79–80
reducing object size, 81–82
reducing the number of objects, 81
relocatable objects, 82–83
screen coordinates, 50–51
SetClassLong(), 70
ShowWindow(), 69–70
system timers, 76–78
user control, 80–81
virtual keys, 74–76
programming elements, 87–88
property sheets, 141
protected, 120, 123
PS_DOT, 323
PS_SOLID, 323
public visibility, 125
public, 120, 123
push-button controls, 71
PX_, 480

Q

queue-based input, 8–9

R

R2_ (drawing mode values), 319–320
Radio Button control, 71, 277
RAM memory, 12, 19
RECT, 89, 147–148
Rectangle(), 91, 162, 299, 324
reducing,
object size, 81–82
number of objects, 81
RegisterAll(), 428, 431
RegisterClass(), 164
RegisterClassEx(), 91, 98
RegisterWindowMessage(), 42
ReleaseDC(), 480
relocatable objects, 82–83
Resoruce,
Editor, 46
Compiler, 46–47
resources, 211–243
bitmap editors, 212–225
designing bitmaps, 222–225
designing cursors, 218–222
designing icons, 214–218
fonts, 226–232
CreateFont(), 230–232
CreateFontIndirect(), 232
LOGFONTA structure, 230
TEXTMETRIC structure, 229
TrueType, 230
simple application, 232–243
add a bitmap, 238–240
add a font, 240
add an icon, 236–237
add sound, 237–238
AppWizard files, 233–236
base code, 233
build application, 241–243
ClassWizard, 240–241
sound recorder, 225–226
RoundRect(), 324
run-time object model support, 158–159

S

SBS_BOTTOMALIGN, 66
SBS_HORZ, 66
SBS_LEFTALIGN, 66
SBS_RIGHTALIGN, 66
SBS_SIZEBOX, 66
SBS_SIZEBOXBOTTOMRIGHTALIGN, 66
SBS_SIZEBOXTOPLEFTALIGN, 66
SBS_TOPALIGN, 66
SBS_VERT, 67
scalability, 17
SCRCOPY, 237–240
screen coordinate system, 50–51, 53
screen saver application, 487–503
  build operation, 500
  code, 487–500
  running, 500–503
ScreenToClient(), 54
Scroll Bar control, 73–74, 277
  thumb, 27–28
SCROLLBAR class, 58
Scrollbar control styles, 66–67
  SBS_BOTTOMALIGN, 66
  SBS_HORZ, 66
  SBS_LEFTALIGN, 66
  SBS_RIGHTALIGN, 66
  SBS_SIZEBOX, 66
  SBS_SIZEBOXBOTTOMRIGHTALIGN, 66
  SBS_SIZEBOXTOPLEFTALIGN, 66
  SBS_TOPALIGN, 66
  SBS_VERT, 67
security, 17–18
SelectObject(), 235, 239, 323
serialization, 146
Serialize(), 206, 411, 437
server, 393
  application (OLE), 424–442
SetBarStyle(), 330
SetBkColor(), 319, 324
SetBkMode(), 319, 324, 482
SetCheck(), 267, 269
SetClassLong(), 70
SetCursor(), 493
SetCursorPos(), 53
SetDlgItemText(), 346
SetMapMode(),52, 55, 377, 383, 436
SetOwner(), 439–440
SetPixel(), 323
SetPos(), 345
SetRange(), 346–347, 356
SetRegisterKey(), 490
SetROP2(), 319
SetServerInfo(), 430
SetTextAlign(), 482
SetTextColor(), 299, 317–319, 324
SetTimer(),77–78, 499
SetViewportExt(), 377, 383
SetViewportExtEx(), 55
SetViewportOrg(), 377, 383
SetViewportOrgEx(), 55
SetWindowExt(), 377, 383, 436
SetWindowExtEx(), 55
SetWindowOrg(), 436
SetWindowText(), 346
ShowCaret(), 32
showing a window, 99–100
ShowWindow(), 69–70, 91, 99, 163, 165
simple,
  C++ class, 123–125
  custom control, 458–472
  MFC application, 159–168
sin(), 124
single,
  document interface (SDI), 203
  inheritance, 121
sizeof(), 90, 97, 235
Slider Control, 348–357
SND_ASYNC, 236
sndPlaySound(), 236–238
sockets, 145
sound recorder, 225–226
Spin Button, 348–357
sprintf(), 364
SS_BLACKFRAME, 67
SS_BLACKRECT, 67
SS_CENTER, 67
SS_GRAYFRAME, 67
SS_GRAYRECT, 67
SS_ICON, 67
SS_LEFT, 67
SS_LEFTNOWORDWRAP, 67
SS_NOPREFIX, 67
SS_RIGHT, 67
SS_SIMPLE, 68
SS_USERITEM, 68

SS_WHITEFRAME, 68
SS_WHITERECT, 68
standard,
  message,
    formats, 37–38
    loop, 40–41
  Windows resources, 41–42
STATIC class, 59
Static control styles, 67–68
  SS_BLACKFRAME, 67
  SS_BLACKRECT, 67
  SS_CENTER, 67
  SS_GRAYFRAME, 67
  SS_GRAYRECT, 67
  SS_ICON, 67
  SS_LEFT, 67
  SS_LEFTNOWORDWRAP, 67
  SS_NOPREFIX, 67
  SS_RIGHT, 67
  SS_SIMPLE, 68
  SS_USERITEM, 68
  SS_WHITEFRAME, 68
  SS_WHITERECT, 68
static controls, 71
Static Text control, 277
stdafx.h, 234
stdio.h, 90
stdlib.h, 127
steps for developing programs, 46
stock,
  brushes, 315
  fill patterns, 317
  hatch patterns, 318
  line styles, 316
  pens, 315
storage object, 392
strcpy(), 376
stream object, 392
StretchBlt(), 235, 239
string.h, 90, 128
strlen(), 91, 376
strtok(), 129–130, 376, 382
struct, 118, 122–123
structures, 146
support, 147
SW_HIDE, 69
SW_MINIMIZE, 69
SW_RESTORE, 69
SW_SHOW, 69
SW_SHOWMAXIMIZED, 69
SW_SHOWMINIMIZED, 69
SW_SHOWMINNOACTIVE, 69
SW_SHOWNA, 69
SW_SHOWNOACTIVE, 69
SW_SHOWNORMAL, 69BLACK_BRUSH, 70
switch, 91
switching to MFC, 150–151
synchronization, 145–147
system,
  menu, 26
  timers, 76–78

T

tab dialog objects, 141
tag name, 123
tan(), 124
terminate box, 27
test container, 482–483
text colors, 318–319
TEXTMETRIC structure, 229
TextOut(), 51, 91, 162, 235, 300, 323
thumb (scroll bar), 27–28
time(), 129, 363, 365, 482
time.h, 128
timers (system), 76–78
title bar, 26, 28
tm structure, 129
ToolBar, 327–338
TranslateColor(), 476, 481
TranslateMessage(), 91, 101
TrueType, 230
typed templates, 147
types, 147–148
type-safe wrappers, 147

U

UINT, 88
understanding OLE, 390–391
UNIX, 15
UPDATE_COMMAND_UI, 263–264
UpdateRegistry(), 428
UpdateRegistryAll(), 465
UpdateWindow(), 91, 99, 163, 165, 287
updating a window, 99–100
user control, 80–81

V

ValidateRect(), 92, 107
VBX, 445
vertical scroll bar, 27–28
view classes, 141
viewport, 54
virtual,
  address space, 19
  coordinates, 51
  functions, 122
  keys, 74–76
  member function, 131
  memory, 18–19
Visual C++ compiler, 46
visual editing, 391
vs. procedure-oriented, 116

W

while, 91
WHITE_BRUSH, 90
whole-window coordinate system, 53
Win 95 and NT Concepts and Terminology, 23–47
  a common look, 25–29
    border, 26
    client work area, 29
    control box, 26
    horizontal scroll bar, 28
    maximize box, 27
    menu bar, 28
    minimize box, 27
    system menu, 26
    terminate box, 27
    title bar, 26
    vertical scroll bar, 27–28
  communications via messages, 36–41
    message sources, 38–39
    processing messages, 39–40
    standard message formats, 37–38
    standard message loop, 40–41
  linker, 47
  object classes, 29–30
  object-oriented technology, 30–35
    bitmap objects, 34–35
    brush objects, 35
    caret objects, 31
    cursor objects, 31
    dialog box objects, 33
    font objects, 33–34
    icon objects, 31
    message box objects, 32
    pen objects, 35
  Resource,
    Compiler, 46–47
    Editor, 46
standard Windows resources, 41–42
  steps for developing programs, 46
  Visual C++ compiler, 46
  Windows,
    code style, 44–46
    functions, 42–43
    vs. Windows, 24–25
  windows.h, 43–44
Win 95 and Win NT features, 19–20
Win32, 15
  structures, 89
Win32s, 15
WINAPI, 43, 90, 92
window messages, 102–105
Window states, 69
  SW_HIDE, 69
  SW_MINIMIZE, 69
  SW_RESTORE, 69
  SW_SHOW, 69
  SW_SHOWMAXIMIZED, 69
  SW_SHOWMINIMIZED, 69
  SW_SHOWMINNOACTIVE, 69
  SW_SHOWNA, 69
  SW_SHOWNOACTIVE, 69
  SW_SHOWNORMAL, 69
Window styles, 59–61
  WS_BORDER, 59
  WS_CAPTION, 59
  WS_CHILD, 60
  WS_CHIPCHILDREN, 60
  WS_CLIPSIBLINGS, 60
  WS_DISABLED, 60
  WS_DLGFRAME, 60
  WS_EX_ACCEPTFILES, 60
  WS_EX_DLGMODALFRAME, 60
  WS_EX_NOPARENTNOTIFY, 60
  WS_EX_TOPMOST, 60
  WS_EX_TRANSPARENT, 60
  WS_GROUP, 60
  WS_HSCROLL, 60
  WS_MAXIMIZE, 60

WS_MAXIMIZEBOX, 60
WS_MINIMIZE, 60
WS_MINIMIZEBOX, 61
WS_OVERLAPPED, 61
WS_OVERLAPPEDWINDOW, 61
WS_POPUP, 61
WS_POPUPWINDOW, 61
WS_SYSMENU, 61
WS_VISIBLE, 61
WindowFromPoint(), 53
Windows applications,
ABSOLUTE.cpp, 127–128
AddRes.cpp, 132–243
BarChart.cpp, 365–387
Clock.cpp, 458–483
Colors.cpp, 294–302
Contain.cpp, 406–424
DataEntry.cpp, 277–294
Editor.cpp, 360–365
FRIEND.cpp, 128–131
Intense.cpp, 338–348
MenuColor.cpp, 247–270
NoWiz, 172–185
Saucer.cpp, 487–503
Server.cpp, 424–442
Shapes.cpp, 320–326
Spin.cpp, 348–357
STACK.cpp, 132–134
Tool.cpp, 327–338
TRIGCLASS.cpp, 123–125
WinVer.cpp, 90–107
WinVerMFC.cpp, 159–168
WithWiz, 188–209
Windows,
class, 93–98
code style, 44–46
functions, 42–43
vs Windows, 24–25
windows.h, 43–44, 90
wingdi.h, 226–229
WinMain(), 46, 92–93, 101
winuser.h, 218
WM_DESTROY, 92, 107
WM_PAINT, 91, 105–107, 296
WM_SETHOTKEY, 276
WM_TIMER, 77–78
WNDCLASSEX, 89, 94–96
WndProc(), 105
WNDPROC, 88
word processor project, 360–365
WORD, 88
World Transformations, 326
WOSA, 18
WPARAM, 37–38, 88
wrappers, 148
WS_BORDER, 59
WS_CAPTION, 59
WS_CHILD, 60
WS_CHIPCHILDREN, 60
WS_CLIPSIBLINGS, 60
WS_DISABLED, 60
WS_DLGFRAME, 60
WS_EX_ACCEPTFILES, 60
WS_EX_DLGMODALFRAME, 60
WS_EX_NOPARENTNOTIFY, 60
WS_EX_TOPMOST, 60
WS_EX_TRANSPARENT, 60
WS_GROUP, 60
WS_HSCROLL, 60
WS_MAXIMIZE, 60
WS_MAXIMIZEBOX, 60
WS_MINIMIZE, 60
WS_MINIMIZEBOX, 61
WS_OVERLAPPED, 61
WS_OVERLAPPEDWINDOW, 61, 91, 162
WS_POPUP, 61
WS_POPUPWINDOW, 61
WS_SYSMENU, 61
WS_VISIBLE, 61
wsprintf(), 91, 162

About the Disk

This diskette contains the MFC files for the applications discussed in the book.

The files are stored in several subdirectories, using the following format:

```
a:> MFC\CHP01
        CHP02
        CHP03
          .
          .
          .
        CHP19
```

Chapters containing multiple applications are further sub-divided.

Chapters 1, 2, 3, 6 and 15 do not contain application files.

The files should be copied to your hard disk before attempting to build the applications.

Once the files are transferred, an application's make file can be used to start the build process. Use of the disk requires a system running Windows 95 or Windows NT. No technical support is offered.